PORTRAYING AUTHORSHIP

Portraying Authorship

Juan Manuel and the Rhetoric of Authority

ANITA SAVO

UNIVERSITY OF TORONTO PRESS
Toronto Buffalo London

Toronto Buffalo London
utorontopress.com
Printed in the USA

ISBN 978-1-4875-5323-4 (cloth)
ISBN 978-1-4875-5325-8 (EPUB)
ISBN 978-1-4875-5324-1 (PDF)

Toronto Iberic

Library and Archives Canada Cataloguing in Publication

Title: Portraying authorship : Juan Manuel and the rhetoric of authority / Anita Savo.
Names: Savo, Anita, author.
Series: Toronto Iberic.
Description: Series statement: Toronto Iberic | Includes bibliographical references and index.
Identifiers: Canadiana (print) 20230578187 | Canadiana (ebook) 20230578209 | ISBN 9781487553234 (cloth) | ISBN 9781487553258 (EPUB) | ISBN 9781487553241 (PDF)
Subjects: LCSH: Juan Manuel, Infante of Castile, 1282–1347 – Criticism and interpretation. | LCSH: Authorship in literature.
Classification: LCC PQ6402 .S28 2024 | DDC 863/.1 – dc23

Cover design: John Beadle
Cover image: Adapted from "Paris Writing to Helen," Octovien de Saint-Gelais, *Les XXI épistres d'Ovide* [French translation of Ovid's *Heroides*], miniatures by Robinet Testard, completed in 1497, BnF, MS Français 875, fol. 83r.

We wish to acknowledge the land on which the University of Toronto Press operates. This land is the traditional territory of the Wendat, the Anishnaabeg, the Haudenosaunee, the Métis, and the Mississaugas of the Credit First Nation.

This book was published with the generous assistance of a Book Subvention Award from the Medieval Academy of America.

University of Toronto Press acknowledges the financial support of the Government of Canada, the Canada Council for the Arts, and the Ontario Arts Council, an agency of the Government of Ontario, for its publishing activities.

Canada Council for the Arts
Conseil des Arts du Canada

Funded by the Government of Canada
Financé par le gouvernement du Canada
Canada

For my parents

Contents

Illustrations

Acknowledgments

The book that follows deals with a particular medieval manifestation of the fiction of the solitary author, a fiction that still remains with us today. But like most books, this one could not have been written without the labour and support of many people. I give my heartfelt thanks to all those who have made this work possible and made it better. Whatever failings remain are mine alone.

Thank you to my teachers, whose guidance continues to shape all the work that I do. Rolena Adorno taught me to write with precision and exemplifies the kind of scholar and teacher I strive to be; I am grateful to call her both mentor and friend. I remember with gratitude María Rosa Menocal, whose clarity of vision and voice have, I hope, led me to find a voice of my own. Alastair Minnis has been a key interlocutor, enriching my work with his insights on medieval authorship. And Irene Zaderenko gave me both the knowledge and tools to be a medievalist and the confidence to apply to graduate school.

Fellow *juanmanuelista* Mario Cossío Olavide has been an unfailing source of intellectual exchange and bibliographic recommendations, and he and Delfine Michaud are generous hosts and friends. I am thankful to Olivier Biaggini for reading the entire manuscript in draft and giving incisive comments. Many thanks to Riley Magane for her invaluable assistance with the research and writing of the third chapter, and to BU's Undergraduate Research Opportunities Program for supporting our collaboration. Jonathan Burgoyne, Megan Cook, Irit Kleiman, Deeana Copeland Klepper, Stephanie Nelson, and Joe Stadolnik have engaged with my work on Juan Manuel in myriad ways over the years, and Alani Hicks-Bartlett, Ross Karlan, and Peter Mahoney gave perceptive feedback on chapters in draft. The anonymous readers invested significant time and effort to help sharpen my argument and clarify its impact.

I'm thankful for the continuing support and camaraderie of my colleagues in Colby College's Spanish Department and Boston University's Department of Romance Studies. The Premodern Scholars of Maine provided a convivial atmosphere in which to share my work in progress. The students in my graduate seminar on Juan Manuel – Wiktoria Bryzys, Gonzalo Carretero Martínez, Tijana Čupić, José Dominicci-Buzó, and José Quispe – approached the texts with enthusiasm and fresh insights. Dean Allbritton, ever the community builder, brought me into the fold of a writing group whose members – Mary Kate Donovan, Leslie Harkema, Catalina Iannone, Gabrielle Miller, Martin Repinecz, Evelyn Scaramella, Amaury Sosa, Wan Tang, Sarah Thomas, and Nicholas Wolters – kept me motivated and offered sage advice. Brett White, an instant and steadfast friend, inspired me with her own wonderful book, and has never failed to answer my questions and assuage my doubts.

I wish to thank the programs and institutions that have supported this project at various stages. A grant from the Program for Cultural Cooperation supported a life-changing research trip to Madrid in 2012 to study the manuscripts of Juan Manuel's works in person, and a Humanities Grant for Research and Travel from Colby College enabled me to return to several Spanish libraries and archives in 2015. A Beinecke Rare Book and Manuscript Library Research Fellowship provided access to rare materials and time to write. Generous awards from the Boston University Center for the Humanities and the Medieval Academy of America have enabled the book's publication.

I acknowledge with gratitude and respect the librarians and archivists who have made this work possible. The staff of the Biblioteca Nacional de España, Beinecke Rare Book and Manuscript Library, Real Academia de la Historia, and Real Biblioteca del Monasterio de El Escorial provided essential information and access to manuscripts. Juan Ignacio Pérez Giménez at the Archivo de la Catedral de Valencia offered a wealth of archival support, and both he and María José Ferrer Echávarri at the Biblioteca de la Universidad de Oviedo facilitated access to images.

Laura Portwood-Stacer's Book Proposal Accelerator guided me through the proposal phase and helped me see my project as a publishable book. I have since benefited greatly from the editorial expertise of Suzanne Rancourt, Mary Lui, Emily Reiner, and their colleagues at the University of Toronto Press.

I am grateful for the support of my family, who have waited patiently for this book for as long as it took. Karen Giaquinto, practically a sister, saw me through the ups and downs of this project's early years. My siblings, Maria, Lynda, and Sal, have a special talent for cheering me on and keeping me humble.

To my husband Aidan, thank you for hashing out ideas about medieval authorship with me on our neighbourhood walks, and for your limitless reserves of curiosity and patience.

I dedicate this book to the memory of my parents, Salvatore and Teresa P. Savo, who taught me, each in their own way, the immense value of an education.

Note on Editions and Translations

Readers of Juan Manuel's works are fortunate to have several good scholarly editions to choose from, each with its own advantages. In this book, I quote the *Conde Lucanor*, General Prologue, and anteprologue from Guillermo Serés's 2022 edition because it is a good main text with a rich critical apparatus and a thorough, up-to-date bibliography, and because it is relatively affordable and accessible to scholars. I quote the *Libro del cavallero et del escudero* edited by Mario Cossío Olavide, the *Libro de los estados* edited by Ian R. Macpherson and Robert Brian Tate, and the *Libro infinido* edited by Carlos Mota, all of which are carefully prepared and have the best annotations. I cite the rest of Juan Manuel's works from the *Obras completas* prepared by Carlos Alvar and Sarah Finci, which presents a uniform and readable text following the transcription norms presented in Pedro Sánchez-Prieto Borja's *Cómo editar los textos medievales*. I have silently accepted most emendations made by these editors, and in the rare case where I disagree with an editorial decision, it is noted accordingly.

The surviving manuscripts of Juan Manuel's works are essential to this study and are cited directly when pertinent. I also make reference to other editions on the many occasions when they provide useful information or a convincing variant reading. When quoting medieval Castilian, I prioritize ease of reading over palaeographic or phonetic accuracy, which means that I add modern punctuation and written accents and sometimes override an editor's orthographic choices to provide a more readable text. English translations are my own unless otherwise noted.

PORTRAYING AUTHORSHIP

Introduction

Juan Manuel (1282–1348 or 1349) was perhaps best known in his lifetime as a litigious nobleman, a powerful but unreliable knight, and a shrewd politician, but he shows us a different self-portrait through his writings. In his *Libro infinido,* a book of advice dedicated to his son and heir Fernando, he mounts an impassioned defence of his preferred pastime, writing books:

> Et comoquier que yo sé que algunos profaçan de mí porque fago libros, dígovos que por eso non lo dexaré, ca quiero crer al exiemplo que vos pus en el libro que yo fiz *de Patronio,* en que dize que
>
> Por dicho de las gentes,
> sól que non sea mal,
> al pro tened las mientes
> et non fagades ál.
>
> Et pues en los libros que yo fago ay en ellos pro et verdad et non daño, por ende non lo quiero dexar por dicho de ninguno. Et los que dello profaçarán, quando ellos fizieren su pro et bieren que fago yo mi daño, estonce deven seer creídos que fago lo que me non cae de fazer libro. Ca devedes saber que todas las cosas que los grandes señores fazen, todas deven ser guardando primeramente su estado et su onra. [...] Et pues yo tengo que maguer en mí aya muchas menguas, que aún fasta aquí non he fecho cosa por que se mengüe mi estado, et pienso que es mejor pasar el tiempo en fazer libros que en jugar los dados o fazer otras viles cosas. (176–7)
>
> Although I know that some people criticize me because I write books, I say to them that I will not stop on their account, for I want to believe the example I gave you in the *Book of Patronio* that I wrote, which says:
>
> As long as you do no wrong,
> whatever people say,

keep in mind your interests,
and from that path don't stray.

> And because there is profit and truth and no harm in the books I write, I won't stop on account of what anyone says. As for those who criticize me, when the time comes that they act to their benefit and see me acting to my detriment, then they can be believed that my writing books is inappropriate. For you should know that everything great lords do should always be done in keeping with their estate and honour. [...] And so I believe that in spite of my many flaws, up until now I have done nothing to lessen my estate, and I find it better to spend my time writing books than playing dice or doing other lowly things.

This passage, written relatively late in Juan Manuel's career as a writer, displays many of the hallmarks of his concept of authorship: humility, pride, self-citation, and concern for acting in ways that correspond to his estate or social category. Most of all, he believes in the moral and intellectual benefits of his books (*ay en ellos pro et verdad et non daño*), both for himself as an author and for his readers. But his concept of authorship did not emerge fully formed at a single moment, nor was it devised and promoted by a single individual. His literary corpus attests to an active process of creating an authorial persona by adapting medieval ideas about authorship from a variety of texts and their makers. This book traces the genesis of Juan Manuel's ideas about authorship, their manifestation in the surviving manuscripts of his works, and their impact on how subsequent readers and editors understand the relationship between medieval authors and their works.

While scholars often remark on Juan Manuel's self-presentation as a seemingly modern phenomenon, I make the case that he forged his authorial persona through the accumulation of medieval writerly roles. In doing so, I answer Reinaldo Ayerbe-Chaux's call to disentangle Juan Manuel's medieval concept of authorship from our expectations as modern readers, including modern assumptions about literary property and the author's originality ("Don Juan" 189). During the Castilian nobleman's lifetime, the manuscript culture of Christian Iberia was in a transitional phase between the institutionally sponsored scriptoria of the thirteenth century and the individual humanistic writers of the fifteenth. Making books, previously a collective endeavour carried out in clerical, monastic, or courtly settings, gradually became more accessible – and attractive – to members of the lay nobility, the group he calls *legos*. He played a significant role in this transition by borrowing the strategies that academic and clerical authors used to safeguard their works and applying them to a lay, vernacular context.

Although fourteenth-century book production continued to involve multiple collaborators, Juan Manuel's works portray a model of authorship centred on one individual who is implicated in every step of the bookmaking process. This fictional authorial persona, "Don Juan," assumes at various points the four authorial roles defined by the thirteenth-century theologian Bonaventure – scribes, compilers, commentators, and authors – to assert authorial responsibility and lend his works authority. Similar to the alter egos of other medieval authors such as Dante and Juan Ruiz, Don Juan represents what Leo Spitzer calls the poetic "I," which operates within the fictional world of the text, as well as the empirical "I" out in the real world. However, while Spitzer maintains that the two were not usually combined in medieval Romance literature (421), this is not true for Don Juan, who encourages the conflation of his poetic and empirical selves for the purpose of shaping his authorial reputation. I argue that Juan Manuel and others involved in making his books promote this model of individual authorship through a combination of rhetorical strategies, paratextual elements, and codicological features, which circulate together with his works in manuscript and print.

Taken together, these rhetorical moves can be understood as a discourse of authorship, a cohesive set of utterances that can compete with other discourses and, to some degree, retains its force across time. With Alastair Minnis, I find this Foucauldian sense of "discourse" useful to describe how medieval writers wielded language to achieve effects in the world beyond the page ("Nolens" 47). I also follow Leonardo Funes ("Excentricidad") and Olivier Biaggini ("Stratégies"; "Énonciation") in identifying the discursive or enunciative function of Juan Manuel's statements about authorship, particularly in his paratexts but also throughout his works. His discourse of authorship would prove especially persuasive to later readers and would help shape his position in Spanish literary history by aligning with modern readers' expectations about authorial creativity. This longevity makes the Castilian magnate's works a useful case study for a broader understanding of authorship in medieval Castilian literature.

In Bonaventure's oft-cited passage on authorship, he distinguishes four authorial roles based on the degree to which the writer relies on textual authorities or his own words:

> Quadruplex est modus faciendi librum. Aliquis enim scribit aliena, nihil addendo vel mutando; et iste mere dicitur scriptor. Aliquis scribit aliena addendo, sed non de suo; et iste compilator dicitur. Aliquis scribit et aliena et sua, sed aliena tamquam principalia, et sua tamquam annexa ad

> evidentiam; et iste dicitur commentator non auctor. Aliquis scribit et sua et aliena, sed sua tamquam principalia, aliena tamquam annexa ad confirmationem et debet dici auctor. (14–15)

> There are four ways of making a book. Sometimes a man writes others' words, adding nothing and changing nothing; and he is simply called a scribe. Sometimes a man writes others' words, putting together passages which are not his own; and he is called a compiler. Sometimes a man writes both others' words and his own, but with the others' words in prime place and his own added only for purposes of clarification; and he is called not an author but a commentator. Sometimes a man writes both his own words and others', but with his own in the place of primacy and others' added only for purposes of confirmation; and he should be called an author. (trans. Burrow 29–30)

According to this schema, all types of writers, from the most mechanical to the most creative, use the works of others to some extent: not even the *auctor* merits unqualified autonomy (Burrow 30). Furthermore, the author's freedom to create is circumscribed within the culture of textual authority: authors' words may be primarily their own, but they are supported by the words and works of others.

Bonaventure wrote this passage to introduce his *Commentary on the Sentences of Peter Lombard,* as a reflection on the nature of human authorship (Peter Lombard's and his own) in contrast to the divine authorship of the Bible. For him and other medieval theologians, the authorship of the Bible was a special case understood in Aristotelian terms as a *duplex causa efficiens* or "twofold efficient cause": "God was regarded as the first *auctor* or the unmoved mover of a book, whereas the human *auctor* was both moved (by God) and moving (in producing the text)" (Minnis, *Medieval Theory* 79). In other words, Bonaventure wrote this passage for the specific context of Latin theology and biblical exegesis and did not have lay vernacular writers in mind. According to Matthew Fisher, Bonaventure's schema has other limitations for modern scholars studying medieval authorship: it is "prescriptive rather than descriptive," assumes categorical distinctions without accounting for shades of grey, and constitutes a "self-referential description" of the relationship among the three entities responsible for his own book: God as first mover, Peter Lombard as efficient cause or *auctor,* and Bonaventure as *commentator* (71–2). Given these objections, what is the justification for using his schema to structure a book on Juan Manuel's approach to vernacular authorship?

First, unlike most medieval writings on authorship, which define authors based on who they are, Bonaventure's framework is useful because it describes what writers do. Whereas most medieval definitions focused on the venerated *auctores* of the past, he seeks to capture the actual work of the bookmakers of his day. In this way, his model resembles Harold Love's modern concept of *authemes* – the discrete tasks performed by writers, editors, and publishers – which offers a flexible and "variable model" suitable for describing a wider range of writerly activities (39).

Second, as scholars such as Minnis and Rita Copeland have demonstrated, vernacular writers in Latin Europe imitated the most prestigious models they could find, Latin academic scholarship, to lend authority to their works. Even if they did not know Bonaventure's passage specifically, they could see the division of writerly roles represented spatially on the pages of Latin commentaries, on which the words of authoritative authors occupied prime place, and compilers and commentators were relegated to the margins (Stillinger 26). Juan Manuel was no exception, given his familiarity with Latin doctrinal and exegetical texts such as the *Epistola ad Paulam et Eustochium* attributed to Jerome, Infante Juan of Aragon's commentary on the Lord's Prayer, and the prologue to Nicholas of Lyra's biblical commentary, *Postilla litteralis super Bibliam* (Lida de Malkiel, "Tres notas" 169ff.; Tate 175–9; Rico 410–11).

Finally, as María Jesús Lacarra and Juan Manuel Cacho Blecua demonstrate in their analysis of Castilian prologues from the thirteenth through fifteenth centuries, the writerly roles described by Bonaventure existed as conceptual categories in medieval Castilian literature, although the boundaries between categories were sometimes permeable (261–71). Regardless of whether Juan Manuel knew Bonaventure's work, he and his contemporaries understood that one could write as a scribe, compiler, commentator, or author, and that each way of writing had distinct ethical functions and benefits. Through my analysis of his works, I show how Don Juan claims responsibility for these four authorial roles at different points in his career and accrues their ethical value over time.

Although my approach is not biographical, it is helpful to review the major events of Juan Manuel's life, which spanned the reigns of four kings of Castile: Alfonso X (r. 1252–84), Sancho IV (r. 1284–95), Fernando IV (r. 1295–1312), and Alfonso XI (r. 1312–50).[1] He was born on 5 May 1282 in Escalona to Infante Manuel, younger brother of Alfonso X, and to Beatriz "Contesson" of the House of Savoy. After his father's death in 1283, the almost two-year-old Juan Manuel inherited his title of *adelantado* of Murcia, a royally appointed governorship in a strategic location between the Christian kingdoms of Castile and Aragon and the Islamic kingdom of Granada ruled by the Naṣrid dynasty. He also inherited the lands around Elche, known as the Tierra de Don Manuel, and the town of Peñafiel. His territory in Murcia came under attack from Granada, Castile, and Aragon, and in 1296 he lost Elche and several other towns to Aragon. After a brief marriage to Infanta Isabel of Mallorca, who died in 1301, he married Infanta Constanza of Aragon, forging important alliances with her father, Jaume II of Aragon (r. 1291–1327), and her brother, Infante Juan of Aragon, a prominent clergyman.

As a high-ranking nobleman whose power rivalled that of a monarch, Juan Manuel was a major player in Iberian politics, but perhaps the most significant events of his adult life revolve around his turbulent relationship with Alfonso XI of Castile. Alfonso inherited the throne as a baby, and after the death of his grandmother María de Molina, Juan Manuel became one of three regents appointed to advise the king during his minority. But in 1325, Alfonso ordered the resignation of his regents, sparking their distrust. Although he promised to marry Juan Manuel's daughter Constanza Manuel, he subsequently imprisoned her in the fortress of Toro and instead married Infanta María, daughter of Afonso IV of Portugal. Juan Manuel broke his oath of fealty to the king in December of 1327, initiating a period of hostility and military aggression that finally ended in a truce mediated by Aragon in 1329. Tensions resumed in 1333 and were resolved in 1338, this time through the mediation of Juana Núñez de Lara, the mother of Juan Manuel's third wife, Blanca Núñez de Lara.[2] At the time of his death in late 1348 or 1349, his lands and titles passed to his heir, Fernando Manuel.[3] His legacy included residences, fortifications, a set of municipal ordinances for the town of Peñafiel, and the founding of two monasteries: San Agustín in Castillo de Garcimuñoz, and the Dominican monastery of San Pablo in Peñafiel.[4]

Juan Manuel's literary works are not mentioned in the letters and documents issued by his chancery (*cancillería*, the bureaucratic institution dedicated to the official correspondence of a king, prelate, or noble), perhaps because of the perceived clash with his social position alluded to in the *Libro infinido*. However, as this book will show, his works tend to speak for themselves. His extant literary works in Castilian are, in rough chronological order and listed by their conventional titles:[5]

- *Crónica abreviada* (1320–5), an abbreviated version of Alfonso X's *Estoria de España*;

- *Libro de la caza* (before 1329, possibly revised later), a treatise on practical aspects of falconry, left incomplete;
- *Libro del cavallero et del escudero* (1326–7), an encyclopedic treatise framed as a young knight's education;
- *Libro de los estados* (completed 1332), a mirror for princes (*speculum principis*) that combines political and religious education;
- *Libro de los enxiemplos del conde Lucanor et de Patronio* or *Conde Lucanor* (completed 1335), a five-part collection of advice for noble readers, including exemplary tales with concluding *viessos* or verses (pt. 1), proverbs (pts. 2–4), and a doctrinal treatise (pt. 5);[6]
- *Libro infinido* (1334–40), a work of practical advice dedicated to his son, Fernando;
- *Libro de las tres razones* (after 1337, possibly 1342–5), a propagandistic exposition of three aspects of Juan Manuel's family history;[7]
- the *Prólogo general* or General Prologue (c. 1342) written to introduce a copy of his collected works;
- *Tratado de la Asunción* (c. 1342), a doctrinal treatise defending the Assumption of the Virgin Mary as Catholic dogma.

The General Prologue mentions several more works that are no longer extant:

- *Libro de la cavallería*, a work on knighthood, nobility, and feudal relationships mentioned several times in the *Libro de los estados;*[8]
- *Crónica complida*, another historiographical work, or possibly a reference to Alfonso X's *Estoria de España;*
- *Libro de los engeños*, on war machines and military strategy;
- *Libro de las cantigas*, a book of songs or lyric poetry;
- *De las reglas cómo se deve trobar*, possibly the first treatise on the poetic arts written in Castilian.

He also commissioned the *Cronicón latino*, a brief annalistic compendium in Latin of major events that occurred from 1274 to 1329, and his only literary work to survive in a fourteenth-century copy (Martín Iglesias 134). The earliest copies of his Castilian literary works are preserved in fifteenth-century manuscripts: Biblioteca Nacional de España (BNE), MS 1356 contains the *Crónica abreviada*, while BNE, MS 6376 (known as *S*) contains all his other Castilian works, including the five-part version of the *Conde Lucanor*.[9] Part 1 of the *Conde Lucanor* appears in three more fifteenth-century manuscripts: Real Academia de la Historia, MS 9/5893 (*H*); BNE, MS 4236 (*M*); and Real Academia Española, MS 15 (*P*, the *Códice de Puñonrostro*); while the five-part *Conde Lucanor* survives in a sixteenth-century humanist copy, BNE, MS 18415 (*G*). A sixteenth-century anthology, BNE, MS 19426 (*N*), copies from *S* the *Libro de las tres razones*, *Libro infinido*, some paratexts, and the verses and proverbs from parts 1–3 of the *Conde Lucanor*.[10] There is also a print edition of part 1 of the *Conde Lucanor* prepared by the Andalusian humanist Gonzalo Argote de Molina (Seville, 1575) with one reprint (Madrid, 1642). Finally, two manuscripts of the *Libro de los doce sabios*, Biblioteca de la Universidad de Oviedo, MS M-497 (*O*) and Biblioteca de Menéndez Pelayo, MS M-92 (known as *M* in scholarship on the *Libro de los doce sabios*), contain the *viessos* from part 1 of the *Conde Lucanor*.

Manuscript *S* in particular has played an important role in transmitting both Juan Manuel's works and his concept of authorship. As a deluxe codex organized around its author figure, the oldest witness of the five-part *Conde Lucanor*, and the only witness of his other works apart from the *Crónica abreviada*, it rightfully holds a special status among the extant manuscripts. Alberto Blecua decisively deemed *S* the best copy of the *Conde Lucanor* in his study of the work's textual transmission (127), and editors invariably choose it as the base text for their editions (except for versionist editions of a single manuscript, such as Paul Gloeckner's edition of *G*). However, its authoritative and authorial status is based not just on historical and palaeographic factors, but on what Laurence de Looze calls "its rhetoric, which associates the authorial corpus-volume with the desires and dictates of the real-life author" (33). In the General Prologue with which *S* begins – discussed at length in chapter 1 – Don Juan famously proclaims in the first person that "fizi fazer este volumen en que están scriptos todos los libros que yo fasta aquí he fechos" ("I had this volume made in which are copied all the books I have written up until now"; ed. Serés, 5) and assures readers that he checked the text himself ("yo mesmo [lo] concerté"; 6). Even though scholars have long recognized that *S* is at best a copy of a copy of this author-approved manuscript, its authorial rhetoric may still hold sway in debates about its date of production.

In the absence of a scribal colophon giving the exact year of completion, scholars have proposed two date ranges for *S* based on palaeographic, codicological, and contextual evidence. Alberto Blecua (13), de Looze (5), and the BNE's Inventario General de Manuscritos (PhiloBiblon, BETA manid 1964) date it to the late fourteenth century, while Ayerbe-Chaux ("Manuscritos" 89), Barry Taylor ("*Estoria*" 39), and Charles Faulhaber (PhiloBiblon, BETA manid 1964) date it to the fifteenth.[11] While there are no clear distinctions between a manuscript copied in 1399 and one copied in 1401, I find the later date more convincing for two reasons. First, Taylor is the only scholar who compares

S to examples from palaeography manuals – two manuscripts dated 1434 and 1489 – to support his hypothesis. Second, I believe the earlier date reflects, at least in part, our desire to place the date of production closer to Juan Manuel's lifetime. Dating *S* to the fourteenth century would dispel any doubt regarding its status as the oldest witness of the *Conde Lucanor*, since *M*, *H*, and *P* all date to the fifteenth. It also aligns more closely with how the manuscript announces its proximity to Don Juan's efforts and wishes. To say "fourteenth century" is to evoke the same one in which Juan Manuel composed his works, but to say "fifteenth" highlights the temporal distance between Don Juan's gesture of authorial self-compilation and the copying of the artefact that survives. The earlier date is still plausible, but it is important to be aware of how the manuscript's rhetoric of authority speaks to our expectations as readers. This is just one example of how the manuscripts and editions of Juan Manuel's works transmit and transform his rhetoric of authority, an idea that underpins this book's argument and that will be taken up explicitly in the epilogue.

Juan Manuel's literary production is usually grouped into three main periods.[12] The first, dubbed his Alfonsine period (*período alfonsí*) by Germán Orduna, is characterized by his admiration and imitation of works by his uncle, Alfonso X *el Sabio*, and includes the *Crónica abreviada*, *Libro de la caza*, *Libro de la cavallería* and possibly the lost *Libro de los engeños*.[13] The second can be called his didactic period, and includes the *Libro del cavallero et del escudero*, *Libro de los estados*, and *Conde Lucanor*, three works aimed at the education of the nobility and structured by a dialogic frame – although these dialogues are quite restricted, as Carlos Heusch has shown ("Limites"). The final group, his personal period, includes the *Libro infinido*, *Libro de las tres razones*, *Tratado de la Asunción*, and General Prologue. It is characterized by Don Juan's recurring presence as a first-person narrator and the literary expression of personal concerns: his son's upbringing, the legacy of his family and works, and a point of doctrine (the Assumption of Mary) in which he firmly believed.

This prolific literary career was unprecedented for a member of the Castilian lay nobility, and Juan Manuel openly calls attention to his exceptionality. In the quote with which we began, he confirms that writing provoked the criticism of his peers because it did not correspond to his *estado*, that is, his place within the tripartite medieval model of social classification known as the "estate system" (which he explores in his *Libro de los estados*). Among the three estates of the clergy (*oratores*: those who pray), the nobility (*bellatores*: those who wage war), and workers (*laboratores*: those who labour), someone who wrote books was far more likely to be a member of the clergy thanks to their formal education

(Heusch, "Mala educación" 322). There were also professional copyists, such as the chancery scribes who worked in noble households, whom Juan Manuel classifies as *laboratores*, as in the *Libro de los estados* (285). Juan Manuel recommends that the sons of nobles learn to read chronicles and do simple Latin exercises in their youth, but writing was not a priority, and certainly not in adulthood when warfare and land management took precedence (*Libro de los estados* 198–201).

In the General Prologue, he reflects on his limitations as a writer, describing himself as "sabiendo tan poco de las escripturas commo aquel que, yo juro a Dios verdat, que non sabría hoy gobernar un proverbio de tercera persona" ("knowing as little about learned writings as someone who, honest to God, wouldn't know today how to conjugate a proverb in the third person"; ed. Serés, 6). The "proverb in the third person" refers to one of the Latin exercises he recommends for noble children, but the reference places him on the periphery of scholarly knowledge, familiar with the basic grammar curriculum of his youth but lacking the time to maintain his Latin or pursue further study (Rico 419; Funes, "Excentricidad" 12–13). This is certainly an example of the topos of false modesty (Scholberg, "Modestia" 28). But it also paints a picture of the typical writer of books in the early fourteenth century: an *orator* proficient in one or more languages of authority, such as Latin, and familiar with its *escripturas* or textual traditions. Before the late fourteenth and fifteenth centuries, when it became more common for nobles such as Diego de Valera and Fernán Pérez de Guzmán to take up the pen, it was highly unusual for a *bellator* to be a writer (Gómez-Bravo, *Textual Agency* 19–32). Even the prolific Ramon Llull (1232–1316), technically a layman, cannot be considered a Catalan precedent, as he received tertiary Franciscan orders and devoted his adult life to missionary causes. Then, why did Juan Manuel write? What possibilities did he see in authorship?

One motivation was political. Juan Manuel's most productive period as a writer coincided with his worst time of conflict with Alfonso XI, from 1325 to 1335. While autobiographical readings of imaginative literature should always be approached with caution, his frequent portrayals of kings and princes in need of advice have been productively read in light of the period of tension with the young Castilian king (see, for example, Deyermond, "Cuentística," and Cossío Olavide, "*Algunos moros*"). Undoubtedly, his dedication to writing represented an attempt to recuperate some of the power and influence he had lost after the breakdown of his relationship with Alfonso XI, through the manipulation of "official" discourses of historiography, aristocratic education, and religious doctrine (see, for example, Funes and Qués). But in addition to this political motivation, he was also captivated by the intellectual and spiritual appeal of a burgeoning book culture in the vernacular, which played an ever-expanding role in the lives of the lay nobility.

Alfonso X played a central role in this boom in vernacular book culture in Castile. Alfonso's patronage of a massive new corpus of Castilian literature had left a deep impression on Juan Manuel, as he attests in the prologue to his *Libro de la caza*. After enumerating the king's translations of works of the liberal arts and sciences as well as Jewish and Islamic doctrine and Christian and secular law, the prologue's third-person narrator marvels that "Non podría dezir ningún omne cuánto bien este noble rey fizo señaladamente en acrecentar et alumbrar el saber" ("No one could express how much good this noble king did, especially to increase and illuminate knowledge"; *Obras*, ed. Alvar and Finci, 303). This is the earliest surviving testament to Alfonso X's literary contributions as being both religious and secular, attentive to Jewish and Islamic intellectual traditions, and highly advantageous for the political and cultural advancement of Castile, an evaluation that stands largely unchanged today (see, for example, chs. 2 and 3 of Francisco Márquez Villanueva's *El concepto cultural alfonsí*). He also expresses a personal appreciation for his uncle's works: "Don Joán, su sobrino [...] se paga mucho de leer en los libros que falla que compuso el dicho rey" ("Don Juan, his nephew, greatly enjoys reading from the books he can find by the aforementioned king"; 304). By writing books, Alfonso made a lasting contribution to the collective knowledge of his kingdom and brought pleasure to individual readers. For Leonardo Funes, this portrait of Alfonso is so tied up with Juan Manuel's self-portrayal that it can be read as an early example of *altrobiografía* ("altrobiography" or "other-biography"), a biography of someone else imbued with the characteristics the writer wants to apply to him- or herself ("Primeros trazos" 104).

Another central figure in the creation of this vernacular book culture was Alfonso X's successor, Sancho IV. Juan Manuel does not praise Sancho's contributions to knowledge or cite the books produced under his patronage explicitly, but his works indicate a deep engagement with Sancho's cultural project, particularly the *Castigos de Sancho IV* and *Lucidario* (Kinkade, "Sancho IV"). Sancho's literary production, closely linked to the cathedral school of Toledo under its archbishop Gonzalo Pérez Gudiel (also known as Gonzalo García Gudiel), marked a return to Christian orthodoxy (Orduna, "Élite"). Alfonso X's multiconfessional collective of scholars and sources was replaced by Christian clerics working with Christian forms of knowledge and authority. Upon Sancho's death in 1295, his wife María de Molina provided political stability during the minorities of their son, Fernando IV, and grandson, Alfonso XI, and may also have inspired cultural continuity in the kingdom's literary production during the first half of the fourteenth century, leading Fernando Gómez Redondo and others to dub this orthodox turn *molinismo*.[14] While there are objections to the term, particularly the wide range of "orthodox" ideas to which it refers and the lack of concrete evidence of María de Molina's literary patronage, I find it helpful as a way of identifying points of continuity in the courtly Castilian literature composed during her queenship.[15] Within *molinista* literature, an orthodox approach to authorship meant that writing was depicted as a Christian act and a service to God, in contrast to the primarily secular goals of Alfonso's authorial project.[16]

The prologues of two works written under Sancho, the *Lucidario* and *Castigos de Sancho IV*, described writing as a "service to God": "Ternemos por bien e por derecho de començar este libro a su serviçio" ("We find it good and right to begin this book in His [God's] service"; *Lucidario* 82); "Ordené e fize este libro para mi fijo e dende para todos aquellos que dél algund bien quisieren tomar e aprender a serviçio de Dios" ("I have ordered and composed this book for my son and henceforth for all those who wish to benefit and learn from it in service to God"; *Castigos* 73). Under this orthodox framework, writing books serves God by serving other Christians and keeping them on the path to spiritual salvation. Juan Manuel affirms this belief in the salvific power of writing in the prologue to his *Conde Lucanor*: "Et Dios [...] por la su merced et por la su piadat quiera que los que este libro leyeren que se aprovechen dél a servicio de Dios et para salvamiento de sus almas et aprovechamiento de sus cuerpos" ("May God in His love and mercy make it so that whoever reads this book will benefit from it in service to God, and for the salvation of their souls and the good of their bodies"; ed. Serés, 11). This tenet of *molinista* literature brings authorship in line with several of the seven spiritual works of mercy, mandates for virtuous action that were taught in the basic Christian catechism. Juan Manuel lists them succinctly in his *Libro del cavallero et del escudero*: "Castigar a los errados, e amostrar a los non sabios, e consejar al que ha mester consejo, e ayudar al cuitado, e perdonar al quel ha errado, e sofrir al enojoso, e ser piadoso a todos los que lo an mester e rogar por ellos" ("Admonish those in error, instruct the ignorant, advise those who need counsel, help the afflicted, forgive those who have wronged you, endure the bothersome, and be merciful to all who need it and pray for them"; 50). Authorship has the potential to admonish, instruct, and advise by transmitting didactic content to readers, which Juan Manuel describes as "pro et verdad et non daño" ("profit and truth and no harm") in the passage with which this book begins. It can also comfort the afflicted by providing entertainment and solace, a commonplace of medieval prologues that appears in his *Libro del cavallero et del escudero*: "Cada que só en algún cuidado, fago que me lean algunos libros o algunas estorias por sacar aquel cuidado del coraçón" ("Every time I find myself worrying, I have some books or stories read to me to remove this worry from my heart"; 3). Making books allows Juan Manuel to perform four of the seven spiritual works of mercy in one fell swoop, and in a way that can impact readers for generations to come. Writing therefore constitutes a significant investment in his own salvation.

Thanks in large part to the initiatives of Alfonso X and Sancho IV, books were far more accessible to the lay nobility in the fourteenth century than they had been in the past. Literacy, vernacular book production, and private book collections began to increase in Castilian courtly circles and urban centres, although the most noticeable increases would not occur until the fifteenth century (Lawrance, "Spread" 80–3). A parallel development occurred in the kingdom of Aragon, where the works of Ramon Llull and a series of royal biographies and chronicles had inaugurated a tradition of Catalan literary prose that began in the late thirteenth century and flourished in the fourteenth (Riquer 197, 394). Not all Castilian and Aragonese nobles were literate, but most were "quasi-literate," meaning that they had access to the written word and to some extent depended on it "for the exercise of their socio-political function" (Bäuml 246). Some fourteenth-century works may have been written in the vernacular to address a multiconfessional reading public, such as Ramon Llull's evangelical works in Catalan (Hames 51–2), Shem Tov de Carrión's *Proverbios morales* (Wacks, *Double Diaspora* 97–126), and the anonymous Aljamiado-Aragonese *Poema de Yusuf*, which, though written in Arabic characters for a primarily Muslim audience, was likely accessible to other Romance speakers through oral performances (Wiegers 29–33). Legal and exegetical texts in Latin, Hebrew, and Arabic were not produced with a lay audience in mind, but recent innovations in book production such as indexes, running titles, and commentarial page layout made these tomes both easier to use and visually appealing (Parkes, "Influence"; Rouse and Rouse 198–9; Rodríguez Velasco, "Producción"). A wealthy and well-connected nobleman like Juan Manuel would have been surrounded by books big and small, beautiful and plain, ones he could read (or have read aloud to him) and ones he could not. The materiality of this book culture seems to have attracted Juan Manuel in and of itself, as we will see in chapter 1's discussion of scribal copying and the mechanical act of writing.

Vernacular authorship in Christian Castile is best understood within the context of the theory of authorship that emerged in Latin Europe in the twelfth and thirteenth centuries. For this context, my study joins many others in standing on the shoulders of Minnis's *Medieval Theory of Authorship*, first published in 1984. This pathfinding book shows how scholastic theologians' approach to studying the human authors of the Bible developed into a cohesive literary theory that was applied to the works of other *auctores* – the venerated authors of antiquity – and eventually to the works of living writers. It has thus facilitated the study of medieval authorship, in both Latin and vernacular contexts, using a theoretical vocabulary rooted in medieval ideas about authors, readers, and texts. The studies of Thomas Stillinger on authority in the medieval lyric, Albert Russell Ascoli on Dante Alighieri, Daniel Hobbins on Jean Gerson, and Stephanie Viereck Gibbs Kamath on first-person allegory in France and England, as well as the essays in *Author, Reader, Book*, edited by Stephen Partridge and Erik Kwakkel, are just a handful of examples that engage with Minnis's work to explain how authorship functions in a particular medieval author, text, or genre.

This book complements these studies by illustrating how medieval Castilian writers, including Juan Manuel and the scribes who copied his works, adapted Latin academic texts to the particular needs of an Iberian vernacular tradition. In my analysis of bookmaking culture in thirteenth- and fourteenth-century Castile, I also aim to complement Ana Gómez-Bravo's *Textual Agency*, which explores scribal culture in fifteenth-century Spain. Finally, my epilogue sheds light on how a medieval concept of authorship was refracted through the prism of Romanticism and national literary histories, a combination of ideas that led nineteenth-century scholars such as George Ticknor to posit Juan Manuel as the quintessential "early Spanish genius" whose prose represented "such forms as afterwards became national and characteristic" (64).

Most of the examples discussed in this book place Juan Manuel in dialogue with the academic culture of Latin Europe and with Christian writers working in the various Latin-derived Romance languages, in Iberia and beyond. However, this is not to deny the importance of what David Wacks identifies as a shared culture of "Iberian-ness" among Muslims, Jews, and Christians, especially in the sphere of secular, practical wisdom represented by the *Disciplina clericalis* of Petrus Alfonsi or the *Kalīla wa-Dimna* of Ibn al-Muqaffa‘ (*Framing* 10). Arabic, in particular, still held a lingering prestige as a language of authority in Christian Iberia in the fourteenth century (Szpiech 79), and there is conclusive evidence that part 1 of the *Conde Lucanor* draws upon Arabic stories and storytelling techniques (Ayerbe-Chaux, *"El conde Lucanor"* 118–37; Lacarra, *Cuentística* 49–50; Wacks, *Framing* 129–56; Torollo). Nor do I exclude the possibility that Juan Manuel's other works drew upon Jewish and Islamic textual culture in specific ways yet to be demonstrated. But his concept of authorship is best understood as part of a phenomenon within Latin Europe.

On the one hand, because one of his aims was to assume the ethical benefits of writing, which for a devout Christian meant spiritual salvation through the Church, it is logical that his concept of authorship would take many of its cues from Latin Christian models. For example, although commentarial writing, the subject of chapter 3, was shared by members of all three faiths, the best way for him to explain Christian doctrine to his readers was to imitate Christian exegetical models. On the other hand, by the fourteenth century several works of secular Arabic literature, including *Kalīla wa-Dimna*, had already been translated into Castilian and adapted for a Christian audience, thanks in part to Alfonso X. Despite the king's rumoured heterodoxy, his translation efforts were part of an initiative that "the Church never opposed and to a certain extent had even fostered" (Márquez Villanueva, "Alfonsine" 81). These secular models still bore the traces of their multiconfessional heritage, but Juan Manuel would have encountered them after the process of *translatio studii*, the transfer of learning from one culture to another, was already complete, and they had been fully assimilated into Christian textual culture (Wacks, *Framing* 103–4).

While medieval literary theory forms the core of my study of Juan Manuel's authorship, I am also informed by two twentieth-century essays that loom large in the discipline: Roland Barthes's "The Death of the Author," first published in the American magazine *Aspen* in 1967, and Michel Foucault's "Qu'est-ce qu'un auteur?" ("What Is an Author?") first published in the *Bulletin de la Société française de philosophie* in 1969. For Barthes, the death of the Author-God was a necessary step in breaking from a critical past still "tyranically centered on the author, his person, his life, his tastes, his passions" (875). The removal of the author promised to open up texts to a wider range of meanings, held together in the figure of the reader, but it fell short of explaining how the notion of authorship actually worked. Foucault, in part responding to Barthes, sought to fill that gap by breaking down the "author-function," a component of certain types of discourse that generates special linguistic, literary, and legal relationships between text and author. The author-function, a discursive construct associated with ownership, origins, and creativity, varies according to the historical moment in which it operates and the types of discourse attached to it. Yet despite this contingency,

Foucault shows how it has retained its force over time as an ideological production, a tool for establishing a particular social order.[17] Foucault deals little with medieval authorship and in some instances misrepresents it (Ascoli, *Dante* 26–8). However, his identification of the author-function as both a discourse and an ideological production is essential to my argument that authorship in medieval Castile is best understood as a set of discourses, deployed in various times and ways to give an audience a particular image of a work's author.

This persuasive aspect of authorship invites a parallel between medieval and modern theory and practice. Foucault's notion of discourse has much in common with the medieval discipline of rhetoric, the art of using language to persuade other people that what you are saying is true.[18] In ancient Greece and Rome, rhetoric was most strongly associated with public speaking and politics, but medieval Latin writers also applied it to literature out of a shared concern for artistic expression through language (Auerbach 192–3). Rhetoric thus shares with discourse the aim of distributing power or influence. As Faulhaber has shown, there were three main sources on rhetoric in fourteenth-century Castile: Cicero's *De inventione*, the *Rhetorica ad Herennium* (also attributed to Cicero), and the *artes dictandi* or arts of letter-writing (141). Juan Manuel's advice on letter-writing in the *Libro infinido* suggests that he had some familiarity with *artes dictandi* (Mota, "Introduction" 82), but given his admiration for the cultural projects of Alfonso X and Sancho IV, his source on rhetoric was probably the *Libro del tesoro*, a Castilian translation of the Florentine scholar Brunetto Latini's *Li livres dou trésor* sponsored by Sancho (Kinkade, "Sancho IV" 1047–8).[19] Its third book, adapted from *De inventione*, deals with rhetoric, of which Latini writes that "toda su entençión es dezir palabras en tal manera que onbre faga creer sus dichos a aquellos que los oyen" ("its whole purpose is to say words in such a way that one makes those listening believe what one says"; 178).[20] Latini teaches that the persuasion of rhetoric does not always happen out in the open (*paladinamente*): sometimes it occurs "ascondidamente, quando alguno enbía sus letras guarnidas de buenas razones contra la defensa que cuida que el otro aya" ("covertly, when someone sends their letters fortified with good reasons against the defence they think the other party might have"; 180). For Juan Manuel – a lay nobleman who sought to participate in a culture of learning and bookmaking traditionally considered inappropriate to his estate – rhetoric provided a way to convince readers and listeners that he belonged. Moreover, he did not always need to call attention to his use of rhetoric; sometimes a more subtle approach (*ascondidamente*) was both safer and more persuasive, such as the strategies he adopts to discuss theological subject matter in the *Libro de los estados* (see ch. 3).

Juan Manuel's use of rhetoric has something else in common with the Foucauldian concept of discourse: its longevity. The accidents of literary history have allowed Juan Manuel's concept of authorship to retain its force over time. Some of his rhetorical strategies, such as requesting that his works be reproduced exactly as he wrote them, are similar to the strategies writers would use after the arrival of the printing press to Europe and the emergence of the concept of literary property (Chartier 32–56). Moreover, as discussed in the epilogue, his rhetoric of authorship aligned with both Romantic ideas of originality and philology's preference for authorial texts. Because his self-presentation as an author coincided with one that came to dominate the literary landscape, it began to seem more like truth than rhetoric, and took on the force of a discourse.

This book is also informed by the post-medieval concept of "portraying," the only word in its title that is fully absent from the medieval Spanish sources. In the transitive sense of making an artistic likeness of a person or thing, it first appears in English in 1398 ("Portray," def. I.2.b), and the corresponding meaning for the Spanish *retratar* is not attested until 1570 (Coromines 5: 576). I use the present participle to indicate a process that is "imperfect" in the grammatical sense of being incomplete and ongoing. As formulated in Juan Manuel's works, authorship is a dynamic concept whose portrayal changes over time.

"Portraying authorship" is deliberately ambiguous: who, or what, is doing the portraying? Juan Manuel played a role by creating Don Juan, who speaks in the first person in all but two of his extant works (*Crónica abreviada* and *Libro de la caza*). But his literary persona's near-ubiquity has contributed to the fiction of the historical man as solitary author, thereby eliding the interventions of the many others who collaborated in the composition and transmission of his works. The anonymous medieval copyists and compilers, the early modern editor Gonzalo Argote de Molina, and the many modern editors and translators of Juan Manuel's works all serve as his "associates," working on his behalf and in his name.[21] I borrow the term "associates" (*associés*) from Gérard Genette, who refers to an author's associate as an individual, such as a publisher, who may accept responsibility for "official" paratexts that appear with the author's work (*Paratexts* 9–10).[22] Like Foucault's author-function and Love's authemes, Genette's concept of the author's associates reminds us that our conventional shorthand of the author as a single, flesh-and-blood person responsible for a work masks a collaborative process in which multiple individuals perform various tasks in the author's name. However, it also has the advantage of emphasizing human actors rather than disembodied functions. This is especially helpful in the context of a manuscript culture, in which scribes and patrons reproduce an author's works not for a speculative market, but for a known audience, and perhaps for their personal use. Throughout this book, I aim to shed light on how Juan Manuel and an influential set of associates, ranging from medieval scribes to nineteenth-century editors and translators, contributed to an enduring portrayal of his concept of authorship.

To portray something is also to represent it using some form of mediation, often through an artistic medium. When actors portray characters on stage and screen, they adopt a role that differs from their role in "real life," but that they are able to embody, more or less convincingly, for an audience. A portrait is an artistic representation of a person that combines representational conventions with some sense of the unique individual being evoked. Similar to these senses of creative and representational portrayal, this book explores how Juan Manuel and his associates use language to portray him as an authoritative author. Writing of pictorial author portraits in medieval manuscripts, Sonja Drimmer observes that "an author portrait is a special category of portrait because it both produces a corpus and arises from one. [...] Because it strives to close a gap between the referent that is both 'out there' and 'in here,' it can beguile the viewer into a forgetfulness of the artist responsible for mediating it" (69). Author portraits anchor the author's works to an individual – a body – and in so doing they conjure up an image of direct transmission from author to reader, obscuring the layers of mediation that go into book production. There are no pictorial author portraits in Juan Manuel's extant manuscripts, but Don Juan's verbal portrait has a similar function, attempting to close the gap between author and text while covering up its own artifice. Modern editors, reinforcing this impulse, often reproduce the male donor figure from an altarpiece in the Cathedral of Murcia, long identified as Juan Manuel, as an author portrait (fig. 0.1).[23] With the word "portraying," I highlight the fictionality and mediation involved in this authorial pose.

This book is divided into four chapters, each of which examines how Juan Manuel assumes one of the writerly roles outlined in Bonaventure's schema (scribe, compiler, commentator, and author). Each chapter traces the discursive construction of its respective role in Castilian works of the thirteenth and fourteenth centuries to illustrate how Don Juan's authorial discourse converges with and diverges from existing models. I also show what he stands to gain from adopting each role: as *scriptor,* he helps preserve knowledge for posterity; as *compilator,* he

Fig. 0.1. Portrait of male donor in Barnaba da Modena, *Retablo de la Virgen de la Leche* (c. 1372). Capilla de Santa María de la Claustra, Museo de la Catedral de Murcia.

generates new meanings from existing sources through juxtaposition; as *commentator*, he demonstrates his exegetical abilities; and as *auctor*, he writes his own words to make a personal contribution to knowledge. Each form of authorial discourse is also a rhetoric of authority, aimed at persuading readers that he is qualified to carry out these writerly roles and therefore may receive and transmit their ethical benefits. In the epilogue, I show how scribes, editors, and translators took up Don Juan's rhetoric of authority to perpetuate this authorial self-portrait, in a process that began with the earliest extant manuscripts and lasted well into the nineteenth century. Together, the chapters and epilogue argue that the medieval rhetorical strategies present in the texts interact with the textual and codicological choices of subsequent editors to communicate a coherent notion of Juan Manuel's authorship.

One final observation on this book's organization: given the hierarchical presentation of Bonaventure's four writerly roles, some scholars have interpreted them as a four-step pathway to becoming an author. Writing about vernacular poetry in Latin Europe, Stillinger proposes that authority-seeking vernacular writers might have aspired to "advance through the ranks" of authorship, but could not, due to their choice of a different language (the vernacular) and subject matter (secular lyric and romance) (38). However, Juan Manuel treats the less "creative" authorial roles not as stepping stones to the role of *auctor*, but as valuable in their own right. His literary persona does not simply progress through the ranks as his literary career develops; rather, he occupies each writerly role at different times and in different combinations without abandoning the others, thereby accumulating and retaining all their ethical benefits. For this reason, although the book proceeds in order from *scriptor* to *auctor*, and although later chapters place more emphasis on his later works, each chapter references most or all of his works at one point or another. My argument is not that Juan Manuel began his literary career as a scribe and ended as a full-fledged author, but that he experimented with the rhetoric of all four roles throughout his career. Furthermore, as my epilogue proposes, his success in the role of "author" is largely due to the interventions of scribes and editors who privileged that role over the others.

1 Scriptor

In Bonaventure's schema of the four ways of writing a book, the scribe is a writer who "writes others' words, adding nothing and changing nothing." In medieval Castilian texts, writers used separate verbs to distinguish between copying (*escribir*), associated with scribes and compilers, and authorial creation (*fazer* or *componer*), associated with authors (B. Taylor, "Capítulos" 63). When medieval authors reflected on scribal labour, they consistently attributed little to no creative input to scribes, but this was far from reality. Rather, this was a rhetorical strategy designed to project an idealized model of textual transmission, in which scribes simply reproduced texts composed by those with more authority over the written word. As Matthew Fisher puts it, "medieval authors went to great lengths to maintain the pretense that medieval scribes were invisible, their labors transparent" (6).

Juan Manuel was not interested in making the work of scribes invisible; instead, he sought to shape readers' ideas about the division of labour between scribe and author. In this chapter, I argue that he depicts scribal copying as both an imperfect means of reproducing texts and as a cultural practice that asserts moral value and bestows authority. *Escribir* and its variants can refer both to rote copying and to the recording of knowledge in writing, and Don Juan harnesses this double meaning to make a distinction between "low" mechanical labour and "high" intellectual work. His criticism of scribes, formulated in the General Prologue to his collected works, adapts both academic and popular sources to situate rote copying as the work of *laboratores*, the lowest position in the medieval estate system. On the other hand, his praise of writing in works like his *Libro del cavallero et del escudero* reimagines scholarly and courtly discourse on bookmaking to ascribe prestige to his own works and, by extension, courtly Castilian prose in general. By redefining the role of scribes along this axis of "low" and "high" roles, he projects an illusion of control over the copying of his works while avoiding the reproach that writing is beneath his station. Moreover, this allows him to criticize scribes for their imperfect execution while assuming responsibility for the positive aspects of their labour.

Some scholars of medieval literature have sought to move away from a hierarchical understanding of the relationship between scribes and authors by adopting the concept of "variance," which embraces the textual variants introduced by copyists as part of the richness of a manuscript culture. John Dagenais, building upon the work of Bernard Cerquiglini and Paul Zumthor, advocates for studying a text's variant readings "without attempting to assign any hierarchical or textual-critical preeminence" to them (130). Variance has its limits for certain tasks, such as preparing a readable critical edition, but one significant advantage is that it has encouraged scholars to question how the scribe-author relationship is portrayed. As this chapter will show, Juan Manuel and his near-contemporaries such as Petrarch and Chaucer worked to perpetuate a hierarchical relationship between authors and scribes in their respective vernacular literary traditions. Nonetheless, it is important to contextualize their remarks not as straightforward accounts of medieval bookmaking, but as part of a rhetorical tradition aimed at persuading others.

It is likely that Juan Manuel, as a member of the elite nobility, would have written very little in his own hand, delegating the actual task of writing to scribes in his employ. But he would also have asserted his ability to commission, pay for, and oversee manual labour as a way of assuming responsibility for the fruits of that labour. This resonates with the autheme of "declarative authorship," which Love defines as the function of "appearing in the public sphere as the work's creator, and of shouldering the responsibilities and accepting the benefits that flow from this" (45). A declarative author signs his or her name to a text, and all the other functions of authorship are contingent upon that public act of naming. In medieval Castile, a form of declarative authorship had been articulated in a well-known passage of the *General estoria* produced by the scriptorium of Alfonso X:

> Del escrivir de [los Mandamientos] avedes oído en el començamiento d'este capítulo cómo dixo Nuestro Señor que él las escrivirié. E aquí dize en el XXXIIII° capítulo del Éxodo que las mandó escrivir a Moisén, e avredes otrossí en el libro que á nombre Deuteronomio [...] que diz que Nuestro Señor que él mismo las escrivió; e semeja que son contrallas estas razones. E sobr'esta contralla fabla maestre Pedro, e depártela d'esta guisa: diz que todo es bien dicho, e que podemos entender e dezir que compuso Nuestro

> Señor las razones de los mandados, e que ovo el autoridad e el nombre dend porque las mandó escrivir, mas que las escrivió Moisén, assí como dixiemos nós muchas vezes el rey faze un libro non por quel él escriva con sus manos, mas porque compone las razones d'él e las emienda e yegua e endereça e muestra la manera de cómo se deven fazer, e desí escrívelas qui él manda, peró dezimos por esta razón que el rey faze el libro. Otrossí cuando dezimos el rey faze un palacio o alguna obra non es dicho porque lo él fiziesse con sus manos, mas porquel mandó fazer e dio las cosas que fueron mester pora ello; e qui esto cumple aquel á nombre que faze la obra, e nós assí veo que usamos de lo dezir. (2: 392–3)

> Regarding the writing of [the Commandments], you have heard in the beginning of this chapter how our Lord said that he would write them, and here he states in chapter 34 of Exodus that he ordered Moses to write them. And you will also have heard in the book called Deuteronomy [...] that our Lord himself wrote them, and it seems that these statements are contradictory. Concerning this contradiction, Master Petrus [Comestor] has this to say: this is all correct, and we can understand and say that our Lord composed the content of the Commandments, and he had authority over them and put his name to them because he ordered them to be written, but in fact Moses wrote them. Thus we have said many times that a king writes a book, not because he copies it with his own hands, but because he creates its arguments, emends them, makes them uniform, corrects them, and shows the way they should be done, and so they are written by whomever the king appoints to do so, but for this reason we say that the king writes the book. Moreover, when we say that the king makes a palace or some other work, it is not because he makes it with his own hands, but rather because he ordered it to be made and provided the things necessary for it. And whoever does this is called the work's maker, and this, I believe, is how we usually put it.

Taking as a starting point the aforementioned commonplace of biblical exegesis about the twofold authorship of the Bible, the Alfonsine scribes compare God's authorship of the Commandments to how the king commissions earthly works such as books and palaces. But while the intervention of God, the divine Author, must be accepted on the basis of religious dogma and faith, the king claims a more active and visible role: he participates not only in the intellectual endeavour of determining the book's subject matter, but also in more granular editorial decisions. Additionally, the analogy of palace construction depicts the king as a savvy manager of materials for various types of workmanship, which we can extend to the provision of written source materials as well as the parchment, ink, and other necessary implements for bookmaking. Juan Manuel, as an avid reader of the works patronized by his uncle, would have had a similar understanding of the relationship between the wealthy and powerful nobility of which he was a part, and the workers, including scribes, who laboured under their aegis. This division of labour between nobles and scribes was construed as part of a divinely ordered society. Significantly, though, the Alfonsine text set the precedent for considerable flexibility in how that labour was distributed.

We know a little about the writing handled by Juan Manuel's chancery (*cancillería*), such as the types of correspondence prepared, the rhetorical models they followed, and the names of scribes who prepared them (Pascual Martínez; Lobato López). Giménez Soler edited nearly six hundred letters associated with him, including many issued from his chancery (217ff.). But we have no record of Juan Manuel supervising a scriptorium, consisting of the professionals paid to copy his literary works and the material conditions in which they worked. If he maintained one, it would probably have been comparable to the scriptoria of Alfonso X and Sancho IV, though on a much smaller scale.[1] Given the lack of evidence, I will not conjecture about the labour practices of this fourteenth-century nobleman's scriptorium or the specific scribes in his employ. Rather, by focusing on his remarks about scribes in his works, I aim to show how he remixes rhetorical tropes about scribal labour to redefine the conceptual division between scribes and authors.

"Low" Scribal Labour

It has become a commonplace of Juan Manuel studies that he was critical of the work of scribes, blaming them for the problems of textual transmission in a manuscript culture. This claim is derived from the General Prologue, which he composed near the end of his career to introduce the volume of his collected works.[2] No authorial version of this volume survives, and the General Prologue is extant only in S. Written in the first person, it describes his concern for how his works will be transmitted and interpreted, lamenting the carelessness of scribes who will inevitably introduce errors into his text. Don Juan tries to protect against this by commissioning an authoritative volume of all his works. But as Dagenais notes, "in his very concern for what the process of scribal transmission would inevitably do to his 'libros,' Don Juan, with characteristic pragmatism, recognizes that such a goal cannot be realized" (115). The General Prologue draws from existing literary models to communicate this message, most notably the *Prologus secundus* to

Nicholas of Lyra's biblical commentary, *Postilla litteralis super Bibliam*, as Francisco Rico has shown. This adaptation of a trope from a Latin academic prologue to a vernacular context is innovative in itself (Rico 409–10; Olivetto, "Alonso" 46). But the General Prologue also introduces new ideas about the categorization of scribes and authors in the burgeoning Castilian literary tradition. In combining the authoritative discourse of a Latin prologue with a tale about a troubadour's legal dispute, it seeks to establish a hierarchy of authors, readers, and scribes sanctioned by legal and literary means.

The General Prologue's portrayal of scribes hinges on its adaptation of the story of the knight and the shoemaker. The story is presented in a tripartite narrative structure similar to each chapter or *enxiemplo* of part 1 of the *Conde Lucanor*, in which Count Lucanor recounts a practical problem, Patronio narrates a pertinent exemplum, and Patronio and Don Juan interpret the exemplum and apply it to a broader context.[3] In the General Prologue, Don Juan plays both advice-seeker and advice-giver, addressing the dilemma of a proud creator seeking to protect his work from discredit. Because the exemplum and its introduction do much of the work of communicating the prologue's message, they merit citing in full:

> Así commo ha muy grant plazer el que faze alguna buena obra, señaladamente si toma grant trabajo en la fazer, cuando sabe que aquella su obra es muy loada et se pagan della mucho las gentes, bien así ha muy grant pesar et grant enojo cuando alguno, a sabiendas o aun por yerro, faze o dize alguna cosa por que aquella obra non sea tan preciada o alabada como devía ser. Et por probar aquesto, porné aquí una cosa que acaeció a un cavallero en Perpinán en tienpo del primero rey don Jaymes de Mallorcas.
>
> Así acaeció que aquel cavallero era muy grant trobador et fazié muy buenas cantigas a marabilla, et fizo una muy buena además et avía muy buen son; et atanto se pagavan las gentes de aquella cantiga, que desde grant tienpo non querían cantar otra cantiga sinon aquella; et el cavallero que la fiziera avía ende muy grant plazer. Et yendo por la calle un día, oyó que un çapatero estava diziendo aquella cantiga, et dezía tan mal erradamente tan bien las palabras commo el son, que todo omne que la oyese, si ante non la oyié, ternía que era muy mala cantiga et muy mal fecha. Cuando el cavallero que la fiziera oyó cómmo aquel çapatero confondía aquella tan buena obra commo él fiziera, ovo ende muy grant pesar et grant enojo, et descendió de la bestia et asentose cerca dél. Et el çapatero, que non se guardava de aquello, no dexó su cantar, et cuanto más dezía, más confondía la cantiga que el cavallero fiziera. Et desque el cavallero vio su buena obra tan mal confondida por la torpedat de aquel çapatero, tomó

muy paso unas tiseras et tajó cuantos çapatos el çapatero tenía fechos; et esto fecho, cavalgó et fuese. Et el çapatero paró mientes en sus çapatos, et desque los vido así tajados et entendió que avía perdido todo su trabajo, ovo grant pesar et fue dando vozes en pos aquel cavallero que aquello le fiziera. Et el cavallero díxole:

– Amigo, el rey nuestro señor es aquí, et vós sabedes que es muy buen rey et muy justiciero; et vayamos antél et líbrelo commo fallare por derecho.

Anbos se acordaron a esto; et desque llegaron antel rey, dixo el çapatero cómmo le tajara todos sus çapatos et le fiziera grant daño. El rey fue desto sañudo et preguntó al cavallero si era aquello verdat; et el cavallero díxole que sí, mas que quisiese saber por qué lo fiziera. Et mandó el rey que lo dixiese; et el cavallero dixo que bien sabía el rey que él fiziera tal cantiga que era muy buena et avía buen son, et que aquel çapatero gela avía confondida, et que gela mandase dezir. Et el rey mandógela dezir et vio que era así. Estonce dixo el cavallero que, pues el çapatero confondiera tan buena obra commo él fiziera et en que avía tomado grant dapno et afán, que así confondiera él la obra del çapatero. El rey et cuantos lo oyeron tomaron desto grant plazer et rieron ende mucho, et el rey mandó al çapatero que nunca dixiese aquella cantiga nin confondiese la buena obra del cavallero, et pechó el rey el daño al çapatero et mandó al cavallero que non fiziese más enojo al çapatero. (ed. Serés, 3–5)

When someone writes a good work, especially one that requires a lot of effort, he will take great pleasure in knowing that his work is highly praised and many people like it; in the same way, he will be very annoyed and angered when someone, knowingly or by accident, does or says something to make that work less appreciated or praised than it ought to be. And to demonstrate this, I will recount here what happened to a knight in Perpignan in the time of the king Don Jaume I of Mallorca.

It so happened that this knight was a great troubadour, and he wrote many marvellous songs and one in particular that had a very good tune, and people were so taken with the song that for a long time it was the only one anyone would sing, and this pleased the knight who had composed it very much. And as he was going down the street one day, he heard a shoemaker singing the words and tune of his song so poorly that anyone who had not heard it before would have thought it was a bad song, and badly written too. When the knight who had written the song heard the shoemaker ruining the good work he had written, he felt very hurt and angry, and he came down from his horse and sat down near him. The shoemaker did not notice this and kept singing, and the more he sang, the worse he mangled the song the knight had composed. And when the knight saw his good work so ruined by the incompetence of that shoemaker, he quietly took a pair of scissors and cut up all the shoes the shoemaker had made, and having done this he took off on his horse. When the shoemaker noticed his shoes all cut up and realized that he had lost all his work, he was very annoyed and went yelling after the knight who had done it. And the knight said to him:

– My friend, our king is here, and you know he is a very good and just king, so let's go to him and have him decide what is right.

They both agreed to this, and when they came before the king, the shoemaker told him how the knight had cut up all his shoes and done him great harm. The king was angered by this and asked the knight if this was true; the knight answered that it was, but that surely the king would like to know why he had done it. The king ordered him to explain, and the knight said that the king knew very well that he had written such a good song with a good melody, but the shoemaker had ruined it, and the king should have the shoemaker sing it for him. And the king had him sing it, and saw that it was true. Then the knight said that since the shoemaker had ruined his good work that had cost him such great effort, he had likewise ruined the shoemaker's work. The king and all those who were listening took great pleasure from this and laughed about it a great deal, and the king ordered the shoemaker not to sing that song or mangle the knight's good work anymore, paid the shoemaker for his damages and ordered the knight not to bother the shoemaker again. (trans. Cossío Olavide and Savo, 3–4)

The tale's motif dates back to the *Lives of Eminent Philosophers* by Diogenes Laertius (fl. late second century CE), a Greek collection of biographical anecdotes that circulated in medieval Europe in Latin translation. In this early version, the philosopher Arcesilaus tells the following anecdote about the poet Philoxenus and a group of brickmakers: "[Philoxenus] found them singing some of his melodies out of tune, so he retaliated by trampling on the bricks they were making, saying, 'If you spoil my work, I'll spoil yours'" (IV, 6, 36, p. 413). The story was adapted not only by Juan Manuel, but also by Franco Sacchetti (1332–1400) in his *Trecentonovelle*, with both authors probably drawing inspiration from a common source (Fiorentino; Lalomia).[4] Juan Manuel's adaptation of the tale is unique in introducing a legal dispute that ends with the king's verdict. It is also the only version to make an explicit link to manuscript culture, comparing the inexpert singer to the scribes who introduce errors into an author's creation. It has traditionally been interpreted as his way of expressing pride in his literary creation and attempting to "fix" the written text of his works (Menocal

472–5). However, by situating the story within his contemporary social and cultural context, Juan Manuel sends a message not just about the reception of his corpus, but about the social and intellectual hierarchies of book production.

The story is set in Perpignan during the reign of Jaume II of Mallorca (r. 1276–1311), an Iberian courtly milieu associated with the patronage of vernacular literature.[5] María Rosa Lida de Malkiel interprets this as a way to lend credibility to the story by bringing it closer to the author's lived experience, given that his first wife, Isabel of Mallorca, was Jaume's daughter ("Tres notas" 188n4).[6] Martí de Riquer, while recognizing the traditional motif at the story's core, goes so far as to speculate that the knight character may have been inspired by a real Catalan troubadour (125). But in a more general sense, a fourteenth-century Castilian audience would associate a troubadour from Perpignan with the prestigious tradition of Occitan lyric poetry. In his *Razos de trobar*, composed between 1190 and 1213, the Catalan courtier and poet Ramon Vidal de Besalú declared Occitan songs the most authoritative literary discourse: "Per totas las terras de nostre lengage son de maior autoritat li cantar de la lenga lemosina qe de neguna autra parladura" ("In all the lands with our language, the songs in the Limousin language [Occitan] are of greater authority than any other type of speech"; 6).[7] By associating the knight with Perpignan, Don Juan draws upon the poetic authority of Occitan, a prized language of vernacular lyric and the preferred language of Catalan troubadours. Vidal's work, considered the first poetic treatise in a Romance language, was possibly known to Juan Manuel because of his connections to the Aragonese court through his second wife Constanza of Aragon, daughter of Jaume II of Aragon. Moreover, Juan Manuel showed his familiarity with the genre by composing his own "[libro] de las reglas cómo se deve trobar" ("book of rules for composing poetry").[8] By choosing a Catalan troubadour as his stand-in, Juan Manuel associates his own Castilian prose works with the most prestigious vernacular literature in the Romance-speaking world. Similarly, Sacchetti would attribute the anecdote to Dante, the most authoritative vernacular author of the Italian tradition.

By casting a shoemaker in the role of scribe, Don Juan provides an apt complement to the social and symbolic resonance of the troubadour-knight. In all versions of the tale, the antagonists' low social status is designated by their profession: brickmakers, a shoemaker, a blacksmith, and a donkey driver. Within the medieval estate system, they are clearly situated as *laboratores*, while the knight and Dante are *bellatores*. These lowly antagonists – with the exception of Sacchetti's donkey driver – are are all "makers" in the sense that they create a tangible product.

As Lalomia points out, this notion of shaping raw material into art was a common metaphor for poetic creation (784ff.). Sacchetti's blacksmith evokes a more famous example, Canto 26 of Dante's *Purgatorio*, in which Guido Guinizzelli says of the Provenzal poet Arnaut Daniel, "fu miglior fabbro del parlar materno" ("he was a better smith of the mother tongue"; 26.117) – a line that T.S. Eliot famously adapted to dedicate *The Waste Land* to Ezra Pound. Juan Manuel's choice of a shoemaker may reflect a folkloric motif about the intellectual limitations of members of this profession, echoed in the Castilian refrain "Zapatero, a tus zapatos" ("Shoemaker, to your shoes"; Rico 417n4). But it also establishes a parallel between the two antagonists as craftsmen, each in his own right. Moreover, it evokes the world of bookmaking, since shoemakers, like scribes, turn animal skins into artisanal products with both practical and aesthetic value. The knight destroys his foe's work with a pair of scissors, a tool that would be equally effective against an offending manuscript. By associating the shoemaker with a kind of fine craftsmanship akin to producing a codex, Juan Manuel places him in the same continuum of literary activity that the knight inhabits. Their work is presented as roughly equivalent, as long as their different social categories are taken into account.

In the tale quoted above, the verdict of the king reinforces this notion of rough equivalence, since each party is instructed not to meddle with the other's work in the future. The king himself pays the shoemaker for his damaged wares ("pechó el rey el daño al çapatero"), signalling that the shoemaker's craft is just as valuable to the kingdom as the knight's poetic compositions. Furthermore, although the king prohibits the shoemaker from singing the knight's song, it is a specific prohibition on a specific song. The king could not place a blanket ban on singing poetry without the express approval of the author, because to do so would be equally detrimental to the knight's reputation, which depends in part on the popularity of his verses. Finally, the laughter of the king and his court ("tomaron desto grant plazer et rieron ende mucho") reveals a perspective quite different from the knight's dismay and anger ("muy grant pesar et grant enojo"). What provokes their laughter – that is, the referent of *desto* and *ende* – is not the shoemaker's atrocious singing, but the knight's testimony that since the shoemaker had ruined his work, he ruined the shoemaker's. For those charged with administering justice, it is comical to think that a troubadour has rights over his work once it has begun to circulate.

The story imagines an ideal world in which a "good and just king" implements laws to protect vernacular authors, similar to the regulations on academic textbooks that will be discussed below. However, judging from the humorous conclusion, Juan Manuel recognizes that it is impossible to exert complete control over one's writing, because transmission and reception will inevitably produce modifications. In spite of this potential for error, he needs scribes to copy his work and readers to read it, in order to accrue the ethical benefits of writing. Scribes and readers are also necessary for the earthly fame he alludes to at the start of the prologue, in which the successful author basks in praise and recognition ("ha muy grant plazer el que faze alguna buena obra [...] cuando sabe que aquella su obra es muy loada et se pagan della mucho las gentes"). Although Don Juan cannot control how his works will be copied and read, he can, at least, explore the themes of inaccuracy and misinterpretation through his writing.

In the second half of the General Prologue, Don Juan takes the lesson from the story of the knight and the shoemaker and applies it to the volume of his own collected works, which his prologue was written to introduce:

> Et recelando yo, don Joán, que por razón que non se podrá escusar, que los libros que yo he fechos non se ayan de trasladar muchas vezes; et porque yo he visto que en el transladar acaece muchas vezes, lo uno por desentendimiento del escribano, o porque las letras semejan unas a otras, que en transladando el libro porná una razón por otra, en guisa que muda toda la entención et toda la sentencia, et será traído el que la fizo non aviendo ý culpa. Et por guardar esto cuanto yo pudiere, fizi fazer este volumen en que están scriptos todos los libros que yo fasta aquí he fechos, et son doze. (ed. Serés, 5)

> And I, Don Juan, fear that the books I have written will inevitably be copied many times, because I have seen it happen often in copying that one word is put in place of another, either due to the ignorance of the scribe, or because the letters resemble one another; in this way the whole intention and meaning is changed, and the one who wrote the work will be betrayed without having any blame. So to guard against this as much as I can, I had this volume made in which are copied all the books I have written up until now, and there are twelve in all. (trans. Cossío Olavide and Savo, 4)

This is the passage that, as Rico has demonstrated, is based on a similar one from Nicholas of Lyra's *Prologus secundus* to his *Postilla litteralis super Bibliam*. The *Postilla*, composed between 1322 and 1332, quickly became the most circulated work of biblical exegesis after the *Glossa ordinaria* (Klepper 6). It may have come to Juan Manuel's attention through Ponç Carbonell, a Franciscan friar who studied with Nicholas in Paris and then returned to Aragon to serve as advisor to Jaume II of Aragon and tutor to Infante Juan of Aragon.[9] Infante Juan, the nobleman's brother-in-law through his second marriage, could have plausibly introduced him to parts of the *Postilla*, since he served as a kind of literary mentor to him (Tate). Nicholas's prologue reflects on how changes introduced by scribes and correctors have altered the meaning of the Bible:

> Ulterius considerandum quod sensus litteralis, a quo est incipiendum, ut dictum est, videtur multum obfuscatus diebus modernis: partim scriptorum vitio, qui propter similitudinem litterarum in multis locis aliter scripserunt quam habeat veritas textus; partim imperitia aliquorum correctorum, qui in pluribus locis fecerunt puncta ubi non debent fieri; et versus incoeperunt, vel terminaverunt, ubi non debent incipi et terminari: et per hoc sententia litterae variatur, ut patebit in suis locis infra prosequendo. (col. 29D)

> Furthermore, as for the literal sense [of scripture] on which this [book] is based, as it is said, it is often seen to be obfuscated nowadays, in part due to the fault of scribes, who in many places wrote something different than what the true text had on account of the similarity of letters; and in part due to the ignorance of some correctors, who in many places put punctuation marks where they should not be, and began or ended lines where they should not begin and end. And in this way the meaning of the letter is changed, as will be apparent in the places described below.

Complaints about scribal corruption of texts are so common in ancient and medieval works as to be an obvious literary trope.[10] However, in following Nicholas's language closely, Juan Manuel effects a more specific rhetorical move. Both writers bemoan the intellectual limitations of scribes, which Nicholas calls *imperitia* and Juan Manuel calls *desentendimiento*; both add a tinge of moral opprobrium in assigning blame to scribes (Nicholas's *scriptorum vitio*) or taking it away from authors (Juan Manuel's *non aviendo ý culpa*). By putting scribes down, they effectively situate themselves higher up in the hierarchy of bookmaking.

Yet there is an important difference: Nicholas is not referring to his own work, but to the biblical text, whose twofold authorship is shared between God and human *auctores*. The stakes for accuracy are therefore much higher. A careless mistake could lead theologians astray and impact the very foundations of Christian belief. Don Juan keeps Nicholas's emphasis on meaning (*sententia litterae*) but makes a significant modification: he specifies that in his case, scribal carelessness affects only the intended meaning of the human author (*muda toda la entención et toda la sentencia*), which leads to a type of "betrayal" (*et será traído el que la fizo*). In light of the tale of the knight and the shoemaker, this betrayal might seem like a matter of earthly fame, since the story emphasizes how the shoemaker's inaccurate rendition could affect the opinions of other listeners: "Todo omne que la oyese, si ante non la oyié, ternía que era muy mala cantiga et muy mal fecha" ("Anyone who had not heard it before would have thought it was a bad song, and badly written too"; 4). But in light of his broader vision of writing as an ethical enterprise, there is something more at stake.

The introduction of scribal errors into a lay author's works would probably not run the risk of spreading heretical beliefs (though see ch. 3 for the case of vernacular theology). Nonetheless, it could disrupt the intended goal (*entención*) of transferring ethical benefits to readers, which would in turn endanger the author's spiritual reward. Adapting Nicholas's prologue helps bring the relationship between humans and God into the conversation without mentioning it explicitly. In this way, Nicholas's words help Don Juan articulate the spiritual consequences of scribal error for his own authorship, even as he recognizes the difference between the Bible and a secular work. This reading is further supported by a passage near the end of the General Prologue in which Don Juan attempts to bypass all the vicissitudes of textual transmission – including scribal errors, readers' interpretations, and his own failings – and appeal directly to God: "Lo que fallaren que es ý menguado non pongan la culpa a la mi entención, ca Dios sabe buena la ove" ("Whatever [readers] find lacking here, let them not blame my intentions, for God knows they were good"; 6). Rather than an empty turn of phrase, I read this as Don Juan's earnest request for God to recognize the moral "good work" of his books. Thus, whereas Lida de Malkiel once proposed that Juan Manuel never fully acknowledged authorship as a path to either earthly fame or spiritual benefit (*La idea* 262–4), I see the General Prologue as a definitive acknowledgment of both.

Even though Juan Manuel recognized the impossibility of controlling the transmission of his works, he discovered in academic texts another strategy that promised to keep scribes in check: the *pecia* system of copying manuscripts (Rico 412–14). This practice, which originated at the University of Bologna and spread to other medieval universities, required official booksellers (*stationarii*) to keep copies of textbooks that had been vetted for quality and accuracy, which they lent out in sections for scholars to copy.[11] It had begun to be implemented in Castile in the thirteenth century, as evidenced by a law in the *Siete Partidas* regulating the practices of booksellers:

> Estacionarios ha menester que aya en todo estudio general para ser complido, que tenga en sus estaciones buenos libros e legibles e verdaderos de testo e de glosa, que los loguen a los escolares para fazer por ellos libros de nuevo o para emendar los que tovieren escritos. E tal tienda o estación como esta non la deve ninguno tener sin otorgamiento del rector del estudio. E el rector ante que le dé licencia para esto deve fazer examinar primeramente los libros de aquel que devía tener la estación para saber si son buenos e legibles e verdaderos. E aquel que fallare que non tiene tales libros, non le deve consentir que sea estacionario nin logue a los escolares los libros, a menos de ser bien emendados primeramente. (Alfonso X, *7PartidasDigital* 2.31.11, 1555 ed.)

> Every university, in order to be complete, must have booksellers who should keep in their stores books which are good and legible and accurate both in text and in commentary, to be rented to pupils to make new ones from, or to correct those which are already written. No one has the right to keep a shop or place of this kind without the permission of the rector of the university, and the latter, before he issues a licence for this purpose, should first cause an examination to be made of the books belonging to him who desires to open the store, in order to ascertain whether they are good, legible, and accurate. Where anyone is found not to possess such works, the rector should not give his consent for him to be a bookseller or permit him to rent books to the pupils, unless they have previously been corrected. (trans. lightly modified from Parsons Scott, 2: 531)

In the thirteenth century, the universities (*studia generalia*) of Salamanca, Valladolid, and Valencia would have implemented such a statute; they were later joined by the universities of Lérida (founded in 1300) and Perpignan (founded in 1350), showing the adoption of the *pecia* throughout Castile and Aragon (Weichselbaumer 347–4).

Juan Manuel's request to his readers in the General Prologue echoes the quality control measures of the *pecia* system: "Et ruego a todos los que leyeren cualquier de los libros que yo fiz que, si fallaren alguna razón mal dicha, que non pongan a mí la culpa fasta que vean este volumen que yo mesmo concerté" ("And I ask all those who may read any of the books I wrote, if they should find anything poorly said, not to blame me until they see this volume that I checked myself"; 6). By applying the language of *pecia* statutes to his own works, Juan Manuel places himself in a "position of intellectual preeminence," on par with the *auctores* whose works were studied at the universities (Rico 414). As Biaggini points out, the author's request is more theoretical than practical: it authorizes the imperfect copy in the reader's hands by positing the possibility of checking it against a corrected copy ("Stratégies" 231–2). But regardless of whether Juan Manuel expected readers to consult it, the "volumen que yo mesmo concerté" constitutes a rhetorical strategy that places him in the role of the qualified bookseller. The prologue separates out a "high" way of copying modelled after the *pecia* system, which requires the discernment of someone like Don Juan to ensure that the text is "good and legible and accurate." Don Juan's credentials as a participant in "good" copying also derive from his elite social status as a *bellator* (like the troubadour-knight) and, most importantly, from his identity as the work's author. The General Prologue thus conjures an image of Don Juan participating in the work of the *scriptor*, while setting him apart from the inept scribes whom he and others are quick to criticize.

Those familiar with Juan Manuel's works might expect this analysis of the General Prologue to be followed by a discussion of the so-called anteprologue to the *Conde Lucanor* (which José Manuel Blecua calls the *prólogo primero* and Germán Orduna calls the "A" prologue in their respective editions). The anteprologue echoes in third person many of the concerns about manuscript transmission voiced in Don Juan's first-person perspective in the General Prologue. However, Alberto Blecua has persuasively argued that it is the work of a later scribe who, either at Juan Manuel's behest or independently, compiled some of the General Prologue's ideas into a new prologue (103–4). As a reformulation of Juan Manuel's authorial concerns made by a later scribe/compiler, it tells us less about how Juan Manuel positioned himself in relation to scribes, and more about how scribes tied his concept of authorship to the body of his work. For this reason, I study the anteprologue in my epilogue, alongside other scribal and editorial continuations of Don Juan's discourse of authorship. This not only avoids the common mistake of conflating the two prologues' claims (de Looze 31), but recognizes how Juan Manuel's ideas were mediated by other writers in late medieval and early modern copies of his works.

Juan Manuel's General Prologue shows a marked interest in the trope of the ignorant scribe, who is assigned the blame for the instability of vernacular texts. But did this authorial pose translate into action? In general, "efforts to correct, edit, or stabilize vernacular texts were extremely rare before the days of Dante" (A. Taylor 201). However, beginning in the fourteenth century, some vernacular writers did take steps to create authorized manuscripts and thereby safeguard their works. In particular, scholars of medieval French literature have demonstrated how authors such as Guillaume de Machaut, Jean Froissart, Christine de Pizan, and Jean Gerson left a range of evidence demonstrating their involvement in and supervision of scribal practices, including paratexts, iconography, instructions for order and layout of texts, and autograph copies.[12] While there is no evidence of Juan Manuel doing anything similar in his lifetime, his prologues do show knowledge of the copying practices used for authoritative academic texts, and an interest in the possibilities they could afford lay authors. Moreover, although *S* was copied fifty or more years after Juan Manuel's death, its preparation indicates a care for the text that could reflect the author's interventions in a now-lost antigraph. The *mise en texte* of *S* – including layout, prologues, tables of contents for the *Libro de los estados* and *Conde Lucanor*, and an unrealized plan for miniatures – reinforces the image of Don Juan guiding the book's production, providing an authorized copy that future copyists should emulate.[13] By beginning with the General Prologue, *S* primes readers to see these features as part of Don Juan's attempt to anticipate the sloppiness of scribes and, in his words, "guardar esto cuanto yo pudiere" ("guard against this as much as I can"). As many scholars have observed, manuscript *S* serves to emphasize the authority of Don Juan, the authorial persona in the text. But it also establishes a hierarchical relationship between two types of scribal activity, the mechanical work of the labourer and the intellectual work of the noble, thereby giving Don Juan a socially acceptable way to occupy the role of *scriptor*.

"High" Scribal Labour

In spite of the tradition of scribe-bashing in which Juan Manuel participates, his discourse of authorship also takes up tropes about the ethical benefits of the act of writing. For the Castilian nobleman, putting quill to parchment was both a public service and an individual good: it fostered the preservation of knowledge, offered a diversion from the stress of daily life, and contributed to the earthly and spiritual well-being of the writer. In his works, he imbues words associated with copying, such as *escribir* (to copy or write down) and *poner en un libro* (to put in a book), with these ethical benefits, even as he keeps them distinct from the more creative task of composing a new work, referred to as *componer* (to compose) or *fazer un libro* (to make or write a book). This allows him to inhabit the role of *scriptor* when it is associated with "high" ethical functions. Moreover, it opens the door for him to claim direct involvement in copying his own works, regardless of the extent to which he was actually involved.

Although writing as a memory aid is an ancient trope, the works of Alfonso X's scriptorium offered attractive and sometimes innovative reflections on the relationship between writing and memory.[14] The first prologue to the *General estoria*, in speculating about the origins of historiography, describes writing as a powerful way of recalling the past, almost as if one could relive it: "Trabajáronse los sabios omnes de meter en escrito los fechos que son passados pora aver remembrança dellos como si estonces fuessen, e que lo sopiessen los que avién de venir assí como ellos" ("Wise men laboured to put into writing the deeds of the past to remember them as if they had lived back then, and so that those who came afterwards could know them in the same way"; Alfonso X, *General estoria* 1: 5). The prologue to the *Estoria de España*, adapted from the prologue to Rodrigo Jiménez de Rada's *De rebus Hispaniae*, harks back to the invention of writing, a fundamental technology for preserving human knowledge: "Ca si por las escrituras non fuesse, ¿cuál sabiduría o engeño de omne se podrié membrar de todas las cosas passadas?" ("For if not for writing, what wisdom or human genius could recall all things past?"; Alfonso X, *Estoria de Espanna Digital* 1). Both Alfonsine histories associate writing with the preservation of exemplary deeds. The prologue to the *Estoria de España* explains that the ancients

> [...] escrivieron otrossí las gestas de los príncipes, tan bien de los que fizieron mal cuemo de los que fizieron bien, por que los que después viniessen por los fechos de los buenos puñassen en fazer bien e por los de los malos que se castigassen de fazer mal, e por esto fue endereçado el curso del mundo de cada una cosa en su orden. (1)

> [...] also wrote down the deeds of princes, both those who acted badly and those who acted well, so that those who came afterwards would strive to do right after the deeds of the good and abstain from doing wrong after the deeds of the wicked, and thus the course of the world was made straight, with each thing in its place.

In the Middle Ages, it was widely accepted that exemplary literature pertained to ethics because of its potential to shape readers' conduct. The Alfonsine prologues could therefore claim that writing, as the technology that recorded exemplary deeds for posterity, was an ethical activity, capable of making a positive impact not just on individual readers (*los que después viniessen*) but on society at large (*el curso del mundo*).

Another text produced by the Alfonsine scriptorium, the *Siete Partidas*, makes a similar claim about the relationship between writing, memory, and ethics:

> El antigüedad de los tiempos, es cosa que haze a los omes olvidar los fechos passados. E por ende fue menester que fuesse fallada escritura, porque lo que ante fuera fecho, non se olvidasse, e supiessen los omes por ella las cosas, que eran establescidas, bien como si de nuevo fuessen fechas. [...] E pues que de las scrituras tanto bien viene, que en todos los tiempos tiene pro, que faze menbrar lo olvidado, e afirmar lo que es de nuevo fecho, e muestra carreras por do se endereçar lo que ha de ser; derecho es que se fagan lealmente e sin engaño, de manera que se puedan entender bien e sean cumplidas. (Alfonso X, *7PartidasDigital* 3.18.Prologue, 1555 ed.)

> Antiquity is something which makes men forget past events. For this reason it was necessary for writing to be invented, so that what had been formerly accomplished might not be forgotten, and that men might by means of it become familiar with those things which have been settled, just as if they had been recently done. [...] And since so much benefit is derived from written documents, which are advantageous at all times, and cause what has been forgotten to be remembered, and confirm what has been recently done, and point out the way by which what is to come may be accomplished; it is just that such documents be drawn up faithfully and without fraud, so that they can be easily understood and be complete. (trans. Parsons Scott, 3: 692)

According to Jesús Rodríguez Velasco, this passage is innovative in adding the clause that writing conveys past events "just as if they had been recently done," which introduces a *fictio legis*, a legal fiction that serves as a foundational presupposition for the law: "Discourse is turned into things and human relations that have actual uses, even if they are presented as events from the past" (*Dead Voice* 29). In the *Siete Partidas*, writing (*escritura*) is not limited to remembering past events that may serve as an ethical guide for readers, but transforms those past events into legal obligations with more power to shape present and future outcomes. The broad subject matter of the Alfonsine historiographical and juridical corpus, combined with the projected audience of an entire kingdom, meant that the ethical benefits of his books would reach far and wide, in both space and time.

Although Juan Manuel's works addressed a narrower subject matter, scope, and audience, they adapt from the Alfonsine prologues a useful set of rhetorical strategies for celebrating the mechanical act of writing (*escribir, meter en escrito, poner en un libro*). The ethical and social benefits afforded by writing meant that it could be seen as a "noble" activity suited to kings and princes. Certain types of writing could thus be distinguished from the rote copying for which professional scribes (*escribanos*) were responsible. This made it possible for Juan Manuel to depict himself as personally involved in the copying of his works, even going so far in some cases as to claim the act of writing (*escribir*) for himself. Even though the role of scribe was not compatible with his station, there was no contradiction because of the consistent emphasis on the noble aims of writing.

Juan Manuel's Alfonsine works, the *Crónica abreviada*, the lost *Libro de la cavallería*, and the *Libro de la caza*, already showed interest in this link between writing and nobility. While the *Crónica abreviada* constituted his first foray into reproducing an existing work, its prologue emphasizes the labour of selection and abbreviation, aligning more with the tasks of the *compilator* than those of the *scriptor* (see ch. 2). However, the prologue to the *Libro de la caza* looks back over Don Juan's brief literary career with a shift in emphasis, describing it as mainly the supervision of scribal labour: "Don Joán [...] fizo escrivir algunas cosas que entendía que cumplía para él de los libros que falló que el dicho rey abía compuesto, señaladamente en las crónicas de España et en otro libro que fabla de lo que pertenece al estado de cavallería" ("Don Juan [...] had some things copied that he deemed suitable for himself from the books he found that the king had composed, particularly in the chronicles of Spain and another book that deals with the estate of knighthood"; *Obras*, ed. Alvar and Finci, 304). In one instance, Don Juan is the subject of the verb *escrivir*: "Et lo que él entendió et acordó con los mejores caçadores con quien él departió muchas vegadas sobre esto, et otrosí lo que falló en la arte del venar, [...] escriviólo en este libro" ("Regarding what he knew and confirmed with the best falconers with whom he conversed many times about this, and also what he found about the art of the hunt, [...] he wrote it down in this book"; 305). Although it is tempting to read this as evidence of Juan Manuel's real-life participation in copying the book, Ayerbe-Chaux ("Introduction" xliii–xlvii) and Dennis Seniff ("Así fiz yo" 39) have persuasively argued that the *Libro de la caza* was written by a professional scribe of Juan Manuel's chancery who collaborated with his master to produce the book through a combination of direct dictation and editorial independence. I thus read this line as an example of Love's autheme of declarative authorship (or, in this case, declarative "scribeship"). Regardless of whether Don Juan wrote any part of the book in his own hand, he assumed responsibility for its writing, so commissioning the book (*fizo escrivir*) and writing it (*escrivió*) amount to the same thing. These locutions serve to remind the reader that Don Juan is responsible for the work's copying and any ethical benefits that derive from its production, much as the king lends his name to the books and palaces created under his supervision.

However, the work in which Don Juan makes the strongest claim to the mechanical act of writing is the *Libro del cavallero et del escudero*. Its prologue and first chapter offer Don Juan's metaliterary reflections on the book's genesis and on writing in general. In the first chapter, which appears after the prologue in the surviving manuscript but was likely written first, Don Juan takes up the trope of writing as an essential tool for the preservation of knowledge:

> Porque dizen todos los sabios que la mejor cosa del mundo es el saber, tienen que todo lo que omne puede fazer para lo acrecentar dévelo fazer, mas que si lo dexa de fazer que non faze bien. E otrosí tienen que una de las cosas que lo más acrecenta es meter en escrito las cosas que fallan por que el saber e las buenas obras puedan seer más guardadas e más levadas adelante. Por ende yo, don Joán, fijo del infante don Manuel, fiz este libro en que puse algunas cosas que fallé en un libro. E si el comienço d'él es verdadero o non yo non lo sé, mas que me pareció que las razones que en él se contenían eran muy buenas, tove que era mejor de las escrivir que de las dexar caer en olbido. E otrosí puse ý algunas otras razones que fallé escritas, e otras algunas que yo puse que pertenecían para seer ý puestas. (6)

> Because all wise men agree that the best thing in the world is knowledge, they maintain that one should do everything one can to increase it, and it would not be right to stop. And they also maintain that one of the things that most increases knowledge is to write down the things they find, so that knowledge and good deeds can be better preserved and carried forth. And so I, Don Juan, son of Infante Don Manuel, wrote this book in which I put some things I found in a book. And whether its beginning is true or not, I do not know; but it seemed to me that its arguments were very good, so I thought it better to copy them down than to let them fall into oblivion. Furthermore, I added some other arguments that I found written down, and still others I added that seemed appropriate to put here.

As Mario Cossío Olavide observes in his edition, this passage echoes Alfonsine formulations of the trope, particularly in the way it posits writing as a testament to the writer's intellectual capacity (5–6). Don Juan depicts himself unequivocally as the one responsible for the book, claiming in the first person that he wrote it (*fiz este libro*) and that it was beneficial to copy (*escrivir*) the good ideas he found in other sources. The book he claims to have copied is almost certainly Ramon Llull's *Llibre de l'orde de cavalleria,* whose frame story of a young squire who gets lost in the forest and encounters an old knight closely mirrors his own.

He is also portrayed as a compiler (*puse ý algunas otras razones que fallé escritas*) and even as an author (*e otras algunas que yo puse que pertenecían para seer ý puestas*), roles that will be addressed in the chapters that follow. But the role most praised in this passage is that of *scriptor*, the one who puts knowledge into writing to prevent it from being lost.

The prologue to the *Libro del cavallero et del escudero* gives an unusually vivid portrait of Don Juan as a writer in both the mechanical and intellectual senses. Whereas the Alfonsine corpus was produced for a whole kingdom, Don Juan's book is dedicated to a single reader: his brother-in-law Infante Juan of Aragon, who served as archbishop of Toledo from 1319 to 1328. Don Juan paints an image of himself as preoccupied and away from home: he is in Seville (probably for reasons related to his rocky relationship with Alfonso XI), unable to sleep because his plans are not coming to fruition. Typically, he would ease his insomnia by having his servants read aloud to him, but this time he takes another course of action: "Comencé este libro que vos envío e acabelo depués que me partí dende" ("I began this book that I am sending to you, and I finished it after I departed from there"; 4). The use of the first person and the intimate bedtime setting evoke an image of the nobleman writing alone in his chamber, even though, as we will see, the book was almost certainly dictated to a professional scribe. He then jokes that the book might also alleviate the archbishop's insomnia:

> Envíovoslo por que alguna vez cuando non pudierdes dormir, que vos lean assí como vos dirían una fabliella. E cuando fallardes algunas cosas que non an muy buen recado, tened por cierto que yo las fiz poner en este libro et reidvos ende, e perderedes el cuidado que vos fazía perder el dormir. E non vos marabilledes en fazer yo escrivir cosas que sean más fabliella que muy buen seso. (4)

> I am sending it to you so that sometime in the future when you cannot sleep, you can be read to from this so-called little fable. When you find some parts lacking in good sense, you can be sure that I was the one who had them written in this book, and laugh about it, and so forget the concerns that made you lose sleep. And do not wonder at the fact that I had things written that were more fable than good sense.

This passage imagines two levels of mediation in the reception process: one on the part of the author, who dictates his work to a scribe (*yo las fiz poner; fazer yo escrivir*), and the other on the part of the reader, who has the work read aloud to him (*que vos lean ... una fabliella*). It nonetheless creates a sense of intimacy between author and reader, mediated not by these other individuals, who are barely mentioned, but by the book itself. The humour, which derives from the humility topos so common in Juan Manuel's prologues, strengthens the conceptual association between the nobleman and the physical book. When contemplating the words on the page, the archbishop should imagine not a professional scribe in the nobleman's coterie, but the familiar face of his brother-in-law who, for better or worse, had them written down.

Finally, Don Juan reflects on the materiality of his book:

> E non vos la envío escrita de muy buena letra nin muy buen pargamino, recelando que si vós fallásedes que non era buen recado, cuanto mayor afán tomara en fazer el libro, mucho en esto tanto fuera el yerro mayor. Mas de que lo vós vierdes, si me enviades dezir que vos pagardes ende, entonce lo faré más apostado. (5)

> And I send you this written neither in a very good hand nor on very good parchment, fearing that if you found it lacking in good sense, my error would have been all the greater if I had taken great care in making the book. But once you have seen it, if you send word that it pleases you, then I will make a finer copy.

Don Juan's deployment of the formulaic *captatio benevolentiae* is interwoven with concrete knowledge of book production. He shows an understanding of how a manuscript's material features respond to social and literary cues, including the social status of its author and recipient as well as the perceived value of the work (Olivetto, "Don Juan" 120). Furthermore, he pairs *buena letra*, a high-quality book hand, with *buen recado*, high-quality content, linking a careful writing style to the intelligence of the words. The specific references to the book's material support and physical appearance, together with the directness of the first-person verbs, conjure up an image of the vernacular writer as "a producer of books," to use Sylvia Huot's phrase for how the French poet Guillaume de Machaut, a near-contemporary of Juan Manuel, is portrayed in his manuscripts (235).

In the two-book *Libro de los estados*, also dedicated to Infante Juan of Aragon, the act of writing begins to seep into the text's fictional world, effected through a blending of Don Juan with one of his characters, the Christian preacher Julio (Scholberg, "Juan Manuel" 458; Biaggini, "Stratégies" 221). The prologue to book 1 remains in the extradiegetic universe of Don Juan and his clerical brother-in-law, recalling the creation of the *Libro del cavallero et del escudero*: "Et este libro comiencé luego que ove acabado el otro que vos envié, que llaman del *Cavallero et del escudero*" ("And I began this book after finishing the other one I sent you, which they call [*Book*] *of the Knight and the Squire*"; 74). However, the allusions to the book's making are less vivid: Don Juan refers occasionally to its size, but generally focuses on its "palabras et razones" ("words and arguments"; 73). The plot – a reworking of the legend of Barlaam and Josaphat, itself a Christianized version of the story of the Buddha that circulated in both Latin and Castilian versions – revolves around the education and eventual conversion of the pagan prince Johás.[15]

The prince receives his political and religious education from the Christian preacher Julio, who in this fictional world had previously served as tutor to Don Juan himself. At the end of book 1, the text suggests that Julio and Don Juan share responsibility for the book's production. In concluding the first book, Julio tells the prince: "Porque segund lo que es escrito fasta aquí, si todo lo que pertenece en los estados de la clerizía se escriviese en este libro et fuese todo uno, seríe muy grant libro, et tengo que [...] sería mejor partido en dos partes" ("According to what is written thus far, if everything about the estate of the clergy were written here and made into one book, it would be a very large one, so I think [...] it would be better to divide it into two parts"; 294). The fictional Julio then transgresses his diegetic level by asking Don Juan, the author, to finish the book: "Pues non cumplía nin fazía mengua de poner ý más, dexólo [Julio] por acabado et rogó a don Joán, su criado et su amigo, que lo cunpliese" ("Since there was no need to put any more, [Julio] deemed [the book] finished and asked Don Juan, his pupil and friend, to complete it"; 294–5). In contrast to the more common expression *fizo escrivir*, which makes explicit the intervention of a professional scribe, the use of the passive voice (*es escrito, se escriviese*) takes a middle road, neither admitting to the scribe's mediation, nor claiming the act of writing for Don Juan or his fictional alter ego, Julio. This ambiguity allows for the possibility of imagining Don Juan as *scriptor*, which is strengthened by the similarities between the two dedications to Infante Juan of Aragon.

Allusions to writing or copying in Juan Manuel's later works largely resolve this ambiguity by making scribal intervention explicit. In part 1 of the *Conde Lucanor*, the repeated reminders that Don Juan "fizo escrivir" each exemplum indicate clearly that his relationship to copying is indirect. Yet this does not mean that the act of writing is any less important: as Carlos Heusch has shown, throughout the *Conde Lucanor* there are many signs of the primacy given to writing, reading, and the concept of the book ("Oralité" 131). Moreover, in part 5 of the *Conde Lucanor*, where the conflation of Don Juan with Patronio is most explicit, it is Patronio who assumes the role of *scriptor* by looking back to part 1's story of the seneschal of Carcassonne (ex. 40) and adding another story to complement it. Speaking in the first person to Lucanor, Patronio says: "Et porque en este libro non está escrito este enxienplo, contárvoslo he aquí; et non escrivo aquí el enxienplo del senescal porque está escrito" ("Because this exemplum is not written in this book, I will recount it here; but I will not copy the exemplum of the seneschal because it is [already] written"; 261). For de Looze, this moment is crucial because Patronio "shows an awareness of the *Conde Lucanor* as a five-part written text" (251), as part of a process of signification that "[bridges] the gap from text to real world" (257). Given the spiritual concerns of part 5, which make it crucial that readers apply the book to their lives, I agree with de Looze that this is the primary function of casting Patronio as *scriptor*.

Nevertheless, considering Juan Manuel's demonstrated appreciation for the ethical benefits of writing, we can also read this as a way to reduce the importance of scribal intermediaries and promote the image of the wise and experienced counsellor as the same one who makes the book. Thus, despite the progression of Juan Manuel's works from less personal (the Alfonsine period) to more personal (the didactic and personal periods), the role of *scriptor* never quite fades into the background the way we might expect. Instead, throughout his corpus, he alternates between two different ways to harness the ethical benefits of writing for himself, sometimes adopting the indirect and managerial attitude of Alfonso X, and other times presenting a more hands-on approach.

While Juan Manuel defended the nobility of certain types of writing, his self-defence in the *Libro infinido* passage cited in the introduction suggests that his contemporaries did not perceive the distinction but continued to "[profaçar] de mí porque fago libros" ("criticize me because I write books"; 176). Leonardo Funes has speculated that this criticism was due to Juan Manuel's lack of a clerical education and amateur status as a writer ("Excentricidad" 12). In this interpretation, the problem is that he is a knight (*bellator*) striving to do the work of a cleric (*orator*), his social equal or even his better. But the nobleman's critics considered writing not just ill-suited to his social category (*fago lo que non me cae*), but beneath it (*non he fecho cosa por que se mengüe mi estado*), which suggests they associated it with the lowly estate of workers (*laboratores*) to which scribes belonged. Moreover, the "vile" pastime he presents as an alternative, gambling with dice, was associated with such low-class behaviours as thievery, prostitution, and blasphemy, even if it was practised by members of all social categories (Molina Molina; O. Constable 316, 346). Regardless of Juan Manuel's understanding of himself as a noble writer rather than a labouring scribe, his peers may have associated his work with the latter role, along with the same intellectual and social assumptions that he ascribed to them.

Scribes and Authors in Fourteenth-Century Europe

Juan Manuel was not alone in reflecting on the relationship between his authorial text and the scribes and readers who would subsequently use and modify it. The fourteenth century saw an increase in vernacular writers who addressed this issue in their works. Juan Manuel is most frequently compared with Juan Ruiz, another Castilian writer whose only attributed work, the *Libro de buen amor* (1330/43), is considered a masterpiece of Castilian literature even as it eludes most attempts at a satisfactory interpretation. Towards the end of his poem, he writes:

> Qualquier omne que·l oya, si bien trobar sopiere,
> más á ý [a] añadir e emendar, si quisiere;
> ande de mano en mano a quienquier que·l pidiere,
> como pella a las dueñas, tómelo quien podiere. (422 [1629a–d])
>
> Anyone who hears my book and knows how to write verse
> may add to it or emend it, if they wish.
> May it pass from hand to hand, to whoever asks for it,
> like a ball in a women's game, take it who will.

This stanza has traditionally been interpreted as either a version of the modesty topos in which the author presents his or her work as imperfect and subject to correction, or "a generous, even postmodern, opening of the text" (Dagenais 25). However, due to the inevitability of scribal modification in a manuscript culture – a fact of which Juan Ruiz was well aware – it can also be read as the author's attempt to set the terms for these changes (Dagenais 25). The idea that certain authorities retained the power to modify any text may have been adapted from the context of canon law. For example, in Martín Pérez's *Libro de las confesiones* (1316), a Castilian guide to confession for parish priests, the author asserts that even the most authoritative legal texts are subject to emendation from the pope: "Eñaden los papas en el derecho e a las vegadas tiran dello, e así fincan los libros del derecho que han sienpre mester corregimiento" ("Popes add to the law and sometimes take away from it, and so law books are left always in need of correction"; 8). Moreover, as Inés Fernández-Ordóñez shows, the concept of private property evolved in the thirteenth century to separate ownership from use, and this idea informed medieval notions of authorship: authors were understood to retain the "rights" to their intellectual property by attaching their name to a text, but the modifications that came with copying, reading, and glossing fell under the category of use, which served the common good and was therefore unrestricted ("Texto" 48). This explains why Juan Ruiz extends his invitation to those who "know how to write verse": like Juan Manuel, he acknowledges a "low" and "high" way to intervene in a text, the latter requiring intellectual engagement as well as a commitment to make the text better.

Outside Castile, other authors were also reflecting on their relationship to their works, as evidenced by their prologues, envois, and commentaries both in the vernacular and in Latin. A famous example is Petrarch, who in a dialogue from *De remediis utriusque fortune* (completed in 1366) formulated his own variation on the theme of the incompetent scribe:

> Utque ad plenum auctorum constet integritas, quis scriptorum inscitiae inertiaeque medebitur corrumpenti omnia miscentique, cuius metu multa iam, ut auguror, a magnis operibus clara ingenia reflexerunt, meritoque id patitur ignavissima aetas haec culinae sollicita litterarum negligens, et coquos examinans non scriptores. Quisquis itaque pingere aliquid in membranis manuque calamum versare didicerit, scriptor habebitur, doctrinae omnis ignarus, expers ingenii, artis egens. Non quaero iam, nec queror orthographiam quae pridem interiit, qualitercumque utinam scriberent quod iubentur, appareret scriptoris infantia, rerum substantia non lateret. Nunc confusis exemplaribus et exemplis unum scribere polliciti, sic aliud scribunt, ut quod ipse dictaveris non agnoscas. (*Four Dialogues*, 34–6)

> Even if the integrity of authors were fully assured, who could remedy the ignorance of the scribes and their indolence, which corrupts and confuses everything, in fear of which, I imagine, already many brilliant minds have turned away from great creative projects. These are the just deserts of our rotten age which neglects the needs of learning in favor of the kitchen and scrutinizes cooks but not the scribes. Thus anyone who has learned to scribble something upon parchment and to hold a pen in his hand is thought to be a scribe, although he has no knowledge whatever, no mind, and no skill. I do not look anymore for orthography, nor do I complain that it has perished long ago. If only they would write what they are told to write, which would reveal the writer's inability but not obscure the facts! Now, with their confused copies and drafts, they promise to write one thing but write another, so that you do not recognize what you yourself dictated. (*Four Dialogues*, 35–7)

Petrarch directs far more vitriol at scribes with the hyperbolic claim that many of them have no knowledge, talent, or skill whatsoever. Whereas Juan Manuel focuses on the reproduction of books, Petrarch identifies a problem even earlier in the process of bookmaking, when authors dictate their works to scribes for the first time. Finally, he also lampoons scribes for their social category, suggesting that society cares more about the labour of cooks than that of scribes.[16]

For Petrarch, authorial control is also linked to language. In a letter to Boccaccio (1364–6), he reflects on the instability of "this vernacular writing, just invented, still new," which exposes writers not just to scribal error, but to the ignorance of an untrained audience (*Letters of Old Age*, 162).[17] Looking back on his career as a vernacular poet, he concludes that "it was a waste of effort to build on soft mud and shifting sand, and that I and my work would be torn to shreds by the hands of the mob" (162). In Petrarch's estimation, the singing shoemakers of the world represent not only the inevitable errors incurred in the process of scribal copying, but a threat so severe to the integrity of his verses that writing in Romance was not worth the effort. Petrarch's proposed solution was to write in Latin: "Although those brief and scattered vernacular works of my youth are no longer mine, as I have said, but have become the multitude's, I shall see to it that they do not butcher my major ones" (163). The vernacular presented the lowest bar of entry: whereas reading and copying a Latin text required some degree of formal study, vernacular works could circulate among a wider audience of literate, quasi-literate, and illiterate individuals (Bäuml). Certain genres in the vernacular, including poems, songs, romances, and exempla, were also more conducive to oral transmission. Thus, the lyrics in Petrarch's *Rime sparse* (*Rerum vulgarium fragmenta*) and the exempla of Juan Manuel's *Conde Lucanor* would have been especially vulnerable to the destructive effects of mixing, scattering, and mangling that both authors describe. But while Juan Manuel's coping strategy was to invoke the *pecia* system, Petrarch's was to use Latin, a language that was simultaneously more authoritative and less susceptible to oral transmission. Ultimately, Petrarch's renunciation of the vernacular was just as disingenuous as Juan Manuel's hope that future readers would seek out the authorial manuscripts of his works, since he continued to revise the *Rime sparse* throughout his life (Menocal 473n3). Rather than a sincere expression of the author's intention, it should be taken as a rhetorical pose, designed to address the problem of transmission by elevating the author above scribes and certain lowly readers.

This type of authorial positioning can also be seen in the works of Geoffrey Chaucer. Concluding his *Troilus and Criseyde* in the 1380s,

Chaucer expresses concern about the future of his book in one of its final stanzas:

And for ther is so gret diversite
In English and in writyng of oure tonge,
So prey I God that non myswrite the,
Ne the mysmetre for defaute of tonge;
And red wherso thow be, or elles songe,
That thow be understonde, God I biseche!
But yet to purpos of my rather speche. (584 [bk. 5, lines 1793–9])

And since there is such great diversity
in English and in the writing of our language,
I pray to God that no one miswrites you
or warps your metre out of linguistic deficiency.
And wherever you may be read or sung,
I beg of God that you be understood!
But now to the purpose of my speech.

Like Juan Manuel and Juan Ruiz, Chaucer identifies textual transmission in a manuscript culture as a process that can alter his work. But in contrast to Juan Ruiz, who deems these alterations desirable, Chaucer describes them in negative terms of "miswriting" and "mismetring," which would change the author's original words and, potentially, his meaning. He does allude to changes introduced by scribes (*diversite* [...] *in writyng of oure tonge*) but, unlike the complaints of Nicholas of Lyra and Juan Manuel, this is only one of several ways that an author's text could undergo change. Other sources of corruption include language variation (*diversite in English*) and reception through reading or singing (*red wherso thow be, or elles songe*).

Another Chaucerian poem, "Chaucers Wordes unto Adam, His Owne Scriveyn" (henceforth "Adam Scriveyn") takes up the trope of the careless scribe in a way that reinforces the position of the lowly scribe and lofty author:

Adam scriveyn, if ever it thee bifalle
Boece or Troylus for to wryten newe,
Under thy long lokkes thou most have the scalle,
But after my makyng thow wryte more trewe;
So ofte adaye I mot thy werk renewe,
It to correcte and eke to rubbe and scrape,
And al is thorugh thy negligence and rape. (650)

Adam the scribe, if it ever befalls you
to write *Boece* or *Troilus* anew,
you must have the scale under your long locks,
but do follow my words and write more truly.
Too many times I must redo your work
and correct and rub and scrape it,
all because of your negligence and haste.

This poem survives only in Cambridge, Trinity College, MS R.3.20, and its attribution to Chaucer has been thrown into doubt (Edwards; Weiskott). But as Seth Lerer and Alexandra Gillespie have shown, it sheds light on how the figure of Chaucer as author was constructed by later editors. Lerer associates "Adam Scriveyn" with John Shirley, a copyist and editor responsible for several Chaucerian compilations, including the one with the sole surviving copy of the poem. For Lerer, the poem bears witness to Shirley's "controlling fascination with authority both literary and political, while at the same time giving voice to his tastes for the envoyistic, the epistolary, and the romance narrative of writing itself" (121). If the poem – or its attribution to Chaucer – is Shirley's, then we can postulate that this idealized performance of authorial control, in which the author can successfully "correcte and [...] rubbe and scrape" the work of scribes, is a fantasy of late medieval editors seeking to "lay claim to Chaucerian authority – and to invent the category of Chaucerian literature" (A. Gillespie 272). As I will address in my epilogue, this holds true for the anteprologue to the *Conde Lucanor*, which perpetuates the separation between author and scribe, even in the author's absence.

The Ethical Writer

Although Juan Manuel participated in a widespread literary tradition of criticizing scribes, he also followed Alfonso X in contributing to a Castilian discourse that celebrated the act of writing for its ethical functions. This discourse would remain important in the fifteenth century, when humanists such as the royal secretary Juan Alfonso de Baena drew upon it to justify their own activities as copyists and compilers of vernacular poetry. As Francisco López Estrada (*Poéticas* 29–33) points out, the prologue to Baena's fifteenth-century *Cancionero de Baena* recycles the tropes in praise of writing from the prologues to the *General estoria* and *Estoria de España* almost verbatim:

Porque la pereza es contraria e enemiga del saber, la qual faze a los ommes que non se lleguen a él, nin busquen carreras por donde [lo] conoscan, ovieron los sabios e los entendidos el saber por grand tesoro, e preçiáronlo mucho sobre todas las otras cosas, e toviéronlo por luz para alumbrar a sus entendimientos, e de todos los otros que lo sopiessen, dexándolo todo en memoria e por escriptura. Ca si por las escripturas non fuesse ¿quál sabiduría o quál engeño o memoria de ommes se podríe membrar de todas las cossas passadas? (qtd. in López Estrada, *Poéticas* 32–3)

Because laziness is contrary and inimical to knowledge and prevents men from approaching it and seeking ways to know it, the wise and intelligent men [of the past] considered knowledge a great treasure, and valued it above all else, and considered it a light to illuminate their intellects and those of anyone else who should learn it, leaving it all in memory through writing. For if not for writing, what wisdom or human genius or memory could recall all things past?

Similar to how the Alfonsine prologues extol the benefits of writing for human memory, Baena posits writing as a tool for preserving knowledge and enhancing the soul's intellective faculties (*alumbrar a sus entendimientos*).[18]

But while the Alfonsine scribes emphasized the ethical benefits of historiography, which records exemplary events from the past, Baena proposes that copying secular *cancionero* poetry also has an ethical function, "in so far as it celebrates great poets and exemplifies poetic craft" (Johnston 96). The *Cancionero de Baena* therefore "celebrates in the simple fact of its creation both [Baena's] own service to his monarch and the cultural sophistication of his master's court" (Johnston 96). By Baena's time, being a scribe no longer bore the negative associations with laziness, lack of intelligence, or low social status that it had in antiquity and the Middle Ages. Instead, for professional scribes in the fifteenth century, "the hand and the instruments it wielded were a sign of social class and as such a synecdoche for intellectual and political power" (Gómez-Bravo, *Textual Agency* 15). While Baena does not reference Juan Manuel's works directly, the fourteenth-century nobleman's celebration of writing and bookmaking may have been helpful in articulating the secular and courtly value of scribal work across a wider range of aristocratic – and eventually bureaucratic – roles.[19]

For Juan Manuel, some scribal activities were still inappropriate for members of the nobility, such as the rote copying associated with monastic and professional scribes. However, he helped situate certain types of scribal copying in a new light, emphasizing writing as a tool to strengthen a collective memory of noble deeds. More importantly, he advocated for writing as a way of preserving and disseminating the knowledge and experience of the most elite members of society: monarchs, princes, and elite nobles such as himself and his descendants. Don Juan can present himself as fulfilling the "high" labour of the *scriptor* because it represents the ethical function of writing, a valued aspect of bookmaking culture. In a similar way, the nobleman's authorial persona would identify and lay claim to the ethical benefits of compilation, the meaningful arrangement of the texts of others.

2 Compilator

The role of *compilator* as defined by Bonaventure might seem like one with little creative input. However, much like copying, compilation was a central part of both textual transmission and literary creation. Compilers did not just bring together selections from different existing texts, but also organized them in a meaningful way. Although the authors of antiquity engaged in and wrote about compilation, this authorial function increased in complexity and legitimacy in the thirteenth century, and its strategies were subsequently adapted by vernacular writers. Juan Manuel and his associates drew upon the existing discourse of compilation and applied it to a new end, using it to strengthen the overall assertion of Don Juan's authorship as the mastery of different writerly roles.

Malcolm B. Parkes ("Influence") popularized the use in contemporary scholarship of the Latin *compilatio* to refer to the practice of selecting and combining texts for compilation, and *ordinatio* to refer to the work's organization and *mise en page* (page layout). Parkes defines the medieval compiler as one who "adds no matter of his own by way of exposition (unlike the commentator) but compared with the scribe he is free to re-arrange" ("Influence" 59). *Ordinatio* – also called *forma tractatus* or *divisio textus* by both medieval and modern commentators – can apply to the organization of any medieval text, but it is closely associated with *compilatio* given the latter's reliance on disparate sources.

Medieval practitioners of *compilatio* both responded to the scholarly demand for a more organized page, and saw their work as valuable in its own right, in its capacity to present the words of others in novel ways.[1] Minnis, building on Parkes's work, shows how the Dominican friar Vincent of Beauvais (c. 1184/94–c. 1264) creates a discourse of *compilatio* that "functions to aggrandize the practice of compilation" in competition with other authorial functions ("Nolens" 60). Although

Bonaventure's definition ascribes little originality to compilers, other definitions do recognize their creativity: for example, Isidore of Seville describes a *compilator* as "one who mixes the words of another with his own" ("qui aliena dicta suis praemiscet"), using the metaphor of a paint seller mixing pigments to explain how compilers combine disparate elements into a cohesive whole (216).

The boundaries between compilation and other types of authorship are not as clear as Bonaventure would have it, as compilation "inevitably shades into a form of composition" (Bahr 8). But singling out this authorial role calls attention to how excerpting, dividing, and organizing texts can create new meaning. Arthur Bahr's research on compilations in medieval London brings to the fore this relationship between compilation and literariness: he defines compilation "not as an objective quality of either texts or objects, but rather as a mode of perceiving such forms so as to disclose an interpretably meaningful arrangement, thereby bringing into being a text/work that is more than the sum of its parts" (3). If the order of individual words in a poem can generate the elusive quality of literariness, then the arrangement of texts in a compilation has the potential to achieve a similar effect.[2] I follow Bahr in calling this productive mode of perceiving the literariness of compilations "compilational reading," thereby distinguishing it from the pragmatic activity of compiling texts. In Juan Manuel's works, compilation does not always seek to inspire compilational reading, but when it does, it is tied up with the notion of Don Juan's authorial responsibility.

Just as Don Juan assumes responsibility for the copying of his works, he also seeks to portray himself as a capable compiler. He adopts the rhetoric of compilation in his works, especially in his prologues, to describe the various tasks of the compiler, including selection, organization, division, and abbreviation. In an effort to understand how *compilatio* fits into his concept of authorship as a composite of available ways of writing, this chapter turns to the role of the compiler, addressing four main questions: What models of compilation did Juan Manuel draw from? What does he say about the practices and aims of compilation? How do his works put compilation into practice? Finally, what does he stand to gain from assuming responsibility for the tasks of the compiler?

Models of *Compilatio*

Vincent of Beauvais articulates a strong and influential discourse of *compilatio* in the general prologue to his monumental encyclopedia, the *Speculum maius* (completed between 1240 and 1260):

> Quoniam ipsum opus novum quidem est simul et antiquum, breve quoque simul ac prolixum: antiquum certe materia et auctoritate, novum vero compilatione et partium aggregatione, breve quoquo propter multorum dictorum in brevi perstrictionem, longum vero nichilominus propter immensam materie multitudinem. [...] Non autem hoc ipsum opus utique meum simpliciter non sit, sed illorum potius, ex quorum dictis fere totum illud contexui, nam ex meo pauca et quasi nulla addidi. Ipsorum igitur est auctoritate, nostrum autem sola partium ordinatione. (*Apologia*, ch. 4, pp. 469–70)

> For this work is new, and yet at the same time old, short and at the same time long. It is old in terms of its subject-matter and authority, but new in its compilation and the way in which it puts together the various parts. It is short in that it condenses many words into a narrow compass, but yet long because of the vastness of the material treated. [...] This work is not in the true sense of the word "mine," but is the work of those authors from whose writings I have put together almost the entire book. For I have added little or nothing that is my own. So the authority is theirs, while only the ordering of the various parts is ours. (trans. V. Gillespie, "From the Twelfth Century" 183)

To validate his claim that authority lies not with him but with the original authors, Vincent goes on to list several weighty *auctores*, such as Aristotle, Avicenna, Pliny, Augustine of Hippo, and Gregory the Great. Although he appears to shift the work's authority – along with the moral responsibility for its claims – away from himself, he recognizes that his editorial decisions have created something new. Each choice made by the *compilator*, from the array of authors cited to the selection of quoted passages, and from the order of the parts to their layout on the page, can affect the possible interpretations of the work. For example, medieval Christian compilers like Vincent could select and arrange passages from the works of classical Greek and Roman authors in a way that removed all references to pagan religion and culture, using them to exemplify the values of Christian morality (V. Gillespie, "From the Twelfth Century" 185). His self-effacing rhetoric belies the intellectual labour and, more importantly, the authorial control exercised in *compilatio*. However, he also gives the impression that he worked alone, an image that would be reinforced in the portrait of him writing in solitude included in the fifteenth-century French translation of the part of his encyclopedia known as the *Speculum historiale* (see fig. 2.1). We do not know how much of Vincent's work Juan Manuel knew directly, but in the fourteenth century, partial and full manuscripts of

Fig. 2.1. Portrait of Vincent of Beauvais. British Library, Royal 14 E I, fol. 3r, https://www.bl.uk/catalogues/illuminatedmanuscripts.

the *Speculum maius* circulated widely throughout medieval Europe, including the Castilian and Aragonese courts where Juan Manuel was first introduced to book culture.[3] It is thus likely that he was familiar with Vincent's discourse of compilation, whether directly or indirectly.

In the prologue to Bartholomaeus Anglicus's *De proprietatibus rerum* (*On the Properties of Things*), a widely circulated medieval encyclopedia probably completed between 1242 and 1247, the author similarly describes his role as a compiler:

> In istis XIX libellulis rerum naturalium proprietates summatim et breviter continentur, prout ad manus meas spicae quae effugerunt manus metentium, pertingere potuerunt. In quibus de meo pauca vel quasi nulla apposui, sed omnia quae dicentur de libris autenticis sanctorum et philosophorum excipiens sub brevi hoc compendio pariter compilavi, sicut per singulos titulos poterit legentium industria experiri. (fol. a1r)

> These nineteen books contain in brief a catalogue of the properties of things, like ears of wheat that escaped the reapers' hands and ended up in my grasp. In them I have added little or nothing of my own; rather, everything said here is taken from authentic books of saints and philosophers that I have compiled together in this brief compendium, as diligent readers will see from the individual titles.

This passage displays the same four hallmarks of *compilatio* expressed by Vincent of Beauvais: the compiler's humility, the authority of his sources, the brevity of his work relative to its sources, and the useful arrangement of its parts. Another, more variable, aspect is the portrayal of the compiler's work as solitary: despite the company of the venerated *auctores* he cites, Bartholomaeus, like Vincent, gives the impression that he worked alone. Finally, he calls attention to the paratextual apparatus of rubrics (*titulos*) that will help his readers navigate the work and appreciate his organizational efforts. Even if Juan Manuel did not know Vincent's prologue directly, he knew and admired the prologue to *De proprietatibus rerum* enough to cite it at the start of his *Crónica abreviada*, accidentally attributing to John of Damascus an excerpt cited from Dionysius the Areopagite (Lida de Malkiel 170).[4] He therefore had access to the scholastic discourse of *compilatio* that Latin authors like Vincent and Bartholomaeus helped formulate.

While the compilers of these scholarly encyclopedias emphasize how an individual can reorder texts to create something new, early descriptions of compilation in Castilian indicate a collaborative approach that involved a team of scribes and compilers working together.[5] The prologues of works from the Alfonsine scriptorium credited teams of compilers (*ayuntadores*, from the Latin *iungere*, to join) with the tasks of *compilatio*. For example, the prologue to the *Libro de la octava esfera* declares that Alfonso "hobo por ayuntadores a maestre Joan de Mesina, et a maestre Joan de Cremona, et a Yhuda el [Coheneso], et a Samuel" ("had as compilers Maestre Joan de Mesina, Maestre Joan de Cremona, Yehuda [ben Moshe ha-Kohen], and Samuel"; 180). Another passage from this prologue, often quoted as evidence of Alfonso's interest in the Castilian language, suggests that the king himself also participated in compilation: "[el rey] tolló las razones que entendió que eran sobejanas, et dobladas et que non eran en castellano drecho, et puso las otras que entendió que complían" ("[the king] removed the passages that he thought were unnecessary or repetitive or not in clear Castilian, and added others that he thought were fitting"; 180).[6]

Compilation also figures in the prologue to the *Estoria de España*, in which Alfonso's literary persona declares, "E por end nós don Alfonsso [...]

mandamos ayuntar cuantos libros pudimos aver de istorias en que alguna cosa contasse de los fechos d'España" ("And thus we, Don Alfonso, ordered the compilation of all the history books we could find that dealt in some way with the deeds of Spain"; *Estoria de Espanna Digital*, 1). As does Vincent of Beauvais, Alfonso then lists his authoritative sources, including authors from late antiquity such as Paulus Orosius and Isidore of Seville as well as recent Iberian historians such as Rodrigo Jiménez de Rada and Lucas de Tuy. A similar passage in the *General estoria* refers to the king's authorship in terms of compilation: "Yo don Alfonso [...] después que ove fecho ayuntar muchos escritos e muchas estorias de los fechos antiguos escogí d'ellos los más verdaderos e los mejores que ý sope e fiz ende fazer este libro" ("I, Don Alfonso, after overseeing the compilation of many texts and many histories of ancient deeds, chose from them those I knew to be the most truthful and best, and from them I had this book made"; 1: 5–6). Alfonso's discourse of compilation touches on all the same points as Vincent's: authoritative sources, brevity, and the creation of something new through the process of reordering; however, it differs in that the king's responsibility is often mediated through his collaborators.

Despite the abundance of models from a Latin Christian milieu, it is important to note that compilation was not an exclusively Christian endeavour in medieval Castile. Nowhere is this clearer than in the example of the Alfonsine scriptorium, where both the texts compiled and the compilers themselves could be part of Christian, Jewish, or Islamic literary traditions and communities. Jewish members of the scriptorium, such as the aforementioned Yehuda ben Moshe ha-Kohen, were recognized in prologues for their labour as translators and compilers. Moreover, the Alfonsine translation of *Kalīla wa-Dimna* (*Calila e Dimna*), commissioned in 1251 while Alfonso was still a prince, attests to compilation as a practice that spans religions, cultures, and epochs. Its prologue by Ibn al-Muqaffaʿ, who translated the work from Pahlavi (Middle Persian) into Arabic in the eighth century, recounts the book's origins: the famed Persian philosopher Berzebuey, physician to the king, travels to India in search of medical knowledge, but instead finds books of practical advice and moral philosophy gathered from the most venerated sages of India. After the Indian philosophers explain the value of these materials to Berzebuey, he translates them into Persian. It is revealed that these books were a compilation made at the court of the Indian king by the philosopher Burduben:

> Desí puso [Berzebuey] en este libro lo que trasladó de los libros de India: unas questiones que fizo un rey de India que avía nonbre Diçelem; et al su alguazil dizían Burduben. Et era filósofo a quien él más amava. Et

> mandóle que respondiese a ellas capítulo por capítulo et respuesta verdadera et apuesta, [...] et que lo ayuntase en un libro entero por que lo él tomase por castigo para sí. (*Calila e Dimna* 102)

> And so [Berzebuey] put into this book what he had translated from the books from India: some questions that an Indian king named Diçelem put to his vizier, Burduben, the philosopher he loved most. And he [the king] ordered him [Burduben] to respond to them chapter by chapter, in truthful and eloquent replies, [...] and to compile them all into one book that he could take for his own edification.

This passage in *Calila e Dimna* celebrates compilation as one of the tools (alongside scribal copying and translation) that makes possible the text's journey from India to Sasanian Persia to the Abbasid caliphate to Christian Castile. Alfonso X's sponsorship of the work's translation into Castilian is also an example of the "Alfonsine cultural concept" described by Francisco Márquez Villanueva, in which the king promoted encyclopedic knowledge beyond the bounds of Christian clerical culture through translation and collaboration among Christians, Jews, and Muslims. The prologue subsumes the discourse of compilation under this multiconfessional quest for knowledge, in a format readily available to fourteenth-century Castilian writers.

Literary production under Sancho IV, as with many other aspects of his reign, was both deeply indebted to Alfonso's legacy and committed to the establishment of a new aristocratic paradigm, and this dynamic is reflected in the discourse of compilation that emerged from his scriptorium. Brunetto Latini's *Libro del tesoro*, translated into Castilian at Sancho's behest in the late thirteenth century, introduced the Castilian elite not only to the work's encyclopedic knowledge gathered from classical and medieval authorities, but also to its rhetoric of compilation:

> Et non digo yo que el libro sea sacado de [mon pauvre] entendimiento ni de mi pequeño saber, mas es asý commo un panar de miel que es cogido de muchas maneras de flores, ca este libro es fecho de los maravillosos dichos de los sabios que ellos dexieron et conposieron ha grande tienpo pasado, segund los saberes que cada uno dellos avía de filosofía; ca toda conplidamente non la podié saber ningund onbre ternal. (11–12)

> And I do not say that this book is taken from my meager intellect or my limited knowledge, but rather that it is like a honeycomb collected from many types of flowers, for this book is made of the marvellous sayings uttered and written by wise men a long time ago, according to each one's

> knowledge in philosophy; for no earthly human can know everything perfectly.

This floral metaphor, a commonplace found in Seneca and throughout classical and medieval literature, points out the problem with such an ambitious intellectual endeavour – the limits of the human mind – and offers a solution in the form of compilation, which organizes the wisdom of many *auctores* in an ordered and comprehensible way.[7] The compiler is like an industrious bee who collects pollen from the flowers of many sources and transforms it into honey, a new product that is both nourishing (useful) and sweet (aesthetically pleasing). Moreover, while Seneca had applied this metaphor to the reader, Latini applies it to the compiler, whose work in turn activates compilational reading and inspires an appreciation for the compiler's craft.

In the *Castigos de Sancho IV* (c. 1293), a book of wisdom literature that Sancho addressed to his son, the future king Fernando IV, the king's literary persona assumes the role of compiler and author for himself, while recognizing the collaborative assistance of others:

> Nós el rey don Sancho, [...] con ayuda de çientíficos sabios *ordené e fize este libro* para mi fijo e dende para todos aquellos que dél algund bien quisieren tomar e aprender a serviçio de Dios e de la virgen gloriosa Santa María. (73–4; my emphasis)

> I, King Sancho, [...] with the help of wise men of science, *have ordered and composed this book* for my son and henceforth for all those who wish to benefit and learn from it in service to God and the glorious and holy Virgin Mary.

To describe his authorship, Sancho uses not only the verb *fazer*, a common way to refer to composing a book, but also the more ambiguous *ordenar*. Although *ordené* could mean that he commissioned the volume, I read it as a reference to *ordinatio*, a sense seen in the prologue to another work attributed to Sancho, the *Lucidario*: "Porque este libro es todo razón de preguntas e de respuestas que vienen sobre aquellas preguntas, seméjanos de lo ordenar en manera de un diçípulo que estudiese ante su maestro, e sobre cada cosa que le preguntase, el maestro quel respondiese a ello" ("Since this book is comprised of questions and their answers, we see fit to organize it in the form of a student in the presence of his teacher, and for each question the student asks, the teacher responds"; 82). Sancho's depiction of authorship is thus characterized by his hands-on approach to *compilatio* and *ordinatio*, relegating the *çientíficos sabios* to an auxiliary role.

He also associates both authorship and compilation with service to God. This fits into the broader return to Christian orthodoxy dubbed *molinismo*, which characterized his court's literary production and remained influential in Castilian literature in the decades after his death.[8] In the prologues to both the *Castigos* and the *Lucidario*, compilation and other ways of writing are acts of Christian devotion, which means they can contribute to saving the writer's soul as well as the souls of his or her readers.[9] When writing takes on these spiritual stakes, it becomes even more important for the compiler's work to be recognized. Moreover, since the responsibility is shared between tried-and-true authorities and the compiler, compilation is a particularly effective way to reap the ethical benefits of writing.

The Christian cultural project of *molinismo* continued after Sancho's death in 1295, as did its discourse of *compilatio* that gave considerable credit to the compiler. In the early fourteenth-century *Libro del consejo e de los consejeros*, the author, known as Maestre Pedro, outlines the labour he invested in *compilatio* and *ordinatio*: "Pugné en estudiar con grand femencia en muchos libros e ayunté razones e autoridades de santos e de sabios e fiz este libro, que se ordena por cuenta de seis, que es más acabado que otro cuento" ("I made a great effort to study many books, and I compiled arguments and authorities by saints and wise men, and I wrote this book organized around the number six, which is more perfect than other numbers"; 112). He thus highlights both the intellectual accomplishment of his compilation and the artfulness with which he organized it around a symbolic number.[10] By encouraging readers to appreciate the aesthetic and functional aspects of his work, Maestre Pedro's discourse of *compilatio* spotlights the creative contribution of the compiler.

Juan Manuel as *Compilator*

Given Juan Manuel's literary debt to Alfonso X and Sancho IV and his interest in book culture, he likely knew most or all of these various approaches to *compilatio* and *ordinatio*: collaborative and individual, secular and Christian. When he began to formulate his own concept of authorship, he drew upon these models, experimenting with how compilation could best serve his aims of political and literary legitimation. The clearest picture of his engagement with *compilatio* and *ordinatio* is found in how he writes about these tasks in his prologues. In his early works, he approaches compilation primarily as a reader: although he assumes responsibility for the selection and abbreviation of materials, he locates the authority of his works with his sources rather than with his arrangement of them. However, in the *Conde Lucanor* and subsequent works, Don Juan takes charge of *compilatio* in ways that further his didactic message. Furthermore, he reflects on the intellectual value of the compiler's work, especially insofar as it can bolster a text's claim to veracity.

The prologues to the *Crónica abreviada* and *Libro de la caza* both use the conventions of the academic *accessus ad auctores*, a formulaic introduction to an *auctor*, to depict Alfonso X as an authoritative author.[11] But, to modify slightly a quote from Rita Copeland, "the standard *accessus ad auctorem* is always really an *accessus ad* [*compilatorem*]" (110). In other words, the prologues serve to depict Juan Manuel as an admiring reader – and successful compiler – of his uncle's works. In the *Crónica abreviada*, the third-person prologue focuses on the virtues of Juan Manuel's abbreviated version of the *Estoria de España*:

> Porque don Joán, su sobrino, se pagó mucho d'esta su obra e por la saber mejor, porque por muchas razones non podría fazer tal obra como el rey fizo, ni el su entendimiento non abondava a retener todas las estorias que son en las dichas crónicas, por ende fizo poner en este libro en pocas razones todos los grandes fechos que se ý contienen. E esto fizo él porque non tovo por aguisado de començar tal obra e tan complida como la del rey, su tío; antes sacó de la su obra complida una obra menor, e non la fizo sinon para sí en que leyese. (*Obras*, ed. Alvar and Finci, 68)

> Since Don Juan, his nephew, enjoyed his work very much and wanted to know it better, and because for many reasons he could not write a work like the king's, nor was his memory sufficient to retain all the histories in the aforementioned chronicles, he had someone put into this book all the great deeds contained there, in fewer words. And he did this because he didn't think it suitable to begin a work as complete as that of the king, his uncle, so instead he took from his complete work a lesser work, and he did this so that he himself could read from it.

Although Don Juan clearly delineates his role as patron or supervisor rather than scribe, he nonetheless assumes declarative authorship, following in the footsteps of Alfonso and Sancho. He declares that his compilation is for no one but himself, and that anyone else who reads his work should consult his source: "Si alguno otro leyere en este libro e non lo fallare por tan complido, cate el logar onde fue sacado en la *Crónica*, en el capítulo de que fará mención en este libro" ("If anyone else should read from this book and find it less than complete, look in the place where it was taken from the *Chronicle*, in the chapter indicated in this book"; 68).

His modest aims and deferential attitude are complicated, however, by his appeal to brevity through the rhetorical commonplace of *abbreviatio*. Since brevity was considered a rhetorical virtue throughout antiquity and the Middle Ages, producing an abbreviated version of an authoritative work was considered a praiseworthy endeavour in itself (Curtius 493). Moreover, as Orduna ("Fablar") has shown, Juan Manuel's appeal to brevity echoes not only the traditional principles of Latin rhetoric, but also Castilian translations of Arabic wisdom literature that viewed abbreviated (*breve*) and subtle (*oscuro*) discourse as a sign of the author's wisdom. Brevity also has benefits for the reader: Don Juan's abbreviated version of the *Estoria de España* might help readers remember some of its anecdotes more easily, since as medieval and modern thinkers agree, brevity aids memorization (Carruthers 83–4). At 149 folios in two columns, the *Crónica abreviada* is still far too long to be memorized. Nonetheless, Don Juan presents it as an aide-mémoire, thereby invoking the moral virtue that medieval thinkers ascribed to both writing and memorization (Carruthers 156). Thus, while he describes the *Crónica abreviada* as a "derivative" compilation made by scribes in his employ, he also ascribes literary and ethical merit to it on account of its brevity.

The *Libro de la caza* is far less dependent on an Alfonsine model, but its prologue establishes a similar relationship between Alfonso X and his nephew. It begins with a famous panegyric on Alfonso's contributions to Castilian learning, a literary and intellectual legacy that Don Juan positions himself to inherit (Orduna, "Prólogos" 115; Burgoyne, "Imagining" 118). As in the *Crónica abreviada*, Don Juan is depicted in the third person as an admiring reader of Alfonso's works. He presents *compilatio* as the best way to assimilate the vast knowledge that Alfonso made available:

> Et porque don Joán, su sobrino, [...] se paga mucho de leer en los libros que falla que compuso el dicho rey, fizo escrivir algunas cosas que entendía que cumplía para él de los libros que falló que el dicho rey abía compuesto, señaladamente en las crónicas de España et en otro libro que fabla de lo que pertenece al estado de cavallería. (*Obras*, ed. Alvar and Finci, 304)

> And because Don Juan, his nephew, [...] enjoys reading from the books he can find by the aforementioned king, he had some things copied that he deemed suitable for himself from the books he found that the king

> had composed, particularly the chronicles of Spain and another book that deals with the estate of knighthood.

Nevertheless, his approach to *compilatio* stands in contrast to Alfonso's encyclopedic arrangement of knowledge in that it is more selective, more readily assimilated, and personalized to the compiler's needs:

> Et cuando llegó a leer en los dichos libros que el dicho rey *ordenó* en razón de la caça, porque don Joán es muy caçador, ley[ó][12] mucho en ellos et falló que eran *muy bien ordenados* además; et quien pudiesse usar de la caça como la él *ordenó*, non erraría en ninguna cosa en arte de la caça, tan bien en la teórica como en la prática. [...] Et porque don Joán entendió que él et los otros caçadores que agora son non an complidamente la teórica de aquesta arte, et otrosí porque entendió que lo que más cumple para esta arte es la prática, que quiere dezir el uso, fízola escrevir en este libro. (304; my emphasis)

> And because Don Juan is an avid falconer, when he began to read from the aforementioned [books] that the king had *ordered* about falconry, he read from them often and found that they were *very well organized*; and whoever practised falconry following *the way he laid it out* would not go astray in anything related to this art, either in theory or in practice. [...] But because Don Juan understood that he and other falconers of today do not know the theory of this art perfectly, and also because he understood that what is most fitting for this art is its practice, that is to say its use, he had it written in this book.

Alfonso's *ordinatio* of the complete art of falconry, evoked in the three instances of *ordenar*, is described as a praiseworthy endeavour encompassing theory and practice. However, the prologue implies that Don Juan's more selective process of *compilatio*, gathering only practical information, is more beneficial to the kinds of readers who would consult a treatise on falconry in the first place.

In the same vein, Don Juan presents his *Libro de la caza* as a compilation gleaned not from books containing theories of falconry, but from conversations with experienced falconers of his day:

> Et lo que [don Joán] entendió et acordó con los mejores caçadores, con quien él departió muchas vegadas sobre esto, et otrosí lo que falló en la arte del venar, que quiere dezir la caça de los venados que se caçan en el monte, escriviólo en este libro segund lo acordó con Sancho Ximenes de Lanchares et con Garci Álvarez et con Roy Ximenes de Mesco et con

Ferrant Gomes, fijo del dicho Garci Álvarez, et con otros cavalleros de Gallicia que saben mucho d'esta arte et con otros monteros que andan en casa del rey nuestro señor et con don Joán et con estos omnes bonos dichos que saben d'esta arte. (*Obras*, ed. Alvar and Finci, 305)[13]

Regarding what [Don Juan] knew and confirmed with the best falconers, with whom he conversed many times about this, and also what he found about the art of the hunt [*venar*], which means the hunting of deer in the mountains, he copied it down in this book according to what he confirmed with Sancho Ximenes de Lanchares, Garci Álvarez, Roy Ximenes de Mesco, and Ferrant Gomes, son of the aforementioned Garci Álvarez, as well as other knights of Galicia who know a great deal about this art, and other hunters in the household of our lord the king, and Don Juan [of Aragon] and these aforementioned good men who know this art well.

Don Juan thus adapts the rhetoric of compilation, developed for organizing a wealth of written texts, to the context of the nobility's practical expertise, expressed orally through courtly networks. Like Vincent of Beauvais or Alfonso X, he claims that the authority of his work resides with the *auctores* he cites; however, he expands the definition of an *auctor* to include contemporary experts who transmit knowledge face-to-face. The selection of subject matter also aligns with aristocratic values in another way: he plans to discuss falconry and deer hunting but omits fishing "porque tovo que non fazía mengua" ("because he deemed it unnecessary"; 304–5), alluding to the courtly perception that fishing was more for subsistence than for leisure.[14] While the section on deer hunting does not survive and may never have been completed, the prologue indicates a thoughtful selection of subject matter according to the interests of the compiler and his anticipated readers.

Juan Manuel's *Libro del cavallero et del escudero* moves away from Alfonso as a literary model, but still mentions compilation as a key factor in the work's genesis. It is also the first prologue in which Don Juan writes in the first person, a subtle way in which his authorial persona gains autonomy.[15] The first chapter, quoted at length in chapter 1, explains Don Juan's process of compilation as the combination of "some things I found in a book" ("algunas cosas que fallé en un libro") with "some other arguments that I found written down, and still others I added that seemed appropriate to put here" ("algunas otras razones que fallé escritas, e otras algunas que yo puse que pertenecían para seer ý puestas"; 5–6). Making the book will prevent these sources from "falling into oblivion" ("caer en olbido"; 5). Here, Don Juan echoes the mnemonic function of compilation seen in the *Crónica abreviada* and *Libro de la caza*, but with two important modifications. First, he acknowledges his reliance on several written sources rather than a single model, which requires a broader reading and selection process. Second, he adds some original arguments ("otras algunas que yo puse"), thereby expanding his authorial role to mix the words of others with his own.

The two-book *Libro de los estados* does not describe compilation as one of Don Juan's authorial tasks (but as we will see in the next section, his life experience is treated as an authoritative source to be compiled). However, the prologue to book 2 uses a colourful hunting metaphor to allude to another trope of the *compilator*, the reader's freedom of choice. Dedicating the book to his brother-in-law Infante Juan of Aragon, who by this time held the title of patriarch of Alexandria, Don Juan instructs him and other readers in how to approach his work:

> Vós et los que este libro leyéredes, fazed como el vallestero que cuando quiere tirar a alguna vestia o ave en algún lugar que non sea tan aguisado como él querría, tira un virote o una saeta de que se non duele mucho; et si mata aquella caça que tira, tiene por bien empleado aquel virote, et sil yerra, tiene que á poco perdido. Et vós, si de las mis palabras mal doladas vos pudiéredes aprovechar, plégavos ende et gradecedlo a Dios; et de lo que ý fallaredes que non sea tan aprovechoso, fazet cuenta que perdedes ý tanto como el vallestero que desuso es dicho. (297–8)

> As for you and whoever else may read this book, make like the crossbowman when he aims at a beast or bird in a less-than-ideal location and shoots an arrow or dart that he does not mind losing: if he kills his prey, he can say the arrow was put to good use, and if not, he can say he has lost little. Likewise, if you can gain some profit from my roughly hewn words, be happy and thank God; and whatever you should find that is not so profitable, accept the loss as would the crossbowman described above.

This invitation to focus on the good passages and ignore the bad is part of Don Juan's near-ubiquitous use of *captatio benevolentiae*, but it also reframes the shared ethical responsibility of *compilatio* to include readers alongside compilers and their source texts. Geoffrey Chaucer similarly invokes this shared responsibility in the *Canterbury Tales* when he invites readers uninterested in the Miller's Tale to "turne over the leef and chese another tale," a passage that Minnis links to the rhetoric of *compilatio* (*Medieval Theory* 201–2). In comparing the "grab bag" aspect of compilation to the element of chance in hunting, Juan Manuel's metaphor adapts the discourse of *compilatio* to a pastime appropriate to his station. It is also an effective rhetorical move: while Juan Manuel remains responsible for any useful passages in his book, he places part of the burden on his readers, including Infante Juan of Aragon, to separate the profitable wheat from the worthless chaff.[16]

The five-part structure of the *Conde Lucanor* lends itself to the kind of compilational reading described by Bahr, in which disparate texts come together to make a whole that is greater than the sum of its parts. Don Juan recognizes this in the prologue to part 1, in which he describes how he mixes the roles of compiler and author: "Yo, don Johán, [...] fiz este libro conpuesto de las más apuestas palabras que yo pude, et entre las palabras entremetí algunos exienplos de que se podrían aprovechar los que los oyeren" ("I, Don Juan, wrote this book in the most beautiful style I could, and among my words I interspersed some exempla that may be profitable to those who hear them"; ed. Serés, 10). While Serés observes in a footnote that *exienplos* could refer either to Patronio's exempla or to the concluding verses, it makes more sense that the words in a "beautiful style" would encompass the verses, which aspire to an aesthetically pleasing form. The *exienplos*, then, are the exempla that circulated independently in Latin compilations for preachers as well as in frametales such as *Calila e Dimna* and *Sendebar*. When Don Juan says that he "interspersed some exempla" into his book, he is laying claim to them not as their author, but as their arranger. Although he is notoriously silent about his sources, he sees the exempla as *auctoritates*, authoritative texts, whose arrangement in his book can instruct readers and provide moral benefit.[17] The prologue to part 2 makes explicit this notion that the combination of disparate materials produces a meaningful whole:

> Et bien cuido que el que leyere este libro et los otros que yo fiz, que pocas cosas pueden acaecer para las vidas et las faziendas de los omnes que non fallen algo en ellos, ca yo non quis poner en este libro nada de lo que es puesto en los otros, mas qui de todos fiziere un libro fallarlo ha ý más conplido. (216)

> I believe whoever reads this book and the others I have written will be hard-pressed to find something in the lives and affairs of people that is not represented somehow in them, for I did not put anything in this book that I have put in the others, but whoever should make of them all a single book will find it most complete.

Earlier in the prologue, Don Juan had announced a drastic change in style from the clearly expressed exemplary tales ("las razones et enxienplos [...] asaz llanas et declaradas") to a more obscure way of writing ("[fablar] más oscuro"; 213–14). For Orduna, this shift in style illustrates the tension between facilitating the reader's understanding and fulfilling the artistic requirements of an author ("Fablar" 144–5).[18] But when read in light of the discourse of compilation, variety emerges as an end in itself. Don Juan suggests that a variety of styles and content is necessary to provide a comprehensive guide for the Castilian nobility, and compilation serves as the technique that will ultimately ensure the success of his didactic program. He also urges readers to see the *Conde Lucanor* as part of his broader authorial corpus, in a gesture of self-compilation that would culminate in the General Prologue, and that his associates would reinforce in the scribal anteprologue to the *Conde Lucanor* and the preparation of *S* as a single-author codex. Here, for the first time in his career, Don Juan gives more credit to his creativity as a compiler than to the authority of his sources, laying the groundwork for more innovative uses of compilation in his later works.

While the *Libro infinido*, *Libro de las tres razones*, and *Tratado de la Asunción* all refer to the activities of *compilatio* and *ordinatio*, they abandon the traditional definition of *auctoritas* in favour of something new. The *Libro infinido*, addressed to Juan Manuel's son Fernando Manuel, returns to and expands the notion of compiling lived experience that he had previously explored in the *Libro de la caza*. Rather than collecting and organizing passages excerpted from written texts, here Don Juan compiles his lived experience together with the experiences of others: "Asmé de componer este tractado que tracta de cosas que yo mismo provę́ en mí mismo et en mi fazienda et bi que conteció a otros, de las que fiz et vi fazer" ("I saw fit to compose this treatise that deals with things I experienced in myself and in my affairs, and things I saw happen to others; of what I did and what I saw done"; 117). Although not all the experiences are his own, his perspective as compiler always takes centre stage, as indicated by the repetition of *vi*, "I saw." The problem with compiling life experience, though, is that the author will continue to have new experiences to add to the book:

> Et porque este libro es de cosas que yo provę́, pusi en él las de que me acordé. Et porque las que d'aquí adelante provaré non sé a qué recudrán, non las pude aquí poner, mas, con la merced de Dios, ponerlas he como las provare. Et porque esto non sé cuándo se acabará, pus nombre a este libro *El libro enfenido*, que quiere dezir libro sin acabamiento. (118–19)

> Because this book is about things I experienced, I put in it the ones I remembered. And because I do not know how things will turn out in the future, I could not include those; but with the mercy of God I will put

> them here as they happen. And because I do not know when this will end, I gave this book the name *Libro infinido*, which means book without end.

Unlike the parodic autobiography of Ginés de Pasamonte in Miguel de Cervantes's *Don Quixote*, the device of the unfinished book in the *Libro infinido* aims at an earnest portrayal of the "book of one's life."[19] As I discuss in chapter 4, writing his life is a key way in which Don Juan performs the work of an *auctor*; nevertheless, compilation is an important part of this project, since it is the way he organizes his life experience into a meaningful and readable text. Moreover, whereas early works like the *Crónica abreviada* sang the praises of brevity, in the *Libro infinido* he takes this principle a step further, experimenting with the advantages of incompleteness. In writing down only the experiences he remembers, he suggests that writing a truly exhaustive account of any subject, even one's own life, is an impossible task.[20] Instead, he promotes a more flexible notion of compilation that allows for omission, change, and growth. Distinct from the all-encompassing scholastic *summae*, the *Libro infinido* calls attention to its own incompleteness, leaving open the possibility for an authorized reader, such as his son Fernando, to return and add more to the book. While the discourse of *compilatio* in the *Libro de los estados* instructs its audience in how to read like a compiler, this passage invites its readers, especially Fernando, to put quill to parchment and write.

The *Libro de las tres razones* also purports to compile experience in the form of oral accounts of events that Don Juan either experienced himself or heard about from "personas que eran de crer" ("trustworthy people"; *Obras*, ed. Alvar and Finci, 979). These oral sources are similar to the ones cited in the *Libro de la caza* and *Libro infinido*, but his method of checking them against one another is presented as so rigorous that it approximates the *compilatio* of scholarly works:

> Et non lo oí todo a una persona, mas oí unas cosas a una persona, et otras a otras; et ayuntando lo que oí a los unos et a los otros, con razón ayunté estos dichos. [...] Et así contece en los que fablan de las escrituras: que toman de lo que fallan en un lugar et acuerdan en lo que fallan en otros lugares, et de todo fazen una razón; et así fiz yo de lo que oí a muchas personas, que eran muy crederas, ayuntando estas razones. (*Obras*, ed. Alvar and Finci, 979–80)

> And I did not hear everything from one person, but rather some things from one person and others from another, and by putting together what I heard from each one, I compiled these sayings in a meaningful way. [...]

> And so it happens with those who discuss authoritative texts [*escrituras*]: they take what they find in one place and check it against what they find in other places, making one sense of everything; and that is just what I did with what I heard from various trustworthy people, compiling these arguments.

Many scholars have interpreted *escrituras* as Holy Scripture, concluding that Juan Manuel audaciously compares his writing practices with those of biblical commentators and scholastic philosophers.[21] However, Barry Taylor ("Review" 156) and Cossío Olavide (*El que toma* 277n282) propose that they could be authoritative historical texts such as the ones used in the Alfonsine scriptorium, a hypothesis made more compelling by Don Juan's repetition of the verb *ayuntar*, Alfonso X's preferred term for compilation. Juan Manuel needed look no further than the historiographical works sponsored by his uncle for examples of *compilatio* and *ordinatio* expertly executed to create new meanings (Fernández-Ordóñez, "*Ordinatio*" 249–56). While this passage should still be considered part of Juan Manuel's claim to authority, what he seeks is not the authority of scriptural exegesis – the highest level of intellectual achievement in his culture – but rather of a textual culture broadly construed, in which lay nobles could productively participate.

The discourse of *compilatio* in the *Libro de las tres razones* values sources not for their reputation, social status, or education, but for their putative presence at the events narrated. Alan Deyermond describes the persuasive force of Juan Manuel's sources as their "authenticity," that is, the close connection between the witness and the events that he or she witnessed ("Cuentos" 77). Thus, for example, the aged Alfonso García, who was raised alongside Juan Manuel's father, Infante Manuel, lends credence to a narrative of events that occurred during Manuel's youth (*Obras*, ed. Alvar and Finci, 980). Likewise, "Doña Savrina de Bedes," lady-in-waiting to Juan Manuel's second wife, Constanza of Aragon, confirms the bitter rivalry between Queen Violante, wife of Alfonso X, and her younger sister Constanza, Manuel's first wife (986).[22] Most remarkably, Sancho IV is the authority who bears witness to his own cursed lineage, passed on from his father Alfonso X, who allegedly failed to earn the blessing of his father Fernando III (995–7).

It is important to note that Don Juan's various claims to authenticity do not ensure historical accuracy, especially because by the time of the book's composition, most of the supposed eyewitnesses were deceased, making his claims impossible to refute (Ruiz 76; Kinkade, *Dawn* 3, 44). Nonetheless, Don Juan presents their testimony as the most credible source to be had, drawing a parallel between these personal contacts and the *auctores* gathered in scholarly compilations. The concluding words of the *Libro de las tres razones* hammer home the connection between compilation and truth:

> Et porque las palabras son muchas et oílas a muchas personas, non podría ser que non oviese ý algunas palabras más o menos, o mudadas en alguna manera; mas cred por cierto que la justicia et la sentencia et la entención et la verdat así passó como es aquí escrito. (*Obras*, ed. Alvar and Finci, 997)

> And because there are many words and I heard them from many people, there are surely some words in excess, missing, or altered in some way; but know for certain that the justice, meaning, intention, and truth all happened just as is written here.

In this way, he assures his audience that despite any shortcomings in his arrangement of sources, the truth can be uncovered through the proper compilational reading.

The *Tratado de la Asunción* puts into practice the strategies of compilation by bringing together disparate sources, including the Bible and popular Christian and Muslim sayings, to make one coherent argument. Yet Don Juan does not describe his activities in terms that resonate with the discourse of compilation, preferring to portray himself as an author writing his own words. To write about the Assumption of Mary, a contentious point of doctrine that would remain unresolved in the Catholic Church until 1950, it might have been safer to shift the authority and much of the blame for this treatise onto his sources.[23] Instead, Don Juan prefers to assume full authorial responsibility, in spite of the fact that "segunt el mío estado, que me caía más fablar en ál que en esto" ("according to my estate it would be better for me to speak of something else"; *Obras*, ed. Alvar and Finci, 1003).

While Juan Manuel used the discourse of compilation throughout his literary career, beginning with his earliest works, his self-presentation as a compiler changed over time. In all his works, he valued compilation both because it allowed him to create new meaning and because it promised to communicate the truth through the reconciliation of authoritative sources (whether the books of *auctores* or the experience and oral testimony of credible individuals). One aspect of compilation, however, gradually lost its appeal: the shared ethical responsibility between compilers and their sources. As I have shown in this section, the discourse of *compilatio* does some of the work of aggrandizing Don Juan's role as compiler, highlighting the virtues of selectivity, brevity, and even incompleteness. But to assume a more active role and greater responsibility, he also experimented with self-conscious manipulations of the *ordinatio* of his works, a strategy to which I now turn.

The Tools of *Ordinatio*

Ordinatio – also known as *forma tractatus* or *divisio textus* – is a central aspect of *compilatio* that encompasses a work's division into parts and the organization of those parts.[24] I will use *divisio textus* to single out the act of dividing the text, and *ordinatio* to encompass both division and organization. *Ordinatio* consists of chapter divisions and other organizational cues within the text, as well as rubrics, marginalia, enlarged or decorated initials, paragraph marks, and other paratextual or visual features. These tasks were often, though not always, assigned to a compiler; furthermore, they foreground the compiler's primary way of making meaning, the arrangement of texts. Although Barry Taylor uses evidence from *S* to speculate that Juan Manuel may have played a role in designing the layout of a collected-works codex ("*Estoria*"), we cannot definitively attribute *ordinatio* to him for two reasons. First, no manuscripts from his lifetime survive, so there is no evidence of his direct intervention. Second, someone of his station typically would have delegated these tasks to professional scribes in his employ, possibly in a small-scale version of the royal scriptoria of Alfonso X and Sancho IV. For these reasons, I propose that his associates – including professional scribes and subsequent editors – were invested in attributing the *ordinatio* of his works to Don Juan, in a process of declarative authorship that used the authority of his name, regardless of whether or not the historical Juan Manuel was involved. This perpetuated the image of Don Juan as *compilator*, thereby contributing to the creation of a literary persona adept at multiple writerly roles.

While the concept of *ordinatio* originated in scholarly works in Latin and Arabic, especially texts in the Latin scholastic tradition, vernacular writers quickly adopted it. Inés Fernández-Ordóñez acknowledges the influence of Latin and Arabic sources, but ultimately credits the Alfonsine scriptorium with disseminating a comprehensive system of *ordinatio* in Castile that included the division of larger works into books and chapters, navigational tools such as indexes and rubrics, and visual features such as alternating red and blue initials ("*Ordinatio*"). Other vernacular writers adopted these strategies, both to lend their works authority and to make them easier to navigate. For example, Spurgeon Baldwin observes in his edition of Brunetto Latini's *Libro del tesoro* that the author frequently calls attention to his work's chapter divisions, "comunicando así al lector que el autor está perfectamente y en todos momentos consciente de la totalidad de su obra, y creando esa misma conciencia en el lector" ("thereby communicating to the reader that the author is always completely aware of the totality of his work, and creating that same awareness in the reader"; ii).

Another strategy involved paratextual markers such as rubrics and decorated initials, features that were often added by specialized rubricators and illuminators but that came to be seen as an integrated part of the work. The *incipit* of the religious polemic *Sobre la secta mahometana*, attributed to Pedro Pascual and composed around 1300, celebrates these tools of *ordinatio*:

> En los libros los títulos y las rúbricas alumbran los coraçones de los que leen y oyen los libros para entender, para fablar[25] de ligero lo que escrito es en ellos. Y los parágrafos y las letras capitales y los puntos ynterrogantes y los otros aguzan y abivan los leedores para entender y leer de entendimiento. (ed. González Muñoz, 83)

> The titles and rubrics of books illuminate the hearts of their readers and listeners, so they can understand and discuss easily what is written in them. Furthermore, paragraphs, capital letters, question marks, and the rest serve to sharpen and heighten readers' abilities to understand and read with intelligence.

The author of *Sobre la secta mahometana* thus acknowledges the relationship between *ordinatio* and hermeneutics: *ordinatio* helps readers derive meaning from a text. Also noteworthy is the recognition that page layout could benefit both readers (*los que leen*) and those who heard the text read aloud (*y oyen*). These listeners were likely not illiterate and uneducated peasants, but rather "learned and sophisticated" members of the nobility (Lawrance, "Audience" 222). Juan Manuel's works are not unique in deploying the textual and paratextual strategies of *ordinatio* in the vernacular, but they are innovative in using them to elevate Don Juan's authorial role, especially considering his background as a *lego* or lay author. Furthermore, particularly in his later works, *ordinatio* is designed not just to aid comprehension but to be reproducible in subsequent manuscript copies, privileging the author's organizational plan.

Juan Manuel's *Crónica abreviada* follows closely the *ordinatio* of its exemplar, the *Crónica manuelina* version of the *Estoria de España*.[26] The extant manuscript (BNE, MS 1356) is divided into three books, each of which is subdivided into chapters, and folios 1r–20r contain an index of chapter numbers and titles. Throughout the text, the chapters are numbered and highlighted with decorated initials in alternating red and blue, in a humbler version of the *ordinatio* implemented by the Alfonsine scriptorium (Fernández-Ordóñez, "*Ordinatio*" 251ff.). The abbreviation of the longer Alfonsine text results in the suppression of content from many chapters, typically announced with formulas like this one: "En el LXXV capítulo e en el LXXVI e en el LXXVII capítulos non dize ninguna cosa que cumpla para poner en este libro" ("In chapters 75, 76, and 77 it does not say anything suitable to put in this book"; *Obras*, ed. Alvar and Finci, 86). As Pablo Enrique Saracino points out, the implied subject of *dize* is Alfonso's *Estoria de España*, making Alfonso's work an ever-present touchstone for his nephew's compilation (6). Sometimes a chapter's contents are left out because "non cuenta ninguna cosa d'estas que acaeciese en España" ("it does not recount anything that occurred in Spain"; *Obras*, ed. Alvar and Finci, 86–7).

The ideological implications of these selection criteria have been well documented: Saracino (4) shows how Juan Manuel's work "hangs" ("cuelga") a more narrowly focused peninsular history onto the framework of Alfonso's more universal history, while Carmen Benito Vessels (110) and Cossío Olavide ("Reescritura") reveal how the omissions shift the ideological focus of the work by foregrounding the political failures of monarchs and the agency of the nobility. Yet in spite of these numerous omissions, the formal structure remains the same, accounting for every chapter both in the text and the table of contents, regardless of whether its content makes the cutoff. One reason for this is ease of comparison with the *Estoria de España*, which Don Juan recommends in his prologue (68). But it also suggests that Juan Manuel had not yet begun to explore the potential of *ordinatio* as a signifying strategy, preferring to imitate the tried-and-true organization of an existing model.

In contrast, his other works do show evidence of using *ordinatio* to create new meaning and project the author's vision of a unified work. Through rhetorical formulas in the text as well as rubrics and other paratextual features, Don Juan makes visible his efforts to lend coherence to his works. With the exception of the *Conde Lucanor*, this evidence is limited to *S*, which might make his project of *ordinatio* seem more uniform than if more manuscript witnesses were available for comparison. Nevertheless, analysing *S* in this way can still provide useful insights, since much of its uniformity comes not from paratextual features that would change from copy to copy, but from textual features that would remain largely the same.

The *ordinatio* of the *Libro de la caza* is standard for a work of its length and genre: it is divided into twelve chapters, with a table of contents that lists each chapter number along with a brief summary. It lacks chapter numbers and rubrics but was probably designed to have them, as indicated by the table of contents, lacunae between chapters, and the overall incompleteness of the work.[27] In its prologue, the division of the text into chapters is attributed to Don Juan himself: "Et partió este libro en doze capítulos" ("And he divided this book into twelve chapters"; *Obras*, ed. Alvar and Finci, 305). Decorated initials appear at the start of each chapter and also at mid-chapter section breaks, running the risk of obscuring the author's *divisio textus*. However, most chapters begin with a variation on this formulaic declaration: "Pues en el capítulo ante d'éste dize cuáles et cuántas son las maneras de los falcones con que al tiempo de agora usan caçar, dirá en este capítulo por cuál razón se pone ante la caça et la conocencia de los falcones que de los azores" ("Since in the previous chapter he describes the kinds of falcons used in hunting nowadays and how many there are, in this chapter he will explain why the knowledge of falconry and falcons has been placed before that of goshawks"; 307).

These formulas are similar to those of an important predecessor in Castilian falconry treatises, the Castilian translation of the *Libro de los animales que cazan* by Baghdadi scholar al-Bayzār (Muḥammad ibn ʿAbdullah ibn ʿUmar al-Bayzār, known in Castilian as Moamín): "E aquí se acaba el segundo capítolo. III. Aquí comiença el tercero capítolo, que fabla de las sazones en que se engendran las aves que caçan [...]" ("And here ends the second chapter. III. Here begins the third chapter, which deals with the times when hunting birds breed [...]"; n. pag.). But while al-Bayzār's transitions only announce the topic of the upcoming chapter, Don Juan also provides a brief summary of the previous chapter to orient the reader. Moreover, he occasionally reflects on the logical order of the chapters, as in the example quoted above. Finally, in a variation on the formulaic use of *dize* in the *Crónica abreviada*, the subject of the repeated verb is no longer a source text, but Don Juan himself (Ayerbe-Chaux, "Introduction" xliii). This strategy establishes a subtle parallel between Alfonso X, whose *Estoria de España* served as the source of the *Crónica abreviada*, and Don Juan, whose falconry experience provides much of the source material for the *Libro de la caza*. What is more, it persuades us that Don Juan is responsible for the text's clear and efficient organization, regardless of the actual division of labour between author and scribes.

While Don Juan describes his *Libro del cavallero et del escudero* as "una manera que llaman en Castiella 'fabliella'" ("a style that in Castile is called a 'little fable'"; 4), its form is more accurately described as a series of questions and answers.[28] The plot is driven by a young squire who poses questions to an old knight about various subjects related to knighthood and the natural world. The work is organized into fifty-one numbered chapters, many of which correspond to the knight's answers in an *ordinatio* that helps the reader locate the work's didactic content.[29] The chapters that follow this pattern – chapters 17–21, 32–8, and 40–8 – are marked by the rubric "Cómo el cavallero ançiano responde al escudero/cavallero novel ..." ("How the old knight responds to the squire/novice knight ...": the squire is knighted in chapter 24, and subsequent rubrics reflect his promotion). Additional structure is provided by the old knight, who begins these chapters with the formula "A lo que me preguntastes" ("In response to what you asked me"). With minor variations, this question-and-answer format will become Juan Manuel's preferred *ordinatio* for all his future works except the anomalous *Tratado de la Asunción*.[30]

The question-and-answer format is so common in medieval frametales and wisdom literature – including Petrus Alfonsi's Latin *Disciplina clericalis*, Sancho IV's *Lucidario*, and the Castilian *Barlaam e Josafat*, to name just a few Iberian examples – that it might be taken for granted as a method of organization. Yet Juan Manuel adds a passage to the *Libro del cavallero et del escudero* that draws attention to the art of asking questions, which stands in for his art of *divisio textus*. The old knight criticizes the inexperienced squire's questions, which fail to divide topics into appropriate units:

> Fijo, fasta aquí todas las preguntas que me vós fiziestes fueron senziellas et dobladas. Ca eran senziellas porque non preguntávades si non por una cosa, mas otrosí eran dobladas porque me preguntávades qué era aquella cosa e para qué fuera fecha. Mas en estas a que aún non vos he respondido non feziestes así, ante me preguntastes muchas cosas en uno. [...] E *pues vos yo reprehendo porque mudastes la manera en las preguntas,* non lo quiero yo mudar en las respuestas, ante vos quiero responder a cada una sobre sí. (53–5; my emphasis)

> Son, up until now all the questions you have asked me were both single and double; they were single in that you were only asking about one thing, but double in that you were asking what that thing was and why it was made. As for the ones I have not answered, you did not ask them that way, but rather asked me about many things at once. [...] And *seeing as I am reprehending you for changing the form of your questions,* I will not change how I answer them, but will proceed in answering each one individually.

As Gómez Redondo points out, Juan Manuel often uses *manera* to refer to the organization of his books ("Géneros" 112). Here, the old knight uses it to refer to the form of the squire's questions, thereby linking the fictional device of the questions to the book's organization. Within the narrative, the old knight takes the squire's jumble of questions (lost to the lacuna that affects chs. 3–16) and reorganizes them into logically divided sections that are easier to learn. This expert editing is then reflected in the material form of the book, particularly in the rubrics that announce the subject of the old knight's responses. In other words, the old knight plays a role in the *ordinatio* of the book in which he is a character, in a blurring of diegetic levels common in the works of Juan Manuel's didactic period. If, as Kenneth Scholberg observes ("Juan Manuel"), the wise authority figures in his framing narratives are typically conflated with the author, then the knight's deployment of *ordinatio* becomes a way for Don Juan to claim responsibility for the book's effective organization.

In contrast to the orderly structure of the *Libro del cavallero et del escudero*, the *ordinatio* of the *Libro de los estados* is more uneven. It underwent at least two phases of composition and revision from 1327 to 1332, the period Juan Manuel described as a "doloroso et triste tienpo" ("painful and sad time") of conflict and open warfare with Alfonso XI (72). At first glance, its two books appear to be arranged in multiples of ten: the first book, comprised of one hundred chapters, corresponds to the conversion story of Prince Johás and a description of the lay estates (*bellatores* and *laboratores*), while the second, with fifty chapters, describes the estate of the clergy (*oratores*). Such large, round numbers were used for various literary effects throughout antiquity and the Middle Ages (Curtius 501–9). In Castilian wisdom literature such as the *Libro de los cien capítulos* (fifty chapters, despite its title), *Lucidario* (one hundred), and *Castigos de Sancho IV* (fifty), chapter divisions in multiples of ten both facilitated learning and evoked the Ten Commandments (Gómez Redondo, *Historia de la prosa* 1: 425–8). Arabic and Hebrew collections of *maqāmāt*, though distant in language and genre from the *Libro de los estados*, illustrate another function of such numbers: the display of artistic virtuosity. James Monroe writes in the introduction to his translation of al-Saraqusṭī's Arabic *Luzūmīyya* that, after al-Ḥarīrī's celebrated collection of fifty *maqāmāt*, this number "came to be viewed as canonical, in the sense that, whereas a lightweight might try his hand at composing a *maqāmah* or two, serious writers [...] were expected to compose at least fifty" (2).[31]

The chapter divisions of the *Libro de los estados* play on the religious and aesthetic appeal of fifty and one hundred, evoking both the perfection of God's creation and the author's ability to imitate it on a smaller scale. However, they were not part of Juan Manuel's original plan for the work: Leonardo Funes has shown how the chapter divisions in *S* disrupt the grouping of thematic units ("Capitulación") and has reconstructed the original thematic divisions ("Sobre la partición").[32] Nevertheless, both the initial thematic organization of the work and its subsequent partition into numbered chapters share the common goal of highlighting the author's involvement in arranging and presenting information. Moreover, since this thematic *ordinatio* is embedded in the text itself, it ensures that future readers (such as Funes) can identify and appreciate Juan Manuel's organizational strategies in spite of subsequent scribal interference.

In *S*, the chapters of the *Libro de los estados* are numbered and indicated by red rubrics and collected in two tables of contents, one for each book (fols. 43v–46v and 102r–103r). While these were not written by Juan Manuel, he may have commissioned them so he could cite specific chapters in his later *Libro infinido* (B. Taylor, "*Libro infinido*" 570–1). Either way, the rubrics work to strengthen his portrayal as a direct participant in *ordinatio*. Some, like the introductory rubric, emphasize his authorship alongside the work's organization: "Este libro compuso don Joán, [...] et á nonbre el *Libro del infante* o el *Libro de los estados*, et es puesto en dos libros: el primero libro fabla de los legos et el segundo fabla de los estados de los clérigos. Et en el primero ha cient capítulos et en el segundo, cincuaenta" ("This book was composed by Don Juan, [...] and it is called the *Book of the Infante* or *Book of Estates*, and it is divided into two books: the first deals with laypeople and the second with the estates of the clergy. And the first has one hundred chapters, while the second has fifty"; 69). Similarly, the rubrics for I.1–2 and II.1 mention his authorship as well as the work's form ("en manera de preguntas et de respuestas"; 72) and intended recipient ("envía este libro a don Joán, fijo del rey de Aragón, patriarcha de Alexandría"; 296). The rubrics for I.60, I.67, and I.82 highlight Don Juan as an exemplary figure who serves as a model for the prince. For instance, Julio's lesson in I.81 on how an emperor should inspire love and fear in his subjects continues in I.82 with an example from Don Juan's life, introduced by the following rubric: "El lxxxii° capítulo fabla en cómo Julio dixo al infante que le dixiera don Joán, aquel su amigo, que en la su casa, si fallava aquél por cuya culpa se volvía la pelea que firiera âlguno, quel mandava luego cortar la mano" ("Chapter 82 tells of how Julio told the Infante that Don Juan, his friend, told him that in his household, whenever someone responsible for a fight injured someone else, he would order that person's hand cut off"; 242). Finally, in the rubric for I.91, Don Juan the character and Don Juan the author collide when Julio recommends two of his other books to Prince Johás: "El xci° capítulo fabla en cómo Julio dixo al infante que buscase el *Libro de la cavallería* que fiziera don Joán, et otro que llaman el *Libro del cavallero et del escudero*, porque en estos yazen cosas muy marabillosas" ("Chapter 91 tells of how Julio told the Infante to look for the *Book of Chivalry* that Don Juan had written, and another called *Book of the Knight and the Squire*, because they contain very marvellous things"; 270).

These attention-grabbing rubrics highlight Don Juan's dual presence as author and exemplary character. Moreover, they promote his authorial status through the creation of an organizational apparatus that resonates visually with prestigious manuscripts. Finally, they facilitate cross references between Juan Manuel's works, anticipating the eventual compilation of the author's entire corpus. In the words of Georgina Olivetto, this self-referential system "se correspondería con una etapa avanzada de compilación y con una idea unitaria y acabada de *corpus*, como el reunido por don Juan en su códice concertado y prologado, y no con un estadio primitivo de libros sueltos" ("corresponds to an advanced phase of compilation and a unified and complete idea of a corpus, like the one collected by Don Juan in his corrected and prologued codex, and not to a primitive phase of separate books"; "Don Juan" 124). The rubrics of the *Libro de los estados* thus illustrate how interventions that are not authorial or "original" can make a significant contribution to a work's authorial discourse.

The *Conde Lucanor*, the Manueline work with the most complex transmission history, also attests to the widest variety of *ordinatio*. Its eight extant manuscripts – two of parts 1–5, three of part 1, and three that extract the *viessos* or proverbs – display different approaches to the division and organization of the work, some of which will be discussed in the epilogue. For now, I will leave aside its prologues and paratexts and focus on *ordinatio* in the main text (the one most likely to remain similar from copy to copy). As Burgoyne shows, part 1 deploys repetitive formulas that divide each exemplum into four easily identifiable parts: the count's problem, Patronio's exemplum, Patronio's advice, and Juan Manuel's concluding verses (*Reading the Exemplum* 33–7). These formulas were known in classical manuals of rhetoric as *(ep)anaphora*, the repetition of an initial word or phrase, and *antistrophe*, the repetition of a final word or phrase (*Rhetorica ad Herennium* 274–7). Paul Zumthor calls them "litany" and highlights their capacity to give a sense of structure or progression to the work as a whole (84). While modern readers might dismiss the formulas in part 1 as monotonous, Burgoyne vindicates them as "a deliberate and refined use of language that calls attention to patently homologous parts, the discursive ties that bind parts into whole narratives, and finally each narrative into a whole book" (*Reading the Exemplum* 38).

Parts 2–5 are less formulaic in their approach, but they nevertheless use the dialogue between Count Lucanor and Patronio, with the repeated discourse markers "Señor conde Lucanor – dixo Patronio" and "Patronio – dixo el conde Lucanor," to mark textual divisions. Whereas the symbolic chapter structure in the *Libro de los estados* was a later addition, the *Conde Lucanor* both integrates meaningful numbers into the *divisio textus* and mentions them in the narrative frame: as Patronio informs Lucanor after each section, part 1 contains fifty exempla, and parts 2–4 contain one hundred, fifty, and thirty proverbs respectively.[33] At the start of part 4, Patronio summarizes the book's *ordinatio* thus far:

> Señor conde Lucanor, [...] trabajé de vos dezir algunas cosas más de las que vos avía dicho en los enxienplos que vos dixe en la primera parte deste libro, en que ha cincuenta enxienplos que son muy llanos et muy declarados. Et pues en la segunda parte ha cient proverbios, et algunos fueron yacuanto oscuros, et los más, asaz declarados; et en esta tercera parte puse cincuenta proverbios, et son más oscuros que los primeros cincuenta enxienplos nin los cient proverbios. Et así, con los enxienplos et con los proverbios, hevos puesto en este libro dozientos. (ed. Serés, 241–2)

> My lord Count Lucanor, [...] I have labored to tell you some things beyond what I already told you in the exempla that I related in the first part of this book, which has fifty very plain and clear exempla. That is why there are one hundred proverbs in the second part, some quite obscure and others rather clear; and in this third part I have put fifty proverbs, which are more obscure than the first fifty exempla and even the hundred proverbs. And so, taking the exempla and proverbs together, I have put in this book for you two hundred in all.

By drawing attention to the pleasing numerical symmetry and varied style of the first three parts, Patronio attracts praise for the work's *ordinatio*. This strategy also serves to safeguard the work against the inevitable scribal additions and subtractions. Given the decades-long scholarly debate about the number of "authentic" tales in part 1, it seems to have been at least partially effective, convincing some readers to take at face value this claim to structural perfection.[34]

If Patronio's textual references to *ordinatio* are one way in which Juan Manuel receives credit for compiling the *Conde Lucanor*, the other way is through the fictionalization of his authorial role. This is prominent in the paratexts, where both medieval and modern readers would expect it: the prologues to parts 1 and 2 and the colophon at the end of the work all name Don Juan as the book's declarative author and compiler. His name also appears in a formula at the end of each exemplum in part

1, expressed more or less like this: "Et porque entendió don Johán que este enxienplo era muy bueno, fízolo poner en este libro et fizo estos viesos que dizen así" ("And because Don Juan understood that this was a very good exemplum, he had it copied in this book and wrote the following verses"; ed. Serés, 39).[35] Of the numerous scholars who have remarked on this fictional portrayal of authorship, the one whose work I find most useful is Laurence de Looze, who reads Don Juan's authorial presence in the five-part *Conde Lucanor* as an exemplary act in itself:[36]

> The composition and dissemination of the [*Conde Lucanor*] is an admirable example of an action performed in the real, social world that also seeks to do the work of salvation. The active interest of the implied author, Juan Manuel, in Book I's exempla concerning how to act when one's interests are at stake transforms into an affirmation of *caritas* and a divesting of self-interestedness in Book V. The writing of that progression becomes not only a good act ("buena obra") but one that seems to have been charitably performed ("la fizo bien"). (256)

But we can be more precise about this performance of "composition" as a charitable act: it is, in large part, the performance of compilation (as well as commentary, the subject of ch. 3).

Don Juan is portrayed as the author of the concluding verses (*fizo estos viesos*), but his relationship to the exempla is more akin to that of a compiler. While the most common version of the formula is the one stated above, in other versions he enjoys the exempla ("Et porque don Johán *se pagó* deste exienplo ... "; 41) or simply finds them ("Et cuando don Johán *falló* este exienplo ... "; 25; my emphasis). The exempla are presented as existing material that Don Juan encounters, evaluates, and selects for inclusion.[37] In the absence of an attribution, the reader wonders who, if anyone, authored them. Did they come from a written source, or from oral tradition? Are we meant to understand that Patronio invented them? This is not to say that the historical Juan Manuel did not write them; at the very least, he took existing motifs and significantly enriched them, as Ayerbe-Chaux has demonstrated in his comparative study of the exempla with other existing versions (*"El conde Lucanor"*). However, his self-presentation in the text clearly distinguishes between two different authorial activities: compiling the exempla, and authoring the verses.

Despite being a less creative authorial activity, the effective deployment of *ordinatio* is clearly valued in the *Conde Lucanor*. In part 1, Don Juan is repeatedly credited with selecting "good" exempla for inclusion in his book.[38] As many scholars have noted, their order is sometimes meaningful, with ex. 1, 25, and 50 serving as effective beginning, middle, and end points (ed. Serés, 194). In the five-part *Conde Lucanor* in *S* and *G*, the juxtaposition of different text types also contributes to the work's artistic unity, seen as a progression from comprehensible exempla to obscure proverbs to spiritual salvation (Gimeno Casalduero, "*Conde*"; de Looze 251–7). The cues of *ordinatio* described above serve to help readers recognize this artful and effective organization and attribute it to Don Juan. And although readers of the one-part *Conde Lucanor* in manuscripts *M*, *H*, and *P* could not appreciate the full "thematic, artistic, or ideological unity" of its five-part version (Burgoyne, "Reading and Writing" 489), they were nonetheless privy to a portrait of Don Juan as a skilled *compilator* thanks to part 1's repeated formulas.

Similarly, the *Libro infinido* and the *Libro de las tres razones* use the tools of *ordinatio* both to assert Juan Manuel's authorship and to encourage subsequent copyists to reproduce a structure perceived as authorial. In the prologue to the *Libro infinido*, Don Juan announces his plan for the book's structure: "Et porque sea más ligero de entender et estudiar es fecho a capítulos" ("To make it easier to understand and study, it is divided into chapters"; 119). Its organization fulfils a clear didactic function, facilitating comprehension for his projected reader, his son Fernando. The use of decorated initials and litany makes the chapter divisions clear: each one begins with a brief summary of the previous chapter and the topic of the present one, and concludes with the following formula: "Et la prueva es que todos los que lo así fizieron se fallaron ende bien, et el contrario" ("And the proof is that everyone who did it this way enjoyed success, and the contrary"; 137). The scribe of *S* also leaves a blank of four to five lines between each chapter, suggesting that rubrics were intended. The book is organized into thematic sections, beginning with spiritual salvation (ch. 1), then physical and mental health (chs. 2–3), maintaining social relationships (chs. 4–14), the responsibilities of the nobility (chs. 15–23), and effective communication (chs. 24–5), concluding with a special chapter on the nature of social bonds (ch. 26, "De las maneras de amor"). As narrator, Don Juan occasionally calls attention to this organization, as when he justifies the order of the first three chapters: "Et pues el alma es tan noble cosa et ha tantas avantajas del cuerpo, es razón de fablar primeramente en el alma que en el cuerpo" ("Since the soul is such a noble thing and is so superior compared to the body, it is fitting to speak first about the soul and not the body"; 120–1). He values this orderly structure so much that he retains it even when it does not suit his message of dynastic superiority: chapters 4–7 discuss, respectively, his son's relationships with kings, superiors, equals, and inferiors, even though he insists that his son has no superiors aside from monarchs and no equals whatsoever (Díez de Revenga, "*Libro enfenido*" 369). The final chapter begins with a numbered list of fifteen forms of friendship and love (*maneras de amor*) that provides an informal table of contents (*Libro infinido* 178–9). These organizational features embedded in the authorial text recall how Brunetto Latini's *Libro del tesoro* makes readers aware of their progression through a carefully organized work. Díez de Revenga ("*Libro enfenido*") goes perhaps too far in comparing the *Libro infinido*'s structure to that of a Gothic cathedral, but its *ordinatio* is clearly designed to attract admiration and praise for its arranger.

In the *Libro de las tres razones*, Juan Manuel's manipulation of *ordinatio* for literary effect is at its finest. What makes this work unique is its combination of different elements that can be characterized as historical, personal, autobiographical, and literary (Díez de Revenga, "*Libro de las armas*" 109). The three arguments (*razones*) are, first, the story of Juan Manuel's coat of arms; second, a defence of his family's right to confer knighthood while not being knights themselves; finally, Sancho IV's deathbed confession to a young Don Juan that his lineage is inferior to that of the Manuels. As several scholars have pointed out, all three work together to communicate a central message: the royal dynasty represented by the current king, Alfonso XI, and inherited from his great-grandfather and namesake Alfonso X, is corrupt, while Infante Manuel and his descendants are politically and morally pure.[39]

The juxtaposition of three disparate topics to generate a single meaning constitutes a masterful use of *ordinatio*. The work begins with a list of the three *razones*, each marked with a decorated initial and formula: "La primera cosa que me preguntastes"; "La otra [razón] que me preguntastes"; "La terçera razón que me preguntastes" (*Obras*, ed. Alvar and Finci, 980, 985, 992). The number three symbolizes the Holy Trinity, while also evoking the interlocking concepts of power, knowledge, and goodness (*poder, saber, bondad*) mentioned in the prologue to the *Libro infinido*. Moreover, as Deyermond has demonstrated, the second *razón* builds on the first, and the third makes reference to the first and second, creating a network of internal references that strengthen the work's structure ("Cuentos" 85). What gives meaning to this compilation of stories and sources is Don Juan's intellect (*entendimiento*). As Seniff puts it: "Words flow from oral sources – some of which are certainly more credible than others – and are then judged by the faculty of understanding, which acts as a filter and synthesizer; the results are then recorded" ("Así fiz yo" 51). Through its use of *ordinatio*, the work not only elevates the author's lineage, but also highlights his ability to create a coherent and truthful narrative through the combination of disparate texts.

As early as the *Libro de la caza*, Juan Manuel and his associates deployed *ordinatio* as part of a broad effort to reinforce his portrayal of his authorial role. They accomplished this in two ways. First, they used the tools of *ordinatio*, such as the rubrics in the *Libro de los estados* and the chapter divisions in *Libro infinido*, to make readers aware of Don Juan's organization of his works. Second, they embedded formulaic cues in the text, particularly in the *Conde Lucanor*, *Libro infinido*, and *Libro de las tres razones*, to ensure that the structure of his works would be replicable in future copies, even if paratextual elements were modified. The reproduction of a text's exact layout and paratextual features, or what Matthew Fisher calls "duplicative copying," was a strategy typically reserved for Bibles and texts with a more complex *mise en page*, such as canon law books with commentaries (Fisher 37ff.). The *ordinatio* of Juan Manuel's works does not demand duplicative copying, but it does encourage a more exacting copying process associated with prestigious Latin texts. In this way, those responsible for the transmission of Juan Manuel's works harnessed bookmaking technology to consolidate the author's reputation and ascribe authority to his works. Just as the General Prologue invokes the *pecia* system as a model for the transmission of authoritative texts, Juan Manuel's works use the tools of *ordinatio* to mitigate problems of textual transmission while elevating the author's status.

Compilation and Literariness

Compilation, like scribal copying, may not have been the most creative authorial function in Bonaventure's schema, but the manuscripts of Juan Manuel's works are nonetheless invested in portraying him as a capable *compilator*. What does he stand to gain from assuming responsibility for this authorial function? For one, the borrowed authority of his source texts, evoked in Vincent of Beauvais's description of the dynamic between compiler and sources: "The authority is theirs, while only the ordering of the various parts is ours." Yet after the *Crónica abreviada*, Don Juan is no longer restricted to compiling the written works of others. Throughout the rest of his corpus, he applies the discourse of *compilatio* to oral sources and even to his own lived experience. Additionally, the organization of his works seeks to activate compilational reading, inviting readers to see how his combinations of oral and written material can generate new meaning. Beginning with the five-part *Conde Lucanor* and culminating with the *Libro de las tres razones*, the selection and arrangement of texts produces the effect of literariness, creating a meaningful whole greater than the sum of its parts. What is more, readers are convinced of the fiction of the solitary individual responsible for this aesthetically pleasing *compilatio*, thanks to the persistent presence of Don Juan.

3 Commentator

According to Bonaventure, the commentator wrote "for purposes of clarification," with the text of another author in prime place. A commentary, also known by the Latin *glossa* and its various Romance derivations, served as an introduction to and explanation of a given text. The Bible was the subject of most medieval commentaries, but other texts considered essential for earthly and spiritual well-being also frequently received the treatment, including theological works of the Church Fathers, ancient and medieval philosophical and legal texts, and narrative works prized for their ethical content. The medieval genre of commentary was broad and encompassed many types of texts, but in this chapter I focus on two distinct forms of commentary that Juan Manuel used and adapted. The first, called the *accessus ad auctores* in the Latin academic tradition, was a general introduction to a text and its author, traditionally an authoritative *auctor* of antiquity. The second was a combination of text and commentary that used *mise en page*, or page layout, to indicate the relationship between the primary text and the secondary gloss. Popular formats for this visually oriented commentary included marginal glosses, interlinear glosses, or glosses after each section break. Julian Weiss also makes a distinction between commentaries that are "systematically keyed to the target text" and those that circulate independently ("Vernacular Commentaries ... II" 239). The former type is the one that appears in Juan Manuel's works. Its appeal lay in the dynamic relationship between text and gloss, a relationship made visible by traces, however fragmentary, of the primary text.

Thanks to its association with sacred texts, commentary was recognized as a way to confer authority upon a given work, and to this end authors in the later Middle Ages began to apply the formal and rhetorical elements of commentary to vernacular literature. Some famous examples include Dante's *Commedia,* which began to circulate shortly after his death with a biography by Boccaccio and a gloss by Benvenuto da Imola, and John Gower's *Confessio amantis*, the English poem for which the author wrote his own Latin commentary (Botterill; Hanna et al.). In Castile, Juan de Mena wrote a self-commentary for his poem *Coronación*, and his longer *Laberinto de Fortuna* was glossed several times, most notably in a 1499 version by the humanist Hernán Núñez.[1]

As John Dagenais has pointed out, in Christian Europe "the vast bulk of medieval writing is biblical commentary," and it is not an exaggeration to propose that "there is just one text and one Author for the Middle Ages, to which the rest is gloss" (22). To interpret the Bible, medieval exegetes devised methods of exposition that identified both literal and spiritual meanings of scripture. The spiritual meanings were further subdivided into allegorical, moral, and anagogical senses, giving what is known as the fourfold method of scriptural exegesis (described, for example, in Thomas Aquinas's *Summa Theologiae*, I.1.10). This fourfold method was succinctly summarized in a distich attributed to Augustine of Dacia (d. 1282):

> Littera gesta docet, quid credas allegoria,
> Moralis quid agas, quo tendas anagogia.

> The literal sense provides the historical data; the allegorical, that which one should believe by faith; the tropological or moral, how one should behave; the anagogical, where one is going in terms of spiritual progress. (loose trans. by Minnis, *Medieval Theory* 34)

Although the application of the fourfold method was not monolithic, it dominated scriptural exegesis and also influenced the methods of commentators writing on secular authors such as Ovid (Minnis and Johnson 4–6).

Despite Juan Manuel's lack of an ecclesiastical education, he would have been familiar with biblical exegesis through his contact with members of the Dominican Order, primarily through sermons and conversations (Lida de Malkiel, "Tres notas" 155–63; Ayerbe-Chaux, "Intellectual"). He also knew written sources such as Nicholas of Lyra's *Prologus secundus*, which ponders the distinction between the literal and spiritual senses of the Old Testament, and Infante Juan of Aragon's commentary on the Lord's Prayer (Rico; Tate). It was by no means unusual for vernacular writers to draw from biblical commentary traditions: Hanna et al. have surveyed dozens of examples in European vernaculars, concluding that the writers of vernacular commentaries and self-commentaries "wished to appropriate the values of academic literary criticism and bestow them on their own writings and those of distinguished medieval contemporaries" (421). Juan Manuel fits this model by using the forms and methods of commentary – especially its *accessus* and *mise en page* – to ascribe authority to his works in a secular literary domain.

In the mid-twentieth century, Lida de Malkiel claimed that Juan Manuel was "poco amigo de autorizarse con libros ajenos" ("not prone to authorizing himself with the books of others"; "Tres notas" 174). Her observation continues to inform scholarly approaches to his works, despite Lacarra's recent call to revise this long-standing assumption (*Don Juan* 20). The present chapter attempts to answer Lacarra's call by showing how the Castilian nobleman imitated the discourse of commentary to appropriate authority from written sources. It is true that he occasionally seems to conceal the names of his sources, as when he refers to Llull's *Llibre de l'orde de cavalleria* as "un libro" in the prologue to the *Libro del cavallero et del escudero*. Yet he also used commentary as a way to engage openly with his sources to create something new.

Juan Manuel also used the role of commentator to branch out from secular literature (represented by the works of his Alfonsine period: the *Crónica abreviada*, *Libro de la caza*, and *Libro de la cavallería*) and make forays into theological writing. Scholars such as Peter Dunn ("Framing the Story") and Jonathan Burgoyne (*Reading the Exemplum* 179–82) have shown how the rhetoric of commentary serves as a structural guide for the *Conde Lucanor*'s secular hermeneutics, both in the text itself (Dunn) and in a particular manuscript (Burgoyne, on manuscript *M* of the *Conde Lucanor*). Fewer studies have addressed how he extends the discourse of commentary to theological concerns as part of a broader project of vernacular theology, a term I borrow from scholars of Middle English literature to describe vernacular works written for a lay audience that aspired to sophisticated discussions of theological subjects.[2]

Writing vernacular theology could be considered a devotional act. As discussed in the introduction, the approach to authorship in works associated with Sancho IV and *molinismo*, in which writing books with ethical aims was construed as service to God, encouraged a link between writing and four of the seven spiritual works of mercy: to instruct the ignorant, counsel the doubtful, admonish sinners, and comfort the afflicted. Vernacular theology, if done properly, had a special potential to fulfil the first two by guiding a relatively unschooled group of vernacular readers to a deeper understanding of Christian doctrine. Moreover, as Harvey Hames shows in his study of Ramon Llull's works in Catalan, the vernacular was also seen as an effective tool for the conversion of Iberian Jews and Muslims, who spoke the vernacular but did not study Latin (51–2). Vernacular theology could therefore also admonish sinners, or in Don Juan's words, "castigar a los errados," which encompasses those in the theological "error" of following another religion (*Libro del cavallero*, ed. Cossío Olavide, 50). If a work of vernacular theology managed to strengthen a reader's faith or even convert an unbeliever to Christianity, the individual responsible for the book would receive spiritual benefits through the act of authorship, as I have proposed elsewhere regarding the *Libro de los estados* ("Hidden Polemic" 24). Since the form of commentary, with its focus on clarifying the obscure, was particularly suited to vernacular theology, adopting the discourse of commentary provided Don Juan with a way to serve others and work towards his final spiritual reward.

Although the *Libro del cavallero et del escudero*, *Libro de los estados*, *Conde Lucanor*, and *Libro infinido* are typically categorized as "mirrors for princes" containing secular advice for knights and nobles, they all have an important spiritual component as well. All four present a wise, experienced character – the unnamed old knight, the preacher Julio, the counsellor Patronio, and Don Juan himself – whose role is to explain nature, society, and religious doctrine to a young nobleman and elucidate his place in these larger systems.[3] Similar to how a biblical exegete would gloss a text, these fictional advisors are tasked with glossing the world. However, the old knight, Julio, and Patronio do not limit themselves to the domains of knowledge considered appropriate for laypeople, but also address more esoteric religious and philosophical matters that would normally be discussed in Latin and addressed to a clerical audience. Using these authority figures as avatars of his authorial persona (in the sense of different incarnations of the same entity), Juan Manuel manipulates a discourse of clarity and obscurity aimed at giving the discerning lay reader access to religious subject matter, while protecting the ignorant masses from dangerous ideas that could lead to heterodox beliefs.

In his works, Don Juan assumes clerical authority while retaining his status as a member of the lay nobility, demonstrating his capacity to perform scriptural exegesis safely in the vernacular. This ambitious strategy integrates two different modes of commentary: a secular one derived from the works of the Alfonsine scriptorium, and a religious one that resonated with the Christian intellectual paradigm of *molinismo* associated with Sancho IV and María de Molina. However, given contemporary concerns about theological works in the vernacular, the author's forays into vernacular theology represented an audacious challenge to the Church's control over religious discourse. This could explain why his works other than the *Conde Lucanor* survive in a single medieval manuscript: scribes and readers might have deemed the more theological works, such as the *Libro de los estados* and the *Tratado de la Asunción*, too dangerous to copy or circulate. Moreover, although the first part of the *Conde Lucanor* enjoyed a wider circulation, parts 2–5 (the *Libro de los proverbios* and *Tratado de la doctrina*) appear only in *S* and *G*, perhaps due to the doctrinal content of the fifth part. Because of this limited circulation, Juan Manuel's approach to commentary did not have much impact on later commentaries in Castilian, which are better understood in the context of the humanistic translation projects of the fifteenth century (Weiss, *The Poet's Art*). Nonetheless, the commentary form and its theological content constitute an important component of Juan Manuel's authorship, and one that is too often ignored.

Secular Authority and the *Accessus ad auctores*

One of the rhetorical forms of commentary that Juan Manuel adapted was the *accessus ad auctores*, a general introduction to a text or author that medieval readers considered authoritative.[4] The *accessus* originated in an educational setting as a way to provide pupils with general information to guide their readings of important works of pagan and Christian literature (Quain 217–18). Although it could take the form of an oral lecture, today we know the medieval *accessus* mainly through its written form as a prologue. It followed a template with different categories of introductory information, which the commentator typically addressed using explicit headings. Although the exact format varied from school to school, two templates dominated in the thirteenth century. One, which R.W. Hunt dubbed the "Type C" prologue, had eight headings used in different combinations: title of the book (*titulus libri*), author (*auctor*), author's intentions (*intentio auctoris*), subject matter (*materia*), style of writing (*modus agendi*), order or organization of the book (*ordo libri*), usefulness (*utilitas*), and the branch of knowledge to which the work belongs (*cui parti philosophiae supponitur*). The other, the "Aristotelian prologue," employed as headings the four Aristotelian causes: the efficient cause (author), material cause (subject matter), formal cause (style of writing), and final cause (a combination of the author's intentions and the book's usefulness) (Minnis, *Medieval Theory* 19–33). In general, Aristotle's causes offer four types of explanations for how or why something exists: the efficient cause explains who or what made the thing, be it a human agent or a process; the material cause identifies the matter out of which it is made; the formal cause identifies its shape or form; and the final cause explains the purpose for which it is made. When applied to books, the four Aristotelian causes foreground the notion that remains implicit in the Type C headings: a thorough understanding of a work requires knowledge of its making and its relationship to other works, knowledge that goes beyond the words on the page. In practice, the two schemas overlapped considerably, and commentators were "free to construct new paradigms by combining elements from both the Aristotelian and earlier traditions" (Weiss, *The Poet's Art* 108). Regardless of the exact categories and headings they chose, medieval commentators used the *accessus ad auctores* to introduce, contextualize, and praise the author whose text provided the basis for their gloss.

As Minnis points out, *accessus*-style lectures were a common teaching tool in grammar schools; thus, even pupils who did not progress far in their studies were familiar with the genre in a simplified form (*Medieval Theory* 161). Juan Manuel's first exposure to the *accessus* may have been in such a grammar school setting. In the *Libro de los estados,* he includes Latin grammar instruction in his description of the ideal education for the children of emperors. Noble children should learn not only to read, speak, and understand Latin, but also to perform grammar exercises, including "fazer conjugación, et declinar et derivar, o fazer proverbio o letras" ("doing conjugations, declinations and derivations, or doing proverbs and letters"; *Libro de los estados* 200). This was the education Don Juan himself had received in his youth: "En esta guisa le criara su madre en cuanto fue viva, et después que ella finó, que así lo fizieron los que lo criaron" ("His mother raised him in this way when she was alive, and after she died, those in charge of his upbringing did the same"; 201). As I will show, Juan Manuel's application of *accessus* categories and headings is idiosyncratic, which could suggest a rudimentary familiarity with the genre's formal elements. However, even in academic examples from the twelfth and thirteenth centuries, "the details of the *accessus* had, to some extent, become shadowy and dim" (Quain 262), so it follows that Juan Manuel's attempts – undertaken in the fourteenth century in a lay context – would take a loose approach to the genre. At any rate, his works show a firm grasp of the benefits of commentary, which confers authority both upon the author of the original text and upon the commentator capable of glossing it. His use of *accessus* categories reveals a deeper understanding of how the rhetoric of commentary could be used to elevate the status of lay, vernacular literature.

Before the fourteenth century, nearly all the texts that received the *accessus* treatment – including the Bible as well as literary and philosophical works by pagan and Christian authors – were considered the work of *auctores* and thus bore the authority of antiquity. A work by an ancient *auctor* was considered truthful and morally valuable in large part because it had stood the test of time. The contributions of "modern" writers, considered dwarves standing on the shoulders of giants in the famous phrase attributed to Bernard of Chartres, paled in comparison to the works of the ancient *auctores* (Minnis, *Medieval Theory* 10–12). But this attitude began to change in the early fourteenth century, when authors writing in Latin and the vernacular started using the *accessus* to introduce the works of contemporary authors, and even their own books. Dante's (c. 1265–1321) *Vita nuova* and *Convivio*, as well as the fourteenth-century *Epistle to Can Grande* associated with him, adopted elements of the *accessus* as a way of associating Dante's "modern" works with the prestige of the ancients (Ascoli, *Dante* 183–5, 203–4). John Gower (c. 1330–1408) similarly used *accessus* headings in the prologues and epilogues to his Latin *Vox clamantis* and English *Confessio amantis* to confer authority upon his works and shape his readers' understanding of their usefulness (Minnis, *Medieval Theory* 168–90). In this way, the *accessus* became a way not just to introduce works of literature, but also to lend them authority and argue that readers should approach them with the same attention and reverence they would pay to Virgil or Augustine. The increase in *accessus*-style introductions to "modern" works, in which Juan Manuel participated, represented a significant shift in medieval notions of authorship. By studying Juan Manuel's prologues not just within Castilian literary history, but in the broader context of Latin European book culture, we can continue to expand our knowledge of the fourteenth century as a period of heightened interest in reshaping existing notions of authorship and authority.

The prologues to the *Crónica abreviada* and *Libro de la caza*, the two extant works from Juan Manuel's Alfonsine period, do not make explicit reference to *accessus* headings, but they do deploy *accessus* categories. They follow the standard order, beginning with extrinsic categories that identify the discipline to which a text belongs, followed by intrinsic ones related to the specific text at hand (Minnis, *Medieval Theory* 30). Given the absence of headings, we cannot say with certainty whether they followed the Type C categories, the Aristotelian categories, or a mix of both. I have chosen to refer to the Type C headings because they are more intuitive for modern readers, but similar correspondences can be drawn for the Aristotelian categories.

The prologue to the *Crónica abreviada* attributes the work to Don Juan as its declarative author, the one who "fizo poner en este libro" ("had written in this book") the highlights of Alfonso X's larger work. Don Juan is positioned as the commentator in the sense that he is providing an *accessus* to the king's work. The *Estoria de España* is introduced using most of the Type C categories, proceeding from extrinsic (branch of philosophy, subject matter, utility) to intrinsic (author, title, order, style, author's intention). After reflecting on the nature and limitations of human knowledge, Don Juan lists all the books that the ancients, with God's help, devised to retain the wisdom of the past. This list – including the Bible, secular and canon law, arts and sciences, and historical chronicles – represents all the branches of "philosophy," that is, human knowledge.[5] The *Estoria de España* can be clearly categorized as a chronicle (*cui parti philosophiae supponitur*). Its subject matter (*materia*) is the deeds of Spain, and its usefulness (*utilitas*) is in preserving the memory of these deeds:

> El muy noble rey don Alfonso, fijo del muy bienaventurado e – con razón que podemos dezir por él segunt las sus obras – el santo rey don Ferrando e de la reina doña Beatriz, por que los grandes fechos que pasaron, señaladamente lo que pertenece a la estoria d'España, fuesen sabidos e non cayesen en olvido, fizo ayuntar los que falló que cumplían para los contar. (*Obras*, ed. Alvar and Finci, 67)

> The very noble king Don Alfonso, son of the very fortunate and – as we can rightly say based on his works – the holy king Don Fernando and the queen Doña Beatriz, had [this chronicle] compiled so that the great deeds of the past, especially those dealing with the history of Spain, would be known and not fall into oblivion, compiling those he found fitting to relate.

This passage also introduces Alfonso as the author (*auctor*), combining the king's noble and saintly lineage with the discourse of compilation to depict him as an authority. The prologue then provides the work's title (*titulus*), which he gives as *Crónica de España* rather than the more commonly used *Estoria de España*, and describes its style (*modus agendi*):

> Este muy noble rey don Alfonso [...] ordenó muy complidamente la *Crónica de España*, e púsolo todo complido e por muy apuestas razones e en las menos palabras que se podía poner, en tal manera que todo omne que la lea puede entender en esta obra, e en las crónicas que él compuso e mandó componer, que avía muy grant entendimiento e avía muy grant talante de acrecentar el saber, e cobdiciava mucho la onra de sus regnos e que era alumbrado de la gracia de Dios para entender e fazer mucho bien. (67–8)

> This very noble king Don Alfonso [...] organized the *Crónica de España* perfectly, and wrote it very completely and in very elegant language and

> in the fewest words possible, in such a way that anyone who reads it will understand, through this work and through the other chronicles he composed and commissioned, that he had a great intellect and a great desire to increase knowledge, and he wished for the honour of his kingdoms and was illuminated by the grace of God to understand and do much good.

Don Juan associates the king's accessible style with his intention (*intentio auctoris*) to spread knowledge and bring honour to his kingdom. While the prologue does not discuss the book's organization (*ordo*), the rubric to the table of contents serves this purpose, announcing its division into three books. By using *accessus* headings to introduce the *Estoria de España*, Don Juan achieves three related goals. First, he portrays the king as an authoritative author worthy of admiration and imitation (Funes, "Don Juan"). Second, he establishes a precedent for applying the *accessus* to a new literary context: works written in the vernacular within a courtly milieu. Finally, as the one responsible for creating the *accessus*, Don Juan sets himself up as the heir to Alfonso X's literary legacy.

I pause here to clarify an apparent contradiction. As discussed in the previous chapter, Don Juan's authorial role in the main text of the *Crónica abreviada* is that of compiler, not commentator, of the *Estoria de España*. He provides no commentary in the form of explanations or interpretations, and although he imposes slightly different selection criteria, overall the text is an abbreviated but faithful version of its exemplar.[6] However, the prologue is another matter: as several scholars have observed, it is in the prologue that Don Juan creates his first truly personal and literary text (Funes, "Don Juan Manuel" 783–4; Biaggini, "Stratégies" and "Énonciation"; Hijano Villegas 81–4). As Biaggini points out, the fact that Juan Manuel replaces the Alfonsine prologue with an original one shows his interest in creating an autonomous work, even if that autonomy is not reflected in the body of the text ("Stratégies" 201–2). We can understand this increased authorial autonomy as the adoption of the role of *commentator*: a role on the same continuum as *scriptor* and *compilator*, but with more creativity and more authority.

The prologue to the *Libro de la caza* establishes a similar relationship between Alfonso X and Don Juan, this time in the context of treatises on falconry and hunting. To introduce the now-lost Alfonsine treatises on hunting, the prologue again begins with the extrinsic categories of branch of philosophy and utility. Here, Don Juan places his uncle's work not in the context of all written knowledge, but within the vast corpus of theological, juridical, and scientific works produced in the Alfonsine scriptorium (which for him amounts to more or less the same thing).

Within this corpus, hunting manuals are considered a mechanical art, traditionally seen as less prestigious than the liberal arts.[7] However, Don Juan defends their utility, linking Alfonso's books on hunting to the diffusion of learning as well as "todas las cosas nobles et apuestas et sabrosas et aprobechosas" ("all noble, beautiful, pleasurable, and beneficial things"; *Obras*, ed. Alvar and Finci, 304). Moving on to intrinsic features, he praises the king's style, writing that he "puso muy complidamente la teórica et la prática [de la caça] como conviene a esta arte; et tan complidamente lo fizo, que bien cuidan que non podría otro emendar nin eñader ninguna cosa más de lo que él fizo" ("recorded the theory and practice [of hunting] very completely, as befits this art; and he did it so completely that people rightly think no one else could emend or add anything more to what he wrote"; 304).

The *accessus* categories have a similar function in both prologues. They allow Juan Manuel to assume the role of commentator, giving him an opportunity to describe and, more importantly, evaluate the works of an authoritative author. But in contrast to his role as compiler in the *Crónica abreviada*, in which he faithfully follows the contours of his uncle's work, he presents the *Libro de la caza* as a kind of gloss or supplement to his uncle's work. Whereas Alfonso had provided a comprehensive theory of the hunt, Don Juan offers practical knowledge gained from prominent falconers of his day and from his own experience (304). He also recognizes the need to update the knowledge accumulated by the previous generation of falconers: "Él vio cómo se mudó la manera de la caça de aquel tiempo fasta aqueste que agora está" ("He saw how the ways of hunting have changed from that time to the present day"; 305). Given its secular subject matter, Don Juan's treatise on hunting clearly does not fulfil the spiritual aims of religious commentary. But by providing practical applications and updates to Alfonso X's work, he does follow the basic structure of commentary as defined by Bonaventure, presenting his original contribution as an expansion of an existing authoritative text. This structure does not carry over into the body of the *Libro de la caza*, which interweaves old and new material in such a way that the two are indistinguishable (Orduna, "Prólogos" 119). Nevertheless, the dependent relationship between text and gloss would continue to inform Juan Manuel's later works. Not only did it contribute to the structure of the *Conde Lucanor*, but it also paved the way for more explicitly theological commentary in the *Libro de los estados* and *Tratado de la Asunción*.

Juan Manuel did not abandon the *accessus* in prologues from his post-Alfonsine period; instead, he introduced a major innovation by applying its techniques to his own authorial persona, in a form of self-*accessus*.

As Salvatore Luongo has shown, Don Juan invokes *accessus* categories in the paratexts to the *Conde Lucanor* (6–13). Luongo identifies his declarations of authorship, authorial intentions, subject matter, and style as the Aristotelian categories of efficient cause, final cause, material cause, and formal cause, respectively. Using the Type C headings makes the strategy even clearer, because some of them are invoked explicitly. For instance, in the prologue to part 2, Don Juan gives the exact Castilian translation of the heading *materia libri*: "d'aquí adelante comencaré la *materia del libro*" ("from here on I will begin the *matter of the book*"; 228; my emphasis). Nevertheless, because the distinctions between the two templates were often blurred, it matters little which one is followed here; what is most important is Don Juan's continued and consistent application of the *accessus* as a strategy for self-authorization.

The *Libro infinido*'s prologue provides the clearest and most cohesive self-*accessus* (I indicate each category in square brackets after its occurrence):

> Et porque yo, don Johán, fijo del infante don Manuel [*auctor*] [...], quería cuanto pudiese ayudar a mí et a otros a saber lo más que yo pudiese [*utilitas*], teniendo que el saber es la cosa por que omne más debía fazer, por ende asmé de componer este tractado [*intentio auctoris*] que tracta de cosas que yo mismo prové en mí mismo et en mi fazienda et bi que conteció a otros, et de las que fiz et vi fazer et me fallé d'ellas bien et yo et los otros [*materia*]. [...] Et porque este libro es de cosas que yo prové, pusi en él las de que me acordé. Et porque las que d'aquí adelante provare non sé a qué recudrán, non las pude aquí poner; mas con la merced de Dios ponerlas he como las provare [*modus agendi*]. Et porque esto non sé cuándo se acabará, pus nombre a este libro el *Libro enfenido*, que quiere dezir libro sin acabamiento [*titulus*]. Et por que sea más ligero de entender et estudiar es fecho a capítulos [*ordo*]. (117–18)

> And because I, Don Juan, son of Infante Don Manuel [*auctor*] [...], wanted, as much as possible, to help myself and others to gain knowledge [*utilitas*] – in the belief that knowledge is the thing that men should most strive for – for this reason I decided to compose this treatise [*intentio auctoris*] that deals with what I experienced in myself and in my estate and what I saw happen to others, and what I did and saw others do that worked out well for me and for them [*materia*]. [...] And because this book is about things I experienced, I put in it the ones I remembered. And because I do not know how things will turn out in the future, I could not include those [things]; but with the mercy of God I will put them here as they happen [*modus agendi*]. And because I do not know when this will end, I gave this

> book the name *Libro infinido*, which means book without end [*titulus*]. And to make it easier to understand and study, it is divided into chapters [*ordo*].

The same strategy that Don Juan used in his early prologues to elevate Alfonso X to the status of venerated *auctor* now lends authority to his own works. He pays special attention to the categories of utility and author's intention (the final cause in the Aristotelian model), which indicate the book's purpose. In fact, all his post-Alfonsine prologues emphasize his purpose for writing: to preserve earthly knowledge (*Libro del cavallero et del escudero, Libro infinido*); to help readers attain earthly success and spiritual salvation within their God-given estate (*Libro de los estados, Conde Lucanor*); to reveal the truth about historical events (*Libro de las tres razones*); or to demonstrate a point of Christian doctrine through logical arguments (*Tratado de la Asunción*). Don Juan communicates to his readers that his works are designed to achieve specific ethical and doctrinal aims, and they should read with these aims in mind. Calling attention to them raises the likelihood that his works will achieve them, so that he as the declarative author may reap the benefits of improving his readers' earthly and spiritual well-being.

Self-commentary in an *accessus* mode, whether in Latin or the vernacular, is rare before Dante. Ernst Robert Curtius cites just one eleventh-century example, Warnerius of Basel's *Paraclitus* (221). Other possible precedents, such as Augustine's *Confessions* and Boethius's *Consolation of Philosophy*, model a type of "autobiographical" writing but do not fit the description of self-commentary (Ascoli, *Dante* 182–3, 185). Dante's adaptation of the *accessus* is much more explicit than Juan Manuel's: he makes reference to the practice and its categories in the first book of his *Convivio* (c. 1304–7), and the *Epistle to Can Grande* provides an even clearer example of self-commentary in the *accessus* mode.[8] There is no evidence that Juan Manuel knew or imitated Dante's works, but the comparison is helpful in order to understand what Juan Manuel's adaptation of the *accessus* achieves in the context of his corpus.

As "moderns," neither Dante nor Juan Manuel could take for granted that their works would be read with the careful hermeneutical procedures afforded to the classical *auctores* of antiquity. Their self-introductions communicated to readers that their works were intentionally imbued with a deeper meaning beyond the literal level, encouraging them to read with those intentions in mind. In turn, their adaptations of the traditional relationships between author, text, and reader proved transformative for their respective concepts of authorship. In Ascoli's words:

> Even as Dante assimilates modern poets, such as himself, to the classical *auctores*, he silently transforms the medieval notion of the *auctor*, whose meanings are revealed by the commentary of modern *lectores*, to a proto-modern idea of the *author*, whose conscious intentions govern the meaning of his own work, quite apart from the readings of others. (*Dante* 199)

Juan Manuel's process of self-exegesis differs from Dante's in that he writes primarily in prose and therefore situates himself within a tradition of venerated prose authors, chief among them Alfonso X. Yet his preoccupation with self-commentary suggests a similar attempt to shift where the meaning of a text is situated. In providing an *accessus* that glosses his own works, Juan Manuel, like Dante, invites readers to seek meaning in the author's intentions, rather than sources outside the text or their own interpretations. This consequence of medieval self-exegesis, in which the author is equated to the "final signified," would become the dominant concept of authorship in Western literature for centuries until Barthes rebelled against it more than six centuries later ("Death" 877).

The use of *accessus* categories to introduce works in Castilian for a lay audience would not become widespread until the fifteenth century, when writers used them to introduce original works in Castilian as well as translations of ancient and modern "classics."[9] As Julian Weiss has shown, these fifteenth-century literary practices – exemplified in the prologues of Enrique de Villena, Diego de Valera, Juan Rodríguez del Padrón, and Gutierre Díez de Games – drew upon both the Latin academic tradition and vernacular commentaries from outside Castile, most notably glosses to Dante's *Commedia* (*Poet's Art* 109–17). Because we have little evidence of the circulation of Juan Manuel's works during the fourteenth and fifteenth centuries (with the exception of the *Conde Lucanor*), scholars have not considered his prologues influential: Weiss mentions the *General estoria* and *Libro de buen amor* as precursors to the fifteenth-century *accessus* but omits Juan Manuel's works entirely (109). However, the copyists and rubricators of his works easily identified the *accessus* categories in his prologues and reproduced them in new paratexts.

The manuscript of the *Crónica abreviada* (BNE, MS 1356), which Faulhaber dates to c. 1451–75 (PhiloBiblon), begins with a rubric that extracts its author and organization and gives it a title: "Ésta es la tabla d'este libro que don Joán, fijo del muy noble infante don Manuel, tutor del muy alto e noble rey don Alfonso, su sobrino, adelantado mayor del reino de Murcia, fizo, que es dicho *Sumario de la Crónica de España*, que va repartido en tres libros" ("This is the table of contents of the book written by Don Juan, son of the very noble Infante Don Manuel, tutor of the very high and noble king Don Alfonso, his nephew, and *adelantado mayor* of the kingdom of Murcia; it is called *Sumario de la Crónica de España* and is divided into three books"; 9). (Scholars prefer the title *Crónica abreviada*, which is attested in the General Prologue authored by Juan Manuel and is therefore considered more authoritative.) Likewise, in *S*, the *Libro del cavallero et del escudero* begins with a rubric that lists its author, title, style, and the author's intention to have the work translated:

> Comiença el libro que fizo don Joán, fijo del muy noble infante don Manuel, et ha nombre el *Libro del cavallero et del escudero*, et es compuesto en una manera que dizen en Castiella fabliella, et envíalo al infante don Joán, arçobispo de Toledo, et ruégal que tenga por bien de trasladar este dicho su libro de romance en latín. (377)

> Here begins the book written by Don Juan, son of the very noble Infante Don Manuel, and its title is *Libro del cavallero et del escudero*, and it is composed in a style that in Castile is called a little fable, and he sends it to the Infante Don Juan, archbishop of Toledo, and asks him to see fit to translate his aforementioned book from Romance to Latin.

These rubrics mix phrases from Juan Manuel's prologues with original descriptions to provide an abbreviated *accessus*. In this way, they continue the project of elevating Don Juan to the status of an authoritative author worthy of study.

For the fifteenth-century copyists of BNE, MS 1356 and *S*, the prologues were sources of useful information, including the author's name and nobiliary titles and the style and organization of the work. Whether or not the copyists specifically sought to deploy *accessus* categories, they evidently found them and chose to reproduce them, reinforcing their value for noble writers, readers, and patrons. Thus, while Juan Manuel's prologues were not the most influential model for the fifteenth-century Castilian *accessus*, they do form part of the corpus of textual examples from which fifteenth-century writers could borrow.

Commentary Writing

In addition to the *accessus*, Juan Manuel adopted another form of commentary that had two defining features: first, it identified multiple levels of meaning within the tradition of the fourfold method of scriptural exegesis; and second, it presented commentary keyed to a base text. Juan Manuel may have known Thomas Aquinas's explanation of the fourfold method of scriptural exegesis in *Summa Theologiae*, I.1.10, through Dominican contacts such as Fray Juan Alfonso, to whom Juan Manuel addresses the *Libro de las tres razones* and the last chapter of the *Libro infinido* (Lida de Malkiel, "Tres notas" 185n5; Ayerbe-Chaux, "Intellectual" 154).[10] Additionally, in the prologue to his *Libro del cavallero et del escudero*, he notes that his brother-in-law Infante Juan of Aragon, at the time Archbishop of Toledo, had sent him "la muy buena et muy complida et muy santa obra que vós fiziestes en el *Pater Noster* por que lo trasladasse de latín en romance" ("the very good, complete, and holy work you wrote on the Lord's Prayer, that I might translate it from Latin to Romance"; 376). While no evidence of this vernacular translation survives, it is reasonable to assume that Juan Manuel knew this "elaborate, but expressly not learned, exegesis," which breaks down each phrase of the Lord's Prayer to explain its significance for the salvation of those who recite it (Tate 177).[11] Finally, despite the rarity of scriptural exegesis in Castilian before the late fourteenth century, Juan Manuel may have seen examples in Alfonso X's *General estoria*, which "passed on to a lay audience the methods of biblical exegesis" (Weiss, "Literary Theory" 500). This range of texts in Latin and the vernacular provided examples of commentary in action and informative descriptions of its utility, both of which Juan Manuel adapted to his own ends.

Beginning with the *Crónica abreviada*, Don Juan experiments with commentary as a form of writing subordinated to another, more authoritative text. As Saracino has observed, the entire *Crónica abreviada* takes the form of a commentary keyed to its source text. The text is divided into three books that mirror the division of the *Crónica manuelina*, and each chapter begins by stating the corresponding chapter number(s) of its base text. Even when the abbreviated version does not copy any content from its source text, it still lists the corresponding chapter numbers as placeholders, creating a close structural dependence between the two (Saracino 4). As discussed in the previous chapter, because the main aim of the *Crónica abreviada* is to excerpt and abbreviate the *Estoria de España*, it is best understood as a compilation. However, in the way each chapter is keyed to a corresponding location in a single source text, its form can be compared to that of a commentary.

The prologue to the *Crónica abreviada* offers another example of commentarial writing keyed to a much shorter base text: a quote attributed to "Joán Damasceno en el libro *De las propiedades de las cosas*" ("John of Damascus in the book *On the Properties of Things*"), which Lida de Malkiel has identified as a quote from Dionysius the Areopagite collected in Bartholomaeus Anglicus's thirteenth-century encyclopedia

De proprietatibus rerum ("Tres notas" 170).[12] In Don Juan's version it reads: "Porque los omnes son embueltos en esta carnalidat espessa, non pueden entender las cosas muy sotiles, que son para mostrar las cosas que son fechas, si non por algunas maneras corporales, así como por ingenios o por semejanças" ("Because humans are enveloped in this dense carnality, they cannot understand very subtle things that serve to explain how things come to be, except through corporal ways such as rhetorical devices or analogies"; 65). Although he may have acquired the quote from an oral source such as a sermon (B. Taylor, "Juan Manuel's Cipher" 37), he presents it as a written source, cited by title and author. Moreover, given John of Damascus's status as a venerated Church Doctor, the quote is treated as an *auctoritas*, a statement made authoritative by the status of the *auctor* to whom it is attributed (Biaggini, "Stratégies" 200). This quote serves as the base text of Don Juan's commentary, which unfolds in the first four sections of the prologue, indicated by decorated initials (see fig. 3.1).

Don Juan uses the form and function of commentary to meditate on the passage's significance for the pursuit of human knowledge, particularly the writing of history. His commentary reframes the quote within a new context through an interpretation that hinges on four key terms: *omnes, cosas sotiles, carnalidat*, and *semejanças*. In its original context, the passage refers to comprehending spiritual substances, such as God, the angels, and the human soul, but Don Juan deftly shifts his focus to the challenge of comprehending human history, an apt way to begin his abbreviated history of Spain. First, he pauses on the word *omnes* (humans), observing that if all humans are incapable of understanding more subtle (or divine) forms of knowledge, then it is all the more difficult for laypeople who read books in the vernacular. He then turns to *cosas sotiles* (subtle things), proposing to write with a balance of subtlety and clarity in order to challenge lay readers without confusing or confounding them. Next, he focuses on corporality (*carnalidat, maneras corporales*), explaining that the limitations imposed on the created world – which includes the heavens, man, animals, and human affairs – do not apply to God. By referring to "las obras que fazen los omnes" ("deeds that humans do"), he prepares the reader for the book's historical subject matter (66). Finally, he turns to *semejanças* (similes), comparing God's infinite knowledge to the human knowledge stored in books, while recognizing that "entre Dios e los omnes á muy pequeña comparación" ("between God and humans there is very little comparison"; 66).

In religious commentary, this unpacking of key words (*lemmata*) in narrative form was common. For example, the manuscript of Infante

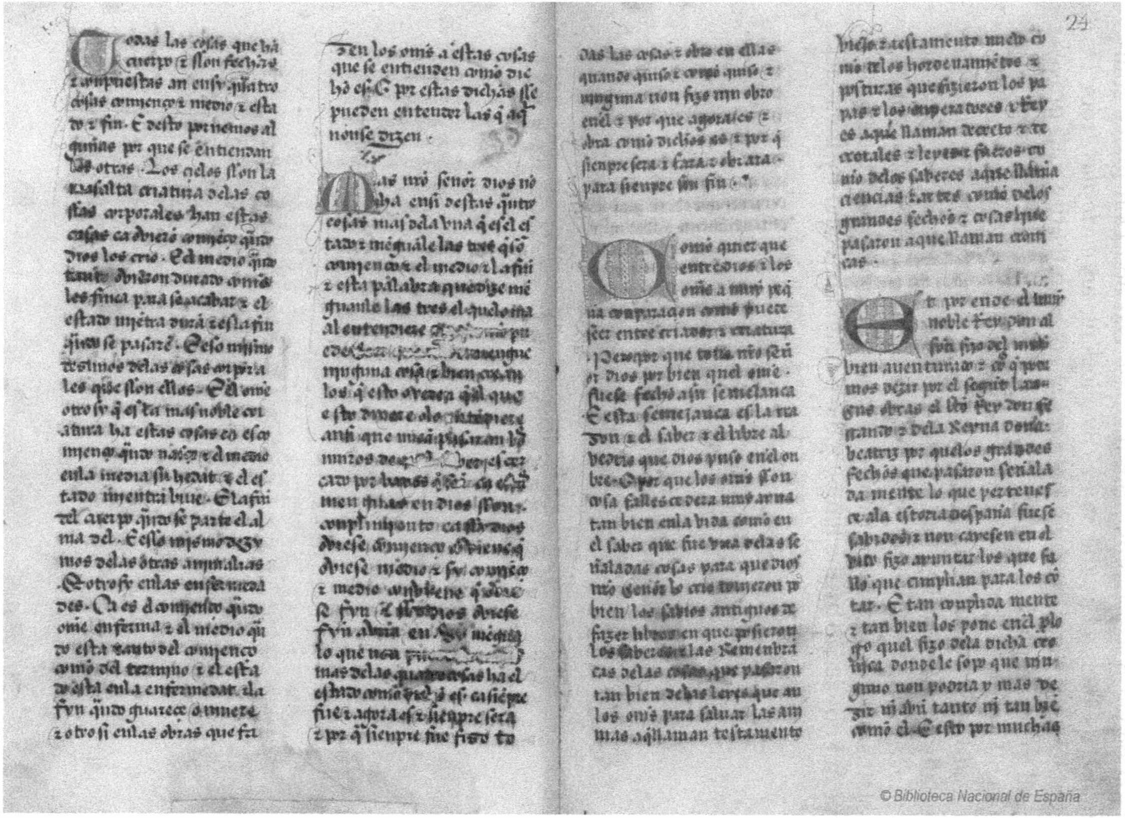

Fig. 3.1. Don Juan's commentary on a quote incorrectly attributed to John of Damascus. BNE, MS 1356, fols. 23r–24r. Image taken from the holdings of the Biblioteca Nacional de España and licensed under the CC by 4.0 licence.

Juan of Aragon's Latin commentary on the Lord's Prayer proceeds this way, with phrases from the prayer underlined in red (see fig. 3.2). Although the *Crónica abreviada* manuscript does not make a visual distinction between key words from the base text and Don Juan's commentary, its method is the same. By glossing an *auctoritas* from *De proprietatibus rerum,* Don Juan bolsters his own authority and proves himself to be a capable commentator.

He will return to this same quote in two of his later works, the *Libro del cavallero et del escudero* (82) and *Libro de los estados* (308–11), but it is especially significant that he chose it as the foundational *auctoritas* to introduce his first foray into writing. Its words perfectly encapsulated the status of lay readers and writers, twice removed from the highest forms of knowledge by the limits of the human mind and by their lack

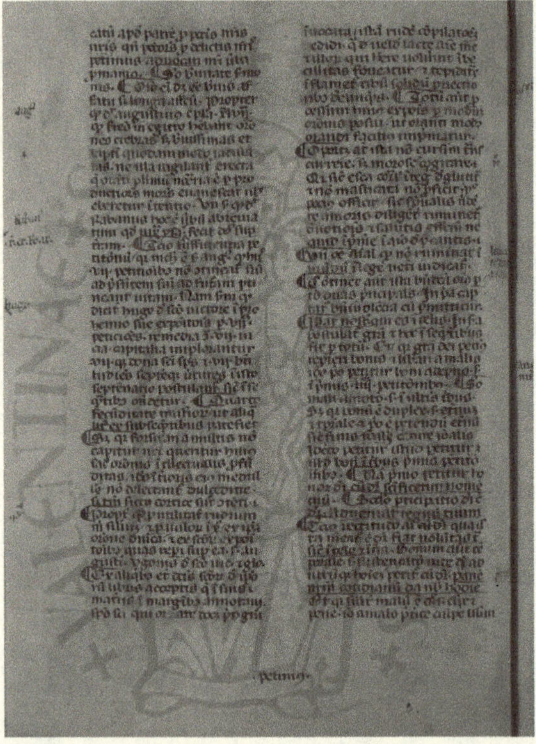

Fig. 3.2. Infante Juan of Aragon's commentary on the Lord's Prayer; note underlining near bottom of right column. Archivo de la Catedral de Valencia, MS 182, fol. 264v.

of a formal Latin education. Yet commentary offered the lay writer an opportunity to reduce the gap between clerical and secular knowledge, because its primary function was to take what seemed obscure and make it clear. In demonstrating the exegetical power of commentary at the outset of his work, Don Juan enacts a partial solution to the problem of his own limitations as a lay author writing in the vernacular, using commentary to mitigate the weaknesses of his authorial persona.

Commentary becomes essential to Juan Manuel's literary project in his most theological work, the *Libro de los estados*. This book harnesses the discourse of commentary to accomplish two goals: first, to introduce theological subject matter into a vernacular work for a lay audience; and second, to demonstrate that Don Juan, the author figure, can treat this material with an appropriate balance of clarity and obscurity. The first goal, glossing theological material for a lay audience, is achieved at the level of the plot by casting a clerical figure, Julio, in the role of commentator. While the plot follows loosely the legend of Barlaam and Josaphat, Juan Manuel's version has less conflict and is driven exclusively by the spiritual journey of the pagan prince Johás, whose quest for a religious and spiritual education leads him to convert to Christianity and seek ever greater knowledge within a Christian world view (Funes and Yoon). Although the prince's father, King Morabán, had sought to protect his son from all knowledge of earthly suffering, one day the inevitable happens: the prince witnesses a passing funeral procession and learns of the existence of death, provoking a spiritual crisis that his pagan upbringing cannot alleviate. His pagan tutor, the knight Turín, realizes that the prince's education should be in the hands of "algún omne muy letrado et muy entendido, et que fuese omne de buena entençión et derechurero" ("someone very learned and intelligent, a righteous man of good intentions"; 97). For this crucial role, Turín nominates Julio, a Christian preacher from Castile who also happens to be the confidant and former tutor of Don Juan, the book's extradiegetic narrator and author figure.

As a preacher, Julio fits the mould of a *letrado* whose knowledge of religious doctrine comes from books. However, his credentials are surprising in that they also include secular knowledge about the obligations of knights, typically the domain of *legos*, the lay nobility. Julio explains that, during his time spent in Don Juan's household, "por las grandes guerras quel acaesçieron [a don Joán] et por muchas cosas que vio et que pasó, despartiendo entre él et mí, sope yo por él muchas cosas que perteneşçen a la cavallería, de que yo non sabía tanto, porque só clérigo, et el mio ofiçio es más de pedricar que usar cavallería" ("on account of the great wars [Don Juan] was involved in and many other things he saw and experienced, discussing them between us, I learned through him many things about knighthood that I did not know before, because I am a clergyman charged with preaching rather than practising knighthood"; 100). This experience has given him some familiarity with *cavallería*, the activities of the lay nobility.[13] He is therefore an ideal figure to "translate" points of theology into language comprehensible to a lay audience, a task he accomplishes using a commentarial mode.

The work's theological content is motivated by Prince Johás's pressing desire to know "en quál estado o en quál manera yo pueda mejor salvar el alma" ("in what estate or in what way I can best save my soul"; 104). Julio initially seeks to satisfy the prince's desire by enumerating the four main *leyes*, or religions – Christianity, Judaism, Islam, and paganism – and presenting arguments for why Christianity is the best one in which to attain spiritual salvation. This section, which Funes dubs the "Discourse on Religions" ("Sobre la partición" 6), spans chapters 26 to 46 of the first book. Julio lays out basic tenets of Christian doctrine, including the existence of God, the Creation, the Fall, and the redemption of sin through Christ's death. He also expounds the philosophy of the dual nature of humans (body and soul) and of Christ (God and man).

Although Julio does not use any technical terms of commentary, such as *glosa* or *fablar espiritualmente*, he describes his method of expounding Christian doctrine in a way that echoes the procedures of biblical exegesis.[14] He explains that his knowledge comes from the Bible: "Aquello que yo sé ende, et lo fallé por las scripturas, dezírvoslo he" ("What I know about this, which I learned from the scriptures, I will tell you"; 110). He occasionally supplements his knowledge with existing biblical commentaries, referring to them as the words of wise men ("et dizen los sabios, algunos d'ellos, que ... "; "et algunos sabios dizen que ... "; "et otros dizen que ... "; 128–9). Recognizing the complexity of these doctrinal concepts, he assumes responsibility for giving the clearest explanation possible: "Por que lo entendades, dezírvoslo he bien declaradamente" ("I will tell you very clearly so that you understand"; 134). These rhetorical gestures reveal Julio's role as a biblical commentator, tasked with illuminating the multiple meanings of scripture for an eager but novice pupil. In the same section, Julio explains that one of Christ's primary tasks among his followers, in addition to preaching, was biblical commentary: "Desplanó las scripturas et amostró por ellas abiertamente que las palabras de la ley que entendían las gentes por los vienes tenporales, que tanbién se entendían por ellas los bienes spirituales" ("He explained the scriptures and through them demonstrated plainly that the words of the law, which the people took to refer to temporal goods, could also be understood as spiritual goods"; 141). This serves as a reminder that the practice of commentary can be considered an imitation of Christ's virtue, aspirational behaviour for medieval Christians.[15] Julio thus not only makes visible his activities as a commentator, but also posits them as spiritually beneficial for both the commentator and his audience.

Julio's exegetical methods are on display in chapters 38 to 41 of book 1, in which he narrates Adam and Eve's expulsion from Paradise (Gen. 2–3). These chapters strike the modern reader as repetitive, but when read as commentary, they take shape as an example of the fourfold method of exegesis adapted to suit the fictional dialogue between Julio and Prince Johás. The chapter divisions do not correspond to the different senses of scripture because they were introduced later and do not follow the work's internal structure (Funes, "Capitulación" and "Sobre la partición"). Chapter 38 focuses on the literal sense, narrating Eve's encounter with the serpent, Adam and Eve's sin, and God's punishment of their disobedience with mortality and suffering. Julio pauses occasionally to clarify elements at the literal level: for instance, he explains that Eve lied about God's command not to eat from the Tree of the Knowledge of Good and Evil by adding an additional command not to touch the tree ("començó a mentir la muger [cuando ...] dixo que Dios les mandara que non tanxiesen aquel árbol"; 128).[16] Chapters 39 and 40 address the moral sense (how Adam and Eve's actions constitute sins), as well as the allegorical sense (how Eve's disobedience to God prefigures Mary's obedience in accepting her miraculous pregnancy). Finally, chapters 40 and 41 elucidate the anagogical sense in which original sin will be resolved for all of humanity: "Et porque al omne fue dada sentençia que muriese, que por la muerte que Jhesu Christo tomó en la cruz por redemir los pecadores, fuesen librados de la muerte" ("And because man was sentenced to die, Jesus Christ underwent death on the cross to redeem sinners and free them from death"; 136). Each time Julio returns to the story's events, he adds another level of exegesis, following the fourfold method roughly in order from literal, to moral and allegorical, to anagogical. If we view this repetition of content as successive levels of commentary, it acquires rhetorical significance as a strategy to initiate the novice reader or listener (Prince Johás, who stands in for Juan Manuel's lay audience) into biblical interpretation.

While Julio's commentary is informed by the fourfold method of scriptural exegesis, its *mise en page* does not imitate the page layout of biblical commentaries. In the twelfth and thirteenth centuries, writers of Latin commentaries had developed complex page layouts that served to separate text from gloss, identify *auctores*, and aid readers in finding information efficiently (Parkes, "Influence"; Rouse and Rouse 198–9). The *Glossa ordinaria*, the standard Bible commentary from this period, adopted a characteristic layout that was reproduced from copy to copy with few variations (see fig. 3.3). In Jesús Rodríguez Velasco's words, "crear un manuscrito glosado es una obra de ingeniería" ("making a glossed manuscript is a feat of engineering"; "Producción" 252). However, the scribe or scribes of *S* use no visual strategies to separate the biblical text from Julio's gloss. They use other organizational tools, such as the chapter rubrics, but as mentioned above, these were added later and thus do not correspond to the different senses of scripture. Rather, the biblical story and its commentary flow together on the page, organized by the simple strategy of repetition (see fig. 3.4). Each time Julio expounds a new spiritual sense of the Adam and Eve story, he begins by repeating the literal sense, reminding the prince – and the reader – of the links between different levels of meaning.

This absence of a more complex *mise en page* suggests the adaptation of commentary for a lay audience more likely to hear the book read aloud. As Ian R. Macpherson observes, "such features as repetition of formulae, words, phrases and sentence patterns are typical of Don Juan's literary style, and ideally designed for a form of presentation in which the listener, unlike the private reader, has no opportunity to turn back the pages in order to remind himself of earlier events" (*Juan Manuel* xxxiv–xxxv). But commentary without a compartmentalized *mise en page* is not unique to Juan Manuel and can be found in other contemporary vernacular works. For example, while some manuscripts of the mid-fourteenth-century *Glosa castellana al Regimiento de príncipes* prepared by Juan García de Castrojeriz used layout to distinguish text from commentary, others simply presented the two in sequence.[17] What is noteworthy about the *Libro de los estados* is that the simple page layout also responds to the work's plot. Its narrative frame, a conversation between Julio and Prince Johás, emphasizes orality as the primary mode of instruction. While the work self-consciously acknowledges the recording of this conversation in written form at the end of book 1, orality nonetheless remains the dominant mode until the introduction of an obscure writing style in book 2 (discussed below).[18] It is therefore logical that the makers of *S* – and, possibly, its antigraphs – would eschew the complex *mise en page* of a scholarly commentary for a simpler layout, which not only facilitates access for a noble audience experiencing the work aurally, but also plays into the fiction of orality that the plot demands. The case of the *Libro de los estados* indicates that authors and their associates do not always imitate the most prestigious forms available, but make decisions based on a variety of factors, thereby complicating narratives of literary imitation and the transfer of authority.

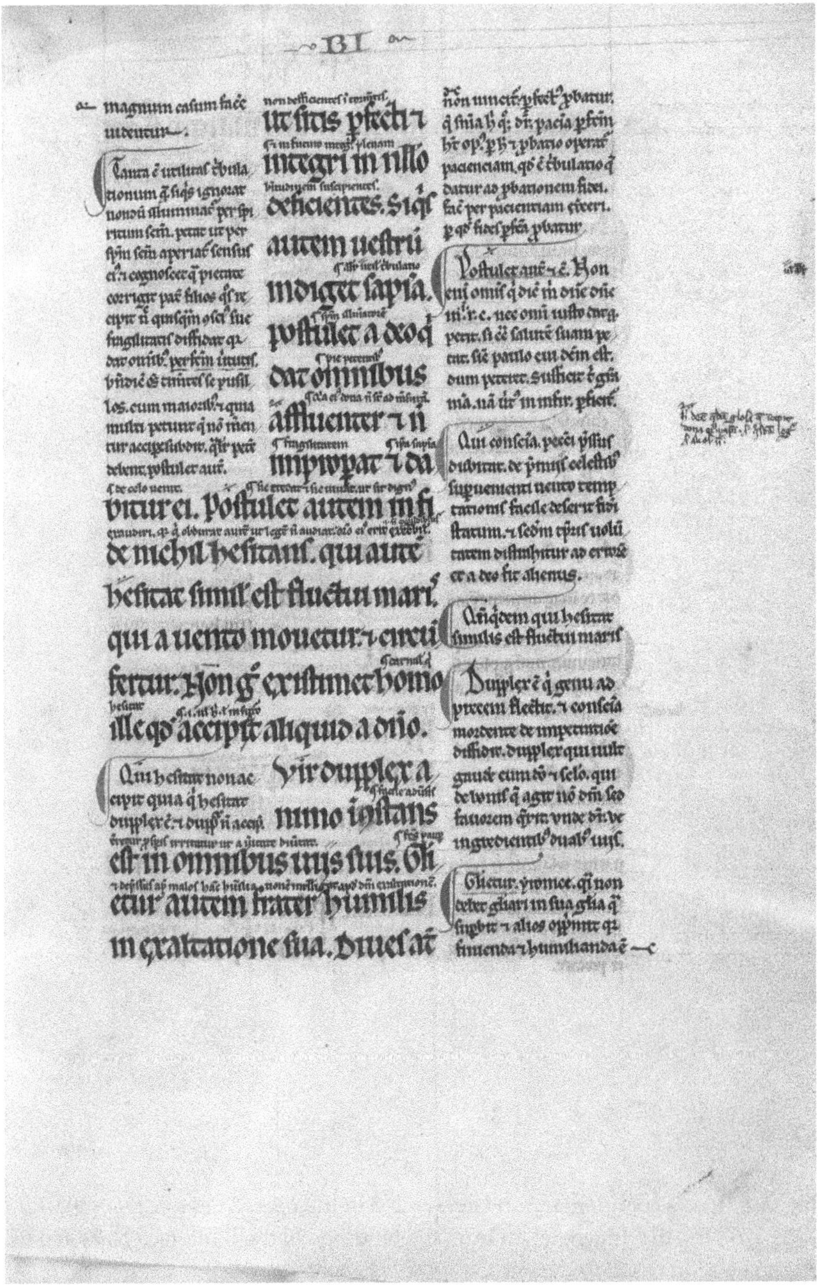

Fig. 3.3. A thirteenth-century Bible with the standard *Glossa ordinaria*. Free Library of Philadelphia, Lewis E 45, fol. 2r.

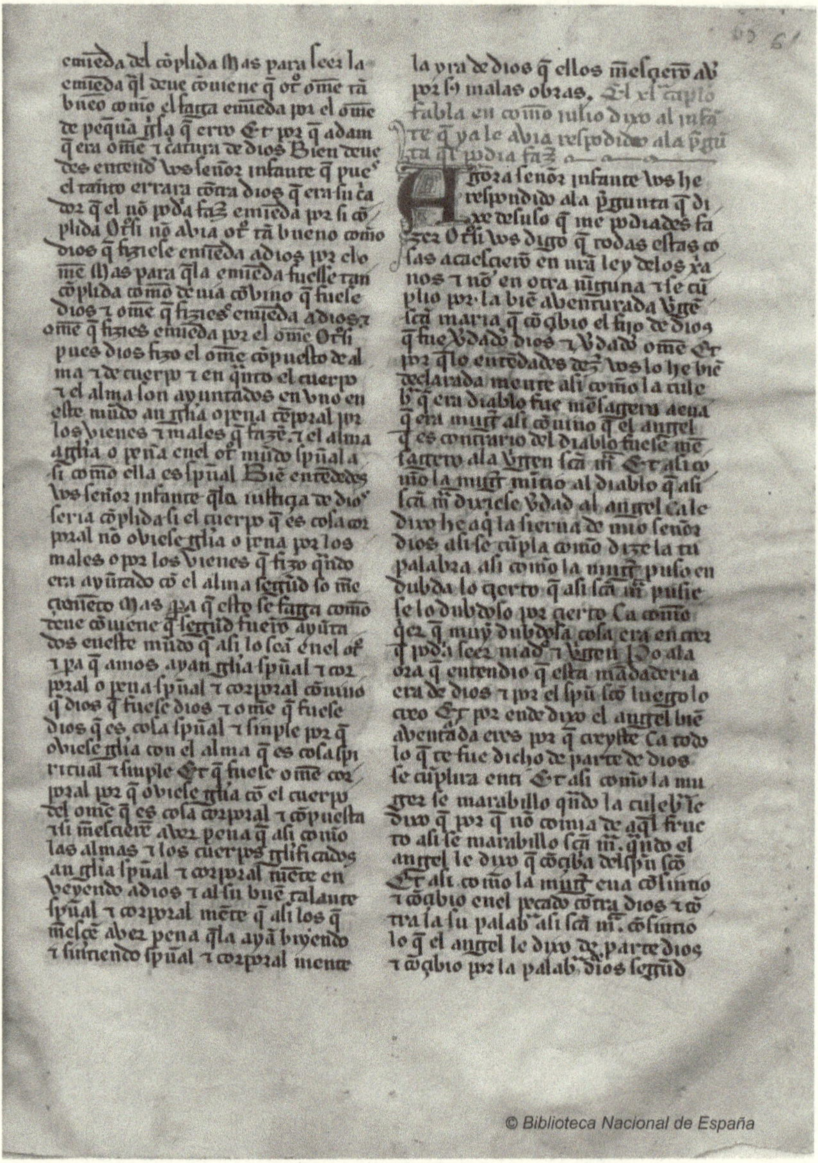

Fig. 3.4. Julio's commentary on Genesis 2–3 in the *Libro de los estados*. *S* (BNE, MS 6376), fol. 61r. Image taken from the holdings of the Biblioteca Nacional de España and licensed under the CC by 4.0 licence.

Julio's exposition of Christian doctrine is so successful that it leads to the swift conversion to Christianity of Prince Johás, the prince's tutor Turín, his father King Morabán, and all the kingdom's subjects. In the remainder of book 1, Julio explains the duties of various members of the lay estates (*bellatores* and *laboratores*), with a special focus on the responsibilities of emperors, Prince Johás's future role. Given the prince's desire for encyclopedic knowledge, Julio is obligated in book 2 to explain the duties of the religious estates (*oratores*), thus completing the panorama of medieval society. But this religious subject matter, particularly the section on religious disputation, necessitates more caution on Julio's part. This portion of the *Libro de los estados* is an example of vernacular theology, a vernacular work for a lay audience that seeks to explore and articulate mysteries of faith (Gillespie, "Vernacular Theology"). Throughout Christian Europe in the later Middle Ages, works of vernacular theology that addressed topics beyond the most basic points of doctrine were held in suspicion and sometimes prohibited outright. This stemmed from a concern that laypeople might accidentally stray from orthodox doctrine or, worse, be persuaded by the arguments of unbelievers or heretics.[19]

In the prologue to book 2, Don Juan, the author figure, acknowledges the challenge of tackling theological topics: "Porque fablar en los estados de la clerezía es ý muy mayor mester el saber, entiendo que es aún mayor atrevimiento que el primero" ("Because speaking about the estates of the clergy requires much more knowledge, I understand it to be a far more daring endeavour than the first [part of the book]"; 296–7). He forges ahead with his vernacular theology, but not without establishing several rhetorical safeguards. First, he submits his work to the correction of Infante Juan of Aragón, who now holds the title of patriarch of Alexandria; second, he affirms his orthodoxy and good intentions; and finally, he appeals to the good judgment of the reader. These rhetorical strategies serve to authorize Don Juan to write about vernacular theology despite his lay status. The theological subject matter in book 2 also takes the form of a commentary, but with a peculiar style that reflects this heightened concern.

At the intradiegetic level of the narrative, Julio dispenses with the usual *captatio benevolentiae* in his opening remarks: "Porque yo muchas vezes me quis escusar de vos responder a otras preguntas que me feziestes et non me tovo pro, ante vos ove después a responder, por ende non quiero agora començar a escusarme" ("Because I tried many times to excuse myself from answering your other questions to no effect, only to answer eventually anyway, this time I will not even begin to excuse myself"; 299). However, when instructing the prince in religious disputation, one of the clergy's main duties, he announces that he will proceed using a "manera estraña de escrivir" ("strange way of writing") that he calls "letras escuras" or "letras estrañas" ("obscure letters" or "strange letters"; 307–16). In *S*, there are three lacunae in II.4, II.5, and II.7 (folios 105v, 106v–107r, and 108r) where he indicates the *letras escuras* should be. I accept Barry Taylor's hypothesis that these strange letters were a code or cipher in an earlier version of the book that the scribe of *S* (or of a previous exemplar) decided to omit ("Juan Manuel's Cipher"). Elsewhere I have argued that Julio's cipher serves a double purpose: it projects an image of compliance with restrictions on religious disputation in the vernacular, while simultaneously arguing that some laypeople have the requisite understanding to participate in theological debates (Savo, "Hidden Polemic"). This was characteristic of many works of vernacular theology, which were obligated to defend their project against the concerns of the clergy. As Nicholas Watson puts it, "writing about religion in the vernacular is a political act; [...] because this is so, all vernacular writing about religion is *connected*, part of a single field or arena of discourse" ("Cultural Changes" 130; emphasis in original). For my purposes here, I will demonstrate how Juan Manuel navigates the tension that arises from combining commentary with vernacular theology, portraying Julio – and, by extension, himself – as a capable mediator between text and reader.

The passages in *letras escuras* deal with three paradoxes of Christian doctrine that were commonly disputed among Jewish, Christian, and Muslim scholars: first, whether the tenets of the faith can be proven using reason; second, whether God can be said to have a face; and third, whether Christ was both fully human and fully divine. Julio affirms that all of Christian doctrine is written in the Bible ("los dichos de la santa Escritura") and clarified in the teachings of the Church Doctors ("los dichos de los santos ductores que fueron de santa Eglesia"; 301). But because these three topics are paradoxes, they require someone to explain them *declaradamente* (clearly) and *llanamente* (plainly). Julio presents himself as not only capable of providing the necessary commentary, but aware of the need to couch it in *letras escuras*:

> Estas cosas en que los que lo non pudiesen entender podrían tomar alguna dubda, por mengua de los sus entendimientos, estas tales cosas quiérolas yo poner por letras tan escuras que los que non fueren muy sotiles non las puedan entender. Et quando viniere alguno que aya entendimiento para lo leer, só çierto que abrá entendimiento para lo entender, et plazerle á por

> lo que fallará escripto, et aprovecharse á dello; et el que lo non entendiere, non podrá caer en dubda por lo que leyere, pues non lo pudiere leer por escuridat de las letras. Et aun he pensado que todo lo que pudiere dezir, fablando segund las maneras que se dizen en la santa Scriptura, segund es la verdad, en que ninguno non puede dubdar, que lo declararé por este nuestro romançe llanamente; et las cosas en que los que las non entendiesen podrían dubdar, non por la cosa que yo diría, mas por la mengua de lo non entender ellos, las tales cosas, scrivirlas he por la manera escura que vos ya dixi. [...] Et si alguno beyere este libro et non pudiere leer estas letras, si fuere omne a qui yo deva o pueda ir, enbíe por mí; et si fuere omne que deva venir a mí, fágalo si quisiere saber lo que las letras quieren dezir. (307)
>
> As for the things that might cause doubt for those who cannot comprehend them due to their lack of understanding, I wish to write them in letters so obscure that those who are not very subtle cannot understand them. And when someone comes along with the understanding to read the letters, I am certain that he will also have the ability to understand [their meaning], and will be pleased with what he finds written and benefit from it. And whoever does not understand will not fall into doubt on account of what he reads, since he will not be able to read the letters on account of their obscurity. Furthermore, I have decided that whatever I can say in the way it is expressed in Holy Scripture, which is the truth that no one can doubt, I will say plainly in our Romance. And whatever might cause doubt for those who do not understand, not because of how I say it but because of their lack of understanding, I will write in the obscure manner I told you about. [...] And if someone should read this book without being able to read the letters and wishes to know what they say, if it is someone I should go to, let him summon me; and if it is someone who should come to me, let him come.

Julio thus divides his theological subject matter into two categories. The first can be expressed openly in the Castilian vernacular because of its close correspondence to the Bible (*fablando segund las maneras que se dizen en la santa Escritura*), while the second must be encoded to protect undiscerning lay readers from falling into doubt. Commentaries in late medieval Castile typically aimed to resolve doubts; for example, the purpose of Pero Díaz de Toledo's translation and commentary of Plato's *Phaedo* was "to set readers right on points of doctrine where Plato's text seems to run counter to Christian teaching" (Round 126–7). But the discourse of commentary in the *Libro de los estados*, with its emphasis on providing clarity and resolving doubt, clashes with the discourse of vernacular theology, whose defensive stance demands a certain measure of obscurity.

Juan Manuel attempts to resolve this tension through two innovations to the commentary form. First, although commentary is written for purposes of clarification, it does not necessarily need to be written in a clear style. If the subject matter is problematic, the commentator can adopt an obscure style, restricting access to readers with a higher level of training. A precedent for this can be found in Martín Pérez's *Libro de las confesiones* (c. 1316), a confession manual for parish priests. While most of the work is in Castilian, the author switches to Latin for potentially dangerous topics: "Porque non se deven todas las cosas que sobre esto dizen [los doctores de la Iglesia] poner en romançe, ca sería grand peligro, ponerlas hemos en latín e entiéndalas quien las pudiere entender" ("Because not everything [the Church Doctors] say about this should be put into Romance on account of the danger it would entail, we will put some things in Latin and let whoever can understand them do so"; 675).[20] In this case, the passage in Latin advises priests on how to deal with men who give fraudulent marriage vows in order to seduce women, so the danger is moral rather than theological. But the recognition that vernacular writing reaches a broader audience, and the rhetorical strategy of changing one's writing or language to restrict access to certain topics, are the same. Juan Manuel may have borrowed this strategy from the *Libro de las confesiones* or from similar works for a clerical audience. However, his choice of *letras escuras* rather than Latin indicates a desire to eschew the established binary of Latin for clerics and vernacular for laypeople in order to create a new community of readers.[21] Access to the *letras escuras* is not mediated by the Church or the schools, but by the one who invented the cipher. Thus, since the key to interpreting the *letras escuras* resides with Julio, who is best understood here as a double of Don Juan, this rhetorical move gives Don Juan a unique "enunciative and interpretive power" separate from clerical forms of authority (Biaggini, "Énonciation" 36).

This brings us to Juan Manuel's second innovation: creating the fiction of an extratextual step necessary to crack the code and understand the commentary. In the passage quoted above, Julio informs both the prince and the book's readers that he himself is the key to deciphering the *letras escuras*. Readers should either send for Julio or seek him out (depending on their social station) so that he can teach them what the letters mean (*lo que las letras quieren dezir*). This introduces an element of orality – a face-to-face interaction – into a passage otherwise dominated by writing and textuality. Given the parallel between the fictional Julio and the authorial persona Don Juan, this suggests that the book's commentary overflows the confines of the page and seeps into the reader's world. With Francisco Bautista, I see this strategy as a way for Don Juan to claim that the most complete gloss of the work lies with its author (11–12). However, while Bautista calls this a moment of self-commentary (*auto-comentario*), I understand it as a gloss on the three paradoxes of Christian doctrine enumerated above (the material purportedly written in *letras escuras*). The result is a rhetorical hide-and-seek in which Don Juan appears to hold the answers to the paradoxes without ever giving a full, satisfactory explanation. If he could persuade readers that he not only understands these mysteries, but could, in some hypothetical face-to-face encounter, explain them clearly, he would have to be considered one of the greatest Christian theologians of his day.

Because Don Juan persistently reminds readers of his lay status, it would seem that his aim is not so extreme. Rather, by merging with Julio in book 2 of the *Libro de los estados*, he assumes responsibility for a form of exegesis specific to vernacular theology. Julio has demonstrated his abilities as a commentator capable of producing biblical exegesis and explaining difficult points of doctrine in a clear, comprehensible style. He has also shown his awareness of the risks of vernacular theology and has proven himself capable of mitigating those risks using a variety of discursive strategies. In book 1, Don Juan's presence as Julio's friend and confidant symbolizes lay knowledge, the complement to Julio's religious expertise. However, by the end of book 2, readers cannot help but attribute Julio's *tour de force* of commentarial writing to Don Juan himself.

A similar strategy can be found in the *Conde Lucanor*, in which Patronio's exegetical talents ultimately reflect back onto Don Juan. In both its one-part and five-part versions, it is first and foremost a work about interpretation. In part 1, the *Libro de los enxiemplos*, Patronio's aim is to teach Count Lucanor how to interpret exempla: exemplary tales designed to entertain and teach at the same time. In parts 2–4, the *Libro de los proverbios*, Patronio challenges Lucanor to extract meaning from succinct and obscure aphorisms and, in the case of part 4, unscramble their syntax as well. Although part 5, the *Libro de la doctrina*, expounds Christian doctrine in a straightforward style that contrasts with the obscurity of parts 2–4, Patronio alludes to the difficulty of explaining spiritual matters (*cosas espirituales*) in a way that goes beyond the blind faith of simple Christians, exemplified by "la vegizuela que está filando a su puerta al sol" ("the old woman spinning thread in her doorway in the sun"; 251). Each of the three "books" of the *Conde Lucanor* borrows from the discourse of commentary in different ways, ostensibly to instruct readers in different types of interpretation. But this also provides benefits for Don Juan, who appropriates the authority of commentary and proves himself a capable commentator of subjects ranging from secular ethics to Christian doctrine.

Don Juan himself, looking back on the completed part 1, assesses its subject matter (*materia* or material cause) as radically different from "teología o metafísica o filosofía natural o aun moral o otras sciencias muy sotiles" ("theology, metaphysics, natural or even moral philosophy, or any other very subtle sciences"; 215). However, this does not prevent him from adapting a commentarial style (*modus agendi* or formal cause) from the discipline of theology. Part 1 of the *Conde Lucanor*, the *Libro de los enxiemplos*, can be understood as a commentary keyed to a base text, with the exempla serving as base text, and Patronio's interpretations and Don Juan's *viessos* serving as commentary. But while biblical commentaries ultimately sought to establish God's truth, the primary function of commentary here is to show readers how to deploy the rhetorical strategies of commentary themselves. As Jonathan Burgoyne argues, the hermeneutical efforts of Patronio and Don Juan primarily serve to teach the reader not a set of specific lessons, but how to deploy these narrative strategies for their own ethical purposes and needs:

> The [*Conde Lucanor*] can be read as a work that teaches the reader how to adopt Juan Manuel's appropriation of the authority associated with the *exemplum* for individual needs and ethical choices. In this way, by providing the reader with a rhetorical strategy that makes use of *exempla*, Juan Manuel's book does indeed aid its readers in performing "such deeds as would be advantageous to their honor, their possessions, and their stations," as well as actions that, if authorized by an illustrative narrative, will benefit their souls. (*Reading the Exemplum* 60)

Moreover, Burgoyne acknowledges that since the exemplum as a narrative strategy is associated with Church doctrine, Juan Manuel, "as the author of the tales, and the inscribed author of the *viessos* that sanction each story, [...] draws the moral authority materialized in the *exemplum* toward himself, and becomes an authority (*auctor*) on Church doctrine as it pertains to princes" (*Reading the Exemplum* 104).[22]

Most of the *enxiemplos*, or chapters, of part 1 adapt the religious authority of commentary to a secular context. When interpreting the exempla, Patronio usually makes the case that the best way for a nobleman like Count Lucanor to achieve spiritual salvation is through actions befitting his estate, such as waging war against Muslims. As Macpherson explains in his classic study of the *Conde Lucanor*'s didacticism, "[Juan Manuel] argues the Thomist case for self-love, that a man has to be what he is, which is what God has made him. If he is born into the world in the *estado* of aristocrat and soldier, it is his duty to himself, to his dependents, his associates and his God, to be a successful aristocrat and soldier" ("Dios y el mundo" 37). One *enxiemplo*, however, foregrounds a more theological form of commentary.

Ex. 48, the story of the half-friend and the full friend, borrows explicitly from the fourfold method of scriptural exegesis, as Pablo Adrián Cavallero has demonstrated. In this popular tale, a father challenges his son to prove the loyalty of his friends in a situation of dire need.[23] The young man shows up on his friends' doorsteps with a slaughtered pig in a sack, pretending to seek assistance in covering up a murder. When none of them will help, his father says they are not true friends, and to try the same trick on the father's half-friend (*medio amigo*). The half-friend agrees to conceal the body and keep it a secret, even after the son tests him further by picking a fight and assaulting him. The son then tests the father's full friend (*amigo complido*), who not only agrees to protect the young man, but, when faced with a real murder accusation, sacrifices his own son, who dies in the young man's place. Patronio first gives a literal interpretation about distinguishing between true friends (*buenos amigos*) and fair-weather friends (*amigos de la ventura*). He then announces that "este enxienplo se puede entender *espiritualmente* en esta manera" ("this exemplum can be understood *spiritually* in this way"; 188; my emphasis), using the exegetical term for the spiritual meaning of scripture. He proceeds to gloss various characters: the young man is likened to the sinner at the moment of his death; his own friends are the laypeople and churchmen who cannot do much to save one's soul; his father's *medio amigo* represents Mary and the saints, who intervene on the sinner's behalf; and the *amigo complido* is God, who sacrifices his only Son to redeem the sinner. Don Juan's *viessos* also refer to the tale's allegorical interpretation: "Nunca omne podría tan buen amigo fallar/commo Dios, que lo quiso por su sangre comprar" ("Man could never find a better friend/than God, who redeemed him with His own blood"; 190). For Cavallero, Juan Manuel's creative reimagining of source materials demonstrates his deft application of biblical exegesis to a new narrative situation, placing the tale and its commentary "en mutua relación de interacción e interdependencia" ("in a mutual relation of interaction and interdependence"; 118). In this case, the rhetoric of biblical exegesis not only shapes the commentaries of Patronio and Don Juan, but also informs the narration of the tale itself. The imitation of biblical commentary in ex. 48 might seem like an outlier in the context of the *Conde Lucanor*, but when seen alongside other instances in the

Crónica abreviada and *Libro de los estados*, it emerges as a significant part of Don Juan's narrative repertoire.

Part 1 of the *Conde Lucanor* is also Juan Manuel's most complex work from the perspective of layout and textual divisions (*divisio textus*). All five manuscripts (*S*, *M*, *P*, *H*, and *G*), as well as Gonzalo Argote de Molina's 1575 print edition, use rubrics, line breaks, and/or decorated initials to demarcate each new *enxiemplo*, the larger narrative unit that encompasses both Patronio's exemplum and its surrounding narrative and exegetical elements. The spaces left for miniatures in *S* also help to divide the text into discrete *enxiemplos*.[24] David Wacks proposes that the structure of the *Conde Lucanor* "owes much to the encyclopedic organization of *exempla* authored by Dominicans" (*Framing Iberia* 145). But is its structure specifically indebted to the *mise en page* of commentary? In other words, does the layout of the *Libro de los enxiemplos* serve to separate the "base text" of Patronio's exempla from the "commentary" represented by the interpretations of Patronio and Don Juan?

As Burgoyne has shown, the fifteenth- and sixteenth-century manuscripts of the *Libro de los enxiemplos* provide evidence of "fragmentary medieval reading practices" that separate, highlight, and recombine the component parts of the different *enxiemplos* ("Reading to Pieces" 245). The divisions in manuscripts *S* and *H* provide the least evidence of a base text/commentary relationship. They mark all sentence-level breaks, including those that begin Patronio's exempla and exegesis, in the same way: *S* with a swipe of yellow ink over the first initial, and *H* with red paragraph marks.[25] Thus, the start of Patronio's "commentary" is marked, but not in a way that distinguishes it from any ordinary sentence-level break. Neither are Don Juan's *viessos* set apart in any special way (see fig. 3.5). However, the other manuscripts do use visual strategies to separate text from commentary. While *P* does not distinguish the verses with line breaks, it does use red paragraph marks consistently to mark where they begin, as well as where Patronio's interpretations begin. It uses them for other paragraph-level breaks as well, but they are less frequent than the ones in *H*, making them more effective dividers between each exemplum and its gloss. *G* does not mark Patronio's interpretations but sets the verses apart with line breaks (see fig. 3.6).

M does the most to establish a base text/commentary relationship: it uses marginal notes in red to mark each narrative unit as a *capítulo* and Patronio's tales as *enxenplos*, while Don Juan's *viessos* are framed with line breaks and marked with red flourishes (see fig. 3.7). Burgoyne sees these visual dividers as "evidence of an educated reading process that recognized a rhetorically discursive structure in the text," a structure modelled after commentary ("Reading to Pieces" 243). Burgoyne reads

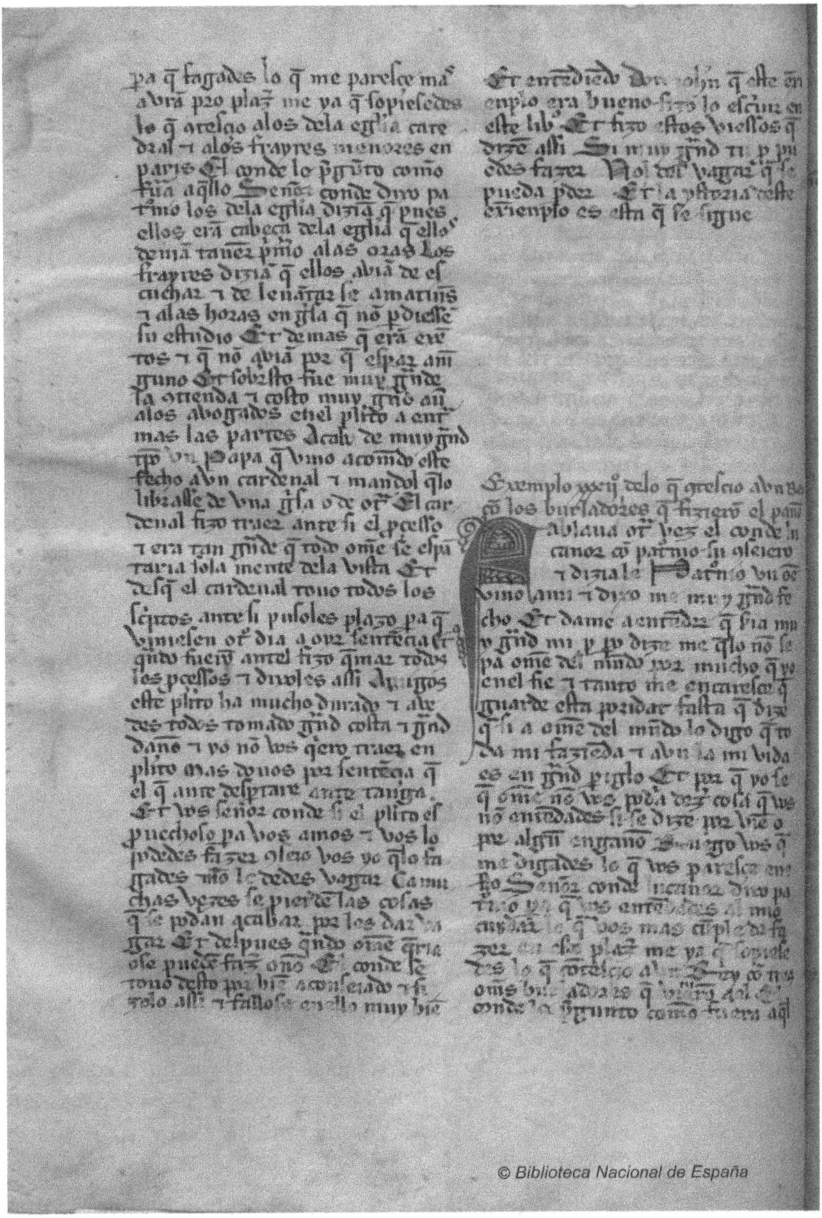

Fig. 3.5. *Viessos* for ex. 31 of the *Conde Lucanor*, MS *S* (BNE, MS 6376), fol. 157v, col. b. Image taken from the holdings of the Biblioteca Nacional de España and licensed under the CC by 4.0 licence.

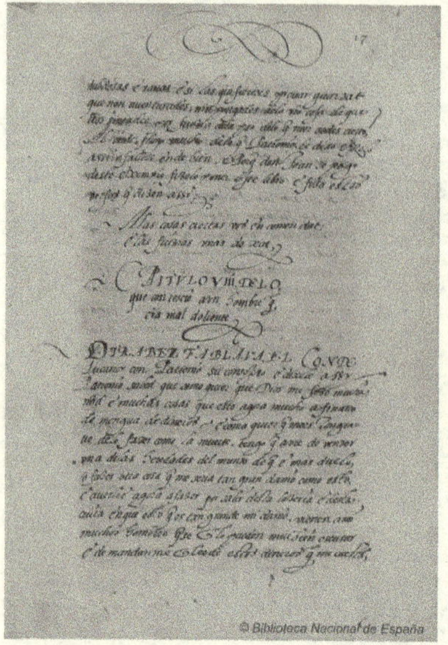

Fig. 3.6. *Viessos* for ex. 7 of the *Conde Lucanor*, MS *G* (BNE, MS 18415), fol. 17r. Image taken from the holdings of the Biblioteca Nacional de España and licensed under the CC by 4.0 licence.

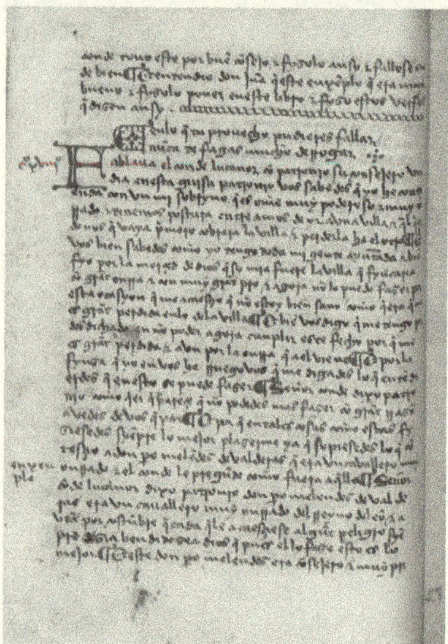

Fig. 3.7. *Viessos* for ex. 17 of the *Conde Lucanor*, MS *M* (BNE, MS 4236), fol. 27v. Image taken from the holdings of the Biblioteca Nacional de España and licensed under the CC by 4.0 licence.

N (BNE, MS 19426), the compilation of selected Manueline works that extracts the *viessos* from part 1, as further evidence of this fragmentary reading, showing how "the scribe could have conveniently scanned his exemplar for Don Juan's anticipated reappearance to locate the desired 'proueruios'" ("Reading to Pieces" 251).

Argote de Molina's 1575 edition also marks internal divisions between text and gloss. In addition to using line breaks for Don Juan's verses, it almost always labels the exempla with the rubric *historia* and marks Patronio's interpretations with a fleuron (see fig. 3.8). In chapters 4, 32, and 38, Patronio's glosses are further highlighted with the rubric *aplicación*.[26] These rubrics were most likely added by the printer, Hernando Díaz (Lacarra, "*El conde*" 235). While they do preserve the separation between text and gloss in the chapters where they appear, the term *aplicación* moves away from the semantic field of biblical exegesis, evoking the practical application of moral advice. Overall, the internal divisions in the early copies of part 1 vary widely from version to version, making it impossible to determine whether Juan Manuel arranged for any particular layout. Nevertheless, his use of repetitive, formulaic language in the text served as a guide for scribes and rubricators, creating some measure of consistency (Burgoyne, *Reading the Exemplum* 37).

The objection might be raised that the separation of Don Juan's *viessos* imitates not biblical commentary, but rather the layout of ancient fable collections in which each exemplary tale was followed by a

LVCANOR. 45

plazermeya que ſupieſſedes lo q̃ conteſcio a los dela yglesia chatredal & a los frayles menores en París. Y el conde le pregunto, como fuera aquello.

HISTORIA.

SEñor conde dixo Patronio, los dela yglesia dezian que pues ellos eran cabeça dela yglesia, que ellos deuian tañer primero a las horas, & los frayles dezian, que ellos auian de eſtudiar & leuantarſe a maytines & a las horas, en guiſa que non perdieſſen ſu eſtudio, & de mas que erã eſſemptos è non auia porque eſperar a ninguno. Y ſobre eſto fue muy grande la contienda, & coſto muy grande auer los aduogados & los pleytos a entramas las partes, è duro muy grande tiempo el pleyto enla corte del Papa & a cabo de gran tiempo vn Papa que vino acomendo, eſte pleyto a vn Cardenal, & mandole que lo libraſſe de vna guiſa o de otra. Y el cardenal fizo traer ante ſi el proceſſo que era tan grande que todo hombre ſe eſpantaria dela viſta. Y deſpues que el cardenal tuuo ante ſi todas las eſcripturas, puſoles plazo para q̃ vinieſſen otro dia a oyr ſentencia. & quando fuerõ ante el, fizo quemar todos los proceſſos, & dixoles aſſi. Amigos eſte pleyto ha mucho durado & auedes tomado grande coſa & gran daño, è yo non vos quiero traer a pleyto, mas do vos por ſentencia que el que antes deſpertare antes tanga.

❧ E vos ſeñor cõde Lucanor, ſi el pleyto es prouechoſo pa amos è vos lo podedes fazer, conſejo vos q̃ lo fagades, & nõ le dedes vagar, ca muchas vezes ſe pierdẽ las coſas q̃ ſe podrian acabar por les dar vagar, & deſpues quãdo hõbre querria, o ſe puede fazer o no. Y el conde ſe tuuo deſto por bien conſejado, & fizolo aſſi & falloſe ende biẽ. Y entendio don Ioan que eſte exemplo era bueno, & fizo eſtos verſos que dizen aſſi.

❧ Si muy gran tu pro pudieres fazer
non le des vagar que ſe pueda perder.

CAPI-

Fig. 3.8. *Viessos* for ch. 20 of Argote de Molina's edition. *El conde Lucanor* (1575), fol. 45r.

corresponding moral in verse known as an *epimythium* (or *promythium*, if it preceded the tale). However, medieval European versions of this layout, such as collections of Aesop's fables, are not attested until the fourteenth and fifteenth centuries (B. Taylor, "*Estoria*" 42). Taylor concludes that the *Conde Lucanor* participated in a larger fourteenth-century trend of combining exempla and distichs, without making any claims of precedence or influence (47). Because there is concrete evidence that Juan Manuel was familiar with biblical exegesis, I see no reason to exclude commentary as a possible model for the textual divisions of the *Libro de los enxiemplos*. Given his eclectic interests and penchant for syncretism, it is plausible that he took inspiration from both commentaries and fable collections, combining their strategies to create a *divisio textus* that suited his needs, and that subsequent copyists could adapt to new contexts.

While part 1, the *Libro de los enxiemplos*, presents both text and commentary in relation to one another, parts 2–4, the *Libro de los proverbios*, provide a base text without a commentary. Appearing only in manuscripts *S* and *G*, these three sets of proverbs give practical and moral advice in a famously succinct and obscure style ("más abreviado et más oscuro"; 231). There are some differences in the types of maxims that dominate each part, but Patronio refers to them all as *proverbios* whose interpretation requires a sharp intellect ("buen entendimiento"; 216).[27] In the prologue to part 2, Don Juan explains that this change in style was suggested by his close friend, Jaime de Jérica, who is "tan sotil et tan de buen entendimiento, que tiene por mengua de sabiduría fablar en las cosas muy llana et declaradamente" ("so subtle and of such a sharp intellect, that he considers it a lack of wisdom to speak of things plainly and clearly"; 214–15). He also playfully invites readers frustrated by the text's impenetrability to blame Jaime, as well as their own deficiencies: "Et los que non las entendieren [las palabras], non pongan la culpa a mí [...] mas pónganla a don Jayme, que me lo fizo así fazer, et a ellos, porque lo non pueden o non quieren entender" ("As for those who cannot understand [the words], they should blame not me but Don Jaime, who made me do it this way, and themselves, for being unable or unwilling to understand"; 216). While there is no reason to doubt the historical accuracy of Juan Manuel's friendship with Jaime de Jérica (B. Taylor, "Don Jaime" 44–5), I concur with Scholberg ("Modestia" 25) and Marta Ana Diz (151) in reading his invocation here as a rhetorical justification for writing a deliberately obscure text.

While scholars disagree about whether this obscure style was inspired by wisdom literature (Orduna, "Fablar") or by formal rhetorical studies (Cherchi; Diz; Serés, "Procedimientos"), they agree that it serves to call attention to the author's command of complex language. For Orduna, parts 2–4 paint a verbal portrait of Don Juan as an intellectual who bedecks his work in "el ropaje propio del decir del hombre sabio" ("clothing befitting the words of sages") and demonstrates a rhetorical prowess that outstrips the unadorned speech of popular preachers ("Fablar" 145). But for this portrait to be persuasive, readers must believe not only that explications of the proverbs are possible, but also that the author has crafted each proverb with at least one possible interpretation in mind. Medieval readers were trained to think this way, since, as de Looze observes, "everything in a medieval reader's formation, beginning with the simplest of Latin sentences, would have taught that if one studied a passage long enough, one could puzzle it out" (229). Furthermore, in the medieval *accessus* paradigm, one of the questions that students asked of a work in order to understand it better was what the author intended (see ch. 2).

I propose that we can understand the proverbs of parts 2–4 as a base text in need of commentary. This contradicts Diz's assertion that they represent a continuation of the exegesis provided by Patronio and Don Juan in part 1: "Los libros de sentencias [...] representan una suerte de lectura que glosa y 'traduce' los múltiples mensajes derivables de los relatos incluidos en el libro primero" ("The books of proverbs [...] represent a way of reading that glosses and 'translates' the multiple meanings derivable from the stories of part 1"; 124). In interpreting Patronio/Don Juan as the proverbs' Barthesian "final signified," the ideal receptacle of their meaning, I am also out of step with Paolo Cherchi, de Looze (185–237), and Heather Bamford ("Meaning"), who set aside the issue of authorial intent to explore the myriad other ways in which readers can make meaning from the proverbs (or, as Bamford proposes, fail to make sense of them at all). However, I am in line with their overall assessment of the proverbs as texts that require the reader's active engagement, whether through analysis of their meaning, syntax, and sonority; the "ethical reading" proposed by John Dagenais; a combination of multiple ways of reading; or an acceptance of their lack of meaning. The proverbs, like any text, can be read in many ways, and the manuscripts attest to these diverse ways of reading. But the paratexts guide readers towards a commentarial mode of reading centred around the figure of Patronio, who promises an authoritative self-exegesis.

The paratexts related to the *Libro de los proverbios* – including Don Juan's prologue to part 2 and Patronio's discussion of the proverbs at the start of parts 2–5 – adopt the discourse of commentary by alluding to an exegesis of the proverbs located outside the text. As discussed above, Don Juan emphasizes the obscurity of the proverbs and the need to put in effort to understand them. Patronio echoes Don Juan in describing the *Libro de los proverbios* as "más abreviado et más oscuro" ("briefer and more obscure"; 241) than the *Libro de los enxiemplos*, but with profitable ethical content "para quien lo estudiare et lo entendiere" ("for whoever should study and understand it"; 242). In his preamble to part 4, Patronio warns Count Lucanor that to understand the upcoming set of proverbs, the most challenging one yet, "vos converná de aguzar el entendimiento" ("you would do well to sharpen your understanding"; 253). Finally, in a key moment in the prologue to part 5, Patronio looks back on the proverbs of part 4 and assesses the difficulty of interpreting them:

> Por afincamiento que me feziestes ove de poner en estos postremeros treinta proverbios, algunos tan oscuramente, que será marabilla si bien los pudierdes entender, si yo o alguno de aquellos a qui los yo mostré non vos los declarare; pero seet bien cierto que aquellos que parecen más oscuros o más sin razón que, desque los entendiéredes, que fallaredes que non son menos aprovechosos que cualesquier de los otros que son ligeros de entender. (249)

> Your insistence obliged me to write these last thirty proverbs, some of them so obscurely that it would be a marvel if you could understand them unless I, or someone to whom I have shown them, were to explain them to you. But be assured that, once you understand them, you will find even the ones that seem most obscure or senseless to be no less profitable than any of the others that are easy to understand.

Scholars typically cite this passage as evidence of the proverbs' obscurity, but when considered in light of commentarial writing, it takes on additional significance. Patronio offers the proverbs as a text in need of a gloss, and himself as the original commentator, the one all future exegetes will cite.

Laurence de Looze rightly identifies Patronio as a teacher and guide who "pushes Count Lucanor (and the reader) to figure out how to understand on his own as much as possible" (234). Yet specifying his role as that of a commentator reframes Patronio's exegesis not as a pedagogical experience, but as a discrete text, a commentary, located beyond the margins of the page and safeguarded in Patronio's memory.[28] This rhetorical move is very similar to the one used in the *Libro de los estados* to approach the subject of vernacular theology, when Julio promises to decipher his *letras escuras* to those readers who seek him out (307). The glosses are not recorded in writing, but rather exist in the "minds" of Julio and Patronio, the authoritative characters who profess to know them. As a result, their creator, Don Juan, is also cast in the role of commentator. The *Libro de los proverbios* thus brings recognition to its author not only for using an obscure style, but also for mastering an authorial role associated with the prestige of religious commentary.

The discourse of commentary in parts 2–4 of the *Conde Lucanor* bears a striking resemblance to Shem Tov de Carrión's *Proverbios morales*, a work that shares Juan Manuel's preoccupation with vernacular theology (Perry 167). The prologue, composed by an anonymous commentator and surviving in one of the five extant manuscripts, promises a commentary on Shem Tov's verses:

> Plaziendo a Dios, declararé algo en las trobas de Rabí Santob, el judío de Carrión, en algunas partes que paresçen escuras – aunque non son escuras, salvo por cuanto son trobas, e toda escritura rimada paresçe escura, e non lo es entrepatada: que por guardar los consonantes, algunas veses lo que ha de dezir después díselo antes. Et esto quiero trabajar en declarar, con el ayuda de Dios, para algunos que pueden ser que leerán e non entenderán sin que otri ge las declare, como algunas vezes lo he ya visto esto. (249)

> God willing, I will explain some of the verses of Rabbi Santob, the Jew from Carrión, in some parts where they seem unclear, although they are only unclear insofar as they are rhymes. All writing in rhyme seems unclear, but it isn't really once it's interpreted, because sometimes, to keep the rhyme, something usually said at the end is placed at the beginning. And this is what I will work to explain, with God's help, for those who might read this but won't understand unless someone else explains it to them, as I have sometimes seen.

Scholars believe the prologue's composer did write this commentary, but it does not survive. Sanford Shepard situates the prologue within the Jewish exegetical tradition, taking into account its treatment of biblical citations as well as its approach to Shem Tov's text (82, note to lines 77–85). Theodore Anthony Perry (177–8) and H. Tracy Sturcken (101) have also drawn comparisons between the obscurity of the *Proverbios morales* and that of the proverbs in parts 2–4 of the *Conde Lucanor*.[29] But the prologue quoted above also gives us clues as to the vocabulary of commentary in Castilian vernacular works, particularly in works that aspire to narrow the gap between theology and lay literature. The obscurity of the base text (*partes que paresçen escuras*), the gap between text and reader's understanding (*leerán e non entenderán*), and the crucial labour of the commentator in explaining the text (*quiero trabajar en declarar; non entenderán sin que otri ge las declare*) are very similar to the language Patronio uses to describe the relationship between the proverbs, Lucanor's comprehension, and Patronio's exegetical efforts. This provides further evidence that parts 2–4 of the *Conde Lucanor* deliberately evoke the discourse of commentary.

Compared to the first four parts of the *Conde Lucanor*, which apply a commentarial style to mainly secular subject matter, part 5 (the *Libro de la doctrina*) is the most explicitly doctrinal and theological. Patronio announces that it will deal with "las cosas espirituales, [que] son mejores et más nobles que las corporales" ("spiritual matters, which are better and more noble than corporal ones"; 250). One of the main topics addressed in part 5 is the need to do good deeds and avoid bad ones in order to attain salvation. This discussion is closely related to part 1, as indicated by the reappearance of the exemplum as a teaching tool. Patronio references two exempla from part 1: the tale of the seneschal of Carcassonne (ex. 40 in manuscript *S*), and the tale of the man who trusts in the Devil (ex. 45). He also narrates a new exemplum about a knight who accidentally kills both his father and his feudal lord in battle, to illustrate how a seemingly wicked action can be motivated by pure intentions.

The relatively few scholars who have offered interpretations of part 5 situate it in relation to the previous four parts. Gimeno Casalduero's initial comparison between the five-part *Conde Lucanor* and a Gothic cathedral, in which the work progressively draws the reader upwards from earthly to spiritual matters ("*Conde*"), has been successfully revised by Diz, who observes how earthly and spiritual concerns inform all three parts of the book (164–5). By reflecting on matters of birth, life, death, and the afterlife directly in part 5, Patronio invites us to see not just this section, but the entire work, as an all-encompassing metaphor of the individual as "lector y hermeneuta del texto de la realidad" ("reader and hermeneut of the text of reality"; Diz 165). De Looze comes to a similar conclusion, asserting that part 5 reframes the ethical content of parts 1–4 in a spiritual light, interpreting people's actions in the social world in terms of their significance for the afterlife (241–2). Finally, Cavallero notes the use of the word *figura* to talk about the relationship between the Old and New Testaments, showing another instance of Juan Manuel using the technical vocabulary of biblical exegesis (120).

In terms of style, part 5 returns to the straightforward prose of part 1, in contrast to the obscurity of parts 2–4 (Cherchi 373). Fernando Degiovanni demonstrates how it uses the rhetorical technique of *amplificatio* (the expansion of ideas) as defined in *artes praedicandi*, treatises written to instruct preachers on the rhetorical strategies used in sermons.[30] But while Degiovanni concludes that part 5 was written to imitate a sermon, this interpretation presents some minor difficulties. First, although sermons were often written down, they were designed to be delivered orally, whereas the five-part *Conde Lucanor* prioritizes textuality, as evidenced in the scrambled syntax of part 4's proverbs, Patronio's references to *este libro*, and part 5's references to exempla from part 1 (Diz 30). Second, Degiovanni cannot account for part 5's references to the *Libro de los estados* as part of *amplificatio*, asserting that this "cita extratextual lleva al límite el procedimiento amplificatorio al desbordar su tradicional metodología" ("extratextual citation takes the amplifying process to its limit, causing it to overflow beyond its traditional methodology"; 14). However, if we take part 5's *amplificatio* as a feature of commentary rather than sermons, these problems can be resolved. As Rita Copeland argues, the rhetorical strategies of the more oral and persuasive genres of oratory and sermon were absorbed into academic commentaries, where they could "exert a certain rhetorical power in their new exegetical environment, to transform commentary into a kind of praxis" (65). *Amplificatio*, in particular, was a technique shared in both preaching and written exegesis (Wenzel 88).

The examples adduced by Degiovanni to show Patronio's use of amplification apply just as easily to commentary. For instance, on the subject of good deeds, Patronio states: "Para que omne [...] aya la gloria de Paraíso, ha mester que se fagan [las buenas obras] en tres maneras: lo primero, que faga omne buena obra; lo segundo, que la faga bien; lo tercero, que la faga por escogimiento" ("To have glory in Paradise, one must do good deeds in three ways: first, they must be good deeds; second, they must be done well; third, they must be done by choice"; 260).

The statement's pithiness and the repetition of *buena/bien/fazer* obscure the meaning, so Patronio explains further:

> Fazer omne buena obra es toda cosa que omne faze por Dios, mas es mester que se faga bien; et esto es que se faga a buena entención, non por vanagloria nin por ipocrisía nin por otra entención, sinon solamente por servicio de Dios. Otrosí, que lo faga por escogimiento; esto es, que cuando oviere de fazer alguna obra, que escoja en su talante si es aquella buena obra o non; et desque viere que es buena obra, que escoja aquella porque es buena et dexe la otra que él entiende [...] que es mala. (260)

> Doing a good deed consists of everything one does for God, but it is necessary to do it well, which means with good intentions, not out of vainglory or hypocrisy or any other intention, but only in service to God. Moreover, one must do it by choice; that is, when about to act, one must decide willingly if the deed is good or not. If he deems it good, he should choose it because it is good, and avoid the alternative that he understands [...] to be bad.

This can be read as *amplificatio* in that it expands on the previous statement, but it also makes sense as a commentary keyed to a base text. Each key term (*buena obra, bien fecha, fecha por escogimiento*) receives a gloss. Moreover, it is delivered in writing as part of a book, likening it more to a commentary than to a sermon. There are certainly elements of orality in part 5, most notably the continued device of the dialogue between Patronio and Count Lucanor, but these are not incompatible with vernacular commentary, as we saw with Julio's biblical exegesis in the *Libro de los estados*.

Reading part 5 as a commentary can also explain the allusions to the *Libro de los estados*. Patronio presents part 5 as a companion to the *Libro de los estados* in that they both deal with the same subject matter, specifically the need to have faith and do good works: "Commo quier que en aquel mismo libro tracta desto asaz conplidamente, pero porque esto es tan mester de saber et cunple tanto, et porque por aventura algunos leerán este libro et non leerán el otro, quiero yo aquí fablar desto" ("Even though that book deals with this [subject] quite completely, I wish to speak of it here because it is so essential and important to know, and because perhaps some people will read this book but not the other"; 254). In other ways, part 5 functions as a supplement by expanding upon subjects that did not receive a thorough treatment in the *Libro de los estados*, such as the spiritual benefits of the sacraments of

Communion and baptism: "Et esto diré aquí porque non fabla en ello tan declaradamente en el dicho libro que don Johán fizo" ("And I will say this here because it is not discussed very clearly in the aforementioned book that Don Juan wrote"; 254). Ultimately, it returns to the central theological question of the *Libro de los estados*: how can princes and nobles possibly save their souls when they cannot fully devote their lives to God, but must fulfil the obligations of their earthly estate?

Degiovanni rightly points out that the multiple subdivisions and digressions of part 5 make its structure far from orderly. But if taken as a gloss of several base texts, including passages from the *Libro de los estados* and specific points of doctrine, its branching structure makes more sense. Perhaps its structure might have been clarified further if it had been copied using a commentarial *mise en page* to illuminate some of the links between base text and gloss. But as it has come down to us, it unfolds in a linear fashion, like a melody, with Patronio's commentary providing variations on a theme.

Self-Commentary

In this chapter I have identified two forms of commentary used in Juan Manuel's works. The first, the *accessus ad auctores*, initially serves as an introduction to Alfonso X as an authoritative *auctor*. But the *accessus* almost always has a subtext of self-interest, serving as "an introduction to the interpretive strategies and interests of the exegete who takes possession of the text of the *auctor*" (Copeland 72). Reading an *accessus* introduces the reader to the commentator's way of reading, which situates the text within specific historical circumstances and gives the commentator licence to create a new interpretation. Juan Manuel's early experiments with the *accessus* in the prologues to the *Crónica abreviada* and *Libro de la caza* are not revolutionary uses of the form, but they do provide a first glimpse into the development of his authorial persona, even when, in the case of the *Crónica abreviada*, the text itself hews closely to its exemplar.

The second form, commentary as a gloss keyed to a base text, provides inspiration for both the form and content of Juan Manuel's works. As a form, it appears in the prologue to the *Crónica abreviada*, in the doctrinal chapters of the *Libro de los estados*, and in the structure of the *Conde Lucanor* in both its one-part and five-part versions. Part of the appeal of commentarial writing is how it casts the commentator – either Don Juan or a proxy such as Julio or Patronio – in the role of an expert capable of explaining difficult or obscure ideas to a less experienced interlocutor.

By manipulating the discourses of clarity and obscurity, these mentor figures became mediators between the work's didactic content and the lay reader's understanding. Given Juan Manuel's aspiration to write vernacular theology, adopting the role of commentator offered a way to communicate mastery of theological subject matter without abandoning the priorities and privileges of his secular estate.

Juan Manuel's most innovative use of commentary appears in the works of his didactic and personal periods, in which he applies both *accessus* categories and commentarial writing to his own works. In the examples discussed above, Don Juan introduces his own *Libro infinido* using *accessus* categories, and in the *Conde Lucanor* Patronio uses commentarial writing to expand upon the theological content of the *Libro de los estados*. Much like Dante's use of self-exegesis in his *Vita nuova* and *Convivio*, these instances of self-commentary serve to associate vernacular works with the prestige of Latin academic texts. They also collapse the hierarchy between the authoritative *auctor* and the humble reader, showing that a single individual can occupy both roles (Ascoli, *Dante* 177–8). Finally, they privilege the author as the individual most capable of glossing his or her own works (Bautista 12).

Dante's self-exegesis in the *Vita nuova* (1292–3) and *Convivio* (1304–7) predates Juan Manuel's by more than twenty years. Compared to his Castilian counterpart, he was a much more creative practitioner, using more technical terms of commentary and delving deeper into explanations of his poetic choices (Ascoli, *Dante* 175ff.). But because there is no evidence that Juan Manuel knew Dante's works, it seems that the two writers came to the same conclusion independently about the usefulness of self-exegesis. So while it still holds true that Dante's use of self-commentary is "virtually unprecedented" (Ascoli, *Dante* 176), we should also ask what shared literary, social, and technological factors may have inspired the two authors to make similar choices. One factor was the landscape of Latin and vernacular literature, in which vernacular writers forged a new literary tradition out of the formal and rhetorical building blocks of the existing Latin tradition. In a culture where authority derived from antiquity, the only way for a "modern" author such as Dante or Juan Manuel to assume the mantle of authority in their lifetime was to speed up the process by applying the rhetorical strategies of commentary to their own writings. Another factor was the increase in literacy, which supported an increase in readers, writers, and books (Lawrance, "Spread"). When confronted with the proliferation of copies of their works and readers to read them, it is logical that writers would seek to guide readers' interpretations by offering self-commentary. This goes hand in hand with Juan Manuel's concern about the inaccuracies of scribal copying analysed in chapter 1, a concern also ascribed to Dante in Franco Sacchetti's tales. Finally, self-commentary allowed the writer to place value not just on traditionally prestigious subject matter, such as theology, but also on topics of personal importance, which for Juan Manuel consisted of his experiences and writings. By adopting the role of commentator and turning an exegetical eye to his own works, he unlocked the possibility of writing his own words, the hallmark of an *auctor* in Bonaventure's schema.

4 Auctor

This chapter attempts to reconcile Juan Manuel's most creative and original writings with medieval statements about what an *auctor* does. Bonaventure's definition is deceptively simple: it is someone who "writes both his own words and others', but with his own in the place of primacy and others' added only for purposes of confirmation." Paul Oskar Kristeller reminds us that medieval Latin literary culture was one in which "creation out of nothing was the exclusive prerogative of God, and a human artist who produced a work out of material given to him could not be remotely compared with the divine creator" (106). However, Bonaventure's schema does account for ways of writing that we would call original or creative. Before the advent of print culture in Latin Europe, what is the relationship between writing one's own words and claiming ownership over those words? When and how does Juan Manuel write his own words? And what was the value of doing this in a culture of letters that, as modern scholars must continually remind ourselves, did not prize creativity and originality in the same way we do?

While Juan Manuel's authorial persona, Don Juan, plays an important role throughout his literary career, I propose that he assumes the role of *auctor* most fully in his later works, adding it to those of scribe, compiler, and commentator, which dominate his earlier writings. The other roles do not fade away but continue to play a part in his discourse of authorship alongside the more creative role of *auctor*. The *Conde Lucanor, Libro infinido, Libro de las tres razones* and, to some extent, *Tratado de la Asunción*, all depict Don Juan as someone who writes his own words. The General Prologue also serves as an important space for his performance of authorship. The rhetorical strategies he uses to position himself in relation to scribes, discussed at length in chapter 1, can help us understand how he privileges the role of *auctor* while depicting himself as a capable participant in other types of writing. Moreover, as I will address near the end of this chapter, his presentation of his own works in the General Prologue sheds light on the ways of writing that he prizes the most.

In this chapter, I explore an aspect of Juan Manuel's authorial practice that has been ignored by contemporary criticism: composing poetry. The *viessos* of part 1 of the *Conde Lucanor* – rhymed verses, usually couplets – stand apart from all his other output, including the pithy *proverbios* of parts 2–4, by their metre and rhyme.[1] Don Juan's poetic efforts have received little recognition in contemporary scholarship due to the accidents of manuscript transmission, by which two other poetic works, his *Libro de las cantigas* and *Reglas de cómo se deve trobar,* have been lost. However, the *Conde Lucanor* provides evidence of a poetic persona tasked not only with interpreting Patronio's exemplary stories, but with putting his interpretations into an aesthetically pleasing form. According to Brunetto Latini's *Libro del tesoro,* verse was considered more challenging than prose due to its restricted form:

> La carrera del fablar en prosa es larga e llana, así commo es la comunal manera de fablar de las gentes. Mas el sendero de fablar en rima es más estrecho e más fuerte, así commo aquel que es çercado e encerrado de muros e de setos, que quiere dezir de puntos e de cuentos e de çierta medida, de que onbre non puede nin deve traspasar. (182)
>
> The path of speaking in prose is broad and flat, since it is the common way that people speak. But the path of speaking in rhyme is narrower and more difficult, since it is a path that is surrounded and closed in by walls and hedges – which represent the accents and counted syllables and a given metre – that one cannot and should not overstep.

By writing in verse, Don Juan sets his words apart from the everyday way of speaking represented by prose, thereby making them his own.

In the *Libro infinido* and *Libro de las tres razones,* Don Juan takes a more radical approach to authorship in the Bonaventuran sense. Instead of manipulating the form, he manipulates the subject matter by electing to write about his life experiences, including his experience as a writer. This shift in subject matter allows him to privilege his own words, relegating the words of other *auctoritates* to an auxiliary status. Finally, although the *Tratado de la Asunción* deals with Christian doctrine, its prologue centres Don Juan's lived experience in a similar way. Ultimately, both the verses of the *Conde Lucanor* and the first-person narratives and self-citations of the *Libro infinido, Libro de las tres razones,* and

Tratado de la Asunción achieve the same end: they portray Don Juan as someone who claims ownership over his words in a way congruent with notions of authorship in a medieval manuscript culture.

Juan Manuel's assertion of his authorship has long been the subject of scholarly interest, inspiring dedicated studies by Mercedes Gaibrois de Ballesteros (*El príncipe*), Harlan Sturm, Scholberg ("Juan Manuel" and "Modestia"), Macpherson ("Don Juan"), Ayerbe-Chaux ("Don Juan"), Funes ("Paradojas" and "Excentricidad"), Bautista, and Biaggini ("Stratégies" and "Énonciation"), as well as many others that address the topic as part of a broader discussion. Our current understanding is based on four tendencies in the nobleman's oeuvre: the omission of names of outside sources, the citation of his own works, a concern for clear and concise language, and the textualization of his lived experience (Funes, "Excentricidad"). My discussion of how Juan Manuel adopts the role of *auctor* is deeply indebted to the work of these scholars, particularly Funes and Biaggini, whose theorization of Juan Manuel's authorship as a discursive function has been foundational to my thinking. Despite the difficulty of providing a comprehensive account of Juan Manuel's idiosyncratic approach to authorship, I believe these scholars provide a convincing analysis of how he "becomes" an author through a discursive process that centres the figure of Don Juan. My contribution lies in distinguishing how the role of *auctor* differs from the others that Don Juan occupies at various moments in his works – *scriptor*, *compilator*, and *commentator* – as well as when and how this difference is signalled. Becoming an *auctor* required claiming ownership over one's words, not in the modern legal sense of intellectual property, but through rhetorical strategies that medieval writers and readers found compelling. This chapter also serves as the foundation of the epilogue, which traces the success of Juan Manuel's authorial self-portrayal among early modern and modern editors, scholars, and readers.

Auctor versus Author

The Latin word *auctor* is used in contemporary scholarship on medieval religious and literary writings to designate a specific category of writers whose reputation guaranteed that their works would be taken as authoritative. In a classic study, M.-D. Chenu traces its etymology to the Latin verbs *augere*, to grow, and *agere*, to make or do, as well as *actor* in the legal sense of one who bears or assumes responsibility for an action ("*Auctor*"). Translated to a literary context, the *auctor* was an *assertor*, one who asserted an opinion or argument and thus held moral responsibility for that statement (Minnis, *Medieval Theory* 100–2).

Medieval writers also made conceptual connections between the word *auctor* and the quality of authenticity (*authenticus*), with *auctores* being those who asserted or wrote things worthy of belief.[2] This appears to be circular logic, or a closed feedback loop: "The work of an *auctor* was a book worth reading; a book worth reading had to be the work of an *auctor*" (Minnis, *Medieval Theory* 12). However, as discussed in the introduction, studies of medieval authorship beginning with Minnis's watershed book have demonstrated again and again how writers manipulated this discourse of authority to claim, often with success, the status of *auctor* for themselves.

This is not to say that the idea of the *auctor*'s authority was always taken seriously. *De disciplina scolarium*, a thirteenth-century advice manual for scholars that claimed Boethius as its author, pokes fun at scholars' reverence for authority by lampooning teachers capable only of parroting what they have read in books. "Boethius" concludes that "obviously, the most miserable nature is always to use what has already been found (*inventis*) and never to use what ought to be discovered (*inveniendis*)," and good scholars should strike a balance between existing *auctoritates* and their own ideas (trans. Hunter 168).[3] As Brooke Hunter observes, the work's advice is often played for laughs, but it is also sincere in "leading readers to think beyond the confines of the authoritatively stated interpretation" (179). This quip by "Boethius," in a work endorsed by more serious scholars such as Vincent of Beauvais (Weijers 32), provides more evidence that medieval writers saw a place for inventiveness alongside more established forms of authority.

Early definitions of authorship in Castilian letters were closely related to the concept as defined in a Latin academic context. Antonio de Nebrija's *Vocabulario español-latino* (c. 1495) shows the influence of the circular logic of authorship and authority: for the Latin *auctor*, he gives the Castilian equivalents "autor o hazedor; autora o hazedora" ("author or maker"), and for *auctoritas*, he gives "autoridad de aquestos" ("the authority of these"), referring to the *autores y autoras* he has just mentioned. Yet Sebastián de Covarrubias's *Tesoro de la lengua castellana o española* (1611) indicates that these definitions had broadened by the seventeenth century. For Covarrubias, the Spanish word *autor* "comúnmente se toma por el inventor de alguna cosa. Autores, los que escriven libros y los intitulan con sus nombres, y libro sin autor es mal recebido, porque no ay quien dé razón dél ni le defienda" ("is commonly taken to be the inventor of something. Authors [are also] the ones who write books and title them with their names, and a book without an author is poorly received, because there is no one to promote or defend it"; 252). He defines *autoridad* as "la razón escrita, que alegamos para fundar algún propósito, y la firmíssima es la que se trae de la Sagrada Escritura, de los Concilios, de las tradiciones de los sanctos Doctores, y en su proporción de los demás que han escrito y escriven" ("the written word that we allege as the basis for some proposition, and the most firm is that of Holy Scripture, the councils, the traditions of the Holy Doctors [of the Church] and, proportionately, all others who write and have written"; 252). Covarrubias's definitions move beyond the circularity of *auctor* and *auctoritas* to encompass anyone who writes a book and claims attribution. Invention – encompassing both creation and novelty[4] – is not auxiliary to the citation of *auctoritates*, as it had been for Bonaventure or the subversive Pseudo-Boethius, but is at the heart of the author's work. Furthermore, although Covarrubias reserves the highest level of authority for Church writings that express doctrinal truths, he accepts that the assertions of other writers have some measure of authority. If authors now have a wider variety of reasons for writing, alluded to by Covarrubias's broad language (*para fundar algún propósito*), it follows that their truthfulness and reliability should be measured in accordance with their specific aims.

Although the Latin academic definitions of *auctor* and *auctoritas* remained relevant to Castilian literary culture in the seventeenth century, it is clear that by this time a more flexible notion of authorship had taken root alongside the older concepts. The arrival of the printing press in western Europe in the mid-fifteenth century had an undeniable impact on notions of authorship and the establishment of literary property rights (Eisenstein 1: 113–26; Chartier 25–59). But this shift in ideas about authorship was more gradual than has sometimes been acknowledged, with significant contributions from the vernacular writers of the thirteenth and fourteenth centuries. In medieval Castilian texts, the lack of precise terminology makes it difficult to distinguish the notion of the Latin academic *auctor* from other ideas about authorship. The word *auctor* or *actor* is documented in Castilian as early as the twelfth century, most often in the legal sense of a person responsible for an act (Corominies 1: 416). In the thirteenth-century *Libro de Alexandre*, the young Alexander uses *actores* to refer to the authoritative authors of antiquity: "De cor sé los actores, de livro non he cura" ("I know the authors by heart, I don't need a book"; 103 [40c]). In Castilian, Aragonese, and Portuguese historiography, practices of authorial attribution were irregular well into the fifteenth century, with *auctor* reserved for authors of source material (Fernández-Ordóñez, "Actores y autores"). Only in the fifteenth century do "modern" vernacular writers such as Gutierre Díez de Games and Diego de San Pedro begin to refer to themselves as *auctores* or *autores* in a way that corresponds to our modern usage, as in the formula "aquí dize el autor" in Díez de Games's *Victorial*, composed between 1431 and 1448 (Coromines credits him with being the first to use the modern spelling). To confuse matters further, the two spellings coexisted well into the sixteenth century, sometimes as synonyms and other times with distinctions related to print culture (Sánchez-Serrano and Prieto de la Iglesia 85–6).

Juan Manuel never uses any variants of *auctor* or *autor* to refer to himself or to other ancient or medieval writers. Nonetheless, he provides us with a crucial point of reference, because in his search for political and literary authority, he reproduces the notion of the *auctor* as a writer whose works are worthy of admiration and imitation. In his later works, he also explores what it means to write one's own words, introducing a Bonaventuran concept of originality that will later align with Renaissance and early modern notions of invention and self-fashioning. To distinguish between the two, I will use *auctor* for the Latin academic concept of an author with authority, and "author" (or Castilian *autor*) for the broader concept, nascent in Bonaventure's suggestions of originality and ownership, that approaches our modern notion of authorship.

Throughout his corpus, Juan Manuel cites or mentions several *auctores* whose works are worthy of admiration or imitation. Sometimes he praises them openly, while other times his admiration is implied in the way he cites them. In chapter 3, I showed how Don Juan portrays Alfonso X as an authoritative *auctor* in the prologues to the *Crónica abreviada* and *Libro de la caza* by adopting the model of the *accessus ad auctores*. I also discussed his commentary on a line attributed to John of Damascus, which he inserts into his own works as an *auctoritas*. Other examples can be found in the *Libro del cavallero et del escudero*, in which Don Juan refers to the *Epitoma rei militaris* of the fourth-century Roman author Vegetius as "un libro que fizo un sabio que dizen Vejecio" ("a book that a wise man called Vegetius wrote"; 12), and praises the commentary on the Lord's Prayer written by his brother-in-law, Infante Juan of Aragon, as "la muy buena e muy complida e muy santa obra que vós fiziestes" ("the very good, very complete, and very holy work you wrote"; 4). In the *Libro infinido*, he recommends that his son read "el libro que fizo fray Gil de la orden de Sant Agostín que llaman *De regimine principum*" ("the book written by Fray Gil of the Order of Saint Augustine, called *De regimine principum*"; 138–9), presenting the work of the Augustinian friar Giles of Rome (d. 1316) as an authoritative account of good kings and tyrants. Finally, in the prologue to the first book of the *Libro de los estados*, he alludes to the first lines of Boethius's (c. 477–526) *Consolation of Philosophy* to explain the relationship between the political tribulations he endured in the late 1320s and the genesis of his book: "Et acaesçe que agora esto acaesçiere, como dixo Boesço: 'Carmina qui quondam,' etcétera" ("And it happens that this has come to pass just as Boethius says: 'Carmina qui quondam,' etc."; 72). According to Lida de Malkiel, Juan Manuel's citations of ancient and medieval Latin authors are remarkably infrequent and imprecise compared to the practices of his contemporaries; she attributes this to his religious orthodoxy, which caused him to avoid the pagan authors of antiquity, as well as to his pride in the knowledge and values of the "modern" Castilian aristocracy ("Tres notas" 169–78). Nevertheless, these vague citations do operate according to the circular logic of *auctores* and *auctoritates*: he quotes them because they are accepted sources of authority, and quoting them both reinforces their status and bolsters the authority of his own works.

In his *Tratado de la Asunción*, Juan Manuel also demonstrates familiarity with the concept of "authenticity" in the context of religious writings. Authenticity, from the Greek-derived *authenticus*, suggested both veracity based on an *auctor*'s reputation, and the idea of origin (Chenu, *Toward Understanding* 131). When defending the doctrinal validity of the Assumption of Mary, he refers to a text attributed to Saint Jerome that casts doubt on other works associated with the Assumption:[5]

> Si alguno [...] dize que el libro que fabla de la vida et de la passión et de la assunción de santa María, *que es apócrifo et non aténtico,* digo yo que en cuanto dizen que el libro es apócrifo que dizen verdat; mas si ellos tienen que sant Jerónimo tovo que santa María non es en cuerpo et en alma en Paraíso, digo que en esto non tienen verdat. (*Obras*, ed. Alvar and Finci, 1007; my emphasis)

> If someone [...] says that the book dealing with the life, passion, and Assumption of Saint Mary *is apocryphal and not authentic,* I respond that when they say the book is apocryphal, they speak the truth; but if they believe Saint Jerome held that Saint Mary is not in heaven in body and soul, in this they are wrong.

Here, "apocryphal" and "not authentic" are not quite synonyms. Rather, by separating them, Don Juan echoes the position of biblical commentators such as Hugh of Saint-Cher (c. 1200–63), for whom a work can be apocryphal – that is, not associated with a known *auctor* – and still be considered true for doctrinal or ethical purposes (Minnis, *Medieval Theory* 11). In other words, while authenticity is usually derived from the reputation of an *auctor*, there is a loophole based on a work's claim to some form of ethical, moral, or spiritual truth. (Don Juan does not discuss whether the apocryphal work in question is authentic, but instead prefers to speculate about Jerome's beliefs.)

Although Juan Manuel uses *a[u]téntico* in a doctrinal context and never openly applies it to his own works, it is plausible that he saw his secular writing in this light, in the same way that he adapted the notion of *auctor* from the Latin academic culture of biblical exegesis. Indeed, in exploring the possibility that a "modern" nobleman – a non-*auctor* by definition – could communicate ethical truths, his later works seek a path to authenticity that circumvents the circular logic of authority that still prevailed in his early writings.

Juan Manuel's "Original" Writings

His Own Verses

Part 1 of the *Conde Lucanor* presents a special case for considering Don Juan as an author because, as demonstrated in chapter 2, his self-presentation in the text differs from how subsequent readers have understood his role and appreciated his work. The concluding formula after each *enxiemplo* distinguishes between two authorial activities, compilation and authorship: "Et entendiendo don Johán que estos exienplos eran muy buenos, fízolos escribir en este libro et fizo estos viesos en que se pone la sentencia de los exienplos" ("And Don Juan, understanding that these examples were very good, had them copied into this book and wrote these verses, which contain the meaning of the examples"; 19). Don Juan compiled the exempla, which are sometimes described as stories he found ("cuando don Johán *falló* este exienplo"; 25; my emphasis), but he composed the *viessos*, or rhymed verses, that conclude each one ("fizo estos viesos"; 19ff.). My reading complements that of Barry Taylor, who observes that the formula uses different verbs of authorship to separate Don Juan's role as supervisor of the scribe who copied each tale (*fízolos escribir*) from his role as author of the verses (*fizo estos viessos*) ("Capítulos" 63). Again, this gives no indication of the historical Juan Manuel's creative input in the exempla, nor does it reflect the consensus, shared by medieval and modern readers, that Juan Manuel can be called the author of the whole work. However, it does point to the *viessos* as exemplifying the creative role of the author within Bonaventure's medieval paradigm. The repeated and almost insistent claim that Don Juan "wrote these verses" links them to his authorial persona in a way that implies the greatest degree of originality and ownership.

As discussed in the previous chapter, the *viessos* are modelled after religious commentary in that each set of verses is associated with a base text and purports to explain its meaning. Their purpose is to gloss the tales: this is what a medieval *accessus* would categorize as their *utilitas* (or, in Aristotelian terms, final cause). However, this does not account for their *modus agendi* or formal cause: their distinct style, unique among Juan Manuel's extant works. Understanding their form will shed light on why Don Juan chose to associate his authorial persona most closely not with the prose writing that makes up the bulk of the collection, but with his foray into poetry.

Despite the lack of critical interest in the *viessos*, Fernando Gómez Redondo has recognized that Don Juan's role as a composer of verse (*versificador*) constitutes an "especial dimensión de su autoría" ("special dimension of his authorship"; "Don Juan Manuel, versificador" 44). In the courtly literature produced under Alfonso X and Sancho IV, Gómez Redondo identifies the emergence of a "versificador entendido" ("intelligent versifier") who draws upon the disciplines of grammar, rhetoric, and music to compose verses that are both beautiful and ethically compelling. By depicting himself as a *versificador*, Don Juan offers proof of his grammatical and rhetorical prowess, privileged skills in the Alfonsine court, as well as the effectiveness of his words for promoting morally and spiritually appropriate conduct, a core value of *molinismo* under Sancho IV and María de Molina (45).

Poetry's ethical function was complemented by its aesthetic function, as the fourteenth-century *Libro de los cien capítulos* attests: "Aquella es nobleza durable la que es contada por viesos rimados e pesados" ("Lasting nobility is that which is narrated in rhymed and accented verses"; 119).[6] Moreover, Ramon Vidal de Besalú claims in his *Razos de trobar* (1190–1213) that distinguishing between good and bad poetry could teach listeners to "lauzar so qe fa a lauzar et blasmar so qe fai a blasmar" ("praise what ought to be praised and blame what ought to be blamed"; 4). Finally, because of their rhyme and metre, the poet's words are unique. They can be paraphrased or modified easily enough, especially through the vicissitudes of oral or textual transmission: indeed, studies by de Looze (18–21) and Daniela Santonocito ("Los 'viessos'") have traced how the *viessos* are modified from version to version in the early transmission history of the *Conde Lucanor*. However, this changes something fundamental about them, as Don Juan's troubadour-knight and Petrarch know all too well (see ch. 1).

Although the didactic function of the *viessos* is important, it has tended to overshadow the significance of their formal aspects, especially their metre. Despite some metrical irregularities, they range from heptasyllabic to hexadecasyllabic verses, offering the widest range of fourteenth-century Castilian verse forms recorded outside of *cancionero* manuscripts (Gómez Redondo, *Historia de la poesía* 637–9).[7] Gómez Redondo differentiates the clerical art of composition (*versificar*) exemplified in Juan Manuel's *viessos* from the works of troubadours, lyric poets, and musicians ("Don Juan Manuel, versificador" 23–4). Nevertheless, seeing the *viessos* as a metrical compendium invites comparisons to the compilations of the French poets Guillaume de Machaut and Jean Froissart. As Sylvia Huot has shown, the manuscripts prepared or overseen by Machaut and Froissart emphasize the diversity of both genres and verse forms, unified only by the poet's authorial persona (232). Don Juan's *viessos* present a far more homogeneous compendium of couplets (distichs) and four-verse *coplas*, all in the genre of moral advice. Still, the diversity of metres composed by a single writer emphasizes the poet's technical expertise. By demonstrating his ability to produce such metrical variety, Don Juan unites the ethical aims of a clerical *versificador* with the aesthetic concerns of a lyric poet, incorporating both into his model of a successful aristocratic author.

If we take this into consideration together with the two lost poetic works mentioned in the General Prologue – the *Libro de las cantigas* and the treatise *Reglas de cómo se deve trobar* – it is no surprise that Don Juan cast a troubadour knight as his stand-in within the exemplum that begins the General Prologue. When composing this prologue to introduce his manuscript of collected works, he chose as his analogue not a wise sage or counsellor who could embody the ethical content of his works, but rather a poet whose works were prized for both content (*palabras*) and form (*son*). His self-presentation in the General Prologue thus reminds us that his poetic accomplishments were a significant facet of his authorial persona, something that was perfectly evident to Gonzalo Argote de Molina when he included his "Discurso sobre la poesía castellana contenida en este libro" ("Treatise on the Castilian poetry contained in this book") in his 1575 edition of the *Conde Lucanor*. Don Juan's poetic persona harks back to Alfonso X's role as troubadour-king in the *Cantigas de Santa María*, which celebrated poetry both as a tool for Christian worship (Galvez 7) and as part of the secular Arabic courtly values of *adab* (Dodds, Menocal, and Balbale 229–30). It also looks forward to debates in the aristocratic circles of fifteenth-century Castile about whether poetic composition was innate or learned, which mirrored debates about the nature of nobility (Gómez-Bravo, *Textual Agency* 47–8). Poetic composition is thus not just a facet of Juan Manuel's authorial self-presentation, but also a key factor in the broader landscape of authorship in late medieval Castile.

His Own Works

The other way in which Juan Manuel claims ownership over his words is by transforming his life experience into literary material. His poetry in the lost *Libro de las cantigas* may have had autobiographical elements comparable to those in Alfonso X's *Cantigas de Santa María*. But because these compositions have been lost, his prose works dominate our understanding of his approach to autobiography.

Before turning to specific examples from the *Libro infinido*, *Libro de las tres razones*, and *Tratado de la Asunción*, it is necessary to address the relationship between medieval life-writing and the modern genre of autobiography. Philippe Lejeune attempts to give a temporally inclusive definition of autobiography as a "récit rétrospectif en prose qu'une personne réelle fait de sa propre existence, lorsqu'elle met l'accent sur sa vie individuelle, en particulier sur l'histoire de sa personnalité" ("retrospective prose account that a real person gives of their own existence, emphasizing their individual life and in particular the story of their personality"; 14). However, as John Fleming points out, medieval European autobiography favours exemplarity over individuality and lacks the modern psychological notion of "personality" (35–6). Elizabeth Bruss's criteria come closer to encompassing the kind of medieval life-writing present in Juan Manuel's later works. She distinguishes autobiography by three situational aspects: truth-value, in which the author asserts the veracity and sincerity of their work; act-value, in which the work is a performance that exemplifies the character of its author; and identity-value, in which the distinct roles of author, narrator, and protagonist are combined into one (299–300). While Germán Orduna limits his analysis of Juan Manuel's autobiographical writing to act-value ("Autobiografía" 247), I propose that all three of Bruss's criteria are helpful in understanding how Juan Manuel textualizes his life experience. Truth-value helps us situate his recurring claim to narrate things he experienced, witnessed, or heard from oral sources, while identity-value helps distinguish genuine autobiographical narration from earlier narrative games in which fictional characters – notably Julio from the *Libro de los estados* and Patronio from the *Conde Lucanor* – reference Don Juan and his works.

I also draw upon Jaume Aurell's study of medieval Catalan autobiography, particularly his study of Jaume I of Aragon's *Llibre dels fets* (composed between 1244 and 1274), a first-person account of the king's exemplary deeds. Aurell classifies Jaume's work as "historical autobiography," defined as

> [...] a retrospective account that stresses the author's historical existence and meaning. This life-writing exercise often produces a new imagined character that may serve as a model for future generations. The literary image that emerges from this form of self-narration is produced by art but functions as historical narration generative of historical reality. (137)

Aurell's work not only accounts for the exemplarity and literariness of medieval autobiography, but also helps establish a concrete precursor to Juan Manuel's most personal works. Given Juan Manuel's close political ties to the Crown of Aragon through his marriages to Isabel of Mallorca (Jaume I's granddaughter) and Infanta Constanza of Aragon (his great-granddaughter), it is likely that he knew the *Llibre dels fets*, whose original composition in Catalan suggests that its intended audience was the king's successors and subjects (Liuzzo Scorpo 7). The Castilian nobleman would have seen in the *Llibre dels fets* an alternative to Alfonso X's comparison between bookmaking and palace construction examined in chapter 1: while Alfonso's authorship was presented as somewhat distant and managerial, Jaume's seemed more intimate, evincing his "real proximity to the drafting of the text" (Aurell 161). Jaume also eschewed written authorities, relying on his memory and occasionally on eyewitnesses who "y avien estat e sabien lo feyt" ("had been there and knew what happened"; 13, par. 9). This Catalan autobiography – infrequently juxtaposed with Juan Manuel's works due to the lingering structural and ideological barriers of "national" language traditions – exemplifies the personal subject matter, creative autonomy, and focus on the narrating "I" that also characterize the *Libro infinido*, *Libro de las tres razones*, and *Tratado de la Asunción*.

The *Libro infinido*, with its twenty-five chapters and treatise on love ("De las maneras de amor"), belongs to the same didactic genre as the *Conde Lucanor* and was composed around the same time or shortly thereafter.[8] However, its narrative approach differs drastically. Don Juan dispenses with the entertaining stories and aesthetically pleasing verses that, in the *Conde Lucanor*'s prologue, he had likened to the sugar or honey that sweetens the "medicine" of the didactic content (ed. Serés, 11). Overall, the *Libro infinido* "provides the pill without the sugar," an assessment that Macpherson had applied to the treatise on love ("Amor" 182) and that Carlos Mota applies to the whole book ("Introduction" 48–9). Moreover, while the *Conde Lucanor* represented the culmination of the interdiegetic relationship between Don Juan and his fictional characters, the *Libro infinido* abandons this technique in favour of a more straightforward dynamic between the narrator, Don

Juan, and his addressee, his son Fernando Manuel.[9] But the absence of these specific literary features does not mean the absence of all literary artifice. As Mota observes:

> En el *Libro infinido* [...] don Juan regresa al ámbito de la representación de la experiencia, pero esta vez evitando la narración y sus técnicas, quedándose en el extracto seco de las lecciones derivadas de esa misma experiencia. Una poderosa voz que dice *yo* no deja de oírse en ningún momento. Pero se instala más que nunca en el papel de *magister* al que, de forma más o menos disimulada, siempre había aspirado, al menos desde su pretensión de que el arzobispo don Juan de Aragón tradujese al latín su *Libro del cavallero et del escudero*. ("Introduction" 52)

> In the *Libro infinido* [...] Don Juan returns to the sphere of representing experience, but this time he avoids narration and its techniques, sticking to the dry summary of lessons derived from that same experience. A powerful voice that says "I" never ceases to be heard at any moment. But he positions himself more than ever in the role of *magister* to which he had always aspired, with varying degrees of openness, at least since his ambition to have the archbishop Don Juan of Aragon translate into Latin his *Libro del cavallero et del escudero*.

This "poderosa voz que dice *yo*" and the way in which it shapes and is shaped by a discourse of authorship reflect Juan Manuel's aim to shift the balance between venerated *auctoritates* and his own words.

The *Libro infinido* opens with a celebration of knowledge (*saber*) that echoes the panegyric to Alfonso X in the prologue to his *Libro de la caza*.[10] In that earlier work, Don Juan had observed that while God is the only "sabidor de todas las cosas" ("knower of all things"; 303), Alfonso had made enormous strides to "acrecentar el saber cuanto pudo" ("increase knowledge as much as he could"; 303) by sponsoring the translation of academic, theological, juridical, and technical works into Castilian. After enumerating the many Alfonsine translations, Don Juan exclaims, "¿Qué vos diré?" ("What more can I say?"; 303), a rhetorical question common in medieval Castilian prose to indicate restraint from excessive narration (*Conde Lucanor*, ed. Serés, 132; Garribba 25–9). He thus conveys the exhaustiveness of his uncle's contribution to the emergent vernacular tradition: nothing more can be written; everything has already been said. By placing this question in the mouth of his authorial alter ego, Juan Manuel also plants the seed of a major concern that would shape his subsequent literary career: what can *I* say? What could Don Juan, from his specific social and rhetorical positions, contribute to Castilian letters after the comprehensive body of work left by the scriptoria of Alfonso X and Sancho IV?

The return to the concept of *saber* in the prologue to the *Libro infinido* establishes a link between this text and the earlier *Libro de la caza* and proposes an answer to this question:

> Et porque la vida es corta et el saber es luengo et grande de aprender, punian los omnes de aprender lo que entienden cada unos que les más cumplen, et unos trabajan en un saber et otros en otro. Et porque yo, don Johán, [...] quería cuanto pudiese ayudar a mí et a otros a saber lo más que yo pudiese, teniendo que el saber es la cosa por que omne más debía fazer, por ende asmé de componer este tratado que trata de cosas que yo mismo prové en mí mismo et en mi fazienda et bi que conteció a otros. (117)

> Since life is short and knowledge is vast and difficult to learn, everyone struggles to learn what they deem most suitable for themselves, and some work at one type of knowledge, and others at another. So because I, Don Juan, [...] wanted to help myself and others to acquire knowledge as much as I can – in the belief that knowledge is the thing one should strive for most – for this reason I thought to compose this treatise that deals with things I myself have experienced in my life and my property, and things I saw happen to others.

Don Juan's unique contribution to knowledge is an account of his own experience. Citing the Senecan trope of "ars longa, vita brevis" (*Libro infinido*, ed. Mota, 117n34), he recognizes that his mortal lifespan limits the knowledge he is able to acquire. He also invokes the idea of suitability (*lo que entienden cada unos que les más cumplen*), which in his works typically refers to one's God-given place within the estate system. As a lay noble, Don Juan did not receive a clerical education, and thus cannot claim a deep mastery of clerical knowledge.

Moreover, though powerful, he does not have the vast resources of a monarch like Alfonso, whom he imagines in the prologue to the *Crónica abreviada* as having not only a team of scholars at his command, but also the luxury of time to study:

> Avía muy grant espacio para estudiar en las materias de que quería componer algunos libros, ca morava en algunos logares un año e dos e más, [...] e ansí avía espacio de estudiar en lo qu'él quería fazer para sí mismo, e aun para veer e esterminar las cosas de los saberes qu'él mandava ordenar a los maestros e a los sabios que traía para esto en su corte. (67)

> [Alfonso] had plenty of time to study the subjects on which he wanted to compose books, since he lived in some places for a year or two, or more. [...] And he also had time to study whatever he wanted for himself, as well as to supervise and evaluate everything from the different areas of knowledge that he ordered to be compiled by the experts and sages brought to his court for this purpose.

Within the limitations imposed by Don Juan's estate and his mortal existence, the most valuable knowledge he has acquired derives from his lived experience, which is what he sets out to transmit in the *Libro infinido.* In aligning the length of the book with the span of his life (a quote discussed in ch. 2), he promises to provide a full account of this knowledge. By claiming his experience as a form of *saber,* Don Juan elevates the life of the individual, or at least the noble individual, to a level of cultural importance worthy of written literary expression.

This raises another question: who wants to know about Don Juan's life? Alfonso's contributions to knowledge need no justification, as they align with established disciplines such as the seven liberal arts, law, and theology. But there is no precedent in Castilian for a book of one's life. Don Juan justifies this unusual project by addressing it to his son Fernando, who needs to know about his father's life so he can take charge of his affairs after his death. It will be so useful to the boy, he muses, that "marabilla será si libro tan pequeño pudiere fallar de que se aproveche tanto" ("it will be a marvel if he can find another book so small that benefits him so much"; 118). He also addresses other readers "que non fuesen de mejor entendimiento que yo" ("whose faculty of understanding is no greater than my own"; 118), projecting a noble audience that shares his priorities as well as his limitations. For this specific audience, Don Juan's experience offers concrete examples of good conduct to imitate and bad conduct to avoid. This exemplary value elevates the "things I myself have experienced" (*cosas que yo mismo prové*) to knowledge worthy of recording in a book.

The elevation of "cosas que yo mismo prové" in the prologue is matched in the structure of the work's twenty-six chapters. Each chapter concludes with a variation of the phrase: "Et la prueva de todas estas cosas es que los que esto fizieron se fallaron ende bien, et el contrario" ("And the proof of all these things is that those who acted this way were successful, and the contrary"; 946). This refrain functions as an antistrophe (Zumthor's concept of litany) repeated for rhetorical effect, a technique used with a similar exemplary function in the closing phrases of part 1 of the *Conde Lucanor* (Gómez Redondo, *Historia de la prosa* 1: 1185). In addition to marking textual divisions, it repeatedly reminds readers that the work's main subject matter is the author's experience, and that this experience has an ethical function in helping to guide readers' conduct.

This rhetoric of experience, still relatively rare in medieval literature, would flourish in the Renaissance culture of self-fashioning, making Juan Manuel's "I" seem strikingly ahead of its time. But the *Libro infinido*'s self-fashioning is rooted in medieval notions of selfhood and authority. Unlike the examples of Renaissance self-fashioning studied by Stephen Greenblatt, none of whom "inherits [...] an ancient family tradition or hierarchical status that might have rooted personal identity in the identity of a clan or caste" (9), Don Juan's elevation of his lived experience is very much rooted in his royal-adjacent lineage and high social status. Additionally, within the medieval discipline of dialectic (the science of disputing and proving claims), experience was one of three acceptable methods of proof, along with authority and reason.[11] Reason, according to the twelfth-century philosopher John of Salisbury, uses "propositions which are immediately evident and require no proof" (215). However, in written texts, both authority and experience rely on the reader's acceptance of the writer's credibility. The difference is that authority can only be wielded by an *auctor*, but anyone can lay claim to the validity of experience. This is consonant with Juan Manuel's treatment of experience in earlier works, particularly the *Libro del cavallero et del escudero*, in which the experience of the elderly knight is presented not only as valid, but as the best way of receiving a chivalric education (Heusch, "La 'mala educación'" 321). Knighthood, for which Ramon Llull in his *Llibre de l'orde de cavalleria* had advocated a "sciència scrita en libres" ("science written in books"; 170), becomes in Juan Manuel's works a discipline of lived experience, recorded in writing not by ancient authorities but by contemporary practitioners. Likewise, in the *Libro infinido*, Don Juan's experience confirms that his advice on spiritual, ethical, and practical affairs will have a positive outcome. Because the book deals with the affairs of the present-day nobility, it can dispense with ancient *auctoritates* in favour of a "modern's" experience.

Despite this emphasis on lived experience in the prologue and throughout the work, much of Don Juan's advice is surprisingly generic. There are a handful of references to the particular circumstances of the Manuel family. For instance, Don Juan urges his son to respect the clan's close ties to the Dominican Order (124), the Jewish physician Don Çag (133), the noble Lara and Castro families, and the lords of Vizcaya and Cameros (146–8). He also warns Fernando of the family's insomniac tendencies and vehemently critiques excessive wine consumption, two topics in advice literature that nonetheless take on a more personal tone in the *Libro infinido* (130–2). The most evocative example is a description of their territorial domain: Don Juan boasts that his son can travel "del reino de Navarra fasta el reino de Granada, que cada noche posedes en villa cercada o en castiellos de los que yo he" ("from the kingdom of Navarre to the kingdom of Granada, each night staying in one of the fortified manors or castles I possess"; 144). But even though he "relied on his personal experience to a degree unusual in the fourteenth century" (Macpherson, "Don Juan" 8), the *Libro infinido* is dominated by general recommendations on how to attain spiritual salvation, get along with monarchs and other nobles, and manage the various members of an aristocratic household. Similar recommendations can be found in other mirrors for princes of the thirteenth and fourteenth centuries such as the *Poridat de poridades* and *Castigos de Sancho IV*, to cite just two Castilian examples. But what the *Libro infinido* lacks in personal anecdotes, it makes up for through self-citation of Don Juan's other books.

Don Juan cites the verses from ex. 2 of the *Conde Lucanor* in his famous defence of his writing (the quote with which this book begins). But the work he cites most is the *Libro de los estados*, mentioned in sixteen of the twenty-six chapters of the *Libro infinido*. This repeated self-citation transforms the *Libro infinido* into a compendium or index of this earlier work (Díez de Revenga, "*Libro enfenido*" 371; Seniff, "Así fiz yo" 47; Mota, "Introduction" 75). This reflects Juan Manuel's broader interest in having his works copied, read, and referenced. In Bautista's assessment, the frequent citations of the *Libro de los estados* not only posit it as an authoritative work (similar to what the *Crónica abreviada* had accomplished for Alfonso X's *Estoria de España*), but also project an image of Juan Manuel's collected works as a network of texts held together by the "categoría de autor" ("category of author"; 14). To take this further, these self-citations are a way for Juan Manuel to place his previous literary production within the frame of the *Libro infinido*'s focus on experience. Like his lived experience, the books he has written constitute a unique contribution to knowledge that is purely his own. By citing his work so prominently, he takes a literal approach to giving his own words prime place. What is more, he portrays writing as a central part of his lived experience, encouraging Fernando and other noble readers to see literary composition as a fundamental part of Don Juan's identity and legacy and, potentially, their own.

His Own Life

While the *Libro infinido* does not quite deliver on Don Juan's promise to narrate his lived experience, the *Libro de las tres razones* comes much closer. It does not pretend to relate the author's whole life, as the *Libro infinido* aspired to do, instead focusing on "tres cosas" ("three things") that he has related often and that are worth recording for posterity (979). It was one of Juan Manuel's last works, possibly composed between 1342 and 1345, but almost certainly after the *Libro infinido*.[12] Despite its intriguing and idiosyncratic blend of genres – including historiography, folkloric and hagiographic motifs, and personal and family anecdotes – it remains relatively understudied, but the existing scholarship converges around two points. First, the work's primary aim is to criticize the royal lineage of Alfonso XI of Castile while elevating the Manuel family line (Dunn, "Structures"; Orduna, "*Libro*"; Ruiz; Rosende). Orduna reads it as Juan Manuel's public critique of the injustices brought upon him by Alfonso XI, including his ousting from the king's inner circle, the repudiation and imprisonment of his daughter Constanza, and his portrayal as cowardly and disloyal in the *Crónica de Alfonso XI* and *Gran crónica de Alfonso XI* ("*Libro*").

Second, through a set of discursive practices that highlight experience, eyewitnessing, and oral testimony, it offers an alternative historiography that promises greater access to the truth (Deyermond, "Cuentos" and "*Libro*"; Funes and Qués; Hijano Villegas; Lizabe). Drawing upon Derrida's articulation of the relationship between texts and genres, Funes and María Elena Qués clarify that the work does not belong to the genre of historiography, but rather participates in some of the genre's discursive practices to achieve its political aims (74). This scholarship illuminates the *Libro de las tres razones*'s relationship to other Castilian chronicles, including the histories sponsored by the Crown of Castile as well as Juan Manuel's own early foray into historiography with his *Crónica abreviada*. Manuel Hijano Villegas goes so far as to propose that Juan Manuel's return to historiography constitutes a radical attempt to rewrite nearly a century of Castilian royal history in order to place the Manuel dynasty at its centre (100). However, this focus on the *Libro de las tres razones*'s ties to politics and historiography tends to overshadow other ways in which it responds to Juan Manuel's own oeuvre and to the broader corpus of courtly vernacular prose.

In addition to its political aim of vindicating the Manuel dynasty, the *Libro de las tres razones* fulfils Juan Manuel's authorial aim of writing his own words. The dynamic interplay between one's own words and the words of others, a defining feature of medieval authorship and a central preoccupation for Juan Manuel, emerges here to its fullest extent. As its conventional title indicates, the work depicts Don Juan narrating three *razones* (arguments) about his experience and lineage to the Dominican friar Juan Alfonso, who is affectionately referred to as a family friend in the *Libro infinido*'s treatise on love (176).[13] As examined in chapter 2, its prologue borrows a discourse of compilation from a more learned textual culture of *escrituras*. But seen in the light of the role of author, this same passage also asserts Don Juan's intellect (*entendimiento*) as a unifying force of the work:

> *Con razón* ayunté estos dichos (et *por mi entendimiento* entendí que passara todo el fecho en esta manera que vos yo porné por escrito) que fablan de las cosas que passaran; et así contece en los que fablan de las escrituras: que toman de lo que fallan en un lugar et acuerdan en lo que fallan en otros lugares, et de todo fazen una razón; et así fiz yo de lo que oí a muchas personas, que eran muy crederas, ayuntando estas razones. (*Obras*, ed. Alvar and Finci, 979–80; my emphasis)

> I compiled *in a meaningful way* these sayings that deal with things that happened (and *through my intellect* I knew that the whole affair happened in the way I will put in writing). And so it happens with those who discuss authoritative texts: they take what they find in one place and check it against what they find in other places, making one sense of everything; and that is just what I did with what I heard from various trustworthy people, compiling these arguments.

The work is made up of disparate *razones*, some of which are derived from the words or testimony of others: "Todas estas cosas non las alcancé yo, nin vos puedo dar testimonio que las yo bi" ("I did not experience all these things, nor can I testify that I saw them"; 979). Compared to the forceful rhetoric of experience in the *Libro infinido*, here Don Juan is more distant from the events narrated. However, his ownership over the work is expressed in other ways. First, he emphasizes hearing oral testimony as another form of experience, not quite as direct as eyewitnessing, but more direct than reading about them in the royal chronicles that his work implicitly challenges (Deyermond, "Cuentos" 76–8). Second, the author's intellect serves as an organizing filter, arranging the disparate accounts in a way that makes sense and is "right" (*con razón*). Thus, Don Juan not only presents the *razón* as a coherent literary genre, but also adopts it as an essential element of his discourse of authorship, or what Gómez Redondo calls his *voluntad de autoría* ("Géneros" 97–8).

The autobiographical rhetoric in the *Libro de las tres razones* relies on convincing the reader of a close, intimate connection between the writer, the narrator, and the events narrated (similar to Bruss's notion of identity-value). Ever since Díez de Revenga ("*Libro de las armas*") and Orduna ("Autobiografía") vindicated the work's claim to autobiography despite its historical inaccuracies, scholars including María Cecilia

Ruiz, Qués, Funes and Qués, and Funes ("Paradojas" and "Excentricidad") have continued to explore this aspect. However, the potential of what Dunn memorably calls "private myths and public fictions" has not yet been exhausted in studies of the *Libro de las tres razones* ("Structures" 61–2, 67). The work's discursive strategies can be productively compared to those of Jaume I's *Llibre dels fets*, which dispenses with external sources of authority in favour of the narrating subject's memory and the shaping of that memory into a written account (Aurell 157ff.). Juan Manuel's work makes similar rhetorical moves, despite some differences in its approach to temporality and lived experience. I will elaborate on three examples (one from each *razón*) that show how Don Juan's narration keeps the focus on his experience, memory, and acts of writing, even when dealing with events that happened long before his birth. In the first two razones, Don Juan uses memory, oral testimony, and other narrative strategies to recount events he did not witness, while continuing to centre the narrating voice of "yo, don Juan." In the third, he captures his lived experience in a vivid account that can unambiguously be taken as autobiographical writing.

The events of the first and second *razones* deal with the life of Juan Manuel's father, Infante Manuel – his birth and naming, the bestowal of his coat of arms, and his gain and loss of the title of king of Murcia – and thus unfolded years before the author's birth. Nonetheless, Don Juan adopts other strategies aimed at communicating them with the immediacy of lived experience. In each one, he intensifies his personal claim on the truth by delivering eyewitness testimony through a purportedly unbroken chain of oral transmission. For example, on the origins of the Manuel family coat of arms, he writes of his sources:

> Oí dezir a mi madre, seyendo yo moço pequeño, et después que ella finó, oí dezir a Alfonso García, un cavallero que me crió, que era mucho anciano et se criara con mio padre et era su hermano de leche, et a otros muchos cavalleros et oficiales que fueran de mio padre, et aún oí ende algo al rey don Sancho. (*Obras*, ed. Alvar and Finci, 980)

> I heard tell of it from my mother when I was a young boy, and after she died, I heard about it from Alfonso García, a knight who raised me, who was very old and had grown up with my father and was his milk brother; and also from many of my father's knights and officials, and I even heard something about it from King Sancho.

Since Infante Manuel received his coat of arms as a child, most of these sources (except perhaps Alfonso García, Manuel's *hermano de leche*) could not have been present, and presumably heard the story from Manuel himself. Don Juan's prologue would have us associate this strategy with the compilation of *escrituras*, which, whether a reference to the Bible or to authoritative chronicles, constituted a rhetoric of authority in Christian Iberia (see ch. 2). It is also worth noting a basic structural similarity to the Islamic strategy of *isnād*, the chain of transmission used to affirm the reliability of the sayings of Muḥammad (*ḥadīth*) that was subsequently adapted in secular Andalusī prose.[14] But there is an important difference. While other religious and academic strategies of authorization are rooted in an established consensus about the integrity of the sources, Don Juan's sources are established as trustworthy based on their proximity to himself and his family. Jaume I adopts a similar strategy in the early chapters of his *Llibre dels fets*, which recount his conception, birth, and early childhood, relying on accounts he heard from high-ranking nobles, royal stewards, and "altres qui ho viren per sos uyls" ("others who saw it with their own eyes"; 13, par. 9). When events are narrated orally by an individual with close personal ties to the narrator, they become integrated into his lived experience and can be recounted as such.

In the first *razón*, the crucial role of women narrators, particularly Juan Manuel's mother Beatriz de Saboya (Beatrice of Savoy), contributes to a persuasive narrative that appropriates the lived experience of the author's ancestors (Lizabe 390). The bodily connection between mothers and sons through nursing, which Don Juan evokes by describing his tutor Alfonso García as his father's *hermano de leche* (milk brother), suggests a more direct transmission of lived experience.[15] Beatriz of course did not witness her husband's birth in 1234, roughly sixteen years before she was born, but her account of the pregnancy and delivery of Infante Manuel by Queen Beatriz de Suabia (Beatrice of Swabia, wife of King Fernando III and also mother of Manuel's older brother, Alfonso X) is imbued with the authority of women's shared, embodied experience. Elements such as the queen's prophetic dreams about her two sons – positive for Manuel and negative for Alfonso – are more valuable for their literary and political persuasiveness than for their historical accuracy: maternal premonitory dreams, like scenes of miraculous breastfeeding, are a common trope in Arabic popular epics (Schine 167n7). Nevertheless, Don Juan emphasizes how the participants in each scene, past or present, narrate their own experience. For example, rather than simply recount what the queen dreamed, Don Juan writes that the queen *told* her dream about Infante Manuel to her husband, and the king *told* her that the dream seemed very different from the one she had while pregnant with Alfonso (*Obras*, ed. Alvar and

Finci, 980). Don Juan, in turn, heard this story from his mother "seyendo yo moço pequeño" ("as a small child"; 980), forging bodily, dynastic, and narrative ties that no other writer could possess. The uniqueness of this personal connection between events narrated and narrating subject comes into focus when compared to the version of the prophecy narrated in the *Crónica Geral de Espanha de 1344* by Count Pedro de Barcelos. Despite offering direct discourse in the form of a dialogue between Queen Beatriz and King Fernando, the *Crónica* ultimately projects the narrative distance of the chronicler, in contrast to the intimacy of Don Juan's account (Ruiz 82–3; Funes, "La blasfemia").

The second *razón* strays the furthest from Don Juan's experience, delving into his family history to explain why he and his father enjoyed the privilege of knighting others, despite not technically being knights themselves. Nevertheless, he continues to craft a narrative that centres his own voice and eschews written sources of authority such as royal chronicles or legal texts. The story focuses on three daughters of Jaume I: Infanta Violante, who married Alfonso X; Infanta Constanza, the first wife of Infante Manuel; and Infanta Sancha, who renounced her royal title and became a pilgrim to the Holy Land. In keeping with the work's dichotomy of Infante Manuel as "elect" and Alfonso X as "reprobate" (Dunn, "Structures" 61–2), Don Juan portrays Manuel's wife Constanza as a sympathetic figure, while Alfonso's wife Violante is cast as hateful and wicked. According to Don Juan, Constanza was murdered by her sister shortly after Alfonso had tricked Manuel into relinquishing his claim to the title of king of Murcia (a claim whose main privilege seemed to be the right to confer knighthood).

In relating this story, he continues to emphasize the oral testimony of an intimate group of eyewitnesses, including his tutor Alfonso García, his first wife Isabel of Mallorca, Isabel's ladies-in-waiting, and Savrina de Bedes (Saurina de Bessers or Béziers), the nurse of his second wife Constanza of Aragon (daughter of Jaume II).[16] He occasionally calls attention to how his faulty memory leaves gaps in the narrative: for example, he cannot remember the exact rank of the prelate who miraculously revealed Infanta Sancha's identity (*Obras*, ed. Alvar and Finci, 986), and he can only remember the refrain of a song about the conflict between Jaume I and the Castilian royal family (989). Finally, he concludes the *razón* with a memory of his experience participating in a knighting ceremony as a toddler not even two years old:

> Mandaron el rey don Alfonso, mio tío, e mio padre que fiziese yo cavalleros en su vida de ellos, et fizlos ante que yo oviese dos años; ca cuando mio padre murió, non avía yo más de un año et ocho meses. Ca yo nací en

> Escalona, martes cinco días de mayo, era de mill et ccc et xx años, et murió mio padre en Peñafiel, sábado día de Navidat, era de mill et ccc [et xx] et un año. (991)
>
> Both King Alfonso (my uncle) and my father commanded me to confer knighthood during their lifetime, and I did so before I turned two; for when my father died, I was no more than a year and eight months old. For I was born in Escalona on Tuesday, the fifth of May, in the era of 1320 [1282 CE], and my father died in Peñafiel on Saturday, Christmas Day, in the era of 1321 [1283 CE].

This scene almost certainly exaggerates the facts (Ruiz 110–11), but it nonetheless meets Bruss's criteria for autobiography: the verifiable dates contribute to truth-value; Don Juan's precocious participation in the ceremony provides act-value; and the first-person narration speaks to identity-value. It also gives us another glimpse of how the narrator's memory leaves gaps in the narration: in contrast to the scene of Sancho IV's deathbed speech, there is no description of how the young Don Juan interacted with his father, or how he felt in the moment. The filter of Don Juan's intellect (*entendimiento*) is not perfect, but it lends unity to the narrative in a way that centres its identity-value. This, along with his close personal ties to his oral sources, helps emphasize the literary value of his lived experience.

The second *razón* is also the most fictionalized of the three, borrowing folkloric and hagiographic motifs to tell the three sisters' stories, including the intriguing but fictional detail that Violante killed Constanza through a gift of poisoned cherries (Deyermond, "Cuentos"; Kinkade, *Dawn* 110). However, given the permeable boundaries between history and literature, not only in medieval chronicles but in autobiography from all periods, this does not contradict Don Juan's claim to depict what "really" happened. Jaume I's *Llibre dels fets* had also used literary motifs, drawing upon a now-lost tradition of Catalan *chansons de geste* to embellish the king's military exploits (Riquer 415–18). In the second *razón*, the fictional embellishments paradoxically help bolster the verisimilitude of the sisters' stories by emphasizing their historical specificity and by breaking free from the moralizing confines of exemplarity, as I have shown elsewhere ("It's a Man's World" 1408). In particular, Constanza's chivalric adventures – first as a young lover attempting to elope with Infante Enrique, and later as the persecuted wife of Infante Manuel – resonate as true to life because they align with readers' assumptions about the Aragonese and Castilian royal families, such as the popular image of Enrique as a rebellious knight. Her tragic death also avoids the familiar pattern of rewarding good characters and punishing wicked ones, which lends it a striking singularity. Additionally, the selection of three sisters, rather than two or four, highlights the work's literary artifice by echoing its tripartite division, also repeated several times in the third *razón* (Qués 104). Don Juan does not hide the arbitrary grouping of Violante, Constanza, and Sancha, briefly mentioning a fourth sister and leaving Sancha's story underdeveloped (though Deyermond attempts to justify its presence as lending an "atmosphere of sanctity" to the Manuel dynasty; "Cuentos" 81). But rather than view these traces of creative intervention as "problems" in conflict with the work's claim to truth, we can take them as further evidence of how he makes this work his own.

The third *razón* is the most closely linked to Don Juan's experience, as it recounts his audience with his cousin, Sancho IV of Castile, while the monarch was on his deathbed. Narrating in the first person, Don Juan sets the scene in detail, recounting the year (1294), the political situation at the frontier with Naṣrid Granada, the king's weakened physical condition, and his good will towards his young cousin. By the time Don Juan begins narrating the monarch's speech, he has carefully laid out his own subject position as a young and impressionable but loyal youth. The evocative images that led Deyermond to declare this section a masterpiece ("*Libro*" 102) also serve to convince readers of the author's eyewitness status and the accuracy of his memory. For example, he names the physicians and other nobles present at the scene; describes how Sancho "tomóme de los braços et asentóme cerca sí" ("took me by the arms and sat me close to him"; *Obras*, ed. Alvar and Finci, 994); and recalls a harrowing moment in which "tomól [al rey] una tos tan fuerte, non podiendo echar aquello que arrancava de los pechos, que bien otras dos vezes lo tobiemos por muerto" ("[the king] was overcome by such a strong cough, struggling to get out what was in his lungs, that twice more we took him for dead"; 995). This rhetoric of eyewitnessing and personal testimony develops further when Sancho himself confesses the curse he received from his father, Alfonso X, which had been transmitted a generation earlier from Alfonso's father, Fernando III. Putting this information in the king's voice strengthens Don Juan's self-aggrandizement (Dunn, "Structures" 62). It also allows him to put into practice the narration of experience he had advocated for (but implemented infrequently) in his earlier works. By writing about an event he witnessed, Don Juan realizes his aim of transforming lived experience into literature.

Don Juan's artistic shaping of the *Libro de las tres razones* can be read as part of his broader authorial project, in line with his self-presentation as a poet in the *Conde Lucanor*. Writing in verse provided clear signs – metre, rhyme, and sometimes musical notation – that readers or listeners should attend to the aesthetic qualities of language and admire the poet's ability to manipulate them. In contrast, Juan Manuel's prose works favour a style that is clear (*declarado*) and complete (*complido*) but also succinct (*en las menos palabras que pudiéredes*) (Orduna, "Fablar"). This stylistic preference tends to keep the reader's attention on what is said, rather than on how it is said. However, Don Juan also appreciates the aesthetic qualities of prose: for example, he writes that he composed the *Conde Lucanor* in "las más apuestas palabras que yo pude" ("the most beautiful words I could"), so that readers would be drawn in by the lovely style in the same way that the liver is attracted to sweet things (12). He also experiments with more obscure and abbreviated prose styles in parts 2–4 of the *Conde Lucanor*, in ways that call attention to his artistry (Cherchi; de Looze 116, 185–237). In the closing lines of the *Libro de las tres razones*, he asserts that his account tells the truth (*verdat*) even if there are "algunas palabras más o menos, o mudadas en alguna manera" ("some words in excess, missing, or altered in some way"; *Obras*, ed. Alvar and Finci, 997). A book can be true even if its author omits or embellishes some parts of the story. In light of this, the artistic interventions in the *Libro de las tres razones* are not meant to pass unnoticed: they are Don Juan's way of using the storytelling strategies he developed over the course of his career to tell a story of fundamental personal importance, a story only he could tell.

His Own Devotion

The last of Juan Manuel's extant works, the *Tratado de la Asunción*, was written around the same time as the *Libro de las tres razones*, sometime after 1342 (Ayerbe-Chaux, "Introduction" xvi). In this brief treatise addressed to Fray Remón Masquefa – a Dominican friar who served as prior in Barcelona and Valencia – Don Juan is inspired by the Feast of the Assumption of the Virgin Mary, celebrated annually on 14 and 15 August, to defend the contested point of the Assumption, the belief that Mary was taken up to heaven in both body and soul.[17] Given its doctrinal subject matter, it can be categorized as vernacular theology, making it an outlier among the works of his personal period. Indeed, after the introductory section that serves as its prologue, the treatise imitates a scholastic mode of argumentation, presenting presumed doctrinal truths ("cierto es que ... "; "todos saben que ... ") followed by an exploration of their logical consequences. However, the prologue itself is in keeping with Juan Manuel's earlier prologues in its focus on the author's lived experience, and in its originality compared with the rest of the work.

The conversational tone of the prologue, which comprises nearly a third of this short work, draws the reader in (Lacarra, *Don Juan* 146). Don Juan recounts a discussion he had with his father-in-law, Jaume II of Aragon, about feelings: specifically, feeling aggrieved by the negative actions of others. This conversation leads him to reflect on the word "zeal" (which he spells *zelo*), the difference between zeal and jealousy (which he distinguishes by the spelling *celo*), and the power of religious zeal to make people act righteously. After this brief etymological excursus, he returns to narrating his experience:

> Et por ende vos digo que el otro día, que era la fiesta de la Asuptión, a que llaman en Castiella "Santa María de Agosto mediado," oí dezir a algunas personas onradas et muy letradas que algunos ponién dubda si era santa María en cuerpo et en alma en Paraíso. Et bien vos digo que ove d'esto muy grant pesar, et movido por este buen zelo dicho, comoquier que [...] entendiendo que segunt el mio estado, que me caía más fablar en ál que en esto, peró por el grand pesar que ove d'esto que oí, pensé de dezir et fazer contra ello. (*Obras*, ed. Alvar and Finci, 1003)

> And so I tell you that the other day, which was the Feast of the Assumption, which they call in Castile "Saint Mary of Mid-August," I heard some honourable and very learned people say that some individuals doubted whether Saint Mary was in Paradise in body and soul. And let me tell you that I was very afflicted by this, and, moved by this aforementioned good zeal, even though [...] I know that according to my estate it would be better for me to speak of something else, still, due to this great affliction over what I heard, I decided to say and do something against this.

This scene is sprinkled with personal details, local colour, and the narrator's emotional reactions. The body of the treatise, with its schematic argumentative structure, Gospel quotations, and untranslated use of the Latin adverb *indirecte*, imitates genres that a layperson would not ordinarily compose, including sermons and scholastic theological proofs (Ayerbe-Chaux, "Introduction" xxxviii; Gómez Redondo, *Historia de la prosa* 1: 1201). However, the prologue frames this subject matter within the author's experience of an informal religious disputation, recalling Don Juan's doctrinal debate with "some very wise Muslims" (*algunos moros muy sabidores*) in the *Libro de los estados* II.3 (Gómez Redondo, *Historia de la prosa* 1: 1199). Even when attempting to emulate a scholastic proof, he uses the narration of lived experience as his primary strategy for claiming authority. In this way, the *Tratado de la Asunción* is consistent with his other late works in portraying him primarily as an author who writes his own words.

Don Juan also claims the role of author in the *Tratado de la Asunción* by subtly incorporating the act of writing into his narration. As discussed in chapter 3, Juan Manuel treats the composition of vernacular theology as a devotional act that complies with three of the seven spiritual works of mercy: "Castigar a los errados e amostrar a los no sabios e consejar al que ha mester consejo" ("Admonish those in error, instruct the ignorant, and advise those who need counsel"; *Libro del cavallero et del escudero*, 50). This is especially true of the *Tratado de la Asunción*, which posits that those who doubt the Assumption are approaching heretical beliefs (*Obras*, ed. Alvar and Finci, 1004). In the passage quoted above, Don Juan takes action to correct this error by composing the very treatise we are reading, which is the thing he "decided to say and do" in response to his compatriots' doctrinal doubts. He thus takes moral responsibility for his words, tapping into the ethical and legal implications of the author as *actor* and *assertor*.

Yet even in this mature expression of authorship, he still returns to the rhetoric of scribal copying. He twice refers to his treatise as a *librete* ("little book"; 1003 and 1007), with a diminutive that not only expresses modesty but also emphasizes the work's materiality.[18] Regardless of how readers actually experience the treatise (for modern readers, almost certainly in a larger anthology of Juan Manuel's works), the word *librete* conjures up a small booklet or a folded piece of parchment. In *S*, it takes up just two and a half folios (191v–193v). This recalls Don Juan's strategy of portraying his involvement in the bookmaking process discussed in chapter 1, which helped his audience envision him in the role of scribe. It also evokes the image of the treatise as a portable symbol of his religious devotion. By combining rhetorical strategies corresponding to scribes and authors, he assumes responsibility for both the material and ethical aspects of his treatise.

Don Juan's Words in Prime Place

Juan Manuel's most original works occupy a privileged place in his corpus as it has come down to us in manuscript *S*. Ruiz observes that the *Libro de las tres razones* serves as Juan Manuel's "escudo representativo" ("representative coat of arms"): it is an identifying symbol of his lineage and social persona, as well as a means of defence and self-glorification (109). As one of the last works he composed and the first to be mentioned in the General Prologue's list of works, it undeniably holds a special place in his corpus. I believe this special status extends to the other works discussed in this chapter: the General Prologue gives subtle indications that he prized his most "authorial" works, that is, his most personal and original works, over the others. His list is bookended with his two most personal works (the *Libro de las tres razones* and *Libro infinido*) at the beginning, and his two most poetic works (*Libro de las cantigas* and *Reglas de cómo se deve trobar*) at the end:

> El primero [libro] tracta de la razón por que fueron dadas al infante don Manuel, mío padre, estas armas, que son alas et leones; et por qué yo et mío fijo, legítimo heredero, et los herederos del mi linage podemos fazer cavalleros non lo seyendo nós; et de la fabla que fizo conmigo el rey don Sancho en Madrit ante de su muerte. Et el otro, de castigos et de consejos que dó a mi fijo don Ferrando, et son todas cosas que yo prové; et el otro libro es *De los estados*; et el otro es el *Libro del cavallero et del escudero*; et el otro, el *Libro de la cavallería*; et el otro, de la *Crónica abreviada*; et el otro, la *Crónica conplida*; et el otro, el *Libro de los engeños*; et el otro, el *Libro de la caça*; et el otro, el *Libro de las cantigas* que yo fiz; et el otro, *De las reglas cómmo se deve trobar*. (ed. Serés, 5–6)

> The first [book] deals with the reason why our coat of arms, with wings and lions, was given to the Infante Don Manuel, my father; and why I and my son and legitimate heir and the heirs of my family line can bestow knighthood on others without being knights ourselves; and the speech King Sancho made to me in Madrid before his death. And another is of lessons and advice I give to my son Don Fernando, all based on things I experienced; and another is [called] *De los estados*; and another is the *Libro del cavallero et del escudero*; and another, the *Libro de la cavallería*; and another, the *Crónica abreviada*; and another, the *Crónica complida*; and another, the *Libro de los engeños*; and another, the *Libro de la caza*; and another, the *Libro de las cantigas* that I wrote; and another, *Reglas de cómo se deve trobar*. (trans. Cossío Olavide and Savo, 5)

In this list, which seems to serve as a table of contents for a lost antigraph (B. Taylor, "*Estoria*" 39), Don Juan guides readers to begin with the two works that deal most directly with his experience.[19] Instead of titles, he gives concise summaries that emphasize his personal connection to his subject matter (*mío padre; yo et mío fijo; mi linage*) and the centrality of his experience (*la fabla que fizo conmigo el rey don Sancho; cosas que yo prové*). The "*Libro de las cantigas* que yo fiz" also stands out in a small but significant way: Don Juan has already presented the list as "todos los libros que yo fasta aquí he fechos" ("all the books I have written up until now"; 5), so the extra assertion of authorship with the verb *fazer* is redundant. This suggests that Don Juan, or one of his associates, considered his poetic composition especially noteworthy. It also helps counter the theory that the *Libro de las cantigas* consisted of prose adaptations of Alfonso X's *Cantigas de Santa Maria,* since this unqualified assertion of authorship does not match how Juan Manuel refers to other works from his Alfonsine period.[20]

The *Libro de las tres razones* is significant to the codicological history of Juan Manuel's collected works in another way. Although the *Libro del cavallero et del escudero* precedes it in *S,* its prime position in the lost antigraph means that its program of illumination – brilliantly reconstructed by Cossío Olavide ("*Libro*") – would also have been prominent in an earlier codex.[21] Cossío Olavide argues that its first illumination, designed to appear immediately after the General Prologue, was the Manuel dynasty's coat of arms (9–12). Few such heraldic images survive in medieval Castilian manuscripts before the fifteenth century, but they subsequently became popular marks of ownership for works commissioned by aristocratic patrons. Beginning in the late fifteenth century, they also gained popularity in the *carta ejecutoria de hidalguía,* a type of Spanish legal document asserting an individual's nobility, legitimacy, and "purity of blood" (*limpieza de sangre*).[22] In these documents, heraldic illustrations served as a symbol of the family's noble status, religious devotion, and local ties (Ruiz García 272; Rhodes 57–8).

The illustration of Juan Manuel's coat of arms would have served a similar purpose, but it could also be interpreted as a seal of authorship, providing a visual link between author and book (Cossío Olavide, "*Libro*" 10). This connection between the writer's "real-world" self and the imaginative space of the page recalls Sonja Drimmer's meditation on the medieval author portrait, an image designed to "[embody] the words that purport to emerge from the exogenous body it represents" (69). While the image of Juan Manuel's coat of arms is not a true author portrait, it similarly purports to embody the extratextual author through a recognizable symbol of his family's historical specificity and social status. Its presence in the initial folios of his collected works manuscript would have reinforced the impression that, despite the intervention of scribes and illuminators, he alone was responsible for the book.

As Gómez Redondo observes, Juan Manuel's *Libro infinido* and *Libro de las tres razones* are the sole precursors to the trend of fifteenth-century aristocratic biographies in Castilian, including Leonor López de Córdoba's *Memorias*, Gutierre Díez de Games's biography of Pero Niño (*El Victorial*), and Fernán Pérez de Guzmán's biographical anthology *Generaciones y semblanzas* (*Historia de la prosa* 2: 2334). His way of textualizing the self is distinct from its Castilian, Iberian, and European precursors. It does not function as a Christian allegory of salvation, like Augustine's *Confessions* or Dante Alighieri's *Commedia*. It is neither a self-reflective courtly love persona, like Ibn Ḥazm in his *Ṭawq al-Ḥamāma* or Dante in his *Vita nuova*, nor a parody of this persona, like Juan Ruiz in the *Libro de buen amor*. Its closest predecessor is Jaume I's autobiographical *Llibre dels fets*, but Jaume's work was backed by his authority as monarch, while Juan Manuel needed to build a rhetorical justification for writing about himself. The deeds depicted in the Castilian's late works fulfil an exemplary function, but they also stand as a testament to a life well-lived, by the standards of his noble estate. In writing them down, Don Juan asserts that an individual's life (or at least that of a noble individual) need not be reduced to its exemplarity, but has intrinsic historical and literary value. These late works, possibly the texts of which Juan Manuel was proudest, were in line with the literary endeavours of fifteenth-century humanists, whose biographies and personal chronicles continued to develop strategies for the textualization of personal experience.

The Ethical Author

Juan Manuel's focus on lived experience in his later works is part of a constellation of strategies that serve not only to vindicate the Manuel dynasty, but also to preserve a record of his deeds, particularly his acts of devotion. As mentioned earlier, composing works of vernacular theology such as the *Tratado de la Asunción* could already be construed as an act of devotion, for its potential to spread and strengthen the Christian faith. The counterpart to this was the preservation of his literary works, which would commemorate his ethical and spiritual contributions for future generations. Deyermond ("*Libro*" 92), Ayerbe-Chaux ("Memorias"), and Holly Sims have elucidated this function of the *Libro de las tres razones* through a comparison to Leonor López de Córdoba's *Memorias*, another text that seeks to vindicate its author's family name in response to persecution from the Castilian monarch. As Sims has shown, these two nobles used a combination of strategies to mould their legacies, including the composition of autobiographical narratives and the founding of religious and funerary monuments: Juan Manuel established the monastery of San Pablo in Peñafiel, while López de Córdoba endowed the Chapel of the Rosary in the church of San Pablo in Córdoba. Both figures were buried in their respective monuments, initiating family pantheons that served as "architectural statements of virtue" (Sims 69). The claim that Juan Manuel deposited a copy of his collected works at the monastery of San Pablo comes from the anteprologue to the *Conde Lucanor*, and thus cannot be considered authentic. However, the fact that this anteprologue was copied into most extant premodern copies of his works (*S, H, M, P, G*, and *N*) suggests that the combination of an architectural and funerary monument with a literary testament was consistent with the expectations of late medieval scribes and readers.[23]

The trope of a deceased person laid to rest with a devotional work was shared across confessional lines in Iberia: some Muslims buried their dead with a copy of the Quran or a selection of Quranic verses, and Alfonso X requested that copies of his *Cantigas de Santa María* be stored in the church that held his tomb (Bamford, *Cultures* 117). Alfonso's *Cantigas* provide a close precedent for Juan Manuel in that they were a devotional work for which the king claimed declarative authorship. Still, the miniatures of Alfonso in two of the extant manuscripts – the Códice Rico (Escorial, MS T.I.1) and Florentine Codex (Biblioteca Nazionale Centrale, MS B.R.20) – portray the songs' making as a collective endeavour in which the king in the centre relies upon the collaboration of the scribes, musicians, and scholars that surround him (Galvez 7, 116–25) (see fig. 4.1). Juan Manuel's body of work is similarly devotional and personal, but it offers a different authorial self-presentation, one in which the many collaborators in the bookmaking process recede into invisibility, upstaged by the solitary figure of Don Juan. The preservation of his books serves as tangible evidence not just of his religious devotion and acts of authorship, but of this compelling authorial persona.

Qualities that we would call creativity and self-expression dominate in the works in which Don Juan assumes the role of author. They play an important part in distinguishing his discourse of authorship from the rhetoric of copying, compilation, and commentary deployed throughout his corpus. Yet for this devout medieval writer, these qualities were not an end in themselves. His self-portrayal as a creative author served what was for him a greater purpose: to reap the full ethical and spiritual benefits of writing. In his authorial self-defence from the *Libro infinido*, he affirms that his books contain "pro et verdad et non daño" ("profit and truth and no harm"; 177). Not only are these benefits transmitted to readers, but they also reflect back onto the one responsible for the book. But when cast in the role of *scriptor*, *compilator*, or *commentator*, Don Juan must share the benefits with his sources.

This issue of shared authority is especially visible in part 1 of the *Conde Lucanor*, which has remained his most widely read work from the fifteenth century to the present. Despite Juan Manuel's undeniable

Fig. 4.1. Portrait of Alfonso X in the *Cantigas de Santa María*. Patrimonio Nacional, Real Biblioteca del Monasterio de El Escorial, MS T.I.1, fol. 5r, https://rbdigital.realbiblioteca.es/s/rbme.

creative interventions in the exemplary tales, he portrays them not as his own words, but as *auctoritates* derived from external sources. Many scholars of the *Conde Lucanor*, including Eloísa Palafox, John Dagenais, and Jonathan Burgoyne (*Reading the Exemplum*) – in dialogue with Judson Boyce Allen on ethics and literature, and Larry Scanlon on the authority of the exemplum – have explored how it serves as a rhetorical guide that teaches its audience how to apply the persuasive and powerful language of the exemplum in new contexts. But this lesson would not be possible without the dynamic interplay between the exempla as the "words of others" and Don Juan's own words, nor would his authorial persona be recognized for his prowess as a compiler and commentator. Traditional and repeatable, exempla belonged to no one. Yet for medieval writers, wielding them effectively was an invaluable rhetorical skill.

In contrast, poetry and personal history were two genres that offered a more direct claim to a work's form and content, and thus to its ethical benefits. When writing verse, Juan Manuel drew upon an established tradition of linking poetry with ethics that could be traced back to antiquity. But when writing about his personal experience, his experiments with strategies of self-authorization helped forge a new path of vernacular life-writing for the humanist writers of the fifteenth century to follow. In both cases, claiming the role of *auctor* meant eliminating the layers of mediation between author and book to become an *assertor*, the one who holds full moral responsibility for his words. This would certainly contribute to his earthly fame, as we will see in the epilogue. But as he writes in his *Libro del cavallero et del escudero*, works of mercy should always be done "por amor de Dios verdaderamente, e non por ninguna vana gloria nin alavamiento del mundo" ("out of true love for God, and not out of vainglory or for earthly praise"; 50). For Juan Manuel, becoming an author was, at its core, an act of Christian devotion.

Epilogue: Self-Promotion

The preceding chapters attempt to answer Ayerbe-Chaux's call to extricate Juan Manuel's medieval concept of authorship from our expectations as modern readers, particularly the assumption that he had an "awareness of literary property" that was before his time ("Don Juan" 189). I have provided a revised and comprehensive account of Juan Manuel's concept of authorship as it is portrayed in his works. Through it, I have sought to demonstrate how his authorship is rooted in a medieval manuscript culture in which relationships between books and their makers are not defined exclusively by ownership and are distinct from modern notions of private property. By comparing his works to other texts from medieval Iberia and western Europe, and by considering the manuscript formats in which they circulated, I show that nearly all his descriptions of his authorial activity have literary precedents when taken individually. However, when taken together, his innovation lies in the way he combines the rhetorical strategies of disparate authorial roles and attributes them all to himself. Scribes, compilers, commentators, and authors each had a particular relationship to the books they wrote, which was expressed in the texts themselves, in prologues and other paratexts, and in codicological decisions about order and layout. By deploying the authorial discourse of all four roles, Juan Manuel persuades his readers that his authorial persona, Don Juan, has overseen and is responsible for every step of the bookmaking process.

One of the ironies of studying Juan Manuel's concept of authorship, one that I have been grappling with throughout this book, is that all the manuscript evidence of his literary works comes from at least fifty years after his death. It thus reflects, in varying degrees, the decisions and interventions of the scribes, compilers, commentators, and editors who act in Juan Manuel's name and can thus be dubbed his associates in Genette's sense of the word. In the preceding chapters, I have focused on how Don Juan is portrayed within this corpus, in the hope of approximating the portrayal conveyed by the lost manuscripts made under the aegis of the historical Juan Manuel in the first half of the fourteenth century. In this epilogue, I aim to bring into focus the interventions of the individuals who edited his works in the fifteenth and sixteenth centuries, the same interventions I have tried to mitigate in earlier chapters.

With very few exceptions, most medieval and early modern copyists accepted the notion that Juan Manuel had been involved in every aspect of making his books. They not only assigned a privileged place to his rhetoric of authorship, but also carried it forward through new interventions that transformed it in subtle ways. The popularity of Juan Manuel's works waned in the seventeenth and eighteenth centuries, but when the philologists of nineteenth-century Europe sought to edit and translate the literature of medieval "Spain," they once again took up this language of authorship, amplified it, and made it their own. I will trace how his authorial rhetoric made its way from late medieval manuscripts, to early modern print editions, to nineteenth-century editions and translations, all while accruing updates from copyists, editors, and scholars. Because his self-presentation was so strong, and because these individuals were invested in a culture of authenticity, it is virtually impossible for modern readers to encounter Juan Manuel's writings without at least some of the later interventions that promote his authorial persona. This epilogue aims to excavate the temporal layers of this self-promotion.

Don Juan in the Early Manuscripts

Only one fifteenth-century manuscript omits any reference to Juan Manuel's name or ideas about authorship. It is Biblioteca de la Universidad de Oviedo, M-497, known as the *O* manuscript of the *Libro de los doce sabios*. It contains the thirteenth-century *Libro de los doce sabios* (fols. 1r–33v), the final verses from part 1 of Juan Manuel's *Conde Lucanor* (fols. 34r–36v), and a compendium known as the *Sumario de los reyes de España* that dates from the late fourteenth or early fifteenth century (fols. 37r–121v, not foliated in the manuscript).[1] Based on its watermarks, Gemma Avenoza dates it to the early fifteenth century, possibly between 1412 and 1439 (PhiloBiblon, BETA manid 4898).[2] If manuscripts *P*, *S*, *M*, and *H* were all copied in the mid to late fifteenth century, as is likely, this places *O* among the earliest surviving copies of a work by Juan Manuel.[3]

In some ways, *O* treats the *viessos* from part 1 of the *Conde Lucanor* as a discrete text. The scribe copies them at the start of a new folio (fol. 34r) and does the same for the *Sumario* (fol. 37r). Red paragraph marks set off each of the distichs while line breaks highlight their metre and rhyme, distinguishing them visually from the prose texts that precede and follow. However, unlike the *Libro de los doce sabios*, which begins with a prologue dedicated to its declarative author, Fernando III of Castile and Leon, the verses lack any kind of prologue, introduction, or authorial attribution. A sixteenth-century copy, Biblioteca Menéndez Pelayo, MS M-92 (known as the *M* manuscript of the *Libro de los doce sabios*), also lacks any mention of Don Juan or the *Conde Lucanor*. Jonathan Burgoyne, in a comparative study of early copies of the *viessos*, shows that it was not unusual for medieval and early modern editors to extract them from their context, with or without attribution ("Los versos" 148). However, even in *O*, there are traces of a discourse of authorship quite similar to that of Don Juan.

As Burgoyne notes, there are two interpolations among the *viessos*. After the couplet corresponding to ex. 13, the manuscript reads:

> ¶Sobre esto fizo Rey
> Alfonso estos versos:
> ¶Non pares mientes a ojos que lloran
> mas a manos commo lavoran. (74 [fol. 34v])[4]
>
> On this King Alfonso wrote these verses: Pay no mind to eyes that cry, but to hands that work.

After those corresponding to ex. 31, there is a similar addition:

> ¶Nota Diego García:
> ¶Mientra te dan la cabrilla
> tú con tu soguilla.
> [36r] ¶En lavor de cras
> pon mano e faz. (76 [fol. 35v–36r])
>
> Diego García notes: When they give you a goat, you bring the rope. In tomorrow's work, don't delay; get to work right away.

The copyist of *O* gives the attributions to King Alfonso and Diego García in specially rubricated sections in the body of the text (see fig. 5.1), while the copyist of *M* moves them to the upper margins (Burgoyne, "Los versos" 147). These interpolations are significant for three reasons. First, Burgoyne interprets them as evidence of a tradition of extracting and compiling the *Conde Lucanor*'s verses into collections that can easily incorporate additional proverbs, typically linked through similar ethical messages ("Los versos" 148). Second, the verses of "King Alfonso" link these manuscripts to witnesses *H*, *M*, and *G* of the *Conde Lucanor*, in which they similarly appear as alternative verses for ex. 13, introduced as follows: "E sobre esta razón fizo otro verso Suer Alfonso, fraile de Santiago, que dize así" ("And on this topic Suer Alfonso, a friar from Santiago, wrote another verse that goes like this"; 398).[5] The most likely explanation for the discrepancy between Suer Alfonso and King Alfonso is that someone named Suer Alfonso added the verses to an early manuscript of the *Conde Lucanor*, and subsequent copyists of this branch of transmission, including the scribe of *O*, carried them forward (Burgoyne, "Los versos" 147; Hammer, *Framing* 223). The change from "Suer" to "Rey" is either an error or a deliberate attempt to evoke the literary authority of Alfonso X or Alfonso XI, each known as a poet to differing degrees.[6]

Third, the interpolations show that even when Don Juan is not named as the author of the verses, scribes take care to distinguish his words from the words of others. In the case of the interpolations by Suer/King Alfonso, it is remarkable that five different manuscripts (*O* and *M* of the *Libro de los doce sabios* and *H*, *M*, and *G* of the *Conde Lucanor*) concur in their attribution with only minor variations.

The concern Don Juan expressed for scribal error in his General Prologue, even at the level of the letter (*porque las letras semejan unas a otras*), has not carried over into the surviving manuscripts, in which his *viessos* often exhibit variants that change their form and meaning (de Looze 17–21). But scribes did imitate the ways in which his works incorporated statements of authorial attribution. The presentation of Suer Alfonso's verses echoes the repetition of "Don Johán [...] fizo estos viessos" with which each *enxiemplo* of part 1 concludes. The verses themselves are one syllable away from a decasyllabic couplet (*arte mayor*), making them similar to one of Don Juan's metrical patterns, which imitates the Galician-Portuguese dactylic decasyllable (Gómez Redondo, *Historia de la poesía* 637). In other words, they are the composition of a *versificador* attentive to metre and rhythm, and thus merit attribution as a display of their author's skill.[7]

In contrast, Diego García's additions are not verses in *arte mayor* but popular sayings (*refranes*) in *arte menor* that appear in other sources. For example, the first is cited in the *Libro de buen amor* as "quando te dan la cabrilla, acorre con la soguilla" (212 [870b]), and the second as "En labor de cras, pon mano, y haz" in Hernán Núñez's 1555 *Refranes o proverbios en romance* (fol. 50r). Diego García's contribution is distinguished

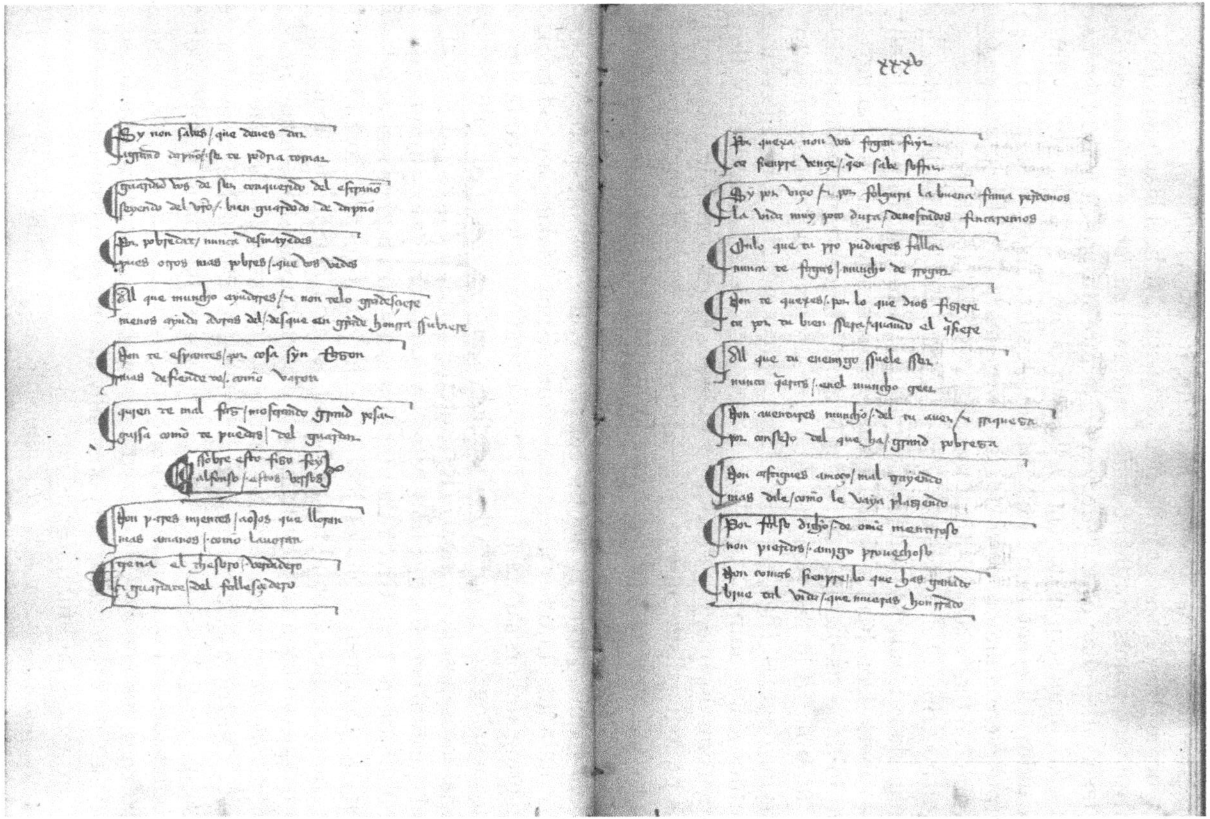

Fig. 5.1. Interpolated verses of "Rey Alfonso." Universidad de Oviedo, CEMs-497, fols. 34v–35r (verses on 34v).

from Don Juan's verses with the verb *notar*, indicating the work of a scribe or compiler rather than an author. These interventions show that fifteenth- and sixteenth-century copyists perceived Don Juan's verses as an "original" corpus belonging to one *versificador*, regardless of whether they knew or indicated his name. Michael Hammer, citing Carruthers, points out that because medieval *auctores* were conceived as texts rather than people, the verses' lack of attribution in the *Libro de los sabios* manuscripts does not take away from their authority or ethical utility ("Decentering" 197). Although silent modifications to this corpus were common, new additions were marked with expressions of attribution that recognized the authorial activities of others.

Manuscripts *O* and *M* of the *Libro de los doce sabios* are outliers among the medieval and early modern copies of Juan Manuel's works. In all the others, Don Juan's name figures prominently, both in paratexts and in the texts themselves. What is more, the concept of authorship he formulated in the General Prologue also appears, transformed to varying degrees. The General Prologue only appears in *S*, the fifteenth-century single-author anthology believed to be a descendant of the copy commissioned by the author himself. As discussed in chapter 1, this prologue distinguishes "high" from "low" scribal labour, placing the two in an interdependent relationship in which intellectual decisions about which books to reproduce go hand in hand with the manual labour required to carry out the copying. Within a short space, it also lays out a host of other ideas about authorship. Making a good book can bring authors satisfaction and praise, and can help them communicate meaning (*sentencia*) to their audience, often through ethically beneficial messages. But scribal errors interfere with the personal, ethical, and spiritual benefits that flow between author and reader through the medium of the text. Given the importance of this author-reader relationship, Don Juan's solution in the General Prologue is to commission a volume centred around his authorial persona, containing "todos los libros que yo fasta aquí he fechos" ("all the books I have made thus far"; *Conde Lucanor*, ed. Serés, 4). Listing his works in a deliberate order can be construed as an attempt to guide the *ordinatio* of this codex. This is also reflected in other aspects of his works: the round numbers of subdivisions announced in the paratexts of the *Libro de los estados* and the *Conde Lucanor*, as well as the tables of contents produced for these and the *Crónica abreviada*, can potentially discourage interpolations and ensure a more faithful transmission.

Juan Manuel's approach to authorship aligns with the increase in author involvement and single-author codices in other European vernaculars in the fourteenth century, particularly in French and Italian.[8]

But while writers like Petrarch took matters into their own hands by creating and editing autograph manuscripts, the Don Juan of the General Prologue never fully rejects the collaborative means of book production characteristic of a manuscript culture. Rather, by imbuing his works with the rhetoric of different types of writers – scribes, compilers, commentators, and authors – he places his authorial persona at the centre of these collaborative networks of book production.

With María Rosa Menocal, we might see some irony in the fact that the surviving manuscripts of Juan Manuel's works contain so many variants, omissions, and additions (488).[9] However, in other ways, Juan Manuel's attempt to establish himself as an author through codicological means evidently took hold. In all the medieval and early modern manuscripts of Juan Manuel's works except for the *Libro de los doce sabios* manuscripts, part 1 of the *Conde Lucanor* is preceded by two prologues. Its "regular" prologue (hereafter simply called the prologue) is a meditation on exemplarity and *similitudo* narrated by Don Juan in the first person.[10] It is preceded by the anteprologue, which meditates on Don Juan's ideas about authorship in the third person and was written by a scribe or compiler who reformulated the General Prologue's ideas (A. Blecua 103–4; Rico 418).

The anteprologue confers authorship on Don Juan just as effectively as its model. It begins with a brief *accessus ad auctores*, declaring the author's name and intention and the work's usefulness: "Este libro fizo don Johán, fijo del muy noble infante don Manuel, deseando que los omnes fiziessen en este mundo tales obras que les fuessen aprovechosas de las onras et de las faziendas et de sus estados, et fuessen más allegados a la carrera por que pudiessen salvar las almas" ("Don Juan, son of the very noble Infante Don Manuel, made this book, with the desire that people would perform deeds in this world that benefit their honour and property and estate, and follow more closely the path to save their souls"; *Conde Lucanor*, ed. Serés, 7). It then turns to the claims from the General Prologue:

> Et porque don Johán vio et sabe que en los libros contece muchos yerros en los transladar, porque las letras semejan unas a otras, cuidando por la una letra que es otra, en escribiéndolo, múdase toda la razón et por aventura confóndese, et los que después fallan aquello escrito ponen la culpa al que fizo el libro. Et porque don Johán se receló desto, ruega a los que leyeren cualquier libro que fuere trasladado del que él conpuso o de los libros que él fizo, que si fallaren alguna palabra mal puesta, que non pongan la culpa a él fasta que vean el libro mismo que don Johán fizo, que es emendado en muchos logares de su letra. E los libros que él fizo son estos que él ha fecho

> fasta aquí: la *Crónica abreviada*, el *Libro de los sabios*, el *Libro de la cavallería*, el *Libro del infante*, el *Libro del cavallero et del escudero*, el *Libro del conde*, el *Libro de la caça*, el *Libro de los engeños*, el *Libro de los cantares*. Et estos libros están en el monesterio de los fraires predicadores que él fizo en Peñafiel. Pero desque vieren los libros que él fizo, por las menguas que en ellos fallaren, non pongan la culpa a la su entención, mas pónganla a la mengua del su entendimiento, porque se atrevió a se entremeter a fablar en tales cosas. (ed. Serés, 7–8)
>
> Don Juan has seen and knows that many errors occur in copying books, because the letters look like one another and can be mistaken for one another in the copying process, and this can change and confuse the whole meaning, and whoever comes along and finds that copy will blame the one who wrote the book. And because Don Juan feared this, he asks whoever reads any copies of the books he composed, if they find some ill-placed word, not to blame him until they see the book that Don Juan himself made, which is emended in many places in his hand. And the books he has written up until now are these: the *Crónica abreviada*, the *Libro de los sabios*, the *Libro de la cavallería*, the *Libro del infante*, the *Libro del cavallero et del escudero*, the *Libro del conde*, the *Libro de la caza*, the *Libro de los engeños*, the *Libro de los cantares*. And these books are in the monastery of the Friars of the Order of Preachers that he founded in Peñafiel. But once they have seen the books he made, they should blame any imperfections in them not on his intentions, but on his lack of discretion, for daring to meddle and speak of such things.

Finally, before transitioning to the text of the *Conde Lucanor*, it adds that Don Juan "fizo todos los sus libros en romance, et esto es señal cierto que los fizo para los legos et de non muy grand saber, commo lo él es" ("wrote all his books in Romance, a sure sign that he made them for laypeople of no great learning, as he is himself"; 8).

De Looze writes that the anteprologue's rhetoric is "that of a witness who speaks with authority *about* Juan Manuel as author and the process of composing the [*Conde Lucanor*], a stance that attests to the degree that the 'author' is, as Michel Foucault would have it, an author-izing and authenticating force/agent more than a sentient, flesh-and-blood creature" (109). How does this rhetoric work? Primarily by recycling and expanding upon the hallmarks of authorship from the General Prologue, including the concern about scribal error, the author-approved codex, the list of Don Juan's works, and the deployment of the humility topos. The *volumen que yo mesmo concerté* becomes a book (or books) *emendado en muchos lugares de su letra*.[11] The third-person narration provides more opportunities to highlight the author's name, which, as shown in the passage above, is repeated three more times after the initial attribution. The sentence that famously announces the deposit of Juan Manuel's collected works in the Dominican monastery at Peñafiel echoes a line in the second version of Juan Manuel's last will and testament, which Gaibrois de Ballesteros dates to 1340: "Acomiendo mi cuerpo que sea enterrado en el monesterio de los frayres Predicadores que yo fiz en Pennafiel" ("I commend my body to be buried in the monastery of the Friars of the Order of Preachers that I founded in Peñafiel"; Gaibrois de Ballesteros, "Testamentos" 49).[12] I cite this parallel not to claim that Juan Manuel wrote the anteprologue, but to propose that his association with the Dominican monastery of San Pablo at Peñafiel was strong enough that the anteprologue's author could reference it to authorize a new compilation of Juan Manuel's works. Sims reminds us that Juan Manuel's fifteenth-century descendants took special pride in the monastery because they lost control over other properties in the *señorío* of Peñafiel (65n100). Moreover, on a metaphorical level, Biaggini rightly identifies this gesture as the forging of a symbolic link between the author's corpse and his corpus (*Le gouvernement* 42). As discussed in the previous chapter, this gesture was not unheard of in Juan Manuel's Castile, but the humanist and antiquarian interests of the fifteenth and sixteenth centuries would continue to strengthen the symbolic importance of the author's body.

The discrepancies between the two lists of works have been studied, but more relevant here is how each list communicates ideas about authorship.[13] In the General Prologue, the list purports to be the table of contents introducing "this volume" (*este volumen*), the single-author codex commissioned by Don Juan. This list confers authority on *S*, the manuscript in which it appears, whose contents and relative luxury reinforce the prologue's message. In contrast, the anteprologue only claims to introduce the *Conde Lucanor*, and its list serves as a catalogue of the copies corrected in the author's own hand and deposited in the monastery at Peñafiel. The authorial version is absent, but it confers authority from a distance by offering readers the possibility of checking their copy against the one at Peñafiel, which would be carefully guarded by the Dominicans whom Juan Manuel had so faithfully supported. As de Looze (33) and Biaggini ("Stratégies" 231) have pointed out, travelling to Peñafiel to check a manuscript would have been costly and impractical. But there was a medieval precedent for depositing important documents at institutions with the resources to preserve them (Olivetto, "Don Juan" 125–6 n44). The anteprologue evokes this practice to create what Biaggini calls an "ideal receptacle" (*écrin idéal*) for the author's intentions ("Stratégies"

231). It conjures up an image of an ideal authorial work whose material conditions are plausible, but whose actual moment of apprehension is postponed indefinitely. This image is kept alive by modern scholars who repeat the unsubstantiated claim that the Peñafiel copy was lost in a fire, reinforcing the notion that Juan Manuel's ideal copy once existed, but was destroyed by a natural disaster beyond human control.

The anteprologue's success compared to the General Prologue can be attributed to its association with the *Conde Lucanor*, but it may also be due in part to this mediated approach to authorship. The anteprologue is prominent in the five main manuscripts of the *Conde Lucanor*, as well as in the single-author anthology of Juan Manuel's works known as *N* (BNE, MS 19426). However, its function varies depending on its placement within the manuscript and the manuscript's overall contents. The manuscripts can be divided into three groups according to their format: the multi-author anthology (*P*, *M*); the single-work codex (*H*, *G*); and the single-author anthology (*S*, *N*).

P and *M* are anthologies of Castilian prose works that both begin with part 1 of the *Conde Lucanor*, starting with the anteprologue. Although I agree with Hammer ("Treating of Virtue" 350) that the *Conde Lucanor*'s role in these anthologies is sometimes overemphasized, the placement, layout, and contents of the anteprologue contribute to the privileged status of Juan Manuel's work. Each codex is unified by a loose thematic relationship: *P* is a "reference tool for orthodox instruction dealing with both secular and religious subject-matter," directed at priests or teachers (Burgoyne, "Reading and Writing" 490), while *M*'s texts are connected by meditations on chivalry, nobility, and virtue (Burgoyne, "Reading to Pieces" 236; Hammer, "Treating of Virtue"). They each contain some anonymous works, such as the *Pater Noster* gloss in *P* and the *Binario de virtudes* in *M*, and some works attributed to named figures, including Infante Fadrique of Castile, who commissioned the Castilian translation of the *Sendebar*, and celebrated authors such as Íñigo López de Mendoza and Francesc Eiximenis.[14] While these anthologies were not designed to be read from cover to cover (de Looze 49–50; Burgoyne, "Reading and Writing" 481), the fact that they both begin with the anteprologue means that the first thing readers encounter is a sustained meditation on Juan Manuel's authorship.

Design features of the manuscripts also emphasize the anteprologue and its discourse of authorship. In *M*, the anteprologue is introduced by the rubric "Aquí comiença el libro que es dicho del conde Lucanor" ("Here begins the book called [the Book] of Count Lucanor") and a red initial with some small flourishes (fol. 1r). It ends with a red paragraph mark and the rubric "el prólogo," signalling the start of the *Conde Lucanor*'s prologue (see fig. 5.2). The early folios of *M* use a red mark (Γ) to indicate pauses, and each title in the list of Juan Manuel's works is set off with this mark, making them stand out on the page.[15] In *P*, the anteprologue is modestly decorated with a red *littera notabilior*, and although there are red marks to indicate section breaks, they are not used to mark the list of works (fol. 1r). Nonetheless, the anteprologue's placement on the first folio calls attention to Don Juan's concerns about the copying of his works. It might seem ironic that *P*, which contains the apocryphal *enxiemplos* 53 and 54 of the *Conde Lucanor*, begins with a paratext that celebrates authorial texts and denounces scribal changes.[16] However, the inclusion of the anteprologue in *P* is consonant with the internal logic of the manuscript for two reasons. First, the apocryphal *enxiemplos* bear no trace of the *Conde Lucanor*'s narrative frame or its built-in authorial attribution ("Et porque entendió don Johán que este enxiemplo era muy bueno ... "), which could represent an attempt to distinguish between authorial and apocryphal tales somewhere along *P*'s chain of transmission. Second, to expand upon a point made by de Looze (51), the anteprologue's function is not to prevent scribes and editors from adapting the *Conde Lucanor* as they see fit, but to perform Juan Manuel's concept of authorship in a way that has the potential

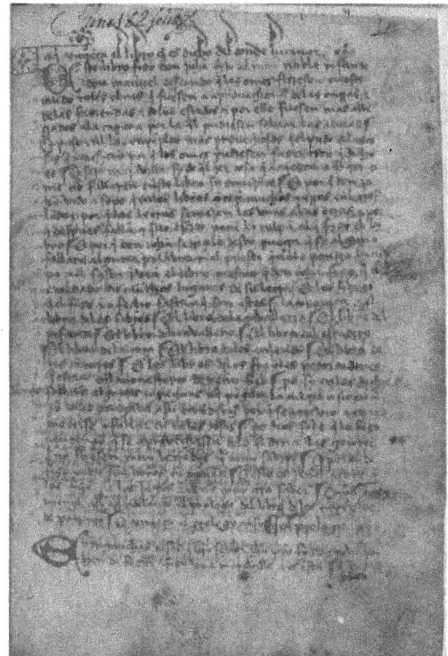

Fig. 5.2. Anteprologue with titles marked, MS *M* (BNE, MS 4236), fol. 1r. Image taken from the holdings of the Biblioteca Nacional de España and licensed under the CC by 4.0 licence.

to persuade readers. Although neither *P* nor *M* is meticulous about authorial attribution, the privileged place of the anteprologue suggests that fifteenth-century editors were interested in the ideas about authorship it conveyed, which could help lend authority to their copies.

Both *H* and *G* are single-work codices that contain only the *Conde Lucanor* (*H* just part 1, and *G* the five-part version).[17] The overall impression of *H*, a fifteenth-century book, is that "someone thought this work by a major author of the previous century worth copying" (de Looze 52). Its first three folios contain the table of contents and are unnumbered, giving them a paratextual status outside the text. Next comes the anteprologue, in which the copyist highlights Don Juan's authorship through a longer variation on the first sentence, written in red ink: "Aquí comiença el libro del conde Lucanor. El qual don Juan fijo del muy noble don Juan [*sic*] Manuel fizo et conpuso" ("Here begins the book of Count Lucanor, which Don Juan, son of the very noble Don Juan [*sic*] Manuel made and composed"; fol. 1r). This eye-catching rubric, with not one but two verbs of authorship (*fazer* and *componer*), prefigures the title page of Argote's 1575 edition, which announces that the work was "compuesto por el excelentíssimo príncipe don Juan Manuel" ("composed by the most excellent prince Don Juan Manuel"). The copyist also minimizes the transition between the anteprologue and prologue, with no line break or red paragraph mark to indicate a new text (de Looze 52; Funes, "Los aportes" 83). Whether an innovation of *H* or of its exemplar, this decision lends authority to the anteprologue by integrating it with the first-person prologue narrated by *yo, don Johán*.

While *G* is also a single-work codex, it is markedly different from *H*. Not only does it contain parts 2–5, but its context and purpose are different: it is a sixteenth-century humanist copy designed for private reading and study rather than for presentation or posterity (de Looze 36–7). The anteprologue begins on fol. 1r, and its first line, "Este libro fizo don Juan" ("Don Juan made this book") is written in larger letters and decorated with a simple pen flourish (see fig. 5.3). We could see this as a way to emphasize the author's name, but it may also be purely decorative, as other folios have such flourishes even when not at section breaks. The anteprologue is separated from the prologue by similar enlarged letters, and its prominent place as the first paratext ensures its consideration by the reader.

S and *N* are single-author anthologies in which Juan Manuel's authorship is the main organizing principle. In *S*, the *Conde Lucanor* appears near the middle of the codex, and the anteprologue immediately precedes it, nestled between the table of contents for part 1 and the *Conde Lucanor*'s prologue (see fig. 5.4). It is written in red ink to

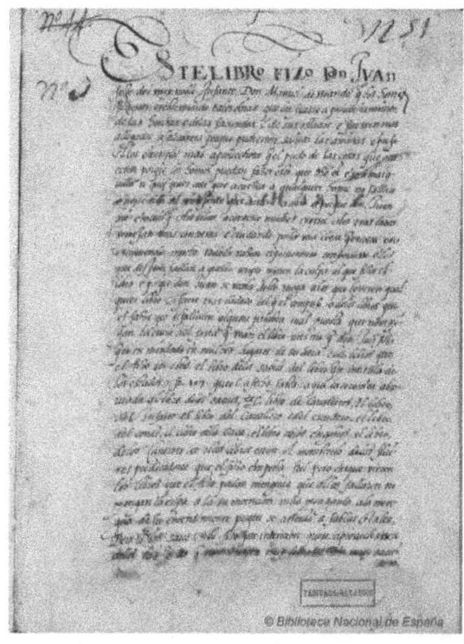

Fig. 5.3. Anteprologue with enlarged declaration of authorship, MS *G* (BNE, MS 18415), fol. 1r. Image taken from the holdings of the Biblioteca Nacional de España and licensed under the CC by 4.0 licence.

mark its status as a paratext "'outside' the text proper" (de Looze 70). *S* has several such "rubricator's prologues" written in red ink: in addition to the anteprologue, there are short, third-person introductions to the *Libro del cavallero et del escudero* and the *Libro de los estados* as well as a colophon in Latin to conclude the *Libro del cavallero et del escudero*.[18] Since *S* begins with the General Prologue, the anteprologue assumes an auxiliary role, referring back to the ideas expressed at the start of the codex. However, given the book's size and length, the red ink also serves to catch the eye of readers who might be paging through at random, rather than reading from start to finish. *S* therefore distinguishes in different ways the two most important texts for communicating Juan Manuel's ideas of authorship, the General Prologue and the anteprologue.

N, first brought to light by Ayerbe-Chaux, is an anthology copied from *S* or a closely related exemplar (Ayerbe-Chaux, "Manuscritos" 92; Burgoyne, "Los versos" 134–7). As a humbly produced copy dating to the first half of the sixteenth century, its material aspects are similar to those of *G*, but it is more akin to *S* in its aim to collect works by Juan Manuel. It begins not with the anteprologue but with the *Libro de las tres razones*, a choice that diminishes the anteprologue's role as a general index. It nevertheless highlights the author figure, since the *Libro de las tres razones* is his most personal work and possibly the one placed first in the collected works manuscript he commissioned.[19] Then, after

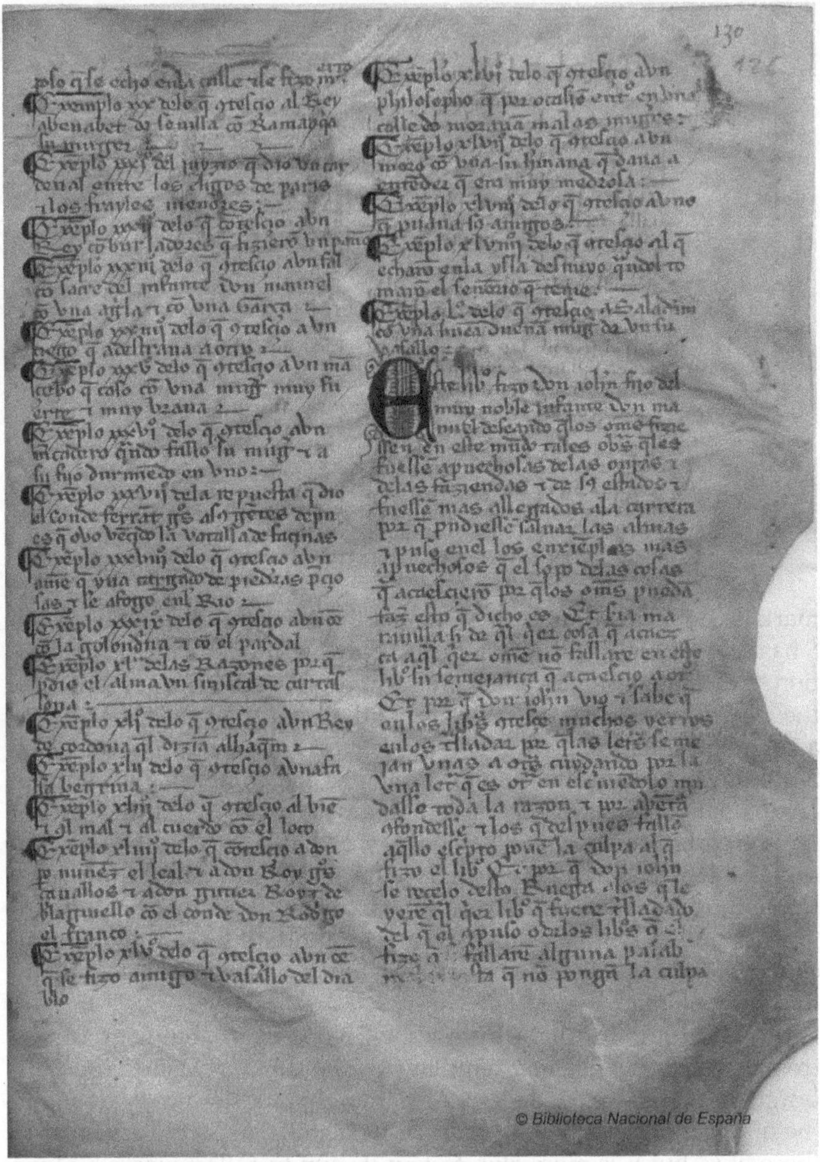

Fig. 5.4. Anteprologue in red ink, MS *S* (BNE, MS 6376), fol. 126r, col. b. Image taken from the holdings of the Biblioteca Nacional de España and licensed under the CC by 4.0 licence.

copying the *Libro infinido* and the rubricator's prologue to the *Libro de los estados*, the scribe of *N* reworks existing texts to transition into the *Conde Lucanor*. I transcribe the two passages most pertinent to the treatment of Juan Manuel's authorship:[20]

> Este don Juan Manuel que conpuso este libro fizo otros muchos que estavan en este mesmo volumen – y el primero dellos tiene por título et nonbre el *Libro del cavallero et del escudero* y es conpuesto en una manera que dizen en Castilla fabliella – y enbíalo al ynfante don Juan arçobispo de Toledo, et ruégal que tenga por bien de trasladar este dicho su libro de romance en latín. El segundo libro es el que va aquí trasladado, y el terçero tiene un título en esta manera: Este libro fizo don Juan [... anteprologue follows] (fol. 34r)

> This Don Juan Manuel who composed this book made many others that were in this same volume; and the first has the title and name *Libro del cavallero et del escudero,* and it is composed in the style that in Castile is called a little fable, and he sends it to the Infante Don Juan, archbishop of Toledo, and asks him to see fit to translate his aforementioned book from Romance to Latin. The second book is the one copied here, and the third has the following title: Don Juan made this book [... anteprologue follows]

Here, the scribe combines language from the General Prologue (*este volumen que yo mesmo concerté* becomes *este mesmo volumen*) with the rubricator's prologue to the *Libro del cavallero et del escudero* and the anteprologue. In doing so, he creates an original paratext that imitates the anteprologue's function by declaring Juan Manuel's authorship, addressing some *accessus* headings (title and style of the *Libro del cavallero et del escudero*), and establishing a connection to a more complete volume of his works. The *N* scribe's list of the works in his exemplar is incomplete and problematic (Burgoyne, "Los versos" 136), but it does follow the order of *S* if we take "the second book ... copied here" to mean the set of three works he has already copied in part or in full: the *Libro de las tres razones, Libro infinido*, and *Libro de los estados*. This would make the *Conde Lucanor* the third book, by the scribe's erroneous count. If the anteprologue borrows the authorial rhetoric of Juan Manuel's General Prologue, then the *N* scribe's paratext repeats this process, resulting in a copy of a copy. While this game of telephone creates confusion as to the scribe's editorial process, it nevertheless retains the main rhetorical strategies that can be attributed to Don Juan himself in the General Prologue.

After the anteprologue, the scribe of *N* writes another original paratext tracing Juan Manuel's lineage:

> Este ynfante don Manuel de que de suso se haze mención fue fijo del rey don Fernando de Castilla, terçero deste nonbre, et de la reyna doña Beatris; el qual dicho rey don Fernando es llamado el Santo y el que ganó a Sevilla. Este dicho ynfante don Manuel, fijo del dicho rey don Fernando et de la dicha reyna doña Beatriz, casó con doña Costança, fija del rey don Jayme de Aragón, et deste matrimonio obieron a este don Juan Manuel *que es autor destos libros*. (fol. 35r; my emphasis)
>
> This aforementioned Infante Don Manuel was the son of the king Don Fernando of Castile, third of this name, and the queen Doña Beatriz, and this king Don Fernando, called the Saint, is the one who won Seville. This Infante Don Manuel, son of the king Don Fernando and the queen Doña Beatriz, married Doña Constanza, daughter of the king Don Jaume of Aragon, and from this marriage they had the same Don Juan Manuel *who is author of these books*.

Despite mistakenly identifying Juan Manuel's mother as Infanta Constanza of Aragon, Infante Manuel's first wife, rather than his second wife Beatriz of Savoy, this passage successfully highlights – and perhaps intentionally exaggerates – the writer's royal lineage. Second, it calls him an *autor*, the earliest surviving text to do so. Given the temporal distance from Juan Manuel's lifetime, the scribe of *N* may be invoking the sense of a venerated "ancient," but as outlined in the previous chapter, by the sixteenth century *autor* had also taken on more modern connotations. Thus, in a handful of lines, the scribe both affirms Don Juan's elite status as the descendant of kings and solidifies his literary reputation as an author, carrying forward the same message his works so ardently defended. What is more, these paratexts in *N* caught the eye of a contemporary reader, whose marginal notes for these sections include *No. del conponedor del libro* ("Note: on the book's composer") and *No. la genealogía de don Juan Manuel* ("Note: genealogy of Don Juan Manuel") (see fig. 5.5). These notes signal that not just the scribe, but also an early modern reader, took an interest in knowing the name and lineage of the author of this collection of Castilian prose works.

In spite of the treachery of transmission, the fact that Juan Manuel's rhetoric of authorship figures prominently in nearly all the surviving manuscripts indicates that it thrived in the manuscript culture of the fourteenth and fifteenth centuries and the hybrid manuscript-print

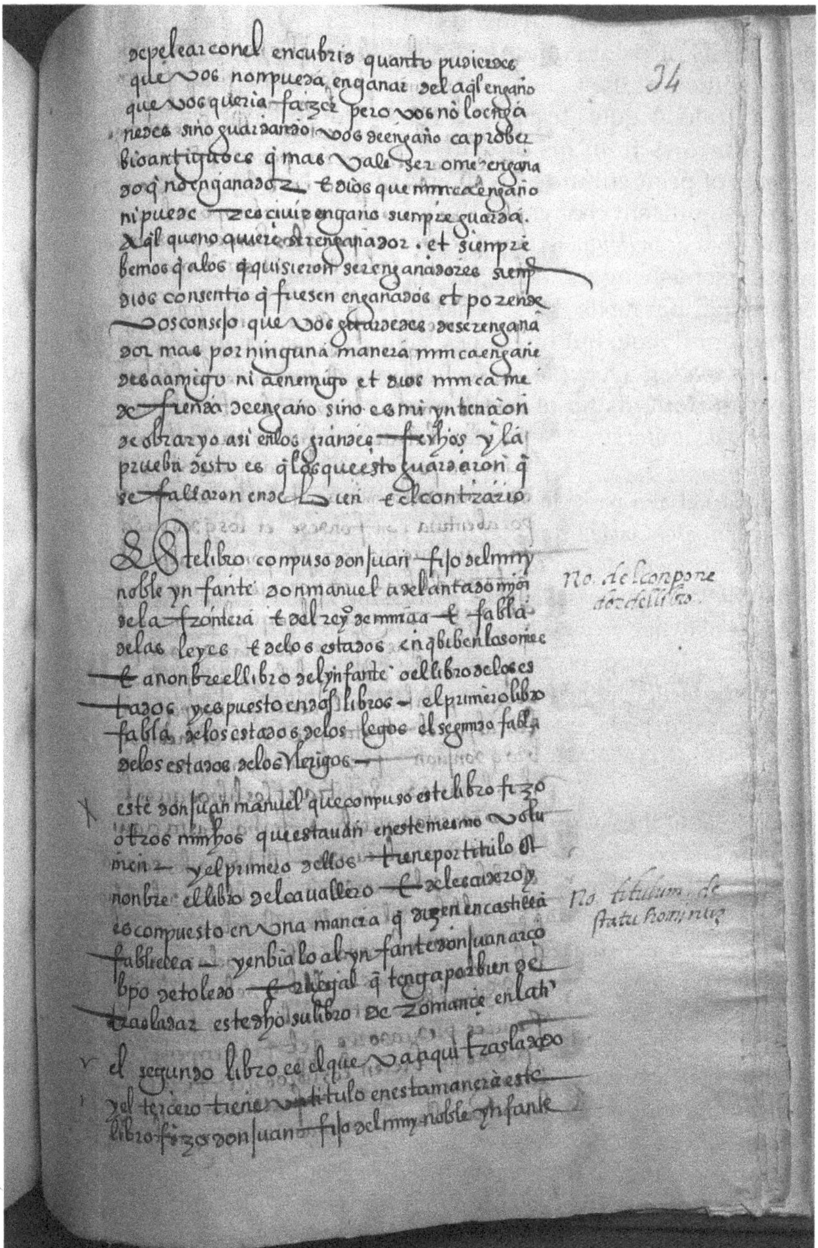

Fig. 5.5. Scribe's prologue and marginal note "del conponedor del libro," MS *N* (BNE, MS 19426), fol. 34r. Image taken from the holdings of the Biblioteca Nacional de España and licensed under the CC by 4.0 licence.

culture of the sixteenth. How did it interact with the affordances and limitations of print culture? The treatment of the author in the 1575 print edition of the *Conde Lucanor*, edited by the Andalusian humanist Gonzalo Argote de Molina (1548–96) and printed by Hernando Díaz, borrows from his discourse of authorship while incorporating aspects of print culture as well as Argote's humanist interests. Argote makes significant changes to the text, including a complete rearrangement of the *enxiemplos* (which he calls *exemplos* or *capítulos*). Yet he simultaneously aggrandizes the figure of the author through a series of original paratexts. He publishes neither the General Prologue nor the anteprologue, but he echoes their rhetoric in his prologue "to the curious reader" (*al curioso lector*), which appears immediately after the standard front matter of publishing licences (*licencias*) and dedication (*epístola dedicatoria*):

> Estando el año passado en la corte de Su Magestad, vino a mis manos este libro del *Conde Lucanor*, que por ser de autor tan ilustre me aficioné a leerle y comencé luego a hallar en él un gusto de la propriedad y antigüedad de la lengua castellana. [...] Solamente me dava alguna pena ver que el libro que yo tenía estuviesse estragado en muchas partes por culpa del escriptor o por no avérsele ofrescido más fiel exemplar; pero esto se remedió fácilmente confiriéndolo con otros dos, [...] de suerte que con tan buen socorro pude corregirlo y emendarlo de muchos lugares que lo avían menester. (1.14)[21]

> Last year at the court of His Majesty there came to my hands this book *Conde Lucanor*, and, since it was by such an illustrious author, I became interested in reading it. [...] The only thing that grieved me was to see that the book I possessed was damaged in many places by fault of the scribe, or for lack of a more faithful exemplar; but this was easily solved by comparing it with two others, [...] such that with this great assistance I was able to correct and emend it in many places.

Argote, like the scribe of *N*, does not hesitate to call Juan Manuel an *autor* in the modern sense of "composer of a literary work," repeating the word four more times in his prologue. Not only had *autor* broadened in meaning by the sixteenth century, but Argote deems it an accurate descriptor of Juan Manuel's relationship to his book. In contrast, in his edition of the *Libro de la montería* (Seville: Andrea Pescioni, 1582), Argote consistently identifies Alfonso XI as the one who "mandó screvir [el libro]" ("ordered [the book] to be written"), clearly distinguishing the king's role as patron.

Admittedly, Argote de Molina's praise of Juan Manuel as an "illustrious" and "excellent" author was motivated by a desire to please his patron, Pedro Manuel, a powerful descendant of the author who served at the court of King Philip II (r. 1556–98). Nevertheless, it also seems driven by sincere admiration, based in part on the impressive authorial self-portrait he found in his exemplars. Argote exalts the author for the edifying content and pleasing style of his works, using rhetoric similar to that of earlier prologues. His description of how he corrected the text (*pude corregirlo y emendarlo*) closely parallels the language of the anteprologue, which describes the authorized manuscript as *emendado en muchos logares* in Don Juan's own hand (de Looze 60). His text does not claim to be based on an authorial manuscript, but he does appeal to the faithfulness of his three exemplars: his own, obtained at the court of King Philip II; one belonging to Jerónimo de Zurita, a royal secretary and official of the Inquisition; and one owned by a certain Doctor Oretano, a Dominican cleric. He probably did not compare the three manuscripts in a systematic way (A. Blecua 79), but listing them served to bolster his editorial credentials by leaning on the institutional prestige of Crown and Church (de Looze 59). His blaming of scribes (*culpa del escriptor*) could be derived from either the General Prologue or the anteprologue; however, his emotional reaction of *pena* at the vicissitudes of textual transmission is paralleled only in the General Prologue, when Don Juan describes the "grant pesar et grant enojo" one feels when one's work is underappreciated. It thus seems that Argote blends elements from both earlier prologues in his presentation of the *Conde Lucanor*'s author.

Argote's other paratexts combine aspects of the Manueline prologues with innovative strategies more in line with his humanist and antiquarian interests. In order, these new paratexts are: a biography of the author; an account of his descendants down to the present; a treatise situating Juan Manuel's verses within a history of early poetry; and a glossary of "ancient" Castilian words. The treatise on poetry places the *viessos* of part 1 within a Mediterranean literary history that cites poetry in French, Italian, Valencian, Basque, Turkish, and Arabic. Argote also includes a section of "Sentencias y dichos notables que don Juan Manuel puso en verso en este libro" ("Notable maxims and sayings that Don Juan Manuel put into verse in this book"; 2.110), which extracts the verses from part 1 and presents them in a numbered list, similar to their treatment in *N* and in the *Libro de los doce sabios* manuscripts. These paratexts represent Argote's interests in genealogy and poetry, typical for a sixteenth-century humanist scholar (Miralles; de Looze 58–9; Santonocito, *Gonzalo Argote* 101).

His biography devotes special attention to Juan Manuel's rocky relationship with Alfonso XI of Castile and to his participation in the "guerra de los moros" ("war with the Moors"; 1.20). These were two topics of interest for sixteenth-century nobles cognizant of their own centralized monarchy and its recent victories over the Ottoman forces at Lepanto in 1571, as well as the Morisco revolt in the Alpujarras from 1568 to 1570. However, Argote's remarks on the nobleman's literary career bear a striking resemblance to earlier prologues:

> Pues si el tiempo que le sobrava de las armas y govierno lo gastava en exercicios no dignos de príncipe, los libros que dexó escriptos dan testimonio d'ello, porque demás d'estę libro, [...] hizo otros muchos libros que dexó en el monasterio de Sant Pablo de la Orden de los Predicadores de su villa de Peñafiel, que él fundó y dotó y eligió para su sepulchro. Los títulos de los cuales son ... (1.20)

> If his time not occupied by matters of arms and governance was devoted to activities not suitable for a prince, the books he left behind bear witness to this, because besides this book, [...] he wrote many others that he left at the monastery of San Pablo of the Order of Preachers in his town of Peñafiel, which he founded and endowed and chose for his tomb. The titles of which are ...

Although Argote did visit Juan Manuel's tomb in Peñafiel as part of his research (Santonocito, *Gonzalo Argote* 103), his identification of the monastery of San Pablo as the author's literary repository seems adapted from some version of the anteprologue, not from firsthand knowledge of any manuscripts there. Moreover, the list of works adopts a visual strategy similar to that of the anteprologue in *M*, using formatting and fleurons to call special attention to each title (see fig. 5.6).[22] Finally, the idea that writing was not a suitable pastime for a high-ranking noble evokes another Manueline paratext, Don Juan's self-defence against criticism from his peers in his *Libro infinido*, a work Argote may have known by the title *Libro de los sabios*.[23] In these ways, Argote's biography reproduces and, in the case of the list of works, heightens the rhetoric of authorship present in earlier manuscripts.

As discussed in chapter 4, Juan Manuel's poetic compositions, including the *viessos* of part 1 of the *Conde Lucanor* and his lost works on poetry, play an important role in his self-portrayal as an author ria de los hombres que auiendo el Infante don Fernando su visnieto puesto su real sobre Antequera, como los moros tuuiessen occupada vna sierra, y fuesse necessario conquistalla, entrando en consejo sobre ello, aunque a todos parescio cosa de gran peligro, acordaron que conuenia ganalla, pero ninguno se offrecio ala empresa, hasta que el Infante don Fernando les dixo. Por cierto mengua faze aqui mi visabuelo don Iuan Manuel.

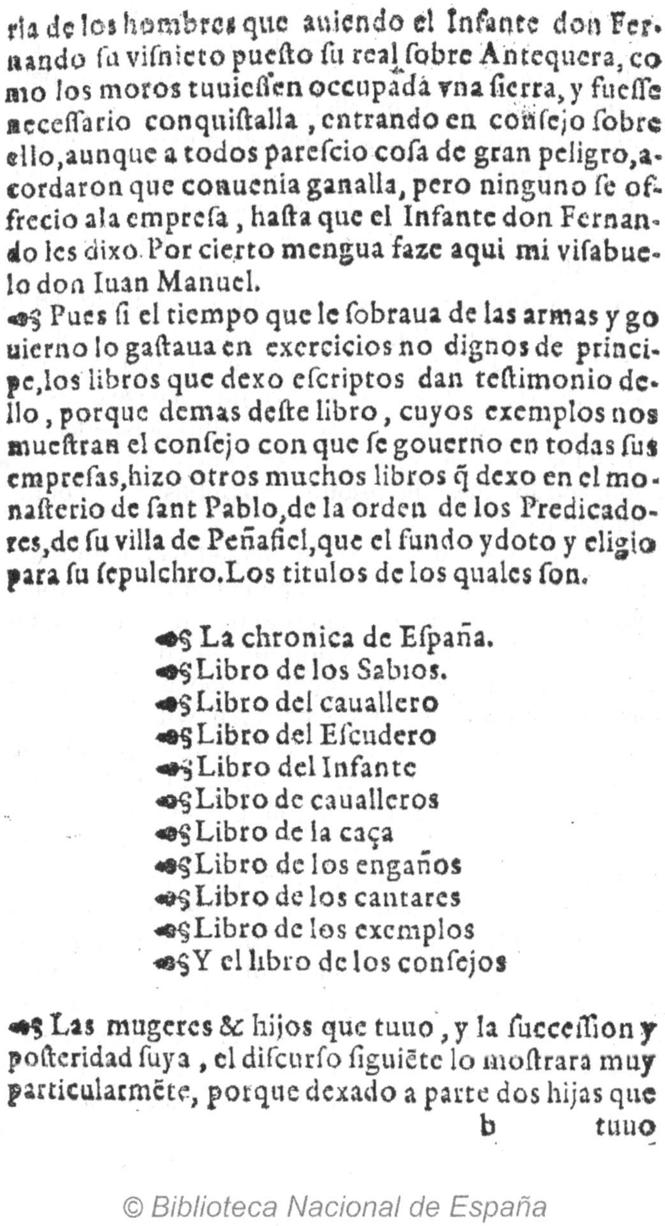

¶ Pues si el tiempo que le sobraua de las armas y gouierno lo gastaua en exercicios no dignos de principe, los libros que dexo escriptos dan testimonio dello, porque demas deste libro, cuyos exemplos nos muestran el consejo con que se gouerno en todas sus empresas, hizo otros muchos libros q̃ dexo en el monasterio de sant Pablo, de la orden de los Predicadores, de su villa de Peñafiel, que el fundo y doto y eligio para su sepulchro. Los titulos de los quales son.

¶ La chronica de España.
¶ Libro de los Sabios.
¶ Libro del cauallero
¶ Libro del Escudero
¶ Libro del Infante
¶ Libro de caualleros
¶ Libro de la caça
¶ Libro de los engaños
¶ Libro de los cantares
¶ Libro de los exemplos
¶ Y el libro de los consejos

¶ Las mugeres & hijos que tuuo, y la succession y posteridad suya, el discurso siguiẽte lo mostrara muy particularmẽte, porque dexado a parte dos hijas que

b tuuo

Fig. 5.6. Argote's list of Juan Manuel's works. *El conde Lucanor* (1575), fol. b1r.

who writes his own words. Argote similarly emphasizes Juan Manuel as a poet in his "Discurso [...] sobre la poesía castellana contenida en este libro" ("Discourse on the Castilian poetry contained in this book"), citing his *viessos* as excellent examples of various Castilian metres (2.117–18). He also states his intention to edit another volume of Juan Manuel's poetry (perhaps the work called *Libro de los cantares* in Argote's list), referring to it as "el libro que don Juan Manuel escrivió en coplas y rimas de aquel tiempo" ("the book Don Juan Manuel wrote of *coplas* and rhymes of that time"; 2.116). Finally, he celebrates Juan Manuel's verses "por su antigüedad y por la autoridad del Príncipe que los hizo" ("for their antiquity and for the authority of the prince who wrote them"; 2.116). Juan Manuel never applied the word *autoridad* to his own works, and he naturally would not have perceived them as ancient. However, his rhetoric of authorship persuaded Argote to equate him with an *auctor*, an authoritative and ancient writer worthy of imitation, and to invest the resources to publish some of his works for a wider audience.

Don Juan's discourse of authorship aligned well with the fixity of print, which contributed to the development of literary property and the valuing of individual innovators (Eisenstein 1: 119–21). But some aspects of print culture may have introduced changes to his authorial self-portrait. Relationships between bookmakers and readers were more commercialized and less personal, with editors and printers catering more to a speculative market than to specific patrons or audiences (Kwakkel 65–6). The scribes copying Juan Manuel's books by hand likely had concrete users in mind, who may have known of him already or even commissioned the copies. *S*, for example, was likely commissioned in Seville by some prominent descendants of the Manuel line (Ayerbe-Chaux, "Manuscritos" 89). Argote and his printer, Hernando Díaz, likewise had a patron from the Manuel family, the aforementioned Pedro Manuel, but they were also invested in persuading new readers to buy the *Conde Lucanor*. One way of doing this was to convince them that Juan Manuel was an excellent author, a talented poet, and an authoritative "ancient" of Castilian literature. Thus, whereas Don Juan's medieval discourse of authorship often took a more intimate tone, invoking members of his immediate social circle, Argote's reformulation of it is more distant and lends a veneer of objectivity.

Argote de Molina's 1575 edition would succeed in making the *Conde Lucanor* – and, with it, a portrait of Juan Manuel as an authoritative author – available to a wider audience for centuries to come.

Though it was nowhere near as popular as the bestsellers of its day, a second printing was eventually issued in 1642 in Madrid by Diego Díaz de la Carrera, with a dedication by the bookseller Pedro Coello. Argote's edition (in its 1575 or 1642 printing) appears in numerous seventeenth-century inventories, and it helped bring the *Conde Lucanor* to the attention of several illustrious early modern readers and writers, including Miguel de Cervantes, Lope de Vega, Pedro Calderón de la Barca, and Baltasar Gracián (Santonocito, *Gonzalo Argote* 143–6). His edition remained enormously influential for nineteeth-century editors and translators of the *Conde Lucanor* (sometimes to a greater extent than they let on, as we shall see). Through this editorial chain of transmission, Juan Manuel's notion of authorship continued to travel with his works, while also accumulating new ideas influenced by Romanticism and the burgeoning discipline of philology.

Juan Manuel in the Nineteenth Century

In Europe and the Americas in the first half of the nineteenth century, two major factors impacted the scholarly understanding of medieval authorship: a Romantic approach to literary history and the new methods of textual editing introduced by Karl Lachmann (Gumbrecht; Altschul, *Geographies*, ch. 1). Romantic literary history, articulated and disseminated by figures such as Friedrich and August Wilhelm Schlegel, Madame de Stäel, and Simonde de Sismondi, affirmed that each European vernacular literature represented a particular *Volksgeist* or national character, visible not just in popular ballads and epics but also in the works of great geniuses such as Cervantes, Shakespeare, and Calderón de la Barca (Wellek; Pérez Isasi). Romantic thinkers imagined the figure of the author as no longer reliant upon the words of others, but a creative force endowed with originality, a shift memorably historicized by Kristeller and Foucault. In the related field of textual editing, Karl Lachmann's rigorous methods of establishing a presumed "authorial" text, disseminated in his 1831 edition of the New Testament and his 1850 edition of Lucretius's *De natura rerum*, called for a break with the humanist editions of the past (Fradejas Rueda, *Introducción* 20; Altschul, "Genealogy" 121). These changes produced what Hans Ulrich Gumbrecht calls a "moment of productive discontinuity" in the discipline of philology, which still stands as a convincing origin story for modern literary criticism (56).

This particular historical moment helped shape how nineteenth-century editors and translators of the *Conde Lucanor* viewed Juan Manuel's discourse of authorship. Three editions in Spanish were published in the nineteenth century: one by the German philologist Adelbert von Keller, first published in Stuttgart in 1839; one by the Catalan literary scholar Manuel Milà i Fontanals, published in Barcelona in 1853; and one by the Spanish scholar Pascual de Gayangos, published in Madrid in 1860 in the anthology *Escritores en prosa anteriores al siglo XV*. There were also three translations: one into German by Joseph Freiherr von Eichendorff, published in 1840; another into French by Adolphe de Puibusque, published in Paris in 1854; and a third into English by James York, first published in London in 1868. These editions and translations (except the German translation, which I have not studied) are informed by their editors' nascent understanding of Lachmannian textual editing, as well as by Romantic notions of the author's creativity. Their editorial decisions amplify Juan Manuel's discourse of authorship in two main ways: by focusing on the figure of the individual author, and by privileging an authorial text.

Two editions, those prepared by Milà i Fontanals and Gayangos, formed part of a series sold by subscription: the *Tesoro de Autores Ilustres* and the *Biblioteca de Autores Españoles desde la formación del lenguaje hasta nuestros días*. The publishers tended to favour authors with name recognition whose works would attract subscribers. For the *Biblioteca de Autores Españoles*, this meant Spanish novelists and playwrights such as Cervantes, Calderón de la Barca, and Moratín, while the *Tesoro de Autores Ilustres* also included authors in translation such as Dante, Goethe, and Harriet Beecher Stowe. In these collections, the author was considered a genius whose creative process was similar to giving birth: the editor of the *Tesoro*, Joan Oliveres i Gavarró, stated that his purpose was to publish "los partos más prodigiosos del entendimiento humano" ("the most prodigious works birthed by the human mind"; Nieto Márquez 1). Many medieval works did not align with this concept of authorship because they lacked an authorial attribution, or because they were attributed to scribes, translators, or patrons rather than an author who claimed some degree of originality. In contrast, Juan Manuel's works presented an author figure whose biography could inform interpretations of his works, and whose intentions editors could strive to obey.

Gayangos's anthology might seem at first glance to be an exception, because most of its works have more complicated authorial attributions. In addition to most of Juan Manuel's extant works, it contains the

Castilian translation of the Arabic *Kalīla wa-Dimna* commissioned by Alfonso X (itself a translation from Middle Persian by Ibn al-Muqaffaʿ); the *Castigos de Sancho IV*; the *Libro de las consolaciones de la vida humana*, a Castilian translation of a Latin work by Antipope Benedict XIII (Pedro de Luna); and two exempla collections Gayangos categorized as anonymous: the *Libro de los enxemplos por a.b.c.* and *Libro de los gatos*.[24] But his preference for a strong author figure is clear. He devotes the vast majority of his general introduction – fifteen out of eighteen pages – to Juan Manuel's life and works. He also claims that "todo lo que este príncipe escribió está de tal manera identificado con su propia persona, hay tal armonía y consonancia entre su vida y sus obras literarias, que a haberse estas hallado sin el nombre de su ilustre autor, no hubiéramos vacilado ni un momento en atribuírselas" ("everything this prince wrote is so identified with his person, and there is such harmony and consonance between his life and his literary works, that if they were found without the name of their distinguished author, we would not have hesitated for a moment in attributing them to him"; *Escritores* vii). For Gayangos, author and works exist in a kind of feedback loop, each one inextricable from the other. Even when attempting to reign in his enthusiasm, he still ends up exalting Juan Manuel as "un personaje que, literariamente considerado, es sin disputa la figura mas notable de todo el siglo XIV" ("a personage who is, in literary terms, without a doubt the most notable figure of the entire fourteenth century"; *Escritores* xxii). Along with the repetition of words like *persona*, *nombre*, *personaje*, and *figura*, this glowing praise places value on the author as both historical individual and creative genius.

The other editions and translations of the *Conde Lucanor* place a similar emphasis on Juan Manuel's authorial persona. With the exception of Keller, whose edition contains no prefatory material, they all begin with an introduction to the author's life and works, perhaps inspired just as much by Argote's example as by contemporary scholarly practice.[25] When describing Juan Manuel's literary career, they quote at length from his prologues, borrowing from his discourse of authorship the tension between his lay estate and his intellectual endeavours. For Milà i Fontanals, Don Juan's famous authorial self-defence in the *Libro infinido* offers "razones muy juiciosas y muy nobles" ("very sensible and noble reasons") to justify the nobleman's literary pursuits (*Libro de Patronio* xi). James York, in his English translation, draws upon the *Libro infinido* and the anteprologue to claim that

> the very thing upon which [Don Juan] probably prided himself least, or looked upon as at best an idle solace from graver toils – the collection of

> stories which he penned in the rare intervals of leisure between the labours of the camp and the council, and which he bequeathed in manuscript to the monks of Peñafiel – still lives to be read, and to afford instruction and entertainment to a generation that follows the arts of peace as nobler than the arts of war. (*Count Lucanor* vi)

York is also echoing the prologue to the *Libro del cavallero et del escudero*, in which Don Juan presents reading and writing as a respite from the troubles of daily life and the insomnia those troubles cause:

> Hermano, señor, el cuidado es una de las cosas que más faze al omne perder el dormir, e esto acaece a mí tantas vezes que me embarga mucho a la salud del cuerpo. E por ende cada que só en algún cuidado, fago que me lean algunos libros o algunas estorias por sacar aquel cuidado del coraçón. [...] E seyendo en aquel cuidado, por lo perder comencé este libro que vos envío. (3–4)

> My brother, my lord, worry is one of the most frequent causes of losing sleep. This happens to me so frequently that it is damaging to my body's health, and so every time I find myself worrying, I have some books or stories read to me to remove that worry from my heart. [...] And during one of those times of worry, to shake it I began this book that I am sending to you.

These rhetorical tropes are not unique to Juan Manuel, but were recycled in Latin and vernacular prologues throughout antiquity and the Middle Ages (Curtius 83–9; Scholberg, "Modestia" 24–7). However, Don Juan and his associates deployed them so convincingly that nineteenth-century editors and translators reproduced them as fact. They remained associated with his biography long into the twentieth century, and it is only in the past twenty years that scholars have succeeded in articulating the discursive functions of these tropes in constructing an authorial self.

In addition to this focus on the individual author, nineteenth-century editors shared with Juan Manuel the idea that an authorial version of a text has special literary value. The main goal of textual criticism, from the mid-eighteenth century onward, has been the establishment of an authorial or authoritative text (Altschul, "Genealogy" 116). Analogous to the king from Juan Manuel's General Prologue, editors were tasked with comparing different versions of a text and determining which variants to preserve and which to discard. The best features of a text were attributed to the talent of the author, whose prestige was comparable to that of Juan Manuel's troubadour-knight, while its worst features were blamed on the intervention of less capable copyists. Although it would take decades for Lachmann's methods to be adopted consistently in the editing of medieval Castilian texts (Bizzarri, "Labor" 82), Lachmannian rhetoric caught on quickly in Spain and across Europe and began to appear in editors' paratexts, regardless of the editorial methods used. In the case of the *Conde Lucanor* and other Manueline works, Argote's edition was relatively accessible to nineteenth-century scholars, but knowledge of the manuscripts remained piecemeal. Moreover, while Spain boasted numerous public libraries and archives, Gayangos, a frontrunner in archival research and manuscript studies, complained in 1834 that his country's collections remained woefully underutilized ("Arabic MSS." 394).

Gayangos had begun to work with *S* at the Biblioteca Nacional sometime in the 1840s, and though he would not publish his edition of Juan Manuel's works until 1860, he was able to divulge its contents to the scholarly community earlier, first by sending a copy to the Bostonian scholar George Ticknor to cite in his 1849 *History of Spanish Literature*, and then in the 1851 Spanish translation that Gayangos and Enrique de Vedia made of Ticknor's work.[26] Ticknor's *History* gives a summary of the contents of *S* and translates almost the entirety of the General Prologue into English, including the tale of the knight and the shoemaker (66–75). Ticknor also mentions Don Juan's request in the prologue to the *Libro del cavallero et del escudero* to have his brother-in-law (erroneously called his brother) Infante Juan of Aragon, archbishop of Toledo, translate his works into Latin (69). Gayangos and de Vedia's translation provides all this, plus an appendix with a more detailed description of *S* and its contents (498–502). They also transcribe two paratexts from the *Libro infinido*: the last part of the prologue, which provides an *accessus* to the work, and Don Juan's self-defence of his writing. By transcribing and translating prologues from an early manuscript, Ticknor and his translators made Don Juan's discourse of authorship available to other editors in a more direct way than the highly mediated paratexts of Argote. They also selectively reproduced the passages in which his self-presentation as an individual author is clearest, while omitting others, such as his request in the *Libro de los estados* that his clerical brother-in-law correct his works.

The nineteenth-century editors of the *Conde Lucanor* found in their exemplars the same aspiration to a complete and correct text that they strove for in their work. Thanks to this consonance, they could use Juan

Manuel's rhetoric to pay lip service to Lachmannian ideals. All the editors (except Keller) express concern for the integrity of Juan Manuel's text, weaving his medieval discourse of authorship together with notions of Lachmannian rigour.

Milà i Fontanals did not use any medieval manuscripts to prepare his 1853 edition, but edited the *Conde Lucanor* from Argote's text, reproducing his unique order of *enxiemplos*. He was not able to consult *S*, but could describe and even cite it thanks to Gayangos and de Vedia's translation of Ticknor's work (*Libro de Patronio* i). He begins his introduction to Juan Manuel's literary career in the same way *S* does, by reproducing the anecdote of the knight and the shoemaker from the General Prologue. He then lists the other works in *S*, faithfully representing the knowledge available to him (viii–ix). Thus, although he was not able to put any philological methods into practice, he still advocated for a return to the manuscripts and took small steps to evoke the compilation of *S* in his edition.

The 1854 French translation by Puibusque came one step closer to consulting *S*, thanks to the transcriptions made by Gayangos and another Spanish scholar, José Amador de los Ríos, to facilitate work with the manuscripts. Puibusque consulted both the copy Gayangos had made for Ticknor, now housed at the Boston Public Library (Ms.fD.9), as well as Amador de los Ríos's copy, now at the Biblioteca Nacional in Madrid (MS 19163). Although his translation is still based on Argote's text, he changes the order of exempla to match *S*, heeding the advice of Amador de los Ríos to follow the "códice más autorizado" ("most authorized codex"; *Historia crítica* 4: 591).[27] He also reproduces the story of the knight and the shoemaker, followed by a reformulation in his own editorial voice:

> Avant l'invention de l'imprimerie, rien n'était moins facile que d'assurer la conservation d'un livre; ignorants ou trop savants, les copistes offraient un égal danger, et combien d'autres causes d'altération ou de perte! [...] Don Juan Manuel prit [des] mesures qui témoignent de ses appréhensions; il fit déposer le volume manuscrit contenant ses oeuvres complètes à Peñafiel, sa résidence favorite, dans le monastère même dont il était le fondateur, et il le confia aux soins des religieux qui devaient être les gardiens de son tombeau. (*Le Comte* 93)
>
> Before the invention of the printing press, nothing was more difficult than ensuring the preservation of a book; scribes, whether ignorant or too clever, could be equally dangerous, and there were so many other causes

> of degradation or loss! [...] Don Juan Manuel took [some] measures that attest to his apprehensions: he had a manuscript copy of his complete works deposited at Peñafiel, his favorite residence, in the very monastery of which he was the founder, and entrusted it to the care of the monks who were to be the guardians of his tomb.

Puibusque takes some liberties with Juan Manuel's concept of authorship by framing his request for a Latin translation of his works as protection against the dangers that "menaçaient la langue vulgaire" ("menaced the vulgar tongue"; 93–4), a sentiment absent from the Castilian's prologues but famously central to Petrarch's discourse about authorship (see ch. 1). Finally, despite the fact that his editorial labour was mediated by copies of copies, he posits his efforts as the beginning of a "resurrection" of Juan Manuel's works, in the face of what he calls the "mutilation" of the prior editions by Argote and Keller (110).

Pascual de Gayangos's 1860 anthology, *Escritores en prosa anteriores al siglo XV*, was a landmark edition of Juan Manuel's works. During the 1850s, he had located and consulted *H*, *M*, and *G* in addition to *S*, and also managed to purchase *G* (whose siglum stands for his last name) for his personal collection.[28] With his access to *S*, which contained all of Juan Manuel's extant works besides the *Crónica abreviada*, he was the first to edit the following texts in their entirety: the General Prologue, *Libro del cavallero et del escudero*, *Libro de las tres razones*, *Libro infinido*, *Libro de los estados*, parts 2–5 of the *Conde Lucanor*, and the *Tratado de la Asunción* (he chose not to edit the incomplete *Libro de la caza*; *Escritores en prosa* 231). Despite the authoritative presentation of *S* and its relative completeness, he rejects any link between it and the authorial codex at Peñafiel. However, he speaks confidently of this ideal text's existence and conjectures, perhaps disingenuously, that his recent acquisition *G* is written "con tal puntualidad y corrección, que no extrañaríamos hubiese sido hecha sobre el códice mismo de Peñafiel" ("with such diligence and accuracy that we would not be surprised if it had been made from the very codex of Peñafiel"; *Escritores en prosa* 232). As for the *Conde Lucanor*, his access to four of the five surviving manuscripts meant that he was perfectly positioned to apply Lachmann's principles and create a true critical edition. This is what he claimed to do in his introduction to Juan Manuel's works:

> Ninguna, pues, de las ediciones de *Los Exemplos de Patronio al conde Lucanor* es tan completa ni tan correcta como la presente, gracias a la feliz

> circunstancia de haber tenido a nuestra disposición los cuatro códices arriba citados, y de habernos además tomado el trabajo ímprobo de cotejarlos escrupulosamente uno con otro. (*Escritores en prosa* 232)
>
> None of the editions of *Los exemplos de Patronio al conde Lucanor* is as complete or as correct as the present one, thanks to the happy circumstance of having at our disposal the four aforementioned codices, and moreover of having undertaken the enormous effort of checking them scrupulously against one another.

This has echoes of Argote's prologue "to the curious reader," but rather than a pleasant humanist pastime, Gayangos portrays his editorial work as a laborious task requiring expertise and stamina (as well as a bit of luck). He also laments the loss of the *Libro de las cantigas*, and complains in all-too-familiar language about the "no escasos errores en que [...] incurrió por descuido u ignorancia el copiante del códice principal" ("not infrequent mistakes [...] made by the copyist of the main codex [*S*] out of carelessness or ignorance"; *Escritores en prosa* 232).

Yet Gayangos misrepresented his editorial labour. It is clear from the edition's foul copy that he used Argote's as his base text, with minor cosmetic changes and the sporadic introduction of variants. His edition fooled James York, whose 1868 translation praised the Spaniard's edition as "the first critical edition presenting a standard text, founded on an elaborate collation of the earlier editions and of the existing manuscripts" (*Count Lucanor* vii). However, other scholars were sceptical of Gayangos's methods. Amador de los Ríos had not been able to read Gayangos's 1860 edition carefully before sending the fourth volume of his *Historia crítica de la literatura española* (1863) to print, but he criticized his compatriot's earlier work on the *Conde Lucanor*, dismissing him as nothing more than a "bibliophile" who lacked editorial rigour (4: 233n1). And in 1900, María Goyri identified the many flaws in Gayangos's edition, decisively revealing the truth behind his rhetorical appeal to completeness and accuracy (Goyri 600; Gloeckner 13–14).

While Juan Manuel's discourse of authorship originally sought to convince an aristocratic audience – and perhaps also a clerical one – that his name stood as a guarantee of morally and spiritually beneficial works, it remained persuasive to nineteenth-century editors because it expressed concerns they shared. A burgeoning interest in Lachmannian textual editing, along with a Romantic fascination with the artist's creativity, made nineteenth-century literary scholars receptive to ideas about an authorial text not just as the best of several exemplars, but as a conveyor of the truth about the author. The editors, in turn, adapted the rhetorical moves of their sources to the context of their own prologues and prefaces, forging an editorial discourse that sometimes, but not always, aligned with their decisions and methods.

Conclusion

Juan Manuel's works have continued to captivate editors, translators, and scholars throughout the twentieth and twenty-first centuries, and their editorial history is still being written. In 1978 Deyermond ("Editors") took stock of the editorial landscape of the *Conde Lucanor*, prompted by the publication of critical editions by José Manuel Blecua (1969) and Germán Orduna (1972). Despite some minor emendations, J.M. Blecua's two-volume critical edition of Juan Manuel's *Obras completas* (1982–3) remains an essential resource. The editorial contributions of Hermann Knust, J.M. Blecua, and Orduna to the Manueline corpus have been studied by, respectively, Hugo Bizzarri ("Labor"), Gómez Redondo ("Obra"), and Funes ("Aportes"). And Juan Manuel's works continue to be edited anew: scholars can now consult Mario Cossío Olavide's richly annotated edition of the *Libro del cavallero et del escudero* (2022) and, for the *Conde Lucanor*, Leonardo Funes's "metacritical" edition (2020), which reflects on some of the salient issues in editing the text, and Guillermo Serés's revised and updated critical edition (2022), which boasts the most complete notes and bibliography to date.

However, I have chosen to end here, with the nineteenth-century editions of the *Conde Lucanor* and particularly with Pascual de Gayangos's 1860 edition of Juan Manuel's works, for several reasons. First, despite the shortcomings of Gayangos's edition, it is the first to make most of Juan Manuel's works accessible to scholars and readers, and it would continue to be cited and referenced well into the twentieth century, until definitively surpassed by J.M. Blecua's *Obras completas* in the 1980s (Gómez Redondo, "Obra" 194). It is recognizable as a modern work of scholarship with modern goals: not just to make the medieval texts accessible, but to give an account of the editor's methods, even if they were not as scientific or rigorous as Gayangos would have us believe. Moreover, the preoccupations of nineteenth-century philology, including national languages and their genealogies as well as the privileged place of the author, remain very much our own. Despite our increasingly successful efforts to transcend linguistic and disciplinary boundaries in our work, literature scholars in the US and Europe still often research and teach within institutional structures organized according to national languages. The editions and literary histories of the nineteenth century stand as our own disciplinary origins, and it is important to understand how this intellectual legacy both shapes and is shaped by its medieval objects of study.

On the other hand, it is tempting to focus on the discontinuity between nineteenth-century philology and our present methods of studying the medieval past. If, as Gumbrecht observed, the nineteenth century marked a significant rupture in the story of Romance philology (56), then perhaps we now find ourselves at a similar turning point. The ways in which our scholarly forebears lionized Juan Manuel as an authoritative author, scrutinized manuscripts in search of his intentions, and held out hope for locating the authorized Peñafiel manuscript, might seem naive from our current vantage point. Historical distance gives us perspective and makes us believe that we can recognize the rhetoric of the past for what it is. But as I have tried to show in this epilogue, the persistence of a medieval discourse of authorship in nineteenth-century editions shows that these moments of discontinuity are perhaps not as decisive as we might think. Juan Manuel's fourteenth-century rhetoric of authority, particularly as expressed in the General Prologue and the self-defence in the *Libro infinido*, has been remarkably pervasive and persuasive right up to the present, reminding us to be attentive to how other types of rhetoric endure, even when disguised in more modern trappings. The persistence of Juan Manuel's discourse of authorship in the books of the fifteenth, sixteenth, and nineteenth centuries attests to how the rhetoric of the past can survive, and even thrive, beyond such moments of rupture.

Notes

Introduction

1 This brief account relies on Andrés Giménez Soler, whose biography remains the most complete to date and includes an appendix of hundreds of letters exchanged between Juan Manuel and the monarchs and courtiers of his day. H. Tracy Sturcken's biography provides a good overview of his life in English.

2 The two instances in which Juan Manuel revoked his fealty to Alfonso XI of Castile, in 1327 and 1336, are analysed in detail by Orduna ("*Libro*" 231–44).

3 On the year of Juan Manuel's death, often given as 1348 based on an unreliable source, see Rubio García.

4 On the founding of these monasteries, see Redondo Cantera.

5 Approximate years of composition are taken from Mota ("Introduction"), whose legwork and sound rationale are particularly convincing.

6 The names for the internal divisions of the *Conde Lucanor* vary from scholar to scholar. Given that the framing conversations between Patronio and Lucanor in *S* suggest a division into five parts, I will refer to them as parts 1–5, following most modern editions. This five-part division is also compatible with the tripartite structure proposed by Orduna ("Notas" 502–3) and explained in Joaquín Gimeno Casalduero ("*Conde*"), with part 1 comprising the *Libro de los exemplos*, parts 2–4 the *Libro de los proverbios*, and part 5 the *Libro de la doctrina*.

7 On *Libro de las tres razones* as a better conventional title than *Libro de las armas*, see Deyermond ("*Libro*" 83–9).

8 On its contents, see B. Taylor ("Capítulos" 56–63).

9 The chapter by Barry Taylor in the forthcoming *A Companion to Don Juan Manuel* provides a fresh look at all the manuscripts ("Manuscript Transmission"). For more detailed descriptions of the *Conde Lucanor*

manuscripts, see de Looze (26–63) and Hammer (*Framing* 44–71), and for perceptive versionist studies of most of them, see Burgoyne ("Fragments," "Reading and Writing," *Reading the Exemplum*, "Reading to Pieces," "Los versos"). On the early transmission of the *Conde Lucanor*, including relationships among manuscripts, see A. Blecua.

10 BNE, MS 19426 was first brought to light by Ayerbe-Chaux ("Manuscritos") and has been studied by Burgoyne ("Los versos"). I accept the siglum *N* proposed by Carlos Mota in his edition of the *Libro infinido*.

11 Many thanks to Olivier Biaggini for raising this issue with me and pointing out that Ayerbe-Chaux's date is based partly on flawed reasoning: the final folio of *S* has a note that refers to the 1483 battle at La Axarquía in the kingdom of Granada, but it is an addition in a different hand and cannot be taken as evidence for the manuscript's date of production. However, I echo Ayerbe-Chaux in questioning the status of *S* as an "idol or icon that we all must revere" ("Critical Editions" 24), a status I believe is due in part to Juan Manuel's persuasive rhetoric of authorship.

12 For an up-to-date overview of bibliography on the three periods, see Serés's edition of the *Conde Lucanor* (292–301).

13 Orduna's influential work on the Alfonsine period includes "Prólogos," "Catálogo," and "El *exemplo*" (122), and has been continued by Diego Catalán ("Don Juan"), Carmen Benito Vessels, Leonardo Funes ("Don Juan"), Manuel Hijano Villegas, and Mario Cossío Olavide ("Reescritura"), among others. For an assessment of Orduna's contribution to Juan Manuel studies, see Funes ("Aportes"). Reinaldo Ayerbe-Chaux ("Don Juan" 187) proposes to place the *Libro de las cantigas* in the Alfonsine period, but I would place it in the personal period, for reasons discussed in chapter 4.

14 Diego Catalán coined the term *molinismo* to refer to María de Molina's influence on post-Sanchine historiography (*Estoria* 13). While the queen's direct impact as a literary sponsor continues to be debated, Gómez Redondo has developed *molinismo* into a productive framework for studying the continuity in Castilian courtly literature under Sancho IV, Fernando IV, and Alfonso XI, including the production of Juan Manuel (*Historia de la prosa* 1: 856–63; "Molinismo"; "Don Juan Manuel, autor molinista").

15 For a critique of *molinismo* that proposes the alternative rubric of "sanchismo," see Linehan (12–13). For one that calls for a more nuanced approach to the literature labeled *molinista*, see North (279–84). The objection of heterogeneity applies to any attempt at literary periodization, but such categories can be productive when thoughtfully used.

16 See Patricia Rochwert-Zuili for an analysis of how Sancho's Christian paradigm of authorship sets up a contrast with the "malos entendimientos" disseminated by Alfonso's works (53–6).

17 My understanding of an "ideological production" is informed by Louis Althusser's "Ideology and Ideological State Apparatuses" and Terry Eagleton's discussion of Althusser's essay (148–50).

18 In understanding Foucault's notion of discourse, I have found helpful Sylvia Wynter's related concept of "adaptive truth-for," a society's invention of an idea with a particular agenda, and subsequent forgetting of the invention, leading to a presentation of that idea as a "truth" existing outside the purview of human agency.

19 While some extant prologues to the *Libro del tesoro* claim that Alfonso sponsored the translation, Gómez Redondo argues convincingly that Sancho both commissioned his own translation (employing the same scholars who wrote the *Castigos de Sancho IV* and *Lucidario*) and deliberately assumed declarative authorship of it (*Historia de la prosa* 1: 866–7).

20 In my translations, I render *onbre* and its variants (*omne, ome, ombre*) in a gender-neutral way when used as a generic pronoun. This usage is attested in Alfonso X's *Siete Partidas,* in which *ome* is glossed as referring "también a la muger como al varón, maguer que non fagamos ý emiente della" ("to a woman as well as to a man, although no mention of her is made"; *7PartidasDigital* 7.33.6, 1555 ed.; trans. Parsons Scott, 5: 1473).

21 While the anonymous medieval associates were far more likely to be men, I avoid gendered pronouns to acknowledge that women did find ways of participating in book culture, a subject studied by Ronald Surtz as well as Isabel Navas Ocaña and José de la Torre Castro.

22 As Jonathan Burgoyne reminds us, in a manuscript culture many individuals can be considered the author's associates, and thus the idea of an "official paratext" applies to all paratexts that "draw authority from the author's work," regardless of the author's involvement (*Reading the Exemplum* 33).

23 Examples include the title page of Gaibrois de Ballesteros's book (*El príncipe*), a colour image in the *Obras completas* edited by Carlos Alvar and Sarah Finci, the cover of *Lectures de El conde Lucanor* edited by César García de Lucas and Alexandra Oddo, and many teaching anthologies. The altarpiece, a work by Barnaba da Modena known as the *Retablo de la Virgen de la Leche* (c. 1372), depicts two donors flanking the Virgin. The female figure is Queen Juana Manuel, Juan Manuel's daughter, and the male figure, though long identified as Juan Manuel, is more likely a portrait of Juan Sánchez Manuel, count of Carrión (Torres Fontes and Torres-Fontes Suárez 106–12).

1. Scriptor

1 On the Alfonsine scriptorium's approach to historiography, see, for example, Catalán (*Estoria*) and Inés Fernández-Ordóñez (*"Ordinatio"*). On the Alfonsine teams of writers and translators who produced scientific works, see the classic study by Gonzalo Menéndez Pidal and the monograph by Fernández Fernández. On the less-studied Sanchine scriptorium, see Hugo Bizzarri ("Historiografía").

2 Lacarra (*Don Juan Manuel* 177) and Fernando Gómez Redondo (*Historia de la prosa* 1: 1198) date the General Prologue to 1342.

3 In referring to the *Conde Lucanor*, I use *enxiemplo* to indicate the chapters of part 1, and exemplum for Patronio's exemplary tales within each *enxiemplo*.

4 Two consecutive tales in Sacchetti's *Trecentonovelle* are protagonized by Dante and deal with his displeasure at modifications to his work. The first, Novella 114, is a closer retelling of the motif from Diogenes: Dante hears a blacksmith singing his *Commedia* "as one sings a song," adding and subtracting verses however he pleases. Dante throws the blacksmith's tools out into the street; the latter demands an explanation, and Dante quips, "You are not singing my work the way that I wrote it; I have no other art, and you are ruining it." The smith decides it is not worth the trouble and takes up singing about Tristan or Lancelot instead of reciting from Dante. In the second, Novella 115, Dante hears a donkey driver singing his *Commedia* interspersed occasionally with an "arri" to encourage his beasts. Dante smacks the man on the back, saying that he did not put that "arri" there; the man insults him with the fig gesture, which Dante does not return, saying that one of his is worth one hundred of the donkey driver's. For a discussion of how the two stories present the same theme with minor variations, see Lalomia (778–9).

5 Some scholars have identified "el primero rey don Jaymes de Mallorcas" as Jaume I of Aragon (r. 1213–76), whose court was a centre for the production of vernacular literature (Lacarra, *Don Juan Manuel* 17; ed. Serés, 3). However, I follow Martí de Riquer in identifying him as Jaume's son, Jaume II of Mallorca (r. 1276–1311), who also patronized authors including Ramon Llull (125; see also Biaggini, *Le gouvernement* 35n1).

6 Elsewhere, Juan Manuel did exploit his ties to Mallorca as a source of political and literary authority, citing his wife Isabel as a source of information about the royal family of Castile in his *Libro de las tres razones* (*Obras*, ed. Alvar and Finci, 986).

7 On "the Limousin language" as Occitan, see Lledó-Guillem (4–5). More broadly, Lledó-Guillem's monograph examines how the Catalan-Aragonese

monarchy exploited linguistic and poetic ties between Catalan and Occitan to serve the monarchy's political interests.

8 The title of Juan Manuel's lost *Libro de las reglas cómo se deve trobar* suggests a deliberate positioning in relation to the thirteenth-century Catalan poetic treatises of Ramon Vidal de Besalú and Jofre de Foixà. Vidal's work is called *Razos de trobar* or *Regles d'En Ramon Vidal* in its manuscript copies, and Jofre de Foixà refers to it as the *Regles de trobar*, which is the same title he gives to his own treatise (Marshall lxvi n1). Juan Manuel's poetic treatise would have been the first of its kind in Castilian.

9 Many thanks to Deeana Klepper for sharing her unpublished work on Ponç Carbonell's role in circulating the *Postilla* in Christian Iberia and helping make this connection.

10 The bibliography on this trope is large and growing. Two years before Rico's essay, Barry Taylor ("Capítulos" 64n1) compared Juan Manuel's version to several Latin examples. See also Fisher (29–30) on its prevalence in medieval Britain, and Hobbins (165–6) for more examples of the "general anxiety" authors faced when handing their work over to scribes for reproduction and circulation.

11 On the *pecia* system in medieval Christian universities, see the classic studies by Destrez and Fink-Errera, as well as Shooner, who traces its origins to a monastic context.

12 Sylvia Huot's pathfinding *From Song to Book*, which examined such authorizing strategies in the works of Jean de Meun, Machaut, and Froissart, has inspired other important research on medieval French literature by scholars such as Deborah McGrady (*Controlling Readers* and "What Is a Patron") and Daniel Hobbins (*Authorship and Publicity Before Print*). For a useful summary of recent scholarship on this topic in vernacular literature more broadly, see Andrew Taylor.

13 I follow Barry Taylor's distinction between *mise en page*, which concerns page layout, textual divisions, and rubrics, and *mise en texte*, which encompasses all these as well as paratexts, indexes, illustrations, and binding ("*Estoria*" 39). For a discussion of how *S* draws on the authority of Don Juan's literary persona, see de Looze (31–2). On the rubrics, tables of contents, and prologues of *S* as signs of its careful preparation, see Barry Taylor ("*Libro infinido*" and "*Estoria*") and Olivetto ("Don Juan" 123–5). For a summary of scholarship on the planned miniatures in the *S* version of the *Conde Lucanor*, as well as evidence that the *Libro de las tres razones* was also meant to have miniatures, see Cossío Olavide, "El *Libro de las tres razones*."

14 For ancient tropes of writing as both memory aid and a metaphor for memory, see Carruthers (16).

15 The relationship between the Castilian *Barlaam e Josafat* and the frame story of the *Libro de los estados* has been well documented; see, for example, Macpherson and Tate's edition (44–8) and Gómez Redondo (*Historia de la prosa* 1: 983). Funes and Yoon have demonstrated that Juan Manuel relies on his readers' familiarity with *Barlaam* to make meaningful changes to the plot and invite comparisons between the two works.

16 Later in the dialogue, Petrarch laments the lack of laws and standards applied to the work of scribes, claiming that "neither the blacksmiths, nor the farmers and weavers, nor most other craftsmen have such unrestricted liberty" ("Non fabris, non agricolis, non textoribus, non ulli fere artium tanta licentia est"; *Four Dialogues*, 38–9). Note that for Petrarch, as for Sacchetti, the archetypal craft is that of the blacksmith.

17 The source is Petrarch, *Letters of Old Age* (*Rerum senilium libri*), bk. 5, lett. 2, "To the same person [Boccaccio], concerning the obsessive appetite for first place." The Latin edition of 1501 reads: "Intellexi tandem molli in limo et instabili arena perdi operam, meque et laborem meum inter vulgi manus laceratum iri. Tanquam ergo qui currens calle medio colubrum offendit, substiti mittamque consilium aliud ut spero rectius atque altius arripui, quamvis sparsa illa et brevia iuuenilia atque vulgaria iam ut dixi non mea amplius sed vulgi potius facta essent, maiora ne lanient providebo" (*Annotatio*, fol. 3.vii.r).

18 In medieval Castilian, *entendimiento* refers to the intellective faculties of the human soul, understood in light of Aristotle's division of the soul into vegetative, sensitive, and intellective faculties, and mediated through medieval commentaries by Avicenna and Thomas Aquinas. Depending on context, I translate it as intellect, memory, understanding, or intelligence.

19 María Guadalupe Campos has proposed that Baena's prologue draws upon the literary education of the nobility expressed in the *Conde Lucanor* (122).

2. Compilator

1 Hathaway argues that compiling did not represent a new genre in the thirteenth century, but rather corresponds to "more prevalent, varied, and sophisticated" methods of compiling (41). However, Minnis provides a convincing rebuttal that the discourse of *compilatio* took on fresh significance in the thirteenth century as one "in deliberate contestation with the discourse of 'authorship'" in academic prologues to the works of *auctores* ("Nolens" 60).

2 Derek Pearsall, writing about the literariness of Chaucer's verse, notes that "words in poetry, in the way they are chosen and arranged, have a wider range of possible meanings than they have in ordinary discourse, and not in any way confined to denotation" (99–100).

3 Both Ayerbe-Chaux ("Introduction" xxiii) and Cossío Olavide (*Libro del cavallero* xli) have pointed out parallels between the *Speculum naturale,* the part of Vincent's encyclopedia on natural history, and passages of Juan Manuel's *Libro del cavallero et del escudero,* but further study is needed in this area. Vincent's work remained popular in Iberia throughout the fourteenth century: Pedro IV of Aragon (r. 1336–87) commissioned a Catalan translation of the *Speculum historiale,* completed around 1384 by the Dominican friar Jaume Domènec (Fernández-Ordóñez, "Actores y autores" 206).

4 *De proprietatibus rerum* was translated into Castilian twice in the later Middle Ages, showing its continuing popularity among Castilian readers. On the circulation and quality of these translations, see Sánchez González de Herrero.

5 Alfonso oversaw a vast collaborative project in two cities (Toledo and Seville) that included many participants: translators made initial translations of works, correctors edited the translators' drafts, compilers gathered and organized material from different sources, rubricators wrote chapter titles and other organizational features of manuscripts, authors added new material as needed, scribes copied the text, and illuminators decorated the manuscripts. The collaborative activities of the members of Alfonso's scriptorium are documented in Menéndez Pidal, Harvey, and Fernández Fernández.

6 Where appropriate, I translate *razón* as "passage" or "argument," following Gómez Redondo's contextualization of the word in the Thomistic tradition as a demonstrative and persuasive method of proving an argument, as well as the literary form this proof takes (*Historia de la prosa* 1: 1192). I translate *drecho* as "clear," following the persuasive reasoning of Cárdenas.

7 As Carruthers explains, this flower metaphor was sometimes maligned as uncreative by Renaissance writers attempting to distance themselves from medieval textual practices, but medieval readers saw the gathering process as an opportunity for new combinations of texts (192).

8 On the guiding principles of the literature categorized under the rubric of *molinismo,* particularly its tendency to centre Castilian literary production around exclusively Christian didactic and ethical materials, see Kinkade ("Sancho IV" 1045–6), Orduna ("Élite"), Gómez Redondo (*Historia de la prosa* 1: 861–3; "Molinismo"), and North (279–84).

9 As in the *Castigos,* the prologue to the *Lucidario* equates authorship with service to God: "Por ende, nós, don Sancho, por la graçia de Dios rey de Castilla, [...] ternemos por bien e por derecho de començar este libro a su serviçio [de Dios]" ("Thus we, Don Sancho, by the grace of God king of Castile, find it good and right to begin this book in [God's] service"; 80–2).

10 Maestre Pedro's *ordinatio* around the number six is obscured by a different medieval editor's subdivision of the work into chapters, as Barry Taylor shows in his edition (76–80). Six was unusual in the numerology of Castilian wisdom literature, but could represent twice the Trinity or, as Gómez Redondo proposes, the letters in "Sancho," imitating Alfonso's arrangement of the *Siete Partidas* around the number seven (*Historia de la prosa* 1: 945).

11 I discuss Juan Manuel's use of *accessus* conventions in chapter 3. On the *accessus* tradition in Latin academic prologues and its adaptations by Chaucer and Gower into English vernacular literature, see Minnis (*Medieval Theory*, chs. 1 and 5). For a panoramic assessment of the *accessus* in European vernacular literature, see Hanna et al.

12 Alvar and Finci's emendation of *leý* to *leyó*, is appropriate, but I call attention to it because it sheds light on the collaborative process of bookmaking: the work was evidently dictated in the first person to a scribe, who then converted it to the third person (Seniff, "Así fiz yo" 39–40; Ayerbe-Chaux, "Introduction" xlv). Whereas Seniff sees the first-person *leý* as the scribe asserting a "personal touch," I read it as one of Juan Manuel's utterances that the scribe failed to correct.

13 Most of the falconers Juan Manuel mentions by name, with the exception of Roy Ximenes de Mesco, have been documented in José Castro y Calvo's edition of the *Libro de la caza* (112–13). Sancho Ximenes de Lanchares (or Lanclares) was a trusted official who served as *adelantado* (governor) and *merino* (magistrate) in Murcia during Juan Manuel's absence (Pascual Martínez 277, 280); he also signed several letters from Juan Manuel's chancery, and a debt to his family is mentioned in the author's second will and testament (Gaibrois de Ballesteros, "Testamentos" 52). Ferrant Gomes is possibly the Ferrando Gómez who served as *camarero mayor* to Fernando IV in 1301, and who complained of Juan Manuel's conduct to Infante Juan of Aragon (*Libro de la caza*, ed. Fradejas Rueda, 131n13).

14 This supports historian Charles Homer Haskins's assertion that fishing "was not a recognized sport of the upper classes" and was therefore generally left out of courtly hunting literature (247–8).

15 This assumes that the *Libro de la caza* was composed early in Juan Manuel's career: Lacarra (*Don Juan* 176) dates its composition to around 1321, and Mota places it before 1329 ("Introduction" 40). Burgoyne raises doubts about this early date, speculating that the work – or a later revision of it – could be read as a defence of the nobility that looks back on the period of 1327–9, Juan Manuel's first rebellion against Alfonso XI ("Imagining" 118).

16 Funes interprets the metaphor differently, drawing a parallel between the "virote del lector ballestero" ("arrow of the crossbowman reader") and Juan Manuel's insomnia, which creates expendable hours in his day that can be devoted to reading and writing ("Excentricidad" 15–17).

17 Devoto and Ayerbe-Chaux ("*El conde Lucanor*") both provide invaluable resources for studying the sources and parallel stories for the exempla of the *Conde Lucanor*. The politics of this aspect of Manueline studies are described astutely by María Rosa Menocal: "But [Juan Manuel] has made gentlemen, *cavalleros*, of those dispersed, anonymous, and 'ethnic' collections which smacked too much of the songs of the *çapatero*, with the sounds of the streets about them even when they were written in Castilian, he has wrestled those pre-literary demons to the ground, and he has tamed that untidy textual past by turning it all into mere footnotes of 'sources' which give rise to his own 'originality'" (476). This is not to say that his sources – the Latin and vernacular exempla collections used by Christian preachers, or the courtly translations of *Calila e Dimna* and *Sendebar* from Arabic – were perceived as low literary forms in fourteenth-century Castile, but rather that nineteenth- and twentieth-century scholars privileged the perceived homogeneity of the *Conde Lucanor* over the sources' more complicated textual history when publishing anthologies and literary histories of medieval Spain.

18 To justify his change in style, Juan Manuel uses the topos common to medieval prologues of writing at a friend's behest, in this case, the Aragonese nobleman Jaime de Jérica. On this historical personage and his rhetorical function in the *Conde Lucanor*, see Barry Taylor ("Don Jaime").

19 The autobiographical project of Ginés de Pasamonte, the reformed criminal and author freed by Don Quijote in the episode of the galley slaves, satirizes the picaresque convention that the *pícaro* inscribes his or her life in a book. When Don Quijote asks whether he has finished the aptly titled *La vida de Ginés de Pasamonte*, he responds: "¿Cómo puede estar acabado [...] si aún no está acabada mi vida?" ("How can it be finished [...] if my life isn't finished yet?"; pt. 1, ch. 22, trans. Grossman).

20 This is related to the topos of the inexpressible in medieval Latin literature, as studied by Curtius (160). However, while Curtius's examples have to do with praise, this particular use by Juan Manuel addresses the conundrum of finishing the book of one's life.

21 Macpherson ("Don Juan Manuel"), Orduna ("*Libro*" 261–2), Ruiz (76), Ramos Nogales (183), Qués (100), Funes and Qués (76), and Deyermond ("*Libro*" 93) all read this passage as a reference to biblical exegesis, with Macpherson asserting that "Don Juan dares to compare his creative process with that of medieval commentators on the scriptures" (5). Rosende brings together the arguments of several of these scholars to propose that the *Libro de las tres razones* adopts an exegetical stance towards its material, invoking the fourfold sense of scripture (202–3). Alvar and Finci promote this reading by capitalizing "Escrituras" in their edition, which I have emended to reflect my dissenting view.

22 On the involvement of Alfonso García de Villamayor in Infante Manuel's affairs, see Kinkade's recent biography of Infante Manuel, *Dawn of a Dynasty*. Giménez Soler identifies Savrina de Bedes as Saurina de Bessers (or Béziers), probably the daughter of Juan de Bessers, a physician employed by Jaume II of Aragon (335).

23 The Assumption continued to be a point of doctrinal debate until 1950, when Pope Pius XII spoke ex cathedra to declare it a tenet of Catholic dogma.

24 Parkes ("Influence") explains how *ordinatio*, initially a practical set of tools to organize twelfth-century scholastic commentaries, developed in the thirteenth century into a theoretical concept of bookmaking technology. Building on this work, Minnis reveals how authors of medieval Latin texts described and rationalized their practice of *ordinatio* (*Medieval Theory* 145–59).

25 The only surviving manuscript of *Sobre la secta mahometana* (Real Biblioteca de El Escorial, MS h.II.25) gives "*fablar* de ligero," reinforcing the relationship between text and orality that appears in the same passage. A divergent reading, "*fallar* de ligero" (*Obras de S. Pedro Pascual, mártir* 4: 1) is worth noting for how it frames paratextual elements as finding aids for readers. Many thanks to the Real Biblioteca de San Lorenzo de El Escorial for providing a digital image of fol. 1r of MS h.II.25.

26 The *Crónica manuelina*, copied between 1295 and 1320, is divided into three books. The first two are related to the *Versión primitiva* of the *Estoria de España*, while the third is associated with a noble patron and survives in British Library, MS Egerton 289. On its transmission and place within the Alfonsine historiographical tradition, see especially Fernández-Ordóñez ("La transmisión" 223–37) and Hijano Villegas (72–80).

27 A modern editor has added chapter numbers in pencil. Barry Taylor has proposed that the *Libro de la caza* in *S* is a complete copy of an incomplete antigraph, or what he calls a "copia incompleta de segunda generación" ("a second-generation incomplete copy"; "Manuscritos" 41). This could explain why the *Libro de la caza* lacks the rubrics and chapter numbers that *S* supplies for the *Libro del cavallero et del escudero*, *Libro de los estados*, and *Conde Lucanor*.

28 For Gómez Redondo, *fabliella* refers not to a concrete literary genre but to a narrative discourse that both creates convincing fictional characters and instructs through simulated oral exchange (*Historia de la prosa* 1: 1111). Barry Taylor ("Fabliella") proposes that Juan Manuel sought to portray his book as trivial in comparison to the Latin commentary on the Lord's Prayer that Infante Juan of Aragon had exchanged with him, but Serés reminds us that he also requested to have his own work translated into Latin, indicating the valuable didactic content of his *fabliella* ("Fundamentos" 184–5).

29 *S*, the only manuscript witness, is missing part of chapter 3, all of chapters 4 through 15, and part of chapter 16. On the contents of these lost chapters, see Barry Taylor ("Capítulos"), who proposes a reconstruction based on the summary provided by Juan Manuel in his *Libro de los estados*.

30 In a polemical essay that calls into question Juan Manuel's authorship of the works written under his name, Vicente Cantarino cites this dialogic structure as evidence of an advanced command of narrative techniques that a *bellator* could not have mastered (56). However, as Lacarra (*Cuentística*) has shown, Juan Manuel's works are predated by a robust corpus of Castilian works with a variety of dialogic frames, all of which were available as vernacular models. Furthermore, as Heusch ("Limites" 186–90) argues, the dialogues between teacher and pupil in the *Libro del cavallero et del escudero, Libro de los estados*, and *Conde Lucanor* are not elaborate and mainly serve to allow the teacher to speak on a given topic without interruption.

31 It is beyond my scope to weigh in on the hypothesis that Castilian authors like Juan Manuel or Juan Ruiz took inspiration directly from Arabic and Hebrew *maqāmāt*. I bring the Iberian *maqāmāt* to bear because they show a secular aesthetic function of chapter numbers that complements the religious and ethical ones evinced by Christian Iberian texts. Other scholars have made stronger arguments for Juan Manuel's use of Andalusī narrative practices in the *Conde Lucanor* (Wacks, *Framing*, ch. 4) and even for reading the *Conde Lucanor* as a collection of *maqāmāt* (Torollo).

32 Funes's work refutes the earlier hypothesis of Gimeno Casalduero, who argued for the work's thematic unity based in part on its extant chapter divisions ("*Libro*").

33 In spite of these textual references to fifty tales, the frame structure of part 1 allowed for flexibility, leaving some early witnesses (*M* and *G*) with fifty, others (*H* and Argote) with only forty-nine, and others (*S* and *P*) with fifty-one (Devoto 296–7). *P*, an unusual case with two apocryphal exempla, has been studied by Burgoyne, who concludes that "the extra *exempla* are witnesses to reading *El Conde Lucanor* within the larger framework of generic collections of didactic short stories intended to be used according to the needs of their readers, rather than read as the artistic expression and unique creation of an individual author" ("Reading and Writing" 484–5).

34 For example, Alvar ("Ay") asserts that the fifty-first tale in *S* was not authored by Juan Manuel and should be excluded from modern editions because it disrupts the work's announced numerical perfection. John England argues the opposing view, proposing that the author did "not mean these numbers to be taken seriously" (19). A summary of this debate can be found in Serés's edition (560–1).

35 A noteworthy variation on this formula occurs in ex. 5, announcing the "viesos en que se entiende abreviadamente la entención de todo este exiemplo" ("verses in which the meaning of the whole exemplum can be understood in brief"; ed. Serés, 37). Although this is often used to support the much-repeated idea in Juan Manuel criticism that Don Juan's verses provide a summary of each tale, Menocal points out that the verses are "grossly reductive" and sometimes fail to map neatly onto the story at hand (487).

36 The scholarship on Don Juan's authorial persona in the *Conde Lucanor* is abundant. Foundational studies on the subject are Scholberg ("Juan Manuel" and "Modestia"), Macpherson ("Don Juan Manuel"), Luongo, Orduna ("Autobiografía"), and Funes ("Excentricidad"). More recently, García de Lucas has contributed a formal analysis of "narrative markers" ("marcadores narrativos") that confirms the work's meticulous structure and its association of that structure with Don Juan.

37 Orduna similarly characterizes Don Juan's relationship to the exempla as one of compilation and a certain degree of distance: "La voz extradiegética crea la ilusión de que el contenido le es ajeno y sólo se [le] atribuye la factura material del objeto" ("The extradiegetic narrator creates the illusion that the content is not his own and the only thing attributed to him is the material making of the object"; "Yo, don Johán" xxvii).

38 In *S*, this repeated formula of compilation holds such sway that the scribe accidentally copies a version of it after the brief *Tratado de la Asunción*, located immediately after the *Conde Lucanor*. I transcribe from *S*: "Et porque don Johán tovo este por buen enxiemplo, fízolo poner en este libro et fizo estos viessos que dizen assí" ("And because Don Juan took this as a good example, he had it put in this book and wrote the following verses"; fol. 194v). The formula is not followed by any verses, just a lacuna of three lines. Ayerbe-Chaux speculates that the scribe wrote it in jest ("Introduction" 175n13), but it is just as likely that the scribe saw the short *Tratado* as one more text in Don Juan's compilation and marked it accordingly.

39 On the dynastic message of the *Libro de las tres razones*, see Deyermond ("Cuentos" and "*Libro*"), Díez de Revenga ("*Libro de las armas*"), Qués, and Rosende.

3. Commentator

1 For a general overview of glosses to Castilian literary works in the fourteenth and fifteenth centuries, see Lacarra and Cacho Blecua (268–9). For an in-depth study of commentarial forms in fifteenth-century Castilian letters, see Weiss (*The Poet's Art*).

2 The term "vernacular theology" was first suggested by A. Ian Doyle and has been developed into a fruitful category of analysis by scholars including Bernard McGinn and Nicholas Watson ("Censorship" and "Cultural Changes"). For a thorough overview of vernacular theology as a scholarly focus in Middle English literature, see V. Gillespie, "Vernacular Theology." For an analysis of vernacular theology in John Gower's *Confessio amantis*, see T. Matthew N. McCabe; for an example of the term's application in an Italian context, see Corbari.

3 For examples from the scriptoria of Alfonso X and Sancho IV of the secular functions of the advisor characters and their interplay with models of good counsel, see Cossío Olavide, "Non ha tan buena escuela."

4 Some comprehensive studies of the Latin academic tradition of the *accessus ad auctores* spanning the twelfth to fifteenth centuries include Quain; Minnis, *Medieval Theory* (especially 15–33); and V. Gillespie, "From the Twelfth Century."

5 In the context of the *accessus*, Bernard of Utrecht and Hugh of St. Victor both define "philosophy" as the discipline concerned with knowledge of all things, both human and divine (Minnis, *Medieval Theory* 23–4).

6 See Benito Vessels, Saracino, and Cossío Olavide ("Reescritura") for arguments about how Juan Manuel's selection criteria differ from Alfonso X's in politically and ideologically meaningful ways. Ultimately, however, I agree with Hijano Villegas that the work's meaning lies in its faithfulness to its model (82).

7 Hugh of St. Victor's twelfth-century *Didascalicon* (2.20) classifies hunting (*venatio*) as one of the seven mechanical arts practised by the lower classes, in contrast to the seven liberal arts practised by the nobility (*Didascalicon* 2.20, trans. J. Taylor, p. 75).

8 On Dante and the *accessus*, see Ascoli (*Dante*, especially ch. 4). The *Epistle*'s attribution to Dante is controversial, but it is nonetheless presented as a self-commentary, and fourteenth-century readers understood it as such (Ascoli, "Access to Authority"; Barański 589).

9 See Weiss's two-part catalogue of Castilian commentaries and glosses ("Vernacular Commentaries ... I" and "Vernacular Commentaries ... II").

10 Ayerbe-Chaux (*Cinco tratados* 109) conflates the Dominican Fray Juan Alfonso with a scribe in Juan Manuel's chancery by the same name, but there is no evidence to support this. For updated information on the Dominicans in Juan Manuel's intellectual circles, see the chapter by Cossío Olavide in the forthcoming *A Companion to Don Juan Manuel*.

11 The text of Infante Juan of Aragon's commentary can be found in Archivo de la Catedral de Valencia, MS 182, fols. 264r–270v. Many thanks to Juan Ignacio Pérez Giménez of the Archivo de la Catedral de Valencia for providing digital images of the pertinent folios.

12 The passage is from the prologue and reads as follows: "Non potest animus noster ad inuisibilium contemplationem ascendere, nisi per uisibilium considerationem dirigatur. Inuisibilia enim Dei per ea que facta sunt intellecta cognoscuntur, ut dicit Apostolus, et ideo theologia proinde sacris et poeticis informationibus usa est, ut ex rerum uisibilium similitudinibus allegorice locutiones et mistici intellectus transumptiones formentur, et sic carnalibus et uisibilibus spiritualia et inuisibilia coaptentur" (cited in Dahan, n39). The misattribution can be explained by the fact that John of Damascus cites the passage in his *Apologia against Those Who Decry Holy Images*, attributing it to Dionysius the Areopagite (B. Taylor, "Juan Manuel's Cipher" 37). Bartholomaeus Anglicus's *De proprietatibus rerum* circulated in Latin in medieval Castile, and was translated into Castilian twice, both times likely in the fifteenth century (Sánchez González de Herrero 349–51).

13 For Juan Manuel, *cavallería* referred not only to the military responsibilities of a knight, but also to a set of aristocratic values including ethical and practical decision-making. This is made clear in chapter 19 of the *Libro del cavallero et del escudero*, in which the old knight's definition of *cavallería* encompasses Vegetius's *Epitoma rei militaris*, the ethical concept of *vergüença*, and practical judgment in managing one's estate and finances (12–15).

14 While the vocabulary of commentaries was by no means standardized, near-contemporaries of Juan Manuel used certain terms to distinguish between types of commentary that overlapped with the fourfold model of scriptural exegesis. For example, in his translation and gloss of Vegetius's *Epitoma rei militaris*, the late-fourteenth-century scholar Alfonso de San Cristóbal uses *glosa* to refer to clarifications of the literal sense, and *fablar espiritualmente* for elucidations of the spiritual sense (allegorical, moral, and anagogical): "La segunda parte será bien como *glosa* puesta en la margen del libro, que es de dichos de los sabidores que concuerdan con lo que dize Vegeçio e declaran sus dichos en algunos logares. La terçera parte será puesta ayuso, que *fablará espiritualmente* trayendo los dichos de Vegeçio, a las vezes a las virtudes e a los pecados e a las costunbres d'esta vida en que bevimos" ("The second part will be a *gloss* in the margin of the book that includes sayings of wise men who agree with what Vegetius says and explain his words in some places. The third part will be placed below, and will *discuss the spiritual meaning* of Vegetius's words, referring to virtues, sins, and practices in this life we live"; 13; my emphasis).

15 As Giles Constable has shown, the Christian ideal of the imitation of Christ was widespread in the late medieval period and encompassed imitations not only of Jesus's suffering, but also of his virtues and earthly behaviours documented in the Bible and in lives of Christ (234).

16 While Juan Manuel does not cite a specific source, this interpretation of Eve's error is a common point of exegesis in both Christian and Jewish traditions. It is discussed by the fourth-century Church Father St. Ambrose (*Paradise*, ch. 12, par. 56; pp. 334–7), as well as by the medieval rabbinical scholars whose work informed Moshe Arragel in his preparation of the fifteenth-century *Biblia de Arragel* (Girón-Negrón 40–3).

17 Fradejas Rueda et al. ("Las versiones") have sorted the manuscripts of the *Glosa castellana al Regimiento de príncipes* into four groups: Series A uses layout to distinguish text from gloss, but Series B, C, and D do not. Juan Beneyto Pérez, in his edition of the *Glosa*, "corrects" the manuscript tradition by making consistent divisions between text and gloss, but acknowledges that these divisions do not appear in all exemplars (xxxvii).

18 Book 1 concludes with Julio petitioning Don Juan to record the events of the narrative as a book, and Don Juan complying. As Scholberg ("Juan Manuel" 458) and Biaggini ("Stratégies" 221) observe, this establishes continuity between the fictional character Julio and the author figure Don Juan as contributors to the book. For further explorations of the role of orality in Juan Manuel's works, see Biglieri; Seniff ("Así fiz yo" and "Orality"); Gerli; and Heusch ("Oralité").

19 For a summary of official legislation and individual positions on vernacular theology in an Iberian context, see Savo ("Hidden Polemic" 11–14).

20 I thank Mario Cossío Olavide for calling my attention to this passage.

21 Although writing in Latin was one available way of restricting readership, there is no reason to believe the encoded writing in the *Libro de los estados* referred either to Latin or to Castilian with a jumbled word order, the technique used in part 4 of the *Conde Lucanor*. As Barry Taylor points out, these strategies would involve the Latin alphabet and would therefore not warrant the description of *letras escuras/estrañas* ("Juan Manuel's Cipher" 39).

22 In ex. 3, the story of King Richard the Lionheart's famous leap against an army of Muslim soldiers, Patronio appropriates ecclesiastical authority not only through the form of the exemplum, but also through the content of his interpretation, which references "doctrines of penance, reconciliation, and the discourse of the Holy Crusade" (Burgoyne, *Reading the Exemplum* 104).

23 The motifs of ex. 48 were widespread in medieval literature and appeared in Iberian collections including the *Disciplina clericalis* by Petrus Alfonsi, *Barlaam e Josafat*, *Castigos de Sancho IV*, *Libro del caballero Zifar*, *Libro de los enxemplos por a.b.c.* by Clemente Sánchez de Vercial, *Espéculo de los legos*, *Esopete historiado*, and others. On Juan Manuel's creative combination of the story of the half-friend from the *Disciplina clericalis* with the allegorical tale of the three friends from *Barlaam e Josafat*, see Ayerbe-Chaux (*"El conde Lucanor"* 161–9).

24 On the unrealized *estorias* or miniatures in *S*, see especially Marcos-Marín; Piccus; Barry Taylor ("*Estoria*"); and Cossío Olavide ("*Libro*").

25 Paragraph marks, also known as paraphs, originated as markers of sections or chapters (the ¶ is a stylized C for *capitulum*), but beginning in the thirteenth century scribes also used them to indicate subdivisions within paragraphs or sections in works for academic and lay readers (Parkes, *Pause and Effect* 44).

26 On Argote's divisions, see Baldissera; Burgoyne (*Reading the Exemplum* 200); Lacarra ("*El conde*" 234–5); and Santonocito (*Gonzalo Argote* 115–16).

27 As Cherchi explains, the units that Patronio calls *proverbios* are not folk proverbs, but rather maxims, the difference being that maxims "are often traceable back to their author and have no spontaneous equivalent in other languages" (367). While this is an important conceptual distinction to make, I follow Patronio's lead in calling them proverbs. Diz provides the most complete analysis of the differences between parts 2, 3, and 4 in her chapter on Patronio's *sentencias* (121–55). On part 4, which introduces a form of extreme hyperbaton known as synchysis, see Cherchi; see also de Looze (225–37) for an analysis of part 4 focused on medieval, early modern, and modern reception.

28 This requires a minor revision of de Looze's claim that "the value of meaning and interpretation lies more in grappling with uncertain or ambiguous text than in arriving at a final conclusion, a *product* of interpretation" (227). I would argue that the reader's hermeneutical process and Patronio's commentary (the hermeneutical product) share equal weight in parts 2–4 of the *Conde Lucanor*. The reader's belief in the existence of Patronio's hermeneutical solution, and faith in the possibility of reaching that solution, give value to the process of grappling with the text.

29 Matthew Raden's comparative study of the *Proverbios morales* and *Conde Lucanor* highlights another parallel: the two authors' negotiation of their political positions through literary expression.

30 Descriptions of rhetorical strategies such as *amplificatio* can be traced back to classical models; in the Middle Ages they circulated in treatises such as Geoffrey of Vinsauf's *Poetria nova* (c. 1208–13). Educated Castilian readers may have learned them through the *Breve compendium artis rethorice*, a treatise on rhetorical theory attributed to a certain Martín de Córdoba and composed probably in the first half of the fourteenth century, during Juan Manuel's lifetime (Faulhaber 132–3).

4. Auctor

1 Only one exemplum, ex. 4, is not paired with verses by Don Juan, but rather with the popular saying "Quien bien se siede non se lieve"

("If you're well seated, don't get up"). Don Juan calls attention to this exception by stating that he "non quiso fazer viesos de nuevo, sinon que puso ý una palabra que dizen las viejas en Castiella" ("decided not to write verses this time, but instead wrote down a saying of the old women of Castile"; 34).

2 On the medieval understanding of the relationship between *auctoritas* and the Greek-derived *authenticus*, Chenu reminds us: "Be their interpretation of objective root-meanings what it may, the medieval grammarians (the true witnesses in this instance) build etymology and semantics upon orthography" (*Toward Understanding* 129n1).

3 "Quippe miserrimi est ingenii semper inventis uti et numquam inveniendis" (ed. Weijers 121). The quote is perhaps best known for its inclusion, slightly modified, in an allegorical drawing by Hieronymus Bosch, *The Wood Has Ears, the Field Eyes* (c. 1502–5, Staatliche Museen zu Berlin).

4 Covarrubias defines *inventar* as "sacar alguna cosa de nuevo que no se aya visto antes" ("to produce something new that has never been seen before"; 1105).

5 This text, the *Epistola ad Paulam et Eustochium*, also known by its incipit "Cogitis me," is now ascribed to Paschasius Radbertus, the ninth-century abbot of Corbie. It adopts the perspective of Saint Jerome writing a letter to the widow Paula and her daughter Eustochium, and cautions against accepting the apocryphal *Transitus Mariae*, a cycle of legends about Mary's Assumption, as truth (Matis). Lida de Malkiel first identified the reference in the *Tratado de la Asunción* ("Tres notas" 169–70).

6 I follow Gómez Redondo's reading of *pesados* rather than *pensados*, referring to the position of the accent in each verse ("Don Juan Manuel, versificador" 44n53).

7 While my subject here is the poetic production of the fourteenth century, it is worth remembering that the surviving manuscripts both of Juan Manuel's works and of *cancionero* poetry date from the fifteenth and sixteenth centuries.

8 Based on internal and external evidence, Mota dates the composition of the *Libro infinido* to the period between 1334, when Juan Manuel's son Fernando was two years old, and 1340, by which time his relationship with the Núñez de Lara family (alluded to positively in the text) had deteriorated decisively ("Introduction" 54–60).

9 On the interdiegetic relationship between Don Juan and Patronio, see especially Scholberg ("Juan Manuel") and de Looze (247–57). De Looze explains that the merging of Patronio with Don Juan can be understood as the assimilation of the writer's task to the quest of a Christian life: "According to Patronio/Juan Manuel, we are all [...] writers, for while we

live we are writing the text of our lives – the books that will be opened and read on Judgment Day" (253).

10 Given Juan Manuel's interest in self-compilation, it is plausible that he would expect readers to observe this connection between the *Libro de la caza* and *Libro infinido*. Moreover, if he revised the *Libro de la caza* sometime in the 1330s, as Orduna ("Prólogos" 119) and Burgoyne ("Imagining" 118) suspect, its prologue may have been fresh in his mind when composing the *Libro infinido*.

11 As C.S. Lewis summarizes in *The Discarded Image*, "in the Middle Ages there are three kinds of proof; from Reason, from Authority, and from Experience. We establish a geometrical truth by Reason; a historical truth, by Authority, by *auctours*. [...] To learn by experience may be to *feel*; or, more misleading, knowledge by experience may be *preve* (that is, proof)" (189; emphasis in original).

12 Both Mota ("Introduction" 40) and Gómez Redondo (*Historia de la prosa* 1: 1191–2) place its composition between 1342 and 1345, in the period after the 1338 peace accord between Juan Manuel and Alfonso XI and the 1340 victory of the Castilians and Portuguese against the Marīnids at the Battle of Río Salado.

13 "Argument" captures the polysemy of Juan Manuel's use of *razón* here reasonably well: it is both a coherent discourse on a topic and a form of rhetorical expression aimed at persuading an audience. On the *razón* as literary genre in Juan Manuel's works, see Gómez Redondo ("Géneros literarios" 93–8 and *Historia de la prosa* 1: 1192).

14 Secular and often parodic versions of the *isnād* appear in Andalusī Arabic narrative, particularly the *maqāmāt* of al-Saraqusṭī, as well as in Aljamiado literature (Lacarra, *Cuentística* 64; Montaner Frutos, *El recontamiento* 68–71). As David Wacks proposes, these parodies of *isnād* may have formed part of a broader repertoire of Iberian storytelling, accessible to Christian Castilian authors through translation, oral performance, and other forms of exchange in a multilingual and multiconfessional literary polysystem (*Framing Iberia* 13, 182–3). Thus, while the similarity is not strong enough to posit the *isnād* as one of Juan Manuel's models, we also cannot discount the possibility entirely.

15 On the link between nursing and dynastic power in Juan Manuel's works, see Kinkade ("Beatrice" 204) and Lizabe (389).

16 Giménez Soler identifies Constanza's nurse as Saurina de Bessers (or Béziers), the daughter of Juan de Bessers, a physician employed by Jaume II of Aragon (335). Saurina's close relationship to Constanza and her important role in Juan Manuel's household are attested in several letters and documents (Giménez Soler 335, 353, 363, 365, 377, and 412), including

one from 1312 in which she assures Jaume II that his daughter is happy and healthy in her recent marriage (407).

17 Beginning in the fifth century, the Assumption was retold in numerous narrative forms (Elliott 471). It is the subject of several Catalan mystery plays originating in medieval Aragon and Murcia, including the *Representació de l'Assumpció de Madona Santa Maria*, first staged in Tarragona in 1388 and now celebrated in La Selva del Camp, and the *Misteri d'Elx*, celebrated in Elche from the fifteenth century to the present (Gómez and Massip 14–15). Juan Manuel's treatise predates the *Misteri d'Elx* by a century, debunking theories that the mystery play inspired him as lord of Elche (Devoto 274; Huerta Tejadas 86). However, his treatise indicates that the Assumption was already a recognized feast day with a popular Castilian name: "Santa María de agosto mediado" ("Saint Mary of Mid-August"; 1003). Remón Masquefa, a friar who occasionally served as intermediary between Juan Manuel and the kings of Aragon (Giménez Soler 108–14), has been documented as prior of Dominican convents in Barcelona and Valencia (Vose 83n109). Masquefa was not prior of the Dominican convent in Peñafiel, contrary to a claim originally made by Pascual de Gayangos (*Escritores* 439n3). For more on his career, see the chapter by Cossío Olavide in the forthcoming *A Companion to Don Juan Manuel*.

18 This diminutive of *libro* is infrequent in medieval Castilian but appears twice in Juan Ruiz's *Libro de buen amor* with similar connotations. Near the beginning, the poet uses *librete* to indicate modesty: "[Dios] me done su graçia e me quiera alunbrar,/que pueda de cantares un librete rimar" ("God give me His grace and enlighten me, so I may rhyme a little book of songs"; 12 [12b–c]). When he brings his book to a close, it also suggests materiality through a play on *punto* as both punctuation and an end point: "Faré/punto a mi librete, mas non lo çerraré" ("I'll put a full stop to my little book, but I won't close it"; 421 [1626c–d]). Juan Manuel uses *librete* once more in his corpus, when the philosopher in ex. 46 of the *Conde Lucanor* composes "un librete pequeño et muy bueno et muy aprovechoso" ("a small, very good, and very beneficial book"; 179) to educate his disciples.

19 For A. Blecua, the list suggests a deliberate "thematic plan," beginning with familial treatises, followed by didactic works, historiography, and manuals for particular "arts" (109). As Huot observes, the organization of medieval single-author codices into subdivisions by genre is significant, as it shows that "these books are at once carefully articulated anthologies and poetically unified wholes" (235).

20 On this theory and its debunking, see Gómez Redondo (*Historia de la prosa*, 1: 1025–6).

21 For descriptions of *S*, see Serés's edition (367–8), A. Blecua (13), Hammer (*Framing* 58–63), de Looze (30–5), and B. Taylor ("Manuscript Transmission"). While it is important to remember that *S* was made at least a century after Juan Manuel's death, scholars agree that it can be used judiciously to study features of the compilation created under the author's supervision (A. Blecua 108–9; B. Taylor, "*Estoria*"; Olivetto, "Don Juan").

22 For an introduction to the *carta ejecutoria de hidalguía*, see Ruiz García. On the religious and racialized concept of *limpieza de sangre* in premodern Iberia, see, for example, Gómez-Bravo ("Origins").

23 Argote de Molina's print edition and manuscripts *O* and *M* of the *Libro de los doce sabios* are the only early witnesses that lack the anteprologue.

Epilogue: Self-Promotion

1 The *Sumario de los reyes de España*, a summary of several chronicles about the monarchs of Castile and León, is included in the *Crónica de Juan Rodríguez de Cuenca*, whose author is identified in the text as head storekeeper of Queen Leonor ("despensero mayor de la reina doña Leonor"), wife of Juan I of Castile (r. 1379–90). For a modern edition, see Jean-Pierre Jardin.

2 Avenoza's watermark analysis (Philobiblon, BETA manid 4898) debunks the theory of Isabel Uría Maqua and Jaime González Álvarez, who proposed, based on a misinterpretation of manuscript evidence, that the *Libro de los doce sabios* and the verses from the *Conde Lucanor* were copied between 1335 and 1350, about fifty years prior to the copying of the *Sumario* (10).

3 As discussed in the introduction, many scholars claim that *S* dates to the late fourteenth century, but B. Taylor uses palaeographic comparisons to date it to the fifteenth century ("Manuscript Transmission"). I echo Ayerbe-Chaux in reasoning that proponents of an earlier date have been swayed by this manuscript's idolization as the *codex optimus et antiquior* of the *Conde Lucanor* ("Critical Editions" 24).

4 I cite from Uría Maqua and González Álvarez's edition. Because the manuscript's layout, line breaks, page breaks, and paragraph marks are significant to my analysis, I attempt to give some sense of them here. For evidence that these verses circulated as a popular proverb, see Alvar ("Dos poemillas" 47–51).

5 See also Ayerbe-Chaux's edition of the *Conde Lucanor* (*Libro del conde Lucanor* 159–60), which prints this interpolation in the main text, and A. Blecua, who groups *H* and *M* into the same branch of his stemma, labelled γ (35–6, 83ff.). Manuscripts *S* and *P* do not contain Suer Alfonso's verses, but *G*, a sixteenth-century humanist copy, does. Argote de Molina's 1575 edition replaces Juan Manuel's verses with Suer Alfonso's verses but attributes them to Don Juan, omitting any reference to the interpolation.

6 James Chatham offers the implausible hypothesis that Juan Manuel originally composed the verses of part 1 without any exempla and had them compiled with the *Libro de los doce sabios*, and subsequently reused them in the *Conde Lucanor*. However, because Juan Manuel adapted many of Patronio's exempla from existing sources, this would require him to find exempla that matched his verses, which seems to me a more difficult task than composing verses to match the tales. Though Juan Manuel's remarks about his writing process should always be taken with scepticism, it is reasonable in this instance to take him at his word: he heard the exempla, adapted them into his book, and then composed his verses. On the love poem attributed to Alfonso XI, see Beltran (163–4).

7 Argote de Molina, who attributes the verses to Don Juan, gives them as: "Non pares mientes los ojos que lloran, mas deves catar las manos que obran" (Santonocito, "Los 'viessos'" 1149–50). His changes adapt the metre to what he calls "versos mayores," verses of eleven or twelve syllables with the stress pattern (u) / u u / u | (u) / u u / u. This fits with Argote's other interventions, which tend to highlight the poetic aspects of Don Juan's verses (1155).

8 On authorship and book production in the French tradition, see Huot; for the Italian tradition, see Petrucci (145–68); on parallels between these traditions and Juan Manuel, see especially de Looze (31–5) and Olivetto ("Don Juan").

9 Menocal cites ex. 51 of the *Conde Lucanor*, which only appears in *S*. Other noteworthy examples include, in *S*, the incomplete *Libro de la caza* and the lacunae in the *Libro del cavallero et del escudero* and *Libro de los estados*; and in *P*, the apocryphal ex. 53 and 54 of the *Conde Lucanor*.

10 The sources and meaning of the prologue to part 1 of the *Conde Lucanor* have been explored elsewhere: see especially Nanu; de Looze (100–4); and Biaggini (*Le gouvernement* 51–61).

11 The anteprologue refers to the books at Peñafiel in the plural ("estos libros"), leading Olivetto ("Don Juan" 120–1) and others to assert that the monastery may have housed not a single-author codex, but a collection of books. I am not convinced on this point, since *libros* can also refer to discrete works within a single codex, but ultimately all conjectures about Manueline works housed at Peñafiel are pure speculation.

12 Given Juan Manuel's expressed pride for works such as the *Libro de los estados* and the *Conde Lucanor*, which had both been completed by that time, it might seem unusual that they are not mentioned in his will. However, there are two possible explanations: first, although Don Juan defends his writing and acknowledges its ethical function, he also recognizes it as a pastime, perhaps unworthy of mention in such an important legal document (Gaibrois de Ballesteros, "Testamentos"

29–30). Second, if the *Libro de las tres razones* and General Prologue were not composed until 1342, he may not have had the idea to make a presentational copy of his works until after issuing his will.

13 Comparisons of the two lists have helped scholars determine the corpus attributed to Juan Manuel, including lost works. For a summary of this scholarship, see Serés's edition (430–1).

14 For the contents of *P*, see PhiloBiblon, BETA manid 1424, and on *P* as an anthology, see Burgoyne ("Reading and Writing"). For the contents of *M*, see PhiloBiblon, BETA manid 1675, and on *M* as an anthology, see Burgoyne ("Reading to Pieces") and Hammer ("Treating of Virtue").

15 *M* gives punctuation in red, and in the early folios (1r–15r) the rubricator consistently uses Γ for final pauses at the sentence level, ¶ for section breaks (such as the start of Patronio's exempla), and four dots for the end of a section (such as the transition between prologue and first *enxiemplo*).

16 For an analysis of these apocryphal *enxiemplos*, see Lacarra ("Copistas").

17 On the version of part 5 in *G*, which incorporates part of a thirteenth-century compilation of wisdom literature known as *Flores de filosofía*, see Burgoyne ("Fragments").

18 The chapter headings for the *Libro del cavallero et del escudero* and the tables of contents and chapter headings for the *Libro de los estados* and *Conde Lucanor* are also written in red ink, marking them as paratexts.

19 A note at the top of the first folio, which to my knowledge has not been correctly transcribed, reads: "aquý está la devysa de los Manueles con sus armas" ("Here is the heraldic device of the Manuel family with their arms"; MS 19426, fol. 1r). This supports the theory defended by A. Blecua (107) and Cossío Olavide ("*Libro*") that an early version of Juan Manuel's collected-works codex, possibly the one designed by the author himself, began with the General Prologue, followed by an illustration of his coat of arms and the *Libro de las tres razones*.

20 I normalize *u* and *v* and modernize accents in my transcription, but otherwise maintain the orthography of the manuscript.

21 I cite Argote de Molina's 1575 edition from the two-part edition by Daniela Santonocito, indicating the part followed by the page number.

22 As Orduna ("Catálogo" 220) correctly observed, Argote's list derives from the anteprologue, but see Serés's edition (430–1) on Orduna's faulty conclusions about the prologues' chronology. The discrepancies in Argote's list are relatively minor and fall within the realm of variation seen in the manuscript copies of the anteprologue.

23 A. Blecua argues convincingly that the *Libro de los sabios* listed in both the anteprologue and Argote's edition refers to the *Libro infinido* (106).

24 The *Libro de los exemplos por a.b.c.* is now attributed to Clemente Sánchez de Vercial (d. 1438), while the *Libro de los gatos* is an anonymous fourteenth-

century Castilian translation of a Latin fable collection by Odo of Cheriton (Gómez Redondo, *Historia de la prosa* 2: 2012–13).

25 Keller uses Argote de Molina's edition as his base text, with light modernization of spelling in words like *caçador/cazador* and *agora/aora*. Based on these choices, the lack of prefatory material, and the octavo format, Keller's aim is not to produce a scholarly edition, but to place an affordable and readable version in the hands of European readers interested in medieval literature.

26 Ticknor's letters to Gayangos, edited by Clara Louise Penney, indicate that he wrote to request the copy of *S* on Christmas Eve of 1844, and received it in September of 1846. On Gayangos's practice of making manuscript copies of Juan Manuel's works as both a modern scholarly endeavour and a way to embody medieval scribal culture, see Savo, "Material Afterlives."

27 Puibusque also consulted Amador de los Ríos's transcription to copy the text of ex. 28, which was excised from *S* and omitted from Argote's edition possibly to censor its controversial murder of a clergyman (*Le Comte* 489).

28 Gayangos designated manuscripts *H, S, M,* and *G* as *A, B i, B ii,* and *C,* respectively. On his purchase of *G*, see Savo ("Material Afterlives" 204–5). Manuscript *P* remained in the private collection of the count of Puñonrostro until about 1900; while Gayangos does not mention it, José Amador de los Ríos was able to consult it for his *Historia crítica de la literatura española* published in 1863 (3: 536n1).

Works Cited

Manuscripts

Main manuscripts of Juan Manuel's works

Biblioteca Nacional de España, Madrid, MS 1356 (*Crónica abreviada*). BETA manid 1965.

G. Biblioteca Nacional de España, Madrid, MS 18415. BETA manid 4894.

H. Real Academia de la Historia, Madrid, MS 9/5893. BETA manid 1962.

M. Biblioteca Nacional de España, Madrid, MS 4236. BETA manid 1675.

N. Biblioteca Nacional de España, Madrid, MS 19426. BETA manid 3300.

P. Real Academia Española, Madrid, MS 15. BETA manid 1424.

S. Biblioteca Nacional de España, Madrid, MS 6376. BETA manid 1964.

The Libro de los doce sabios *with verses from the* Conde Lucanor

M. Biblioteca de Menéndez Pelayo, Santander, MS M-92. BETA manid 1963.

O. Biblioteca de la Universidad de Oviedo, Oviedo, MS M-497 or CEMs-497. BETA manid 4898.

Other manuscripts

Archivo de la Catedral de Valencia, Valencia, MS 182, fols. 264r–270v. Infante Juan of Aragon's Latin commentary on the Lord's Prayer.

Biblioteca Nacional de España, Madrid, MS 19163. José Amador de los Ríos's copy of the *Conde Lucanor*. BETA manid 3444.

Biblioteca Nazionale Centrale, Florence, MS B.R.20. Florentine Codex of Alfonso X, *Cantigas de Santa María*. BITAGAP manid 1091.

Boston Public Library, Boston, Ms.fD.9. *Código ... de algunas obras de Don Juan Manuel*. George Ticknor's copy of *S*.

British Library, London, Royal MS 14 E I, vol. 1. Vincent of Beauvais, *Le miroir historial* [*Speculum historiale*], translated by Jean de Vignay.

Real Biblioteca del Monasterio de San Lorenzo de El Escorial, El Escorial, MS h.II.25. [Pseudo] Pedro Pascual, *Sobre la secta mahometana*. BETA manid 1444.

Real Biblioteca del Monasterio de San Lorenzo de El Escorial, El Escorial, MS T.I.1. Códice Rico of Alfonso X, *Cantigas de Santa María*. BITAGAP manid 1090.

Editions of Juan Manuel's works

Juan Manuel. *Cinco tratados*. Edited by Reinaldo Ayerbe-Chaux, Hispanic Seminary of Medieval Studies, 1989.

Juan Manuel. *Le Comte Lucanor: Apologues et fabliaux du XIVe siècle*. Edited and translated by Adolphe de Puibusque, Librarie d'Amyot, 1854.

Juan Manuel. *El conde Lucanor*. Edited by Adelbert von Keller, Imle and Liesching, 1839.

Juan Manuel. *El conde Lucanor*. Edited by Leonardo Funes, Colihue, 2020.

Juan Manuel. *El conde Lucanor*. Edited by Guillermo Serés, Real Academia Española, 2022.

Juan Manuel. *El Conde Lucanor, compuesto por el excelentíssimo príncipe don Juan Manuel, hijo del Infante don Manuel, y nieto del santo rey don Fernando*. Edited by Gonzalo Argote de Molina, Hernando Díaz, 1575.

Juan Manuel. *El Conde Lucanor, compuesto por el excelentíssimo príncipe don Juan Manuel, hijo del Infante don Manuel, y nieto del santo rey don Fernando*. Edited by Gonzalo Argote de Molina, Diego Díaz de la Carrera, 1642.

Juan Manuel. *Count Lucanor: or, The Fifty Pleasant Stories of Patronio*. Translated by James York, Gibbings, 1868.

Juan Manuel. *Der Graf Lucanor*. Translated by Joseph Freiherr von Eichendorff, Simion, 1840.

Juan Manuel. *Libro de la caza*. Edited by José María Castro y Calvo, Consejo Superior de Investigaciones Científicas, 1947.

Juan Manuel. *Libro de la caza. Don Juan Manuel y el* Libro de la caza, edited by José Manuel Fradejas Rueda, Seminario de Filología Medieval – U de Valladolid, 2001, pp. 127–208.

Juan Manuel. *Libro del cavallero e del escudero*. Edited by Mario Cossío Olavide, Iberoamericana Editorial Vervuert, 2022.

Juan Manuel. *Libro del conde Lucanor*. Edited by Reinaldo Ayerbe-Chaux, Alhambra, 1983.

Juan Manuel. *Libro del conde Lucanor et de Patronio*. Edited by Germán Orduna, Huemul, 1972.

Juan Manuel. *Libro de los estados*. Edited by Ian R. Macpherson and Robert Brian Tate, Editorial Castalia, 1991.

Juan Manuel. *El libro de Patronio o el conde Lucanor*. Edited by Manuel Milà i Fontanals, Juan Oliveres, 1853.
Juan Manuel. *Libro infinido*. Edited by Carlos Mota, Cátedra, 2003.
Juan Manuel. *Obras completas*. Edited by José Manuel Blecua, Gredos, 1982–3. 2 vols.
Juan Manuel. *Obras completas*. Edited by Carlos Alvar and Sarah Finci, Fundación José Antonio de Castro, 2007.

Other Works Cited

al-Bayzār, Muḥammad ibn ʿAbd Allah ibn ʿUmar (Moamín). *Libro de los animales que cazan (Kitāb al-yawariḥ)*. Edited by José Manuel Fradejas Rueda. *Archivo Iberoamericano de Cetrería*, U de Valladolid, 2006–17, http://www.aic.uva.es/clasicos/yawarih/yawarih-intro.html.
Alfonso de San Cristóbal. *La versión castellana medieval de la Epitoma rei militaris (de Flavio Vegecio Renato y Alfonso de San Cristóbal)*. Edited by José Manuel Fradejas Rueda, Cilengua, 2014.
Alfonso X of Castile. *Estoria de Espanna Digital. Versión primitiva de lectura*. Edited by Aengus Ward, version 1.1, U of Birmingham, 2020, https://blog.bham.ac.uk/estoriadigital/.
Alfonso X of Castile. *General estoria. Primera parte*. Edited by Pedro Sánchez-Prieto Borja, Fundación José Antonio de Castro, 2001. 2 vols.
Alfonso X of Castile. *Libro de la octava esfera. Antología de Alfonso X el Sabio*, edited by Antonio G. Solalinde, Espasa-Calpe, 1965, pp. 180–5.
Alfonso X of Castile. *Las Siete Partidas*, vol. 2: *Medieval Government: The World of Kings and Warriors (Partida II)*. Edited by Robert I. Burns, translated by Samuel Parsons Scott, U of Pennsylvania P, 2000.
Alfonso X of Castile. *Las Siete Partidas*, vol. 3: *The Medieval World of Law: Lawyers and Their Work (Partida III)*. Edited by Robert I. Burns, translated by Samuel Parsons Scott, U of Pennsylvania P, 2000.
Alfonso X of Castile. *Las Siete Partidas*, vol. 5: *Underworlds: The Dead, the Criminal, and the Marginalized (Partidas VI and VII)*. Edited by Robert I. Burns, translated by Samuel Parsons Scott, U of Pennsylvania P, 2001.
Alfonso X of Castile. *7PartidasDigital. Edición crítica digital de las Siete Partidas*. Edited by José Manuel Fradejas Rueda, U de Valladolid, 2016–, https://7partidas.hypotheses.org.
Alighieri, Dante. *Purgatorio*. Edited by Giorgio Petrocchi, Princeton Dante Project, 1997–9, https://dante.princeton.edu/.
Allen, Judson Boyce. *The Ethical Poetic of the Later Middle Ages: A Decorum of Convenient Distinction*. U of Toronto P, 1982.
al-Saraqusṭī. *Al-Maqāmāt al-Luzūmīyah*. Translated by James Monroe, Brill, 2002.

Althusser, Louis. Selection from "Ideology and Ideological State Apparatuses." Translated by Ben Brewster. *The Critical Tradition: Classic Texts and Contemporary Trends*, edited by David H. Richter, 3rd ed., Bedford/St. Martin's, 2007, pp. 1264–72.

Altschul, Nadia R. "The Genealogy of Scribal Versions: A 'Fourth Way' in Medieval Editorial Theory." *Textual Cultures*, vol. 1, no. 2, autumn 2006, pp. 114–36. *Project MUSE*, https://doi.org/10.2979/tex.2006.1.2.114.

Altschul, Nadia R. *Geographies of Philological Knowledge: Postcoloniality and the Transatlantic National Epic*. U of Chicago P, 2012.

Alvar, Carlos. "Ay cinquenta enxiemplos." *Bulletin hispanique*, vol. 86, nos. 1–2, 1984, pp. 136–41. *Persée*, https://doi.org/10.3406/hispa.1984.4522.

Alvar, Carlos. "Dos poemillas medievales en castellano." *Dejar hablar a los textos: homenaje a Francisco Márquez Villanueva*, edited by Pedro M. Piñero Ramírez, U de Sevilla, 2005, pp. 47–56.

Amador de los Ríos, José. *Historia crítica de la literatura española*. Vol. 3, Madrid, José Rodríguez, 1863.

Amador de los Ríos, José. *Historia crítica de la literatura española*. Vol. 4, Madrid, José Fernández Cancela, 1863.

Ambrose. *Hexameron, Paradise, and Cain and Abel*. Translated by John J. Savage, The Catholic U of America P, 2003.

Aquinas, Thomas. *Summa Theologiae*. Blackfriars and McGraw-Hill, 1963. 61 vols.

Aquinas, Thomas. *The Summa Theologiae of St. Thomas Aquinas*. Translated by the Fathers of the English Dominican Province, online edition, 2017, https://www.newadvent.org/summa/.

Argote de Molina, Gonzalo, editor. *Libro de la montería que mandó escrevir el muy alto y muy poderoso rey don Alonso de Castilla y de León*. Seville, Andrea Pescioni, 1582.

Ascoli, Albert Russell. "Access to Authority: Dante in the *Epistle to Cangrande*." *Seminario dantesco internazionale/International Dante Seminar 1*, edited by Zygmunt Barański, Le Lettere, 1997, pp. 209–52.

Ascoli, Albert Russell. *Dante and the Making of a Modern Author*. Cambridge UP, 2010.

Auerbach, Erich. *Literary Language and Its Public in Late Latin Antiquity and in the Middle Ages*. Translated by Ralph Manheim, Bollingen, 1965.

Aurell, Jaume. *Authoring the Past: History, Autobiography, and Politics in Medieval Catalonia*. U of Chicago P, 2012.

Ayerbe-Chaux, Reinaldo. *"El conde Lucanor": materia tradicional y originalidad creadora*. José Porrúa Turanzas, 1975.

Ayerbe-Chaux, Reinaldo. "Critical Editions and Literary History: The Case of Don Juan Manuel." *The Politics of Editing*, edited by Nicholas Spadaccini and Jenaro Talens, U of Minnesota P, 1992, pp. 22–38.

Ayerbe-Chaux, Reinaldo. "Don Juan Manuel y la conciencia de su propia autoría." *La corónica*, vol. 10, no. 2, 1982, pp. 186–90.

Ayerbe-Chaux, Reinaldo. "The Intellectual and Spiritual Relationship of Don Juan Manuel to the Dominicans." *Monks, Nuns, and Friars in Medieval Society*, edited by Edward B. King, Jacqueline T. Schaefer, and William B. Wadley. P of the U of the South, 1989, pp. 153–60.

Ayerbe-Chaux, Reinaldo. Introduction. *Cinco tratados*. By Juan Manuel, edited by Reinaldo Ayerbe-Chaux, Hispanic Seminary of Medieval Studies, 1989, pp. vii–lxiv.

Ayerbe-Chaux, Reinaldo. "Manuscritos y documentos de Don Juan Manuel." *La corónica*, vol. 16, no. 1, 1987, pp. 88–95.

Ayerbe-Chaux, Reinaldo. "Las memorias de doña Leonor López de Córdoba." *Journal of Hispanic Philology*, vol. 2, 1977, pp. 11–33.

Bahr, Arthur. *Fragments and Assemblages: Forming Compilations of Medieval London*. U of Chicago P, 2013.

Baldissera, Andrea. "Argote de Molina editore del *Conde Lucanor*: Un fortunato 'repéchage' anticuario." *L'Europa del libro nell'età dell'umanesimo. Atti del XIV Convegno Internazionale (Chianciano, Firenze, Pienza 16–19 luglio 2002)*, edited by Luisa Rotondi Secchi Tarugi, Cesati, 2004, pp. 397–407.

Bamford, Heather. *Cultures of the Fragment: Uses of the Iberian Manuscript, 1100–1600*. U of Toronto P, 2018.

Bamford, Heather. "Meaning and Reading in the Proverbs of *El conde Lucanor*." *Revista de Estudios Hispánicos*, vol. 55, no. 3, Oct. 2021, pp. 777–97. *Project MUSE*, https://doi.org/10.1353/rvs.2021.0039.

Barański, Zygmunt G. "The Epistle to Can Grande." *The Cambridge History of Literary Criticism*, vol. 2: *The Middle Ages*, edited by Alastair Minnis and Ian Johnson, Cambridge UP, 2005, pp. 583–9.

Barthes, Roland. "The Death of the Author." Translated by Stephen Heath. *The Critical Tradition: Classic Texts and Contemporary Trends*, edited by David H. Richter, 3rd ed., Bedford/St. Martin's, 2007, pp. 874–7.

Bartholomaeus Anglicus. *De proprietatibus rerum*. Strasbourg, Jordanus von Quedlinburg, 1491.

Bäuml, Franz H. "Varieties and Consequences of Medieval Literacy and Illiteracy." *Speculum*, vol. 55, no. 2, Apr. 1980, pp. 237–65. *U Chicago P Journals*, https://doi.org/10.2307/2847287.

Bautista, Francisco. "Autoría, niveles literarios y autocita. El *Libro de los estados* en la obra de don Juan Manuel." *Voz y letra*, vol. 25, nos. 1–2, 2014, pp. 7–15.

Beltran, Vicenç. *Edad Media: lírica y cancioneros*. Centro para la Edición de los Clásicos Españoles – Visor, 2009.

Beneyto Pérez, Juan, editor. *Glosa castellana al "Regimiento de Príncipes" de Egidio Romano*. Instituto de Estudios Políticos, 1947–8.

Benito Vessels, Carmen. *Juan Manuel: escritura y recreación de la historia*. Hispanic Seminary of Medieval Studies, 1994.

Biaggini, Olivier. "Énonciation et figure de l'auteur dans les premières oeuvres de don Juan Manuel." *Voz y letra*, vol. 25, no. 1–2, 2014, pp. 17–39.

Biaggini, Olivier. *Le gouvernement des signes:* El Conde Lucanor *de don Juan Manuel*. Presses universitaires de France, 2014.

Biaggini, Olivier. "Stratégies du paratexte dans les oeuvres de don Juan Manuel." *Cahiers d'études hispaniques médiévales*, no. 35, 2012, pp. 195–232. *Persée*, https://doi.org/10.3406/cehm.2012.2281.

Biglieri, Aníbal A. "*El conde Lucanor*, ejemplo 36: (el autor), (la realidad), el texto." *Revista Canadiense de Estudios Hispánicos*, vol. 113, no. 3, 1987, pp. 461–75.

Bizzarri, Hugo O. "La historiografía castellana en el entorno de Sancho IV: continuidad y ruptura." *Actas del XI Congreso Internacional de la Asociación Hispánica de Literatura Medieval (Universidad de León, 20 al 24 de septiembre de 2005)*, edited by Armando López Castro and María Luzdivina Cuesta Torre, vol. 1, U de León, 2007, pp. 323–34.

Bizzarri, Hugo O. "La labor crítica de Hermann Knust en la edición de textos medievales castellanos: ante la crítica actual." *Incipit*, vol. 8, 1988, pp. 81–97.

Blecua, Alberto. *La transmisión textual de* El conde Lucanor. 2nd ed., U Autónoma de Barcelona, 1982.

Bonaventure. *In Primum Librum Sententiarum.* Vol. 1 of *Opera Omnia*, Florence, Quaracchi, 1882.

Botterill, Steven. "The Trecento Commentaries on Dante's *Commedia*." *The Cambridge History of Literary Criticism*, vol. 2: *The Middle Ages*, edited by Alastair Minnis and Ian Johnson, Cambridge UP, 2005, pp. 590–611.

Bruss, Elizabeth W. "Eye for I: Making and Unmaking Autobiography in Film." *Autobiography: Essays Theoretical and Critical*, edited by James Olney, Princeton UP, 1980, pp. 296–320.

Burgoyne, Jonathan. "Fragments of Flowers: *Flores de filosofía* in Early Modern Spain and the Scribal Revision of *El conde Lucanor*." *La corónica*, vol. 37, no. 2, spring 2009, pp. 5–31. *Project MUSE*, https://doi.org/10.1353/cor.0.0030.

Burgoyne, Jonathan. "Imagining Nature and Nobility in Law and Literature: *Siete partidas* (Alfonso X), *Libro de la montería* (Alfonso XI), and *Libro de la caza* (Juan Manuel)." *Romance Quarterly*, vol. 66, no. 3, 2019, pp. 114–23. *Taylor & Francis Online*, https://doi.org/10.1080/08831157.2019.1637214.

Burgoyne, Jonathan. "Reading and Writing Patronio's Doctrine in Real Academia Española MS 15." *Hispanic Review*, vol. 71, no. 4, autumn 2003, pp. 473–92. *JSTOR*, https://doi.org/10.2307/3247017.

Burgoyne, Jonathan. *Reading the Exemplum Right: Fixing the Meaning of* El Conde Lucanor. U of North Carolina Department of Romance Languages, 2007.

Burgoyne, Jonathan. "Reading to Pieces: *Divisio Textus* and the Structure of *El conde Lucanor*." *La corónica*, vol. 32, no. 1, fall 2003, pp. 231–55. *Project MUSE*, https://doi.org/10.1353/cor.2003.0003.

Burgoyne, Jonathan. "Los versos de don Juan: la transmisión del *Conde Lucanor* y el *Libro de los doce sabios* en el siglo XVI (Biblioteca Nacional de Madrid, ms. 19.426 y Biblioteca Menéndez Pelayo, ms. M-92." *eHumanista*, vol. 17, 2011, pp. 134–60, https://www.ehumanista.ucsb.edu/volumes/17.

Burke, James F. "Frame and Structure in the *Conde Lucanor*." *Revista Canadiense de Estudios Hispánicos*, vol. 8, no. 2, 1984, pp. 263–74.

Burrow, J.A. *Medieval Writers and Their Work: Middle English Literature, 1100–1500*. Oxford UP, 1982.

Calila e Dimna. Edited by Juan Manuel Cacho Blecua and María Jesús Lacarra, Castalia, 1984.

Campos, María Guadalupe. "Lírica vernácula y saber: consideraciones sobre el lugar de la lectura y la escritura en el 'Prologus Baenensis.'" *Letras*, nos. 61–2, 2010, pp. 119–28.

Cantarino, Vicente. "Más allá de *El conde Lucanor*: un infante desconocido." *Josep Maria Solà-Solé: homage, homenaje, homenatge*. Vol. 1, Puvill, 1984, pp. 55–66.

Cárdenas, Anthony J. "Alfonso X nunca escribió *castellano drecho*." *Actas del X Congreso de la Asociación Internacional de Hispanistas: Barcelona, 21–26 de agosto de 1989*, edited by Antonio Vilanova Andreu, Promociones y Publicaciones Universitarias, 1992, pp. 151–60.

Carruthers, Mary J. *The Book of Memory: A Study of Memory in Medieval Culture*. Cambridge UP, 1990.

Catalán, Diego. "Don Juan Manuel ante el modelo alfonsí: El testimonio de la *Crónica abreviada*." *Juan Manuel Studies*, edited by Ian R. Macpherson, Tamesis, 1977, pp. 17–51.

Catalán, Diego. *La* Estoria de España *de Alfonso X: creación y evolución*. Seminario Menéndez Pidal, U Complutense de Madrid – Fundación Ramón Menéndez Pidal – U Autónoma de Madrid, 1992.

Cavallero, Pablo Adrián. "*El conde Lucanor* y el método exegético." *Thesaurus*, vol. 43, no. 1, 1988, pp. 112–21.

Cervantes y Saavedra, Miguel de. *Don Quijote de la Mancha*. Edited by Francisco Rico, Real Academia Española, 2004.

Cervantes y Saavedra, Miguel de. *Don Quixote*. Translated by Edith Grossman, Ecco, 2005.

Chartier, Roger. *The Order of Books: Readers, Authors, and Libraries in Europe between the Fourteenth and Eighteenth Centuries*. Translated by Lydia G. Cochrane, Stanford UP, 1994.

Chatham, James R. "Escorial Ms. T.I.1 of the *Cantigas de Santa Maria* and Two MSS of *El conde Lucanor*." *Revista de Estudios Hispánicos*, vol. 18, no. 3, 1984, pp. 441–53.

Chaucer, Geoffrey. *The Riverside Chaucer*. Edited by Larry D. Benson et al., 3rd ed., rev., Oxford UP, 2008.

Chenu, Marie-Dominique. "*Auctor, actor, autor.*" *Bulletin du Cange*, vol. 3, 1927, pp. 81–6. *Persée*, https://doi.org/10.3406/alma.1927.2044.

Chenu, Marie-Dominique. *Toward Understanding Saint Thomas*. Translated by A.-M. Landry and D. Hughes, Henry Regnery, 1964.

Cherchi, Paolo. "*Brevedad, Oscuredad,* Synchysis in *El Conde Lucanor* (Parts II–IV)." *Medioevo Romanzo*, vol. 9, no. 3, 1984, pp. 361–74.

[Cicero]. *Rhetorica ad Herennium*. Translated by Harry Caplan, Harvard UP, 1954. Loeb Classical Library 403.

Constable, Giles. *Three Studies in Medieval Religious and Social Thought*. Cambridge UP, 1998.

Constable, Olivia Remie. "Chess and Courtly Culture in Medieval Castile: The *Libro de ajedrez* of Alfonso X, el Sabio." *Speculum*, vol. 82, no. 2, 2007, pp. 301–47. *U Chicago P Journals*, https://doi.org/10.1017/s0038713400009404.

Copeland, Rita. *Rhetoric, Hermeneutics, and Translation in the Middle Ages: Academic Traditions and Vernacular Texts*. Cambridge UP, 1991.

Corbari, Eliana. *Vernacular Theology: Dominican Sermons and Audience in Late Medieval Italy*. De Gruyter, 2013.

Coromines, Joan. *Diccionario crítico etimológico castellano e hispánico*. With José A. Pascual, Gredos, 1983–91. 6 vols.

Cossío Olavide, Mario. "*Algunos moros muy sabidores*: Virtuous Muslim Kings in Examples 30 and 41 of *El conde Lucanor*." *Bulletin of Spanish Studies*, vol. 97, no. 2, 2020, pp. 127–38. *Taylor & Francis Online*, https://doi.org/10.1080/14753820.2020.1729619.

Cossío Olavide, Mario. *"El que toma candela del fuego ajeno": Don Juan Manuel y la refundación castellana del mundo cortesano en el siglo XIV*. 2020. U of Minnesota, PhD dissertation.

Cossío Olavide, Mario. "El *Libro de las tres razones*, obra 'estoriada.'" *Translat Library*, vol. 3, no. 3, 2021. https://doi.org/10.7275/6e6d-ga26.

Cossío Olavide, Mario. "'Non ha tan buena escuela cuemo casa de señores.' El consejero caballeresco en el *Libro del cavallero et del escudero* de don Juan Manuel." *Lexis*, vol. 43, no. 2, 2019, pp. 517–59. https://doi.org/10.18800/lexis.201902.007.

Cossío Olavide, Mario. "*Ubi est thesaurus tuus*: Don Juan Manuel, Latin Culture, and the Dominicans." *A Companion to Don Juan Manuel*. Brill, forthcoming.

Cossío Olavide, Mario. "Una reescritura aristocrática de la *Estoria de España*. La *Crónica abreviada* de don Juan Manuel." *Olivar*, vol. 21, no. 34, 2021, e105. https://doi.org/10.24215/18524478e105.

Cossío Olavide, Mario, and Anita Savo, editors and translators. *Libro de los enxiemplos del conde Lucanor et de Patronio (ca. 1335)*, by Juan Manuel. *Open*

Iberia/América Teaching Anthology. 2020, *Humanities Commons*, https://doi.org/10.17613/ra2g-8011.

Covarrubias Orozco, Sebastián de. *Tesoro de la lengua castellana o española*. Edited by Ignacio Arellano and Rafael Zafra, Iberoamericana, 2006.

Curtius, Ernst Robert. *European Literature and the Latin Middle Ages*. Translated by Willard R. Trask, Routledge and Kegan Paul, 1979.

Dagenais, John. *The Ethics of Reading in Manuscript Culture: Glossing the* Libro de buen amor. Princeton UP, 1994.

Dahan, Gilbert. "Encyclopédies et exégèse de la Bible aux XIIe et XIIIe siècles." *Cahiers de Recherches Médiévales et Humanistes*, vol. 6, 1999. *OpenEdition Journals*, https://doi.org/10.4000/crm.927.

Degiovanni, Fernando. "Retórica de la predicación e ideología dominica en la quinta parte de *El conde Lucanor*." *Bulletin hispanique*, vol. 101, no. 1, 1999, pp. 5–18. *Persée*, https://doi.org/10.3406/hispa.1999.4990.

de Looze, Laurence. *Manuscript Diversity, Meaning and Variance in Juan Manuel's* El Conde Lucanor. U of Toronto P, 2006.

Destrez, Jean. *La pecia dans les manuscrits universitaires du XIII*[e] *et du XIV*[e] *siècle*. Jacques Vautrain, 1935. 2 vols.

Devoto, Daniel. *Introducción al estudio de don Juan Manuel y en particular de* El conde Lucanor*: una bibliografía*. Castalia, 1972.

Deyermond, Alan. "Cuentística y política en Juan Manuel: *El conde Lucanor*." *Studia in honorem Germán Orduna*, edited by Leonardo Funes and José Luis Moure, U de Alcalá, 2001, pp. 225–39.

Deyermond, Alan. "Cuentos orales y estructura formal en el *Libro de las tres razones* (*Libro de las armas*)." *Don Juan Manuel, VII Centenario*. U de Murcia – Academia Alfonso X el Sabio, 1982, pp. 75–87.

Deyermond, Alan. "Editors, Critics, and *El conde Lucanor*." *Romance Philology*, vol. 31, no. 4, May 1978, pp. 618–30.

Deyermond, Alan. "The *Libro de las tres razones* Reconsidered." *"Never-ending Adventure": Studies in Medieval and Early Modern Spanish Literature in Honor of Peter N. Dunn*, edited by Edward H. Friedman and Harlan Sturm, Juan de la Cuesta, 2002, pp. 81–107.

Díez de Revenga, Francisco Javier. "El *Libro de las armas* de don Juan Manuel: algo más que un libro de historia." *Don Juan Manuel, VII Centenario*. U de Murcia – Academia Alfonso X el Sabio, 1982, pp. 103–16.

Díez de Revenga, Francisco Javier. "El *Libro enfenido* de don Juan Manuel: estructura y significación literarias." *Homenaje al profesor Juan Torres Fontes*. Vol. 1, Academia Alfonso X el Sabio, 1987, pp. 365–74.

Diogenes Laertius. *Lives of Eminent Philosophers*. Translated by R.D. Hicks, preface and introduction by Herbert S. Long, vol. 1, Harvard UP, 1972.

Diz, Marta Ana. *Patronio y Lucanor: la lectura inteligente "en el tiempo que es turbio."* Scripta Humanistica, 1984.

Dodds, Jerrilynn D., María Rosa Menocal, and Abigail Krasner Balbale. *The Arts of Intimacy: Christians, Jews, and Muslims in the Making of Castilian Culture*. Yale UP, 2008.

Doyle, Anthony Ian. *A Survey of the Origins and Circulation of Theological Writings in English in the 14th, 15th, and Early 16th Centuries with Special Consideration of the Part of the Clergy Therein*. 1953. Cambridge, PhD dissertation. 2 vols.

Drimmer, Sonja. *The Art of Allusion: Illuminators and the Making of English Literature, 1403–1476*. U of Pennsylvania P, 2018.

Dunn, Peter. "Framing the Story, Framing the Reader: Two Spanish Masters." *Modern Language Review*, vol. 91, no. 1, Jan. 1996, pp. 94–106. *JSTOR*, https://doi.org/10.2307/3733999.

Dunn, Peter. "The Structures of Didacticism: Private Myths and Public Fictions." *Juan Manuel Studies*, edited by Ian R. Macpherson, Tamesis, 1977, pp. 53–68.

Eagleton, Terry. *Literary Theory: An Introduction*. U of Minnesota P, 2008.

Edwards, A.S.G. "Chaucer and 'Adam Scriveyn.'" *Medium Ævum*, vol. 81, no. 1, 2012, pp. 135–8. *JSTOR*, https://doi.org/10.2307/43632904.

Eisenstein, Elizabeth L. *The Printing Press as an Agent of Change*. Cambridge UP, 1979. 2 vols.

Elliott, J.K. "The 'Apocryphal' New Testament." *The New Cambridge History of the Bible*, edited by James Carleton Paget and Joachim Schape, Cambridge UP, 2012, pp. 455–78.

England, John. "*Exemplo* 51 of *El Conde Lucanor*: The Problem of Authorship." *Bulletin of Hispanic Studies*, vol. 51, no. 1, 1974, pp. 16–27. https://doi.org/10.1080/1475382742000351016.

Faulhaber, Charles. *Latin Rhetorical Theory in Thirteenth and Fourteenth Century Castile*. U of California P, 1972.

Fernández Fernández, Laura. *Arte y ciencia en el scriptorium de Alfonso X el Sabio*. Seville, Cátedra Alfonso X el Sabio – Secretariado de Publicaciones de la U de Sevilla, 2013.

Fernández-Ordóñez, Inés. "Actores y autores en la historiografía regia de la Baja Edad Media ibérica: 1200–1450." *Histoires, femmes, pouvoirs: Péninsule Ibérique (IXe–XVe siècle)*, edited by Jean-Pierre Jardin, Patricia Rochwert-Zuili, and Hélène Thieulin-Pardo, Classiques Garnier, 2018, pp. 201–22.

Fernández-Ordóñez, Inés. "La lengua de los documentos del rey: del latín a las lenguas vernáculas en las cancillerías regias de la Península Ibérica." *La construcción medieval de la memoria regia*, edited by Pascual Martínez Sopena and Ana María Rodríguez López, U de València, 2011, pp. 323–62.

Fernández-Ordóñez, Inés. "*Ordinatio* y *compilatio* en la prosa de Alfonso X el Sabio." *Modelos latinos en la Castilla medieval*, edited by Mónica Castillo Lluch and Marta López Izquierdo, Iberoamericana – Vervuert, 2010, pp. 239–70.

Fernández-Ordóñez, Inés. "El texto medieval: propiedad y uso." *Medioevo romanzo*, vol. 38, no. 1, 2014, pp. 45–68.

Fernández-Ordóñez, Inés. "La transmisión textual de la *Estoria de España* y de las principales 'Crónicas' de ella derivadas." *Alfonso X el Sabio y las crónicas de España*, edited by Inés Fernández-Ordóñez, U de Valladolid – Centro para la Edición de los Clásicos Españoles, 2000, pp. 219–60.

Fink-Errera, Guy. "Une institution du monde médiéval: la 'pecia.'" *Revue philosophique de Louvain*, vol. 60, no. 66, 1962, pp. 184–243. *Persée*, https://doi.org/10.3406/phlou.1962.5153.

Fiorentino, Luigi. "Don Juan Manuel e Franco Sacchetti." *Ausonia: rivista di lettere e arti*, vol. 31, no. 1–2, 1976, pp. 17–23.

Fisher, Matthew. *Scribal Authorship and the Writing of History in Medieval England*. Ohio State UP, 2012.

Fleming, John V. "Medieval European Autobiography." *The Cambridge Companion to Autobiography*, edited by Maria DiBattista and Emily O. Wittman, Cambridge UP, 2014, pp. 35–48.

Foucault, Michel. "What Is an Author?" Translated by Josué Harari. *The Critical Tradition: Classic Texts and Contemporary Trends*, edited by David H. Richter, 3rd ed., Bedford/St. Martin's, 2007, pp. 904–14.

Fradejas Rueda, José Manuel. *Introducción a la edición de textos medievales castellanos*. U Nacional de Educación a Distancia, 1991.

Fradejas Rueda, José Manuel, Isabel Acero Durántez, and María Jesús Díez Garretas. "Las versiones A y B de la traducción castellana del *De regimine principum* de Gil de Roma." *Actas del IX Congreso Internacional de la Asociación Hispánica de Literatura Medieval, A Coruña, 18–22 de septiembre de 2001*, edited by Carmen Parrilla García and Mercedes Pampín Barral, vol. 1, Toxosoutos, 2005, pp. 227–34.

Funes, Leonardo. "Los aportes de Germán Orduna a la crítica juanmanuelina." *Incipit*, vol. 40, 2020, pp. 79–103. https://doi.org/10.5281/zenodo.7830091.

Funes, Leonardo. "La blasfemia del Rey Sabio: itinerario narrativo de una leyenda (primera parte)." *Incipit*, vol. 13, 1993, pp. 51–70.

Funes, Leonardo. "La capitulación del *Libro de los estados*: consecuencias de un problema textual." *Incipit*, vol. 4, 1984, pp. 71–91.

Funes, Leonardo. "Don Juan Manuel y la herencia alfonsí." *Actas del VIII Congreso Internacional de la Asociación Hispánica de Literatura Medieval*, edited by Margarita Freixas, Silvia Iriso Ariz, and Laura Fernández García, vol. 1, Asociación Hispánica de Cultura Medieval, 2000, pp. 781–8.

Funes, Leonardo. "Excentricidad y descentramiento en la figura autoral de don Juan Manuel." *eHumanista*, vol. 9, 2007, pp. 1–19, https://www.ehumanista.ucsb.edu/volumes/9.

Funes, Leonardo. "Paradojas de la voluntad de autoría en la obra de don Juan Manuel." *Actas del XIII Congreso de la Asociación Internacional de Hispanistas: Madrid 6–11 de julio de 1998*, edited by Florencio Sevilla Arroyo and Carlos Alvar Ezquerra, vol. 1, Editorial Castalia, 2000, pp. 126–33.

Funes, Leonardo. "Primeros trazos de una altrobiografía en la Baja Edad Media castellana: el caso de don Juan Manuel." *Revista Diálogos Mediterrânicos*, vol. 20, 2021, pp. 88–108.

Funes, Leonardo. "Sobre la partición original del *Libro de los estados.*" *Incipit*, vol. 6, 1986, pp. 3–26.

Funes, Leonardo, and María Elena Qués. "La historia disidente: el lugar del *Libro de las armas* en el discurso historiográfico del siglo XIV castellano." *Atalaya*, vol. 6, 1995, pp. 71–8.

Funes, Leonardo, and Sun-Me Yoon. "Motivación y verosimilitud en el relato-marco del *Libro de los estados*." *La corónica*, vol. 19, no. 2, 1991, pp. 100–11.

Gaibrois de Ballesteros, Mercedes. *El príncipe don Juan Manuel y su condición de escritor*. Editorial Magisterio Español, 1945.

Gaibrois de Ballesteros, Mercedes. "Los testamentos inéditos de don Juan Manuel." *Boletín de la Real Academia de la Historia*, vol. 99, no. 1, 1931, pp. 25–59.

Galvez, Marisa. *Songbook: How Lyrics Became Poetry in Medieval Europe*. U of Chicago P, 2012.

García de Lucas, César. "El marco expositivo en el *Libro de los enxemplos*." *Lectures de* El Conde Lucanor *de Don Juan Manuel*, edited by García de Lucas and Alexandra Oddo, Presses Universitaires de Rennes, 2014, pp. 19–33.

García de Lucas, César, and Alexandra Oddo, editors. *Lectures de* El Conde Lucanor *de Don Juan Manuel*. Presses Universitaires de Rennes, 2014.

Garribba, Aviva. "La voz del narrador en el 'Cuento de la Santa Emperatriz.'" *Revista de poética medieval*, vol. 4, 2000, pp. 11–49.

Gayangos, Pascual de. "Arabic MSS. in Spain." Review of *Disertación histórica sobre los Archivos de España y su antigüedad, con algunas reglas para su coordinación*, by Facundo de Porras Huidobro. *Westminster Review*, vol. 21, no. 42, 1834, pp. 378–94.

Gayangos, Pascual de, editor. *Escritores en prosa anteriores al siglo XV*. Madrid, Manuel Rivadeneyra, 1860. Biblioteca de Autores Españoles 51.

Gayangos, Pascual de, and Enrique de Vedia, translators. *Historia de la literatura española*. By George Ticknor, vol. 1, Madrid, Imprenta de la Publicidad – Rivadeneyra, 1851.

Genette, Gérard. *Paratexts: Thresholds of Interpretation*. Translated by Jane E. Lewin, Cambridge UP, 1997.

Gerli, E. Michael. "Textualidad y autoridad: hacia una teoría de los orígenes de la escritura señorial (el caso de *El libro del Conde Lucanor*)." *Propuestas teórico-metodológicas para el estudio de la literatura hispánica medieval*, edited by

Lillian von Der Walde Moheno, U Nacional Autónoma de México, 2003, pp. 335–49.

Gillespie, Alexandra. "Reading Chaucer's Words to Adam." *The Chaucer Review*, vol. 42, no. 3, 2008, pp. 269–83. *Scholarly Publishing Collective*, https://doi.org/10.2307/25094401.

Gillespie, Vincent. "From the Twelfth Century to *c.* 1450." *The Cambridge History of Literary Criticism*, vol. 2: *The Middle Ages*, edited by Alastair Minnis and Ian Johnson, Cambridge UP, 2005, pp. 145–236.

Gillespie, Vincent. "Vernacular Theology." *Middle English: Oxford Twenty-First Century Approaches to Literature*, edited by Paul Strohm, Oxford UP, 2007, pp. 401–20.

Giménez Soler, Andrés. *Don Juan Manuel: biografía y estudio crítico.* Tipografía La Academia de F. Martínez, 1932.

Gimeno Casalduero, Joaquín. "*El Conde Lucanor*: composición y significado." *Nueva revista de filología hispánica*, vol. 24, no. 1, 1975, pp. 101–12. https://doi.org/10.24201/nrfh.v24i1.458.

Gimeno Casalduero, Joaquín. "El *Libro de los estados* de don Juan Manuel: composición y significado." *Don Juan Manuel, VII Centenario.* U de Murcia – Academia Alfonso X el Sabio, 1982, pp. 149–62.

Girón-Negrón, Luis M. "Voz y escritura en la Edad Media: lecciones del archivo hispano-judío." *Ilusión y materialidad: perspectivas sobre el archivo*, edited by Jerónimo Pizarro and Diana Paola Guzmán, U de los Andes, 2018, pp. 23–45.

Gloeckner, Paul B. *An Edition of Don Juan Manuel's* El conde Lucanor *According to MS 18.415 in the Biblioteca Nacional: "The Gayangos Manuscript."* 1972. New York U, PhD dissertation.

Gómez, María del Carmen, and Francesc Massip, with Jesús Massip Fonollosa, editors. *Misteri d'Elx, Misterio de Elche. Consueta de 1709.* Tirant lo Blanch, 2010.

Gómez-Bravo, Ana M. "The Origins of 'Raza': Racializing Difference in Early Spanish." *Interfaces*, no. 7, 2020, pp. 64–114. https://doi.org/10.13130/interfaces-07-05.

Gómez-Bravo, Ana M. *Textual Agency: Writing Culture and Social Networks in Fifteenth-Century Spain*. U of Toronto P, 2013.

Gómez Redondo, Fernando. "Don Juan Manuel, autor molinista." *Actas del VIII Congreso Internacional de la Asociación Hispánica de Literatura Medieval*, edited by Margarita Freixas, Silvia Iriso Ariz, and Laura Fernández García, vol. 1, Asociacíon Hispánica de Cultura Medieval, 2000, pp. 827–42.

Gómez Redondo, Fernando. "Don Juan Manuel, versificador." *A prosa didáctica medieval*, edited by Marta Teixeira Anacleto and Elsa Branco, U de Coimbra, 2011, pp. 13–46. Cadernos de literatura medieval 2.

Gómez Redondo, Fernando. "Géneros literarios en don Juan Manuel." *Cahiers de linguistique hispanique médiévale*, vol. 17, 1992, pp. 88–125. *Persée*, https://doi.org/10.3406/cehm.1992.1078.

Gómez Redondo, Fernando. *Historia de la poesía medieval castellana,* vol. 1: *La trama de las materias*. Cátedra, 2020.

Gómez Redondo, Fernando. *Historia de la prosa medieval castellana,* vol. 1: *La creación del discurso prosístico. El entramado cortesano*. Cátedra, 1998.

Gómez Redondo, Fernando. *Historia de la prosa medieval castellana,* vol. 2: *El desarrollo de los géneros. La ficción caballeresca y el orden religioso.* Cátedra, 1999.

Gómez Redondo, Fernando. "El molinismo: un sistema de pensamiento letrado (1284–1350)." *Estudios de literatura medieval: 25 años de la Asociación Hispánica de Literatura Medieval,* edited by Antonia Martínez Pérez and Ana Luisa Baquero Escudero, U de Murcia, 2012, pp. 43–73.

Gómez Redondo, Fernando. "La obra de don Juan Manuel y la obra de José Manuel Blecua." *Dicenda,* no. 2, 1983, pp. 193–200.

Goyri de Menéndez Pidal, María. Review of *El conde Lucanor,* edited by Hermann Knust. *Romania,* vol. 29, no. 116, 1900, pp. 600–2.

Greenblatt, Stephen. *Renaissance Self-Fashioning: From More to Shakespeare.* U of Chicago P, 1980.

Gumbrecht, Hans Ulrich. *The Powers of Philology: Dynamics of Textual Scholarship*. U of Illinois P, 2003.

Hames, Harvey. "The Language of Conversion: Ramon Llull's Art as a Vernacular." *The Vulgar Tongue: Medieval and Postmedieval Vernacularity,* edited by Fiona Somerset and Nicholas Watson, Penn State UP, 2003, pp. 43–56.

Hammer, Michael. "De-Centering the Narratives and Privileging Proverbs: Two Early Modern Readings of the *Conde Lucanor.*" *Viator,* vol. 40, no. 1, 2009, pp. 185–200. *Brepols Online,* https://doi.org/10.1484/j.viator.1.100350.

Hammer, Michael. *Framing the Reader: Exemplarity and Ethics in the Manuscripts of the* Conde Lucanor. 2003. UCLA, PhD dissertation.

Hammer, Michael. "Treating of Virtue: Intertextuality in a Fifteenth-Century Spanish Miscellany." *Viator,* vol. 40, no. 2, 2009, pp. 349–66. *Brepols Online,* https://doi.org/10.1484/j.viator.1.100433.

Hanna, Ralph, et al. "Latin Commentary Tradition and Vernacular Literature." *The Cambridge History of Literary Criticism,* vol. 2: *The Middle Ages,* edited by Alastair Minnis and Ian Johnson, Cambridge UP, 2005, pp. 363–421.

Harvey, L.P. "The Alfonsine School of Translators: Translations from Arabic into Castilian Produced under the Patronage of Alfonso the Wise of Castile (1221–1252–1284)." *Journal of the Royal Asiatic Society,* vol. 109, no. 1, Jan. 1977, pp. 109–17. *Cambridge Core,* https://doi.org/10.1017/s0035869x00154656.

Haskins, Charles Homer. "The Latin Literature of Sport." *Speculum,* vol. 2, no. 3, July 1927, pp. 235–52. *U of Chicago P Journals,* https://doi.org/10.2307/2847715.

Hathaway, Neil. "Compilatio: From Plagiarism to Compiling." *Viator,* vol. 20, 1989, pp. 19–44. *Brepols Online,* https://doi.org/10.1484/j.viator.2.301346.

Heusch, Carlos. "Les limites du dialogisme dans *El conde Lucanor* de don Juan Manuel." *Voz y letra*, vol. 25, nos. 1–2, 2014, pp. 185–200.

Heusch, Carlos. "La 'mala educación' en el *Libro del cavallero et del escudero* de don Juan Manuel." *Librosdelacorte*, vol. 22, 2021, pp. 309–25. *UAM Ediciones*, https://doi.org/10.15366/ldc2021.13.22.011.

Heusch, Carlos. "Oralité et refus de l'oralité dans *El conde Lucanor* de Juan Manuel." *Pandora*, vol. 2, 2002, pp. 125–39.

Hijano Villegas, Manuel. "Historia y poder simbólico en la obra de don Juan Manuel." *Voz y letra*, vol. 25, no. 1–2, 2014, pp. 71–110.

Hobbins, Daniel. *Authorship and Publicity Before Print: Jean Gerson and the Transformation of Late Medieval Learning*. U of Pennsylvania P, 2009.

Huerta Tejadas, Félix. "Un escrito mariológico del Infante Don Juan Manuel." *Revista española de teología*, vol. 8, no. 1, 1948, pp. 81–116.

Hugh of St. Victor. *Didascalicon: A Medieval Guide to the Arts*. Translated by Jerome Taylor. Columbia UP, 1991.

Hunt, R.W. "The Introductions to the 'Artes' in the Twelfth Century." *Studia mediaevalia in honorem admodum Reverendi Patris Raymundi Josephi Martin*. De Tempel, 1948, pp. 85–112.

Hunter, Brooke. "Boethian Humor and the Pseudo-Boethian *De disciplina scolarium*." *Viator*, vol. 46, no. 1, 2015, pp. 161–80. *Brepols Online*, https://doi.org/10.1484/j.viator.5.103505.

Huot, Sylvia. *From Song to Book: The Poetics of Writing in Old French Lyric and Lyrical Narrative Poetry*. Cornell UP, 1987.

Isidore of Seville. *The Etymologies of Isidore of Seville*. Edited by Stephen A. Barney, W.J. Lewis, J.A. Beach, and Oliver Berghof. Cambridge UP, 2011.

Jardin, Jean-Pierre, editor. *Suma de reyes du despensero: Édition et présentation*. e-Spania Books, 2013. *OpenEdition Books*, https://doi.org/10.4000/books.esb.481.

Jaume I of Aragon. *Llibre dels fets del rei en Jaume*, vol. 2: *Text i glossari*, edited by Jordi Bruguera, Barcino, 1991.

John of Salisbury. *The Metalogicon, a Twelfth-Century Defense of the Verbal and Logical Arts of the Trivium*. Translated by Daniel D. McGarry, Paul Dry Books, 2009.

Johnston, Mark D. "Poetry and Courtliness in Baena's Prologue." *La corónica*, vol. 25, no. 1, 1996, pp. 93–105.

Juan Ruiz. *Libro de buen amor*. Edited by Alberto Blecua, Cátedra, 2012.

Kamath, Stephanie A.V.G. *Authorship and First-Person Allegory in Late Medieval France and England*. Boydell and Brewer, 2012.

Kinkade, Richard P. "Beatrice 'Contesson' of Savoy (c. 1250–1290): The Mother of Juan Manuel." *La corónica*, vol. 32, no. 3, summer 2004, pp. 163–225. *Project MUSE*, https://doi.org/10.1353/cor.2004.0017.

Kinkade, Richard P. *Dawn of a Dynasty: The Life and Times of Infante Manuel of Castile*. U of Toronto P, 2020.

Kinkade, Richard P. "Sancho IV: Puente literario entre Alfonso el Sabio y Juan Manuel." *PMLA*, vol. 87, no. 5, Oct. 1972, pp. 1039–51. *Cambridge Core*, https://doi.org/10.2307/461181.

Klepper, Deeana Copeland. *The Insight of Unbelievers: Nicholas of Lyra and Christian Reading of Jewish Text in the Later Middle Ages*. U of Pennsylvania P, 2007.

Kristeller, Paul Oskar. "'Creativity' and 'Tradition.'" *Journal of the History of Ideas*, vol. 44, no. 1, Jan.–Mar. 1983, pp. 105–113. *JSTOR*, https://doi.org/10.2307/2709307.

Kwakkel, Erik. "Decoding the Material Book: Cultural Residue in Medieval Manuscripts." *The Medieval Manuscript Book: Cultural Approaches*, edited by Michael Johnston and Michael Van Dussen, Cambridge UP, 2015, pp. 60–76.

Lacarra, María Jesús. "*El conde Lucanor* (1575) de Argote de Molina: el rescate de un texto medieval." *Formas narrativas breves: lecturas e interpretaciones*, edited by Carlos Alvar, Cilengua, 2014, pp. 221–45.

Lacarra, María Jesús. "Los copistas cuentistas: los otros ejemplos de *El conde Lucanor* en el códice de Puñonrostro." *"Entra mayo y sale abril": Medieval Spanish Literary and Folklore Studies in Memory of Harriet Goldberg*, edited by Manuel da Costa Fontes and Joseph T. Snow. Juan de la Cuesta, 2005, pp. 231–58.

Lacarra, María Jesús. *Cuentística medieval en España: los orígenes*. U de Zaragoza, 1979.

Lacarra, María Jesús. *Don Juan Manuel*. Síntesis, 2006.

Lacarra, María Jesús, and Juan Manuel Cacho Blecua. *Historia de la literatura española*, vol. 1: *Entre oralidad y escritura. La Edad Media*. Crítica, 2012.

Lalomia, Gaetano. "La difesa del proprio lavoro letterario. Diogene Laerzio, Franco Sacchetti e Juan Manuel." *Estudios de literatura medieval en la Península Ibérica*, edited by Carlos Alvar, Cilengua, 2015, pp. 773–88.

Latini, Brunetto. *Libro del tesoro: versión castellana de Li Livres dou Tresor*. Edited by Spurgeon W. Baldwin, Hispanic Seminary of Medieval Studies, 1989.

Lawrance, Jeremy N.H. "The Audience of the *Libro de buen amor*." *Comparative Literature*, vol. 36, no. 3, summer 1984, pp. 220–37. *JSTOR*, https://doi.org/10.2307/1770261.

Lawrance, Jeremy N.H. "The Spread of Lay Literacy in Late Medieval Castile." *Bulletin of Hispanic Studies*, vol. 62, no. 1, 1985, pp. 79–94. *Taylor & Francis Online*, https://doi.org/10.1080/1475382852000362079.

Lejeune, Philippe. *Le pacte autobiographique*. Seuils, 1975.

Lerer, Seth. *Chaucer and His Readers: Imagining the Author in Late-Medieval England*. Princeton UP, 1993.

Lewis, C.S. *The Discarded Image*. Cambridge UP, 2007.

Libro de Alexandre. Edited by Jesús Cañas Murillo, Editora Nacional, 1978.

Libro de los cien capítulos. Edited by Agapito Rey, Indiana UP, 1960.
Lida de Malkiel, María Rosa. *La idea de la fama en la Edad Media castellana*. Fondo de Cultura Económica, 2006.
Lida de Malkiel, María Rosa. "Tres notas sobre don Juan Manuel." *Romance Philology*, vol. 4, nos. 2–3, 1950–1, pp. 155–94.
Linehan, Peter. *At the Edge of Reformation: Iberia Before the Black Death*. Oxford UP, 2019.
Liuzzo Scorpo, Antonella. "Emotional Memory and Medieval Autobiography: King James I of Aragon (r. 1213–76)'s *Llibre dels fets*." *Journal of Medieval Iberian Studies*, vol. 10, no. 1, 2018, pp. 1–25. *Taylor & Francis Online*, https://doi.org/10.1080/17546559.2016.1239832.
Lizabe, Gladys. "El poder del entorno femenino de don Juan Manuel en la construcción de su discurso historiográfico." *Debates actuales del hispanismo: balances y desafíos críticos*, edited by Germán Prósperi, U Nacional del Litoral, 2016, pp. 382–93.
Lledó-Guillem, Vicente. *The Making of Catalan Linguistic Identity in Medieval and Early Modern Times*. Palgrave Macmillan, 2018.
Llull, Ramon. *Llibre de l'orde de cavalleria*. Edited by Albert Soler i Llopart, Barcino, 1988.
Lobato López, María Luisa. "El arte de 'façer cartas' de Juan Manuel." *Actas del XII Congreso de la Asociación Internacional de Hispanistas, 21–26 de agosto de 1995*, edited by Aengus Ward, vol. 1, U of Birmingham, 1998, pp. 230–9.
López Estrada, Francisco. "Don Juan Manuel y Marcial (un apunte comparatista)." *Revue de Littérature Comparée*, vol. 52, no. 2, 1978, pp. 247–54.
López Estrada, Francisco. *Las poéticas castellanas de la Edad Media*. Taurus, 1984.
Love, Harold. *Attributing Authorship: An Introduction*. Cambridge UP, 2002.
Luongo, Salvatore. *"En manera de un grand señor que fablava con un su consegero": Il* Conde Lucanor *di Juan Manuel*. Liguori, 2006.
Macpherson, Ian R. "Amor and don Juan Manuel." *Hispanic Review*, vol. 39, no. 2, Apr. 1971, pp. 167–82. *JSTOR*, https://doi.org/10.2307/471602.
Macpherson, Ian R. "*Dios y el mundo*: The Didacticism of *El conde Lucanor*." *Romance Philology*, vol. 24, no. 1, Aug. 1970, pp. 26–38.
Macpherson, Ian R. "Don Juan Manuel: The Literary Process." *Studies in Philology*, vol. 70, no. 1, 1973, pp. 1–18.
Macpherson, Ian R., editor. *Juan Manuel: A Selection*. Tamesis, 1980.
[Maestre] Pedro. *Libro del consejo e de los consejeros*. Edited by Barry Taylor, Cilengua, 2014.
Marcos-Marín, Francisco. "*Estoria* como 'representación secuencial.' Nota sobre el *Libro de buen amor*, desde Alfonso X, el *Libro de Alexandre* y *El conde Lucanor*, y otras referencias." *Archivum*, vols. 27–8, 1977, pp. 523–8.
Márquez Villanueva, Francisco. "The Alfonsine Cultural Concept." *Alfonso X of Castile, the Learned King (1221–1284). An International Symposium, Harvard*

University, 17 November 1984, edited by Francisco Márquez Villanueva and Carlos Alberto Vega, Department of Romance Languages and Literatures of Harvard U, 1990, pp. 76–109.

Márquez Villanueva, Francisco. *El concepto cultural alfonsí*. Edicions Bellaterra, 2004.

Marshall, J.H. Introduction. *The "Razos de trobar" of Raimon Vidal and Associated Texts*. Oxford UP, 1972.

Martín Iglesias, José Carlos. "El denominado *Cronicón* latino de don Juan Manuel: nueva edición y estudio." *Cahiers d'études hispaniques médiévales*, vol. 38, no. 1, 2015, pp. 131–65. *Cairn.info*, https://doi.org/10.3917/cehm.038.0131.

Matis, Hannah W. "The Seclusion of Eustochium: Paschasius Radbertus and the Nuns of Soissons." *Church History*, vol. 85, no. 4, Dec. 2016, pp. 665–89. *Cambridge Core*, https://doi.org/10.1017/s0009640716000767.

McCabe, T. Matthew N. *Gower's Vulgar Tongue: Ovid, Lay Religion, and English Poetry in the* Confessio Amantis. D.S. Brewer, 2011.

McGinn, Bernard. Introduction. *Meister Eckhart and the Beguine Mystics: Hadewijch of Brabant, Mechthild of Magdeburg, and Marguerite Porete*. Continuum, 1994, pp. 1–16.

McGrady, Deborah. *Controlling Readers: Guillaume de Machaut and His Late Medieval Audience*. U of Toronto P, 2006.

McGrady, Deborah. "What Is a Patron? Benefactors and Authorship in Harley 4431, Christine de Pizan's Collected Works." *Christine de Pizan and the Categories of Difference*, edited by Marilynn Desmond, U of Minnesota P, 1998, pp. 195–214.

Menéndez Pidal, Gonzalo. "Cómo trabajaron las escuelas alfonsíes." *Nueva revista de filología hispánica*, vol. 5, no. 4, 1951, pp. 363–80. https://doi.org/10.24201/nrfh.v5i4.196.

Menocal, María Rosa. "Life Itself: Storytelling as the Tradition of Openness in the *Conde Lucanor*." *Oral Tradition and Hispanic Literature: Essays in Honor of Samuel G. Armistead*, edited by Mishael M. Caspi, Garland, 1995, pp. 469–96.

Minnis, Alastair. *Medieval Theory of Authorship: Scholastic Literary Attitudes in the Later Middle Ages*. 2nd ed., U of Pennsylvania P, 1988.

Minnis, Alastair. "Nolens auctor sed compilator reputari: The Late-Medieval Discourse of Compilation." *La méthode critique au Moyen Âge*, edited by Mireille Chazan and Gilbert Dahan, Brepols, 2006, pp. 47–63.

Minnis, Alastair, and Ian Johnson. Introduction. *The Cambridge History of Literary Criticism*, vol. 2: *The Middle Ages*, edited by Alastair Minnis and Ian Johnson, Cambridge UP, 2005, pp. 1–12.

Miralles, Enrique. Prologue. *El conde Lucanor (Sevilla, 1575, Hernando Díaz)*. Puvill, 1978, pp. 9–38.

Molina Molina, Ángel Luis. "El juego de dados en la Edad Media." *Murgetana*, vol. 100, 1999, pp. 95–104.

Montaner Frutos, Alberto. *El recontamiento de al-Miqdâd y al-Mayâsa. Edición y estudio de un relato aljamiado-morisco aragonés*. Institución Fernándo el Católico, 1988.

Mota, Carlos. Introduction. *Libro infinido*. By Juan Manuel. Cátedra, 2003, pp. 11–110.

Nanu, Irina. "Sobre las huellas del didacticismo latino en el 'Prólogo' de *El conde Lucanor*." *Bulletin of Hispanic Studies*, vol. 80, no. 2, 2003, pp. 149–60. *Liverpool UP*, https://doi.org/10.3828/bhs.80.2.1.

Navas Ocaña, Isabel, and José de la Torre Castro. "Prosistas medievales castellanas: autorías, auditorios, genealogías." *Estudios filológicos*, vol. 47, June 2011, pp. 93–113. *SciELO*, https://doi.org/10.4067/s0071-1713 2011000100006.

Nebrija, Elio Antonio de. *Vocabulario español-latino*. Salamanca, [1495]. *Biblioteca Virtual Miguel de Cervantes*, 2005, https://www.cervantesvirtual.com/nd/ark:/59851/bmcvm466.

Nicholas of Lyra. "Prologus secundus: De intentione auctoris et modo procedendi." *Postilla litteralis*, edited by J.-P. Migne, Paris, 1852. Patrologia Latina, vol. 113, col. 29–34.

Nieto Márquez, Inés. *Tesoro de Autores Ilustres, o Colección Selecta y Económica de las Mejores Obras Antiguas y Modernas Nacionales y Extranjeras*. Barcelona, 1842–1899?. *Biblioteca Virtual Miguel de Cervantes*, 2017, https://www.cervantesvirtual.com/nd/ark:/59851/bmc0928688.

North, Janice Renee. *The Construction of a Cultural Legacy: Queen María de Molina of Castile and the Political Discourses of Molinismo*. 2013. U of Virginia, PhD dissertation.

Núñez, Hernán. *Refranes, o Proverbios en romance*. Salamanca, Juan de Cánova, 1555. RODERIC, U de València, Biblioteca Històrica, https://hdl.handle.net/10550/52803.

Olivetto, Georgina. "Alonso de Cartagena: ante el manuscrito de autor." *Romance Philology*, vol. 68, no. 1, 2014, pp. 45–63. *Brepols Online*, https://doi.org/10.1484/j.rph.5.103544.

Olivetto, Georgina. "Don Juan Manuel: autor y autoeditor." *Voz y letra*, vol. 25, no. 1–2, 2014, pp. 111–32.

Orduna, Germán. "La autobiografía literaria de don Juan Manuel." *Don Juan Manuel, VII Centenario*. U de Murcia – Academia Alfonso X el Sabio, 1982, pp. 245–58.

Orduna, Germán. "¿Un catálogo más de obras de don Juan Manuel?" *Bulletin of Hispanic Studies*, vol. 50, no. 3, 1973, pp. 217–23. *Liverpool UP*, https://doi.org/10.3828/bhs.50.3.217.

Orduna, Germán. "La élite intelectual de la escuela catedralicia de Toledo y la literatura en época de Sancho IV." *La literatura en la época de Sancho IV: Actas del Congreso Internacional*, edited by José Manuel Lucía Megías and Carlos Alvar Ezquerra, U de Alcalá, 1996, pp. 35–52.

Orduna, Germán. "El *exemplo* en la obra literaria de don Juan Manuel." *Juan Manuel Studies*, edited by Ian R. Macpherson, Tamesis, 1977, pp. 119–42.

Orduna, Germán. "'Fablar complido' y 'fablar breve et escuro': procedencia oriental de esta disyuntiva en la obra literaria de don Juan Manuel." *Homenaje a Fernando Antonio Martínez: estudios de lingüística, filología, literatura e historia cultural*. Instituto Caro y Cuervo, 1979, pp. 135–46.

Orduna, Germán. "El *Libro de las armas*: clave de la 'justicia' de don Juan Manuel." *Cuadernos de historia de España*, vols. 67–8, 1982, pp. 230–68.

Orduna, Germán. "Notas para una edición crítica del *Libro del conde Lucanor et de Patronio*." *Boletín de la Real Academia Española*, vol. 51, no. 194, 1971, pp. 493–512.

Orduna, Germán. "Los prólogos a la *Crónica abreviada* y al *Libro de la caza*: la tradición alfonsí y la primera época en la obra literaria de don Juan Manuel." *Don Juan Manuel y el* Libro de la caza, edited by José Manuel Fradejas Rueda, Seminario de Filología Medieval – U de Valladolid, 2001, pp. 105–19. Originally published in *Cuadernos de historia de España*, vols. 51–2, 1970, pp. 123–44.

Orduna, Germán. "Yo, don Johán, fijo del infante don Manuel ... " *El conde Lucanor*. By Juan Manuel, edited by Guillermo Serés, Galaxia Gutenberg, 2006, pp. ix–xxix.

Palafox, Eloísa. *Las éticas del* exemplum*: Los* Castigos del rey don Sancho IV, El conde Lucanor *y el* Libro de buen amor. U Nacional Autónoma de México, 1998.

Parkes, Malcolm Beckwith. "The Influence of the Concepts of *Ordinatio* and *Compilatio* on the Development of the Book." *Medieval Learning and Literature: Essays Presented to R.W. Hunt*, edited by J.J.G. Alexander and M.T. Gibson, Clarendon, 1976, pp. 115–41.

Parkes, Malcolm Beckwith. *Pause and Effect: An Introduction to the History of Punctuation in the West*. Routledge, 2016.

Partridge, Stephen, and Erik Kwakkel, editors. *Author, Reader, Book: Medieval Authorship in Theory and Practice*. U of Toronto P, 2012.

Pascual Martínez, Lope. "Los oficios y la cancillería en el señorío de don Juan Manuel." *Don Juan Manuel, VII Centenario*. U de Murcia – Academia Alfonso X el Sabio, 1982, pp. 259–85.

Pearsall, Derek. "Towards a Poetics of Chaucerian Narrative." *Drama, Narrative, and Poetry in the Canterbury Tales*, edited by Wendy Harding, Presses Universitaires du Mirail, 2003, pp. 99–112.

[Pseudo] Pedro Pascual. *Obras de S. Pedro Pascual, mártir*. Edited by Pedro Armengol Valenzuela, vol. 4, Imprenta Salustiana, 1908.

[Pseudo] Pedro Pascual. *Sobre la se[c]ta Mahometana*. Edited by Fernando González Muñoz, U de València, 2011.

Penney, Clara Louise, editor. *George Ticknor: Letters to Pascual de Gayangos from the Originals in the Collection of the Hispanic Society of America*. Hispanic Society of America, 1927.

Pérez, Martín. *Libro de las confesiones: Una radiografía de la sociedad medieval española*. Edited by Antonio García y García, Bernardo Alonso Rodríguez, and Francisco Cantelar Rodríguez, Biblioteca de Autores Cristianos, 2002.

Pérez Isasi, Santiago. "Building Nations through Words: Iberian Identities in Nineteenth-Century Literary Historiography." *The Routledge Companion to Iberian Studies*, edited by Javier Muñoz-Basols, Laura Lonsdale, and Manuel Delgado, Routledge, 2017, pp. 333–43.

Perry, Theodore Anthony, translator. *The Moral Proverbs of Santob de Carrión: Jewish Wisdom in Christian Spain*. Princeton UP, 1987.

Petrarch (Petrarca, Francesco). *Annotatio nonnullorum librorum seu epistolarum Francisci Petrarche*. [Venice]: [Simone da Lovere], [1501]. *HathiTrust*, https://catalog.hathitrust.org/Record/009293046. Accessed 8 May 2022.

Petrarch (Petrarca, Francesco). *Four Dialogues for Scholars*. Edited and translated by Conrad H. Rawski, P of Western Reserve U, 1967.

Petrarch (Petrarca, Francesco). *Letters of Old Age*, vol. 1: *Books I–IX*. Translated by Aldo S. Bernardo, Saul Levin, and Reta A. Bernardo, Italica, 2005.

Petrucci, Armando. *Writers and Readers in Medieval Italy: Studies in the History of Written Culture*. Edited and translated by Charles M. Radding, Yale UP, 1995.

PhiloBiblon, directed by Charles B. Faulhaber, Bancroft Library, U of California Berkeley, 1997–, https://bancroft.berkeley.edu/philobiblon/index.html.

Piccus, Jules. "The Meaning of *Estoria* in Juan Manuel's *El conde Lucanor*." *Hispania*, vol. 61, no. 3, Sept. 1978, pp. 459–65. *JSTOR*, https://doi.org/10.2307/341072.

"Portray, *V*. (I.2.b)." *OED: Oxford English Dictionary*, Mar. 2023. https://doi.org/10.1093/OED/1565097214.

Quain, Edwin A. "The Medieval *Accessus ad Auctores*." *Traditio*, vol. 3, 1945, pp. 215–64. *Cambridge Core*, https://doi.org/10.1017/s0362152900016895.

Qués, María Elena. "El *Libro de las armas* de don Juan Manuel: construcción del yo/construcción del texto." *Anuario medieval*, vol. 5, 1993, pp. 96–106.

Raden, Matthew. "Writing from Margin to Center: The Case of Don Juan Manuel and Shem Tov." *Hispanófila*, vol. 135, 2002, pp. 1–17.

Ramos Nogales, Rafael. "Notas al *Libro de las armas*." *Anuario medieval*, vol. 4, 1992, pp. 179–92.

Redondo Cantera, María José. "El convento de San Pablo en Peñafiel (Valladolid). Panteón de los Manuel." *Biblioteca: estudio e investigación*, vol. 26, 2011, 161–99.

Rhodes, Alexander. "Heraldry and Religious Symbolism in a Seventeenth-Century *Carta Ejecutoria*." *Art and Violence in the Middle Ages and the Renaissance*, edited by Robert G. Sullivan and Meriem Pagès, Cambridge Scholars Publishing, 2020, pp. 53–66.

Rico, Francisco. "Crítica del texto y modelos de cultura en el *Prólogo general* de don Juan Manuel." *Studia in honorem prof. Martín de Riquer*. Vol. 1, Quaderns Crema, 1986, pp. 409–23.

Riquer, Martí de. *Història de la literatura catalana*. Vol. 1, Ariel, 1980.

Rochwert-Zuili, Patricia. "D'Alphonse X à Alphonse XI: l'affirmation du pouvoir dans les prologues des oeuvres castillanes aux XIIIe et XIVe siècles." *Cahiers d'études hispaniques médiévales*, vol. 35, 2012, pp. 45–60. *Persée*, https://doi.org/10.3406/cehm.2012.2273.

Rodríguez Velasco, Jesús. *Dead Voice: Law, Philosophy, and Fiction in the Iberian Middle Ages*. U of Pennsylvania P, 2020.

Rodríguez Velasco, Jesús. "La producción del margen." *La corónica*, vol. 39, no. 1, fall 2010, pp. 249–72. *Project MUSE*, https://doi.org/10.1353/cor.2010.0010.

Rosende, Marcelo. "Profecía, figura, consumación y providencia en el *Libro de las tres razones* de don Juan Manuel." *Revista de literatura medieval*, vol. 18, 2006, pp. 199–223.

Round, Nicholas G., editor. *Libro llamado 'Fedrón,' Plato's 'Phaedo' Translated by Pero Díaz de Toledo*. Tamesis, 1993.

Rouse, Mary A., and Richard H. Rouse. *Authentic Witnesses: Approaches to Medieval Texts and Manuscripts*. U of Notre Dame P, 1991.

Rubio García, Luis. "La fecha de la muerte de don Juan Manuel." *Don Juan Manuel, VII Centenario*. U de Murcia – Academia Alfonso X el Sabio, 1982, pp. 325–36.

Ruiz, María Cecilia. *Literatura y política: el* Libro de los estados *y el* Libro de las armas *de don Juan Manuel*. Scripta Humanistica, 1989.

Ruiz García, Elisa. "La carta ejecutoria de hidalguía: un espacio gráfico privilegiado." *Estudios de genealogía, heráldica y nobiliaria*, edited by Miguel Ángel Ladero Quesada, U Complutense, 2006, pp. 251–76.

Sacchetti, Franco. *Il trecentonovelle*. Edited by Valerio Marucci, Salerno, 1996.

Sánchez González de Herrero, María Nieves. "De proprietatibus rerum: Versiones castellanas." *Cahiers de recherches médiévales et humanistes*, vol. 16, 2008, pp. 349–66. *OpenEdition Journals*, https://doi.org/10.4000/crm.11072.

Sánchez-Prieto Borja, Pedro. *Cómo editar los textos medievales: criterios para su presentación gráfica*. Arco Libros – La Muralla, 1998.

Sánchez-Serrano, Antonio, and Remedios Prieto de la Iglesia. "'Auctor,' 'Autor' y otros problemas semánticos concernientes a la autoría, gestación y ediciones de la *Celestina*." *Celestinesca*, vol. 35, 2011, pp. 85–136. https://doi.org/10.7203/celestinesca.35.20134.

Sancho IV of Castile. *Castigos del rey don Sancho IV*. Edited by Hugo Oscar Bizzarri, Iberoamericana, 2001.

Sancho IV of Castile. *Los "Lucidarios" españoles*. Edited by Richard P. Kinkade, Gredos, 1968.

Santonocito, Daniela. "Edición de *El conde Lucanor* (Sevilla: Hernando Díaz, 1575), al cuidado de Gonzalo Argote de Molina (1a parte)." *Memorabilia*, vol. 17, 2015, pp. 1–89.

Santonocito, Daniela. "Edición de *El conde Lucanor* (Sevilla: Hernando Díaz, 1575), al cuidado de Gonzalo Argote de Molina (2a parte)." *Memorabilia*, vol. 18, 2016, pp. 1–132.

Santonocito, Daniela. *Gonzalo Argote de Molina, editor de textos medievales*. Peter Lang, 2020.

Santonocito, Daniela. "Los 'viessos' del *Conde Lucanor*: del manuscrito a la imprenta." *Estudios de literatura medieval en la Península Ibérica*, edited by Carlos Alvar, Cilengua, 2015, pp. 1137–56.

Saracino, Pablo Enrique. "La *Crónica abreviada* de don Juan Manuel, una 'lectura desviada' de la crónica alfonsí." *Medievalia*, vol. 38, 2006, pp. 1–10.

Savo, Anita. "The Hidden Polemic in Juan Manuel's *Libro de los estados*." *La corónica*, vol. 44, no. 2, spring 2016, pp. 5–28. *Project MUSE*, https://doi.org/10.1353/cor.2016.0001.

Savo, Anita. "It's a Man's World: Women and Movement in Juan Manuel's Works." *Bulletin of Spanish Studies*, vol. 98, no. 9, 2021, pp. 1385–1409. *Taylor & Francis Online*, https://doi.org/10.1080/14753820.2021.1975983.

Savo, Anita. "Material Afterlives of the *Conde Lucanor*: Asynchrony in BNE, MS 17788." *Digital Philology*, vol. 9, no. 2, fall 2020, pp. 199–227. *Project MUSE*, https://doi.org/10.1353/dph.2020.0011.

Scanlon, Larry. *Narrative, Authority, and Power: The Medieval Exemplum and the Chaucerian Tradition*. Cambridge UP, 1994.

Schine, Rachel. "Nourishing the Noble: Breastfeeding and Hero-Making in Medieval Arabic Popular Literature." *Al-'Uṣūr al-Wusṭā*, vol. 27, 2019, pp. 165–200.

Scholberg, Kenneth R. "Juan Manuel, personaje y autocrítico." *Hispania*, vol. 44, no. 3, Sept. 1961, pp. 457–60. *JSTOR*, https://doi.org/10.2307/335408.

Scholberg, Kenneth R. "Modestia y orgullo: una nota sobre don Juan Manuel." *Hispania*, vol. 42, no. 1, Mar. 1959, pp. 24–31. *JSTOR*, https://doi.org/10.2307/334690.

Seniff, Dennis P. "'Así fiz yo de lo que oý': Orality, Authority, and Experience in Juan Manuel's *Libro de la caza*, *Libro infinido*, and *Libro de las armas*." *Noble*

Pursuits: Literature and the Hunt, edited by Dennis P. Seniff, Diane M. Wright, and Connie L. Scarborough, Juan de la Cuesta, 1992, pp. 33–57. Originally published in *Josep María Solà-Solé: homage, homenaje, homenatge*, edited by Antonio Torres-Alcalá et al., vol. 1, Puvill, 1984, pp. 91–109.

Seniff, Dennis P. "Orality and Textuality in Medieval Castilian Prose." *Oral Tradition*, vol. 2, no. 1, 1987, pp. 150–71.

Serés, Guillermo. "Los fundamentos de la caballería según don Juan Manuel." *La construcció d'identitats imaginades: literatura medieval i ideologia*, edited by Julián Acebrón Ruiz, Isabel Grifoll, and Flocel Sabaté i Curull, Pagès, 2015, pp. 167–85.

Serés, Guillermo. "Procedimientos retóricos de las partes IIa–IVa de *El conde Lucanor*." *Revista de Literatura Medieval*, vol. 6, 1994, pp. 147–70.

Shem Tov de Carrión. *Proverbios morales*. Edited by Paloma Díaz-Mas and Carlos Mota, Cátedra, 1998.

Shepard, Sanford, editor. *Proverbios morales*. By Shem Tov de Carrión, Castalia, 1986.

Shooner, Hugues V. "La production du livre par la pecia." *La production du livre universitaire au Moyen Âge: Exemplar et pecia. Actes du symposium tenu au Collegio San Bonaventura de Grottaferrata en mai 1983*, edited by Louis J. Bataillon, Bertrand G. Guyot, and Richard H. Rouse, Centre national de la recherche scientifique, 1983, pp. 17–37.

Sims, Holly. *Writing a Past to Remember: Texts as Monuments in Medieval Castile*. 2019. U of North Carolina, Chapel Hill, PhD dissertation.

Spitzer, Leo. "Note on the Poetic and Empirical 'I' in Medieval Authors." *Traditio*, vol. 4, 1946, pp. 414–22. *Cambridge Core*, https://doi.org/10.1017/s0362152900015609.

Stillinger, Thomas C. *The Song of Troilus: Lyric Authority in the Medieval Book*. U of Pennsylvania P, 1992.

Sturcken, H. Tracy. *Don Juan Manuel*. Twayne, 1974.

Sturm, Harlan G. "Author and Authority in *El conde Lucanor*." *Hispanófila*, vol. 52, Sept. 1974, pp. 1–9.

Surtz, Ronald E. *Writing Women in Late Medieval and Early Modern Spain: The Mothers of Saint Teresa of Avila*. U of Pennsylvania P, 1995.

Szpiech, Ryan. "Latin as a Language of Authoritative Tradition." *The Oxford Handbook of Medieval Latin Literature*, edited by Ralph Hexter and David Townsend, Oxford UP, 2012, pp. 63–85.

Tate, Robert Brian. "The Infante Don Juan of Aragon and Don Juan Manuel." *Juan Manuel Studies*, edited by Ian R. Macpherson, Tamesis, 1977, pp. 169–79.

Taylor, Andrew. "Vernacular Authorship and the Control of Manuscript Production." *The Medieval Manuscript Book: Cultural Approaches*, edited by Michael Johnston and Michael Van Dussen, Cambridge UP, 2015, pp. 199–214.

Taylor, Barry. "Los capítulos perdidos del *Libro del cavallero et del escudero* y el *Libro de la cavallería*." *Incipit*, vol. 4, 1984, pp. 51–69.

Taylor, Barry. "Don Jaime de Jérica y el público de *El conde Lucanor.*" *Revista de filología española*, vol. 66, nos. 1–2, 1986, pp. 39–58. https://doi.org/10.3989/rfe.1986.v66.i1/2.462.

Taylor, Barry. "*Estoria* y *viesso* en el manuscrito S de *El conde Lucanor*: una cuestión de *mise en texte.*" *Incipit*, vol. 31, 2011, pp. 35–55.

Taylor, Barry. "La *fabliella* de don Juan Manuel." *Revista de poética medieval*, vol. 4, 2000, pp. 187–200.

Taylor, Barry. "Juan Manuel's Cipher in the *Libro de los estados.*" *La corónica*, vol. 12, no. 1, 1983, pp. 32–44.

Taylor, Barry. "El *Libro infinido* de don Juan Manuel: ¿un texto abierto?" *Actas del IX Congreso Internacional de la Asociación Hispánica de Literatura Medieval (A Coruña, 18–22 de septiembre de 2001)*, edited by Carmen Parrilla García and Mercedes Pampín Barral, vol. 3, Toxosoutos, 2005, pp. 563–72.

Taylor, Barry. "The Manuscript Transmission of Juan Manuel's Works." *A Companion to Don Juan Manuel*. Brill, forthcoming.

Taylor, Barry. "Manuscritos incompletos, obras incompletas: *Libro de los gatos, Siervo libre de amor, Libro de la caza.*" *Incipit*, vol. 30, 2010, pp. 33–47.

Taylor, Barry. Review of Juan Manuel, *Cinco tratados*, edited by Reinaldo Ayerbe-Chaux. *La corónica*, vol. 19, no. 1, 1990–1, pp. 148–59.

Ticknor, George. *History of Spanish Literature*. Vol. 1, New York, Harper and Bros., 1849.

Torollo, David. "*El conde Lucanor*, ¿una colección de *maqāmāt* en castellano?" *eHumanista*, vol. 33, 2016, pp. 330–47, https://www.ehumanista.ucsb.edu/volumes/33.

Torres Fontes, Juan, and Cristina Torres-Fontes Suárez. "Los retablos de Bernabé de Módena en la Catedral de Murcia y sus donantes." *Boletín de la Real Academia de Bellas Artes de San Fernando*, vol. 84, 1997, pp. 89–116.

Uría Maqua, Isabel, and Jaime González Álvarez, editors. *El* Libro de los doce sabios *y relación de los reyes de León y Castilla: Códice Ovetense [O]*. U de Oviedo, 2009.

Vidal de Besalú, Ramon. *The* Razos de trobar *of Raimon Vidal and Associated Texts*. Edited by J.H. Marshall, Oxford UP, 1972, pp. 1–25.

Vincent of Beauvais. *Apologia Totius Operis*. Edited by Anna-Dorothee von den Brincken. "Geschichtsbetrachtung bei Vincenz von Beauvais: Die *Apologia Actoris* zum *Speculum Maius.*" *Deutches Archiv für Erforschung des Mittelalters*, vol. 34, no. 2, 1978, pp. 410–99.

Vose, Robin. *Dominicans, Muslims, and Jews in the Medieval Crown of Aragon*. Cambridge UP, 2009.

Wacks, David A. *Double Diaspora in Sephardic Literature: Jewish Cultural Production Before and After 1492*. Indiana UP, 2015.

Wacks, David A. *Framing Iberia: Maqāmāt and Frametale Narratives in Medieval Spain*. Brill, 2007.

Watson, Nicholas. "Censorship and Cultural Change in Late-Medieval England: Vernacular Theology, the Oxford Translation Debate, and Arundel's Constitutions of 1409." *Speculum*, vol. 70, no. 4, Oct. 1995, pp. 822–64. *U Chicago P Journals*, https://doi.org/10.2307/2865345.

Watson, Nicholas. "Cultural Changes." *English Language Notes*, vol. 44, no. 1, spring 2006, pp. 127–37. *Duke UP*, https://doi.org/10.1215/00138282-44.1.127.

Weichselbaumer, Nikolaus. "'Quod Exemplaria vera habeant et correcta': Concerning the Distribution and Purpose of the Pecia System." *Specialist Markets in the Early Modern Book World*, edited by Richard Kirwan and Sophie Mullins, Brill, 2015, pp. 331–50.

Weijers, Olga, editor. *De disciplina scolarium*. By Pseudo-Boethius. Brill, 1976.

Weiskott, Eric. "'Adam Scriveyn' and Chaucer's Metrical Practice." *Medium Ævum*, vol. 86, no. 1, 2017, pp. 147–51. *JSTOR*, https://doi.org/10.2307/26396502.

Weiss, Julian. "Literary Theory and Polemic in Castile, *c*. 1200–*c*. 1500." *The Cambridge History of Literary Criticism*, vol. 2: *The Middle Ages*, edited by Alastair Minnis and Ian Johnson, Cambridge UP, 2005, pp. 496–532.

Weiss, Julian. *The Poet's Art: Literary Theory in Castile, c. 1400–60*. Society for the Study of Mediaeval Languages and Literature, 1990.

Weiss, Julian. "Vernacular Commentaries and Glosses in Late Medieval Castile, I: A Checklist of Castilian Authors." *Text, Manuscript, and Print in Medieval and Modern Iberia: Studies in Honour of David Hook*, edited by Barry Taylor, Geoffrey West, and Jane Whetnall, Hispanic Seminary of Medieval Studies, 2013, pp. 199–243.

Weiss, Julian. "Vernacular Commentaries and Glosses in Late Medieval Castile, II: A Checklist of Classical Texts in Translation." *Medieval Hispanic Studies in Memory of Alan Deyermond*, edited by Andrew M. Beresford, Louise M. Haywood, and Julian Weiss, Tamesis, 2013, pp. 237–71.

Wellek, René. "The Concept of 'Romanticism' in Literary History." *Comparative Literature*, vol. 1, no. 1, 1949, pp. 1–23.

Wenzel, Siegfried. "The Arts of Preaching." *The Cambridge History of Literary Criticism*, vol. 2: *The Middle Ages*, edited by Alastair Minnis and Ian Johnson, Cambridge UP, 2005, pp. 84–96.

Wiegers, Gerard. *Islamic Literature in Spanish and Aljamiado: Yça of Segovia (fl. 1450), His Antecedents and Successors*. Brill, 1994.

Wynter, Sylvia. "Unsettling the Coloniality of Being/Power/Truth/Freedom: Towards the Human, After Man, Its Overrepresentation – An Argument." *The New Centennial Review*, vol. 3, no. 3, fall 2003, pp. 257–337. *Project MUSE*, https://doi.org/10.1353/ncr.2004.0015.

Zumthor, Paul. "The Text and the Voice," translated by Marilyn C. Engelhardt. *New Literary History*, vol. 16, no. 1, autumn 1984, pp. 67–92. *JSTOR*, https://doi.org/10.2307/468776.

Index

Note: Page numbers in *italics* indicate a figure.

Toronto Iberic

1 Anthony J. Cascardi, *Cervantes, Literature, and the Discourse of Politics*
2 Jessica A. Boon, *The Mystical Science of the Soul: Medieval Cognition in Bernardino de Laredo's Recollection Method*
3 Susan Byrne, *Law and History in Cervantes'* Don Quixote
4 Mary E. Barnard and Frederick A. de Armas (eds.), *Objects of Culture in the Literature of Imperial Spain*
5 Nil Santiáñez, *Topographies of Fascism: Habitus, Space, and Writing in Twentieth-Century Spain*
6 Nelson R. Orringer, *Lorca in Tune with Falla: Literary and Musical Interludes*
7 Ana M. Gómez-Bravo, *Textual Agency: Writing Culture and Social Networks in Fifteenth-Century Spain*
8 Javier Irigoyen-García, *The Spanish Arcadia: Sheep Herding, Pastoral Discourse, and Ethnicity in Early Modern Spain*
9 Stephanie Sieburth, *Survival Songs: Conchita Piquer's* Coplas *and Franco's Regime of Terror*
10 Christine Arkinstall, *Spanish Female Writers and the Freethinking Press, 1879–1926*

11 Margaret E. Boyle, *Unruly Women: Performance, Penitence, and Punishment in Early Modern Spain*
12 Evelina Gužauskyt, *Christopher Columbus's Naming in the* Diarios *of the Four Voyages (1492–1504): A Discourse of Negotiation*
13 Mary E. Barnard, *Garcilaso de la Vega and the Material Culture of Renaissance Europe*
14 William Viestenz, *By the Grace of God: Francoist Spain and the Sacred Roots of Political Imagination*
15 Michael Scham, Lector Ludens: *The Representation of Games and Play in Cervantes*
16 Stephen Rupp, *Heroic Forms: Cervantes and the Literature of War*
17 Enrique Fernández, *Anxieties of Interiority and Dissection in Early Modern Spain*
18 Susan Byrne, *Ficino in Spain*
19 Patricia M. Keller, *Ghostly Landscapes: Film, Photography, and the Aesthetics of Haunting in Contemporary Spanish Culture*
20 Carolyn A. Nadeau, *Food Matters: Alonso Quijano's Diet and the Discourse of Food in Early Modern Spain*
21 Cristian Berco, *From Body to Community: Venereal Disease and Society in Baroque Spain*
22 Elizabeth R. Wright, *The Epic of Juan Latino: Dilemmas of Race and Religion in Renaissance Spain*
23 Ryan D. Giles, *Inscribed Power: Amulets and Magic in Early Spanish Literature*
24 Jorge Pérez, *Confessional Cinema: Religion, Film, and Modernity in Spain's Development Years, 1960–1975*
25 Joan Ramon Resina, *Josep Pla: Seeing the World in the Form of Articles*
26 Javier Irigoyen-García, *"Moors Dressed as Moors": Clothing, Social Distinction, and Ethnicity in Early Modern Iberia*
27 Jean Dangler, *Edging toward Iberia*
28 Ryan D. Giles and Steven Wagschal (eds.), *Beyond Sight: Engaging the Senses in Iberian Literatures and Cultures, 1200–1750*
29 Silvia Bermúdez, *Rocking the Boat: Migration and Race in Contemporary Spanish Music*
30 Hilaire Kallendorf, *Ambiguous Antidotes: Virtue as Vaccine for Vice in Early Modern Spain*
31 Leslie J. Harkema, *Spanish Modernism and the Poetics of Youth: From Miguel de Unamuno to* La Joven Literatura
32 Benjamin Fraser, *Cognitive Disability Aesthetics: Visual Culture, Disability Representations, and the (In)Visibility of Cognitive Difference*
33 Robert Patrick Newcomb, *Iberianism and Crisis: Spain and Portugal at the Turn of the Twentieth Century*

34 Sara J. Brenneis, *Spaniards in Mauthausen: Representations of a Nazi Concentration Camp, 1940–2015*
35 Silvia Bermúdez and Roberta Johnson (eds.), *A New History of Iberian Feminisms*
36 Steven Wagschal, *Minding Animals in the Old and New Worlds: A Cognitive Historical Analysis*
37 Heather Bamford, *Cultures of the Fragment: Uses of the Iberian Manuscript, 1100–1600*
38 Enrique García Santo-Tomás (ed.), *Science on Stage in Early Modern Spain*
39 Marina S. Brownlee (ed.), *Cervantes'* Persiles *and the Travails of Romance*
40 Sarah Thomas, *Inhabiting the In-Between: Childhood and Cinema in Spain's Long Transition*
41 David A. Wacks, *Medieval Iberian Crusade Fiction and the Mediterranean World*
42 Rosilie Hernández, *Immaculate Conceptions: The Power of the Religious Imagination in Early Modern Spain*
43 Mary L. Coffey and Margot Versteeg (eds.), *Imagined Truths: Realism in Modern Spanish Literature and Culture*
44 Diana Aramburu, *Resisting Invisibility: Detecting the Female Body in Spanish Crime Fiction*
45 Samuel Amago and Matthew J. Marr (eds.), *Consequential Art: Comics Culture in Contemporary Spain*
46 Richard P. Kinkade, *Dawn of a Dynasty: The Life and Times of Infante Manuel of Castile*
47 Jill Robbins, *Poetry and Crisis: Cultural Politics and Citizenship in the Wake of the Madrid Bombings*
48 Ana María Laguna and John Beusterien (eds.), *Goodbye Eros: Recasting Forms and Norms of Love in the Age of Cervantes*
49 Sara J. Brenneis and Gina Herrmann (eds.), *Spain, the Second World War, and the Holocaust: History and Representation*
50 Francisco Fernández de Alba, *Sex, Drugs, and Fashion in 1970s Madrid*
51 Daniel Aguirre-Oteiza, *This Ghostly Poetry: History and Memory of Exiled Spanish Republican Poets*
52 Lara Anderson, *Control and Resistance: Food Discourse in Franco Spain*
53 Faith S. Harden, *Arms and Letters: Military Life Writing in Early Modern Spain*
54 Erin Alice Cowling, Tania de Miguel Magro, Mina García Jordán, and Glenda Y. Nieto-Cuebas (eds.), *Social Justice in Spanish Golden Age Theatre*

55 Paul Michael Johnson, *Affective Geographies: Cervantes, Emotion, and the Literary Mediterranean*
56 Justin Crumbaugh and Nil Santiáñez (eds.), *Spanish Fascist Writing: An Anthology*
57 Margaret E. Boyle and Sarah E. Owens (eds.), *Health and Healing in the Early Modern Iberian World: A Gendered Perspective*
58 Leticia Álvarez-Recio (ed.), *Iberian Chivalric Romance: Translations and Cultural Transmission in Early Modern England*
59 Henry Berlin, *Alone Together: Poetics of the Passions in Late Medieval Iberia*
60 Adrian Shubert, *The Sword of Luchana: Baldomero Espartero and the Making of Modern Spain, 1793–1879*
61 Jorge Pérez, *Fashioning Spanish Cinema: Costume, Identity, and Stardom*
62 Enriqueta Zafra, *Lazarillo de Tormes: A Graphic Novel*
63 Erin Alice Cowling, *Chocolate: How a New World Commodity Conquered Spanish Literature*
64 Mary E. Barnard, *A Poetry of Things: The Material Lyric in Habsburg Spain*
65 Frederick A. de Armas and James Mandrell (eds.), *The Gastronomical Arts in Spain: Food and Etiquette*
66 Catherine Infante, *The Arts of Encounter: Christians, Muslims, and the Power of Images in Early Modern Spain*
67 Robert Richmond Ellis, *Bibliophiles, Murderous Bookmen, and Mad Librarians: The Story of Books in Modern Spain*
68 Beatriz de Alba-Koch (ed.), *The Ibero-American Baroque*
69 Deborah R. Forteza, *The English Reformation in the Spanish Imagination: Rewriting Nero, Jezebel, and the Dragon*
70 Olga Sendra Ferrer, *Barcelona, City of Margins*
71 Dale Shuger, *God Made Word: An Archaeology of Mystic Discourse in Early Modern Spain*
72 Xosé M. Núñez Seixas, *The Spanish Blue Division on the Eastern Front, 1941–1945: War, Occupation, Memory*
73 Julia Domínguez, *Quixotic Memories: Cervantes and Memory in Early Modern Spain*
74 Anna Casas Aguilar, *Bilingual Legacies: Father Figures in Self-Writing from Barcelona*
75 Julia H. Chang, *Blood Novels: Gender, Caste, and Race in Spanish Realism*
76 Frederick A. de Armas, *Cervantes' Architectures: The Dangers Outside*
77 Michael Iarocci, *The Art of Witnessing: Francisco de Goya's* Disasters of War

78 Esther Fernández and Adrienne L. Martín (eds.), *Drawing the Curtain: Cervantes's Theatrical Revelations*
79 Emiro Martínez-Osorio and Mercedes Blanco (eds.), *The War Trumpet: Iberian Epic Poetry, 1543–1639*
80 Christine Arkinstall, *Women on War in Spain's Long Nineteenth Century: Virtue, Patriotism, Citizenship*
81 Ignacio Infante, *A Planetary Avant-Garde: Experimental Literature Networks and the Legacy of Iberian Colonialism*
82 Enrique Fernández, *The Image of Celestina: Illustrations, Paintings, and Advertisements*
83 Maryanne L. Leone and Shanna Lino (eds.), *Beyond Human: Decentring the Anthropocene in Spanish Ecocriticism*
84 Jennifer Nagtegaal, *Politically Animated: Non-Fiction Animation from the Hispanic World*
85 Anton Pujol and Jaume Martí-Olivella (eds.), *Catalan Cinema: The Barcelona Film School and the New Avant-Garde*
86 Matthew Bailey, *Speaking Truth to Power: The Legacy of the Young Cid*
87 Hilaire Kallendorf, *Perilous Passions: Ethics and Emotion in Early Modern Spain*
88 Anita Savo, *Portraying Authorship: Juan Manuel and the Rhetoric of Authority*